Munchausen Syndrome by Proxy

Munchausen Syndrome by Proxy

Issues in Diagnosis and Treatment

Edited by

Alex V. Levin, M.D.

Mary S. Sheridan

LEXINGTON BOOKS
An Imprint of The Free Press
NEW YORK LONDON TORONTO SYDNEY TOKYO SINGAPORE

Library of Congress Cataloging-in-Publication Data

Munchausen syndrome by proxy : issues in diagnosis and treatment /
  [edited by] Alex V. Levin, Mary S. Sheridan.
        p.   cm.
  Includes bibliographical references.
  ISBN 0-02-918606-4
  1. Munchausen syndrome by proxy.   I. Levin, Alex V.
II. Sheridan, Mary S.
  [DNLM: 1. Munchausen Syndrome by Proxy—diagnosis.   2. Munchausen Syn-
drome by Proxy—therapy.   3. Pediatrics.   WS 200   M963 1995]
RC569.5.M83M86   1995
616.85'8223—dc20
DNLM/DLC
for Library of Congress   95-3324
                                                                              CIP

Lexington Books
An Imprint of The Free Press
A Division of Simon & Schuster Inc.
1230 Avenue of the Americas
New York, N.Y. 10020

Printed in the United States of America
printing number
1 2 3 4 5 6 7 8 9 10

A project of this magnitude inevitably infringes on time available to the contributors for endeavors beyond the scope of this topic. On behalf of all the contributors, we would like to dedicate this book to the family and friends who graciously supported our work with understanding and patience; and in particular to Michael, Joshua, and Faith.

Contents

33 Summary   433
   Mary S. Sheridan and Alex V. Levin

Preface

There is an African proverb from a culture in which swaddling of an infant on the mother's back is common practice: "It is not in the nature of the mother's back to let the baby fall." The protective obligation of parents, particularly mothers, toward their children may be one of the few universally accepted obligations in society. Certainly, Americans think about motherhood with a romanticism applied to few other subjects. Over the past hundred years, and particularly the past thirty as child abuse has been studied intensively, we have learned that the abrogation of this obligation is not uncommon. The all-loving and ever-patient mother is more a creature of our needs than a real being. We have accepted, albeit reluctantly, that sometimes tired and frustrated parents come to the end of their patience. If they lack parenting skills they may yell when they should chide and hit when they should redirect. The overwhelming majority of physical abuse does not come from a specific desire to harm the child, but from a day that is too long, a support system that is too meager, or a belt buckle that is too convenient. Those whose authoritarian beliefs, sexual desires, or need to control are extreme may create reigns of terror in their homes. Those whose ability to cope is marginal may see it deteriorate entirely in the presence of children.

Munchausen Syndrome by Proxy (MBP) is the deliberate creation of actual or apparent illness or the false reporting of illness in a child or other dependent, done because the caretaker apparently wishes the attention that comes from the association with that illness. When seen in proper context, it is but one form of abuse, although an unexpected form. In contrast to the overwhelmed and neglectful parent, we see the facade of an apparently exemplary caregiver. Rather than the repentant or hostile, we see the ingratiating. Most people can recognize the part of themselves that gets impatient with a child and that might, under extreme circumstances, hit too hard were it not for our sense of control and available resources. It is much harder to empathize with deceit and calculation. It is thus somewhat easier to understand why most acts of physical abuse occur, although we cannot sanction them. It is much harder to empathize with lying and calculated injury, time after time, particularly when children are its victims. Knowing that MBP exists changes our views of what parenting can be, and perhaps our views about our own competence.

There is still much to be learned about MBP. Some of the most basic questions: how frequently it occurs, what dynamics underlie it, how it might be prevented, are still unanswered. Yet, in the years since Dr. Roy Meadow first identified MBP as an entity, some progress has been made. Increasing public and professional attention is leading to increased recognition of cases. The reporting and prosecution of these cases is familiarizing some members of the health care and child protective professions with each other's competencies. Yet there remain pockets of resistance and disbelief. One would like to think that, in time, MBP will be widely recognized, its dynamics understood, and proper interventions designed—just as we recognize, understand and intervene in other forms of abusive behavior. One would also like to believe that greater awareness will serve as a deterrent.

The effort to write this book began at the Fourth National Child Abuse Conference, cosponsored by Children's Hospital of Philadelphia and the University of Toronto, Hospital for Sick Children in Toronto in 1991. Margaret Zusky, our editor from Lexington Books, to whom we are extremely grateful, received the idea with initial skepticism. However, after doing some basic research, she acknowledged that MBP was indeed real and was a topic that had not been adequately covered in a review format.

The failure to recognize, acknowledge, and accept MBP has prevented successful protection of children and prosecution of perpetrators. It has made medical caretakers the unwitting participants in child abuse. We hope that this book—the first attempt at a comprehensive, multidisciplinary perspective—will help to address these problems.

Appreciation is expressed to the chapter authors both for their writing and for their continued efforts to understand, research, and communicate about MBP. We are also grateful to Lexington Books for their support of this project, and particularly to Margaret Zusky, for her patience. Christopher Bools contributed to the Bibliography. Acknowledgment is also due to the various long distance, fax, and express delivery services that helped facilitate the writing of a book whose editors are in Toronto and Honolulu, and whose contributors range between and beyond. We hope that we have bridged the distances to assemble a cohesive book about a wide-ranging disease.

There has been considerable discussion within the community of those studying MBP as to whether the term Factitious Disorder by Proxy, which is used in DSM IV, should replace MBP. We have decided to use the uniform term Munchausen Syndrome by Proxy in this work, and to abbreviate it MBP. This has not always agreed with the personal styles of contributors, but we felt it was important to achieve some internal unity. In making this decision, the editors recognize that there are valid arguments for and against each term.

The careful reader will note that a full list of references is appended to each chapter, in the interests of making scholarly consultation easier. We include a full bibliography of references to MBP at the end of the book.

This book attempts to present the state of knowledge about MBP. However, in a field like this, one could as easily call it the state of ignorance. Much MBP probably goes undetected. Other forms and patterns of the disorder, as yet unrecognized, most likely exist. Hopefully, knowledge of the disorder as it is presented here will inspire alertness, further documentation, research, and creative thought. If, indeed, MBP is truly a disorder inspired by the desperate search for approval and the extreme failure to recognize others as individuals, may this recounting of a relatively rare and sometimes bizarre entity also sensitize us to the hunger for approval of so many around us, and the times that the welfare of one person is sacrificed to the interests of another. Perhaps when we can understand these two motivations, we will understand—and obviate the need for—MBP.

Alex V. Levin
Mary S. Sheridan

I

Definitions and Diagnosis

1

The History of Munchausen Syndrome by Proxy

Roy Meadow

There is no *new* human behavior. That which is claimed to be new either has been unrecognized, unreported, or described in another way in other times. "Munchausen Syndrome by Proxy— The Hinterland of Child Abuse" published in 1977 in the *Lancet*[1] described two children whom I had encountered in my work as a pediatric nephrologist. One was a 6 year old whose mother, throughout the child's life, had provided fictitious information about her symptoms and tampered with her urine samples, causing false results and innumerable investigations, operations, and treatments in different medical centers. The other was a young boy who had presented with recurrent severe illnesses associated with hypernatremia from the age of 6 weeks until he died at the age of 15 months. The cause was repetitive poisoning with salt, given to him by his mother.

Child abuse itself is embedded in history and becomes redefined as society changes its values and decides that a particular form of behavior affecting children is no longer acceptable in their society at that time. Poisoning of children has been reported before.[2,3,4] Similarly, for centuries, patients and their relatives have been known to exaggerate symptoms. Unknown to me, even the phrase Munchausen by Proxy had been used before in an article about psychosocial dwarfism.[5] The apparent originality of my 1977 article was that it drew attention to the way in which severe child abuse could occur as a result of a mother persistently fabricating illness

3

stories for her children, thereby obtaining gratification for herself, and also to the way in which modern medical practice could harm children seriously as a result of misdiagnosis from false information. Munchausen Syndrome by Proxy (MBP) is a cumbersome title which, at times, I have regretted. It was chosen for journalistic reasons to capture attention to what I thought might be an important cause of child abuse, and also because of the similarities with Munchausen Syndrome (MS) itself.

The descendants of the original Baron von Munchhausen must wonder about the way in which they have become associated with such infamy. Baron von Munchhausen (1720–1790) retired to the family estate, south of Hannover in Germany, where he was a renowned humorous raconteur. His after dinner stories formed the basis for the travel fantasies, written by R. E. Raspe (see Fig. 1–1) and first published in English as *Baron Munchausen's Narrative of his Marvelous Travels and Campaigns in Russia* in 1785. (The fictitious baron spelled his name in English with a single 'h'.) The tales caused some embarrassment for the real Baron von Munchhausen who died a rather sad and lonely man, almost certainly without children of his own.[6] The tales lived on and are readily available as children's stories in Western Europe and North America, and they have been made into at least three full length films. A London physician, Richard Asher, borrowed the name and wrote in the *Lancet*:

> Here is described a common syndrome which most doctors have seen, but about which little has been written. Like the famous Baron von Munchausen [sic], the persons affected have always travelled widely; and their stories, like those attributed to him, are both dramatic and untruthful. Accordingly the syndrome is respectfully dedicated to the baron, and named after him.[7]

Since then many adults have been given that label of MS. It is more often attached to men than to women, and it often designates persons who migrate from one hospital to another with their untruthful stories of illness. The term tends to have been preserved for adults who have factitious disorder and physical symptoms, rather than those in which the patient produces the symptoms intentionally for financial or other reasons. My original suggestion that the label of MBP might "be applied to anyone who persistently fabri-

FIGURE 1–1

The original English edition of Baron Munchausen's adventures.

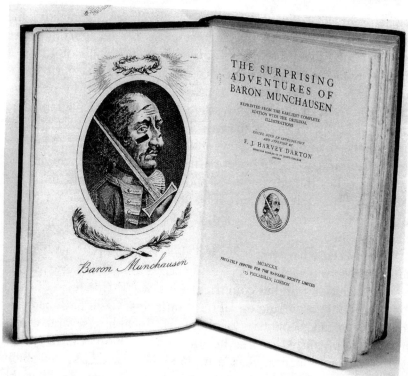

cates symptoms on behalf of another, so causing that person to be regarded as ill" was a wide ranging one, and has been able to accommodate more recent examples of adults (who are usually elderly or dependent) being abused by other relatives, and even—as veterinary surgeons report[8]—of pets being presented in this way by their owners. But the term has been used most where it started, with children. In the light of experience, it has tended to be used when fabricated illnesses of children meet the following criteria:

1. Illness in a child which is fabricated by a parent, or someone who is *in loco parentis*.
2. The child is presented for medical assessment and care, usually persistently, often resulting in multiple medical procedures.
3. The perpetrator denies knowing the etiology of the child's illness.

4. Acute symptoms and signs of illness cease when the child is separated from the perpetrator.

The original 1977 article led to several colleagues contacting me about other families, but the main impetus for recognizing more cases stemmed from the opportunity to present details of 12 cases at the Annual Scientific Meeting of the British Paediatric Association in York in 1980. It was a large meeting attended by pediatricians from most of the health districts in the United Kingdom. The paper finished with the challenge "There is probably at least one such family in your district now—have you recognized it?" During the remaining days of the meeting many pediatricians came to me saying that they thought they had such examples of child abuse occurring within their practices. This enabled the first series of 25 consecutive cases to be published; it is still one of the largest series to be described.[9]

We only see what we know, and descriptions of a "new condition" always lead to more cases being recognized. Publicity also led to its recognition in other countries. It is a worldwide form of child abuse, certainly occurring on all the continents. Cases have been reported from most countries of the world including several where there is no organized or free health service. The literature review by Rosenberg, which appeared in 1987,[10] provided an excellent picture of the many different varieties of MBP abuse as well as the methods by which they were perpetrated. In some countries too much reliance was placed upon the apparently high mortality and other adverse outcomes reported in that paper. This was unfortunate, because such a literature review inevitably includes the more severe cases that have been reported, and inadvertently includes them more than once as a result of the case appearing as an individual case report and also as part of a series. In the ensuing years it has become clear that although MBP is a severe form of child abuse, with a significant mortality as well as serious comorbidity for the abused child's siblings, neither the mortality nor the morbidity are as unfavorable as reported in that review.

Over time a clearer picture began to emerge of the different ways in which factitious illness and its consequences could occur. At times the mother might merely repeat a convincing false illness story. In other cases the mother would back up that illness story by fabricating signs of illness or altering samples that had been obtained for investigation. Other mothers would, in addition to the false story of illness, actively harm their child by direct injury including poisoning and smothering. Within these general characters various classical presentations emerged such as fictitious epilepsy, recurrent apnea, repetitive suffocation, and salt poisoning.

The epidemiology is difficult to study. Much depends on the diagnostic criteria. I am involved, at the request of other colleagues, with 30–35 cases per year within the United Kingdom, and I cannot know what percentage of new cases my experience represents. Because of that, we have begun a formal epidemiological study. Through the British Paediatric Surveillance Unit, a postage-paid card is sent monthly to every pediatrician in the United Kingdom and Ireland asking them to notify us of cases they have identified in the previous month. The survey has a response rate of more than 80% each month; therefore, at the end of 2 years, there should be reliable information about the incidence. The cases should be ones in which the probability of abuse is such that a statutory case conference has been convened (case conferences being multidisciplinary meetings organized by Social Work Departments responsible for deciding whether a child has been abused or is at risk of abuse).

There are likely to be national differences in the incidence of abuse, although the epidemiology in Europe is unlikely to be very different from that in North America. It may, however, be different in other countries. The differences are likely to result from different social and hospital practices. Pediatricians in Britain, as well as in North America, encourage mothers to be resident with their children in hospital. Many of us have the strong impression that good facilities and relationships with staff and other resident mothers provide a convenient haven for perpetrating mothers which permits them to continue the abuse. It is not uncommon to find that mothers who have suffocated, or otherwise repeatedly physically harmed their child, have perpetuated more than 90% of the physical harm while resident with their child in hospital. At a personal level this has been a particular irony because the main mission of my early years in pediatrics was to campaign *against* restricted visiting on children's wards and to campaign *for* accommodation for mothers to live in hospital with their children.

In several countries there has been confusion about how to classify MBP abuse. In the United Kingdom, social work departments have been asked to categorize it as a form of "physical abuse." However, those involved with the families will more often be impressed by the inevitable and persistent emotional abuse that is entailed, while recognizing that it often does include physical abuse as well.

For most societies and most countries there have been initial difficulties in recognizing Munchausen Syndrome by Proxy abuse and, in particular, accepting that some of the more extreme behaviors of mothers to their children have actually occurred. In 1982 in the United Kingdom, the pediatric pathologist John Emery caused an uproar that provoked debate in the British Parliament by suggesting that some infants categorized as Sudden Infant Death Syndrome had been "gently battered" or smothered to death. At that time I was encountering many children with fictitious epilepsy whose siblings had died suddenly and unexpectedly in early life, and several of the mothers admitted that they had smothered their children. The link seemed obvious but was too abhorrent for child care agencies to believe or accept as grounds for action. Thus the video recording of a mother smothering her child[11] was of great importance in convincing skeptics. In the United Kingdom, Southall and colleagues refined the video techniques and have been able to report a large series of children being smothered, recorded on videotape in hospital.[12] In the same way that some doctors and child care agencies have needed persuasion to accept that such abuse occurs, so the courts have required legal precedent concerning ways of dealing with it; and that has been established in most countries in the last 10 years. No longer is it inevitable for the pediatrician who has diagnosed the abuse to be faced by disbelieving care workers or sarcastic lawyers.

Confusion has continued about whether the term MBP should be applied to the child or the mother. Originally I had used the term to imply that factitious illness was being caused in the child by another person or substitute (i.e., proxy). Thus, the term was used to describe a form of child abuse. Therefore I felt uncomfortable when asked, in court or by colleagues, whether a mother "has Munchausen Syndrome by Proxy." It seemed no more appropriate than asking if a stepfather, who had sexually abused his stepdaughter, "is suffering from sex abuse." The *Diagnostic and Statistical Manual of Mental Disorders* of the American Psychiatric Association[13] prefers the term "Factitious Illness by Proxy," including it under the main category of factitious illness. This may help to persuade people to use the term MBP in the way originally intended, as a description of a form of child abuse. While it is important to recognize certain prototypes and common personality disorders among the perpetrators, it is equally important to acknowledge disparities, as well as perpetrators other than the child's natural mother.

From personal experience of more than 300 cases it seems to me that the child's biologic mother is the perpetrator in 90%, another female care giver (baby-sitter or nurse) in 5% and the father for the other 5%. At first it was not realized that fathers could behave in this way, but several case reports confirm their behavior[14–18] and the subject has been the basis of a novel.[19] My own experience has been that the male perpetrators, as persons and personalities, have been very similar to the female perpetrators (so much so that I took steps to find out if the first few had male chromosomes and glands). In Britain it has been curious, and perhaps worrying, to observe how differently male perpetrators are treated by the police and the courts. They seem to be regarded as a danger to society; as if they are likely to rampage through the neighborhood killing children. They are locked up until they appear in court and tend to receive long custodial sentences, whereas the female perpetrators are seldom prosecuted and rarely given custodial sentences.

There have also been several reports of serial killings falling within the spectrum of MBP. Few would suggest that it is appropriate to classify a child who is killed suddenly by the parent in that category. But when a child is repetitively poisoned or suffocated, and presented to doctors as having a mysterious natural illness until on a subsequent occasion the child is presented to the doctors and is dead, that does seem to fall within the category of MBP. The deaths of at least some of Mary-Beth Tinning's nine babies fall into that category.[20] In England in 1993 a 24-year-old nurse, Beverly Allitt, was found guilty of killing four children on a pediatric ward, attempting to kill three others, and causing grievous harm to six more.[21] The circumstances fell within the MBP scenario and the perpetrator herself had MS. These cases have led to questions about the safety of children living with persons who have MS or gross somatization disorders. The answer is not known, for although it is certain that a significant minority of those who commit

MBP abuse have MS, there has been no systematic study of the welfare of children in the care of persons with MS.

Some have tried to broaden the spectrum even further. Rand[22] considers that "contemporary" MBP should include false allegations of sexual abuse that occur at the time of custody disputes between parents. Others see that as separate.[23] Nevertheless false allegations of both physical and sexual abuse have been reported outside custody disputes and in the context of other MBP abuse.[24]

Although there are always important lessons from history, we should not dwell on the past nor on the confusing semantics surrounding MBP abuse. The story began with a wish to warn physicians, and particularly pediatricians, that they were in danger of harming children with their investigations and treatments, and of encouraging children to be falsely ill because their mothers were inventing stories of illness. In the early cases the main harm to the children came from the invasive diagnostic actions of well-meaning, but misguided, doctors and therapists. Subsequent reports have tended to dwell upon cases in which the parent actively harmed the child by poisoning, suffocation, and scarification of the skin or other organs in the perpetration of MBP. The number of such reported cases is large and distressing. The reader might gain the impression that this is the commonest form of factitious illness abuse. However, it is important to recognize that the easiest cases to address and to prove in legal proceedings are those in which there is direct forensic evidence by way of toxicological analysis or video recording. Much more difficult are the many cases in which the mother confines herself to inventing a false illness story over a long period of time. As physicians we know that we are most likely to arrive at the correct diagnosis, and to provide effective help, by listening very carefully and believing the mother's story of the child's illness. Nevertheless at the same time we must allow a small corner of our mind to be questioning and skeptical in order to prevent children's suffering from fictitious illness invented by their parents.

References

1. Meadow R. Munchausen syndrome by proxy—the hinterland of child abuse. *Lancet.* 1977; 2:343–345.

2. Lansky LL and Erikson HM. An unusual case of childhood chloral hydrate poisoning. *Am J Dis Child.* 1974; 127:343–345.

3. Kempe CH. Uncommon manifestations of the battered child syndrome. *Br Med J.* 1975; 129:1265–1268.

4. Rogerd D, Tripp J, and Bentovem A, et al. Non-accidental poisoning: an extended syndrome of child abuse. *Br Med J.* 1976; 1:793–6.

5. Money J and Werlwas J. Folie a deux in the parents of psychosocial dwarfs: two cases. *Bull Amer Acad Psychiat Law.* 1976; 4:351–61.

6. Meadow R and Lennert T. Munchausen by proxy or Polle syndrome: which term is correct? *Pediatrics.* 1984; 74:554–6.

7. Asher R. Munchausen's syndrome. *Lancet.* 1951; 1:339–341.

8. Personal communications.

9. Meadow SR. Munchausen syndrome by proxy. *Arch Dis Child.* 1982; 57:92–98.

10. Rosenberg DA. Web of deceit: a literature review of Munchausen syndrome by proxy. *Child Abuse Negl.* 1987; 11:547–563.

11. Rosen CL, Frost JD, Bricker T, et al: Two siblings with recurrent cardiorespiratory arrest: Munchausen syndrome by proxy or child abuse? *Pediatrics* 1983; 71:715–720.

12. Samuels MP, McClaughlin W, and Jacobson RR, et al. Fourteen cases of imposed upper airway obstruction. *Arch Dis Child.* 1992; 67:162–170.

13. American Psychiatric Association. *Diagnostic and Statistical Manual of Mental Disorders,* 4th ed. Washington, DC. APA; 1994.

14. Dine MS and McGovern ME. Intentional poisoning of children-overlooked category of child abuse: report of 7 cases and review of the literature. *Pediatrics.* 1982; 70:32–5.

15. Orenstein DM and Wasserman AL. Munchausen syndrome by proxy simulating cystic fibrosis. *Pediatrics.* 1986; 78:621–4.

16. Zohar Y, Avidan G, Shvili Y, et al. Otolaryngologic cases of Munchausen's syndrome. *Laryngoscope.* 1987; 97–101.

17. Meadow SR. Suffocation, recurrent apnea, and sudden infant death. *J Pediatrics.* 1990; 117:351–7.

18. Makar AF and Squier PJ. Munchausen syndrome by proxy: father as perpetrator. *Pediatrics.* 1990; 85:370–3.

19. Kellerman J. *Devil's Waltz.* New York: Little Brown; 1992.

20. Eggington J. *From cradle to grave: the short lives and strange deaths of Marybeth Tinning's nine children.* New York: Morrow; 1989.

21. Davies N. *Murder on ward 4.* London: Chatto and Windus; 1993.

22. Rand DC. Munchausen syndrome by proxy: integration of classic and contemporary type. *Issues in child abuse accusations* 1990; 2:83–89.

23. Schreier HA and Libow JA. *Hurting for love: Munchausen by proxy syndrome.* New York: Guilford Press; 1993.

24. Meadow R: False allegations of abuse and Munchausen syndrome by proxy. *Archives of Diseases of Childhood.* 1993; 68:444–7.

2

From Lying to Homicide

The Spectrum of Munchausen
Syndrome by Proxy

Donna Rosenberg

Since Dr. Meadow described Munchausen Syndrome by Proxy (MBP) in 1977,[1] hundreds of cases have been detailed in the medical literature, identification of MBP has increased, and attention to the syndrome has heightened. Inevitably, an informal and animated discussion has developed among many professionals as to the range and content of this rather peculiar syndrome, whose hallmark is a mother's persistent fabrication of her child's illness.

The spectrum of MBP is the focus of this chapter. What is reasonably included in this medical category? What is reasonably excluded? How does one sensibly evaluate those situations that appear to fall around the muddier edges of the spectrum? Who perpetrates MBP? What drives them? What are the forms of harm experienced by the child victims? What are the risks confronting these young victims?

But simply defining a spectrum is insufficient to its purposeful use. The process by which information about the spectrum is transcribed into a conclusion about a child's disorder is the *diagnostic process*. It is the process by which we *logically account for the coexistence of all the information* about a particular patient. Almost inevitably, the diagnostic process becomes a focal area of questioning in civil or criminal court. The trier of fact will want a clear answer to one pivotal question: *How* do you know that MBP is the correct diagnosis *in this patient*? More commonly than in other forms of child abuse, the *way* medical diagnosis is made generally, and specifically the way *this* medical diagnosis was made, must be clearly articulated. Unless those involved have a solid understanding of the diagnostic process, one has seen that the diagnosis of MBP may be made to appear one of ineptitude, desperation, obstinacy, ambition, caprice, intimidation, or even revenge. Therefore, because of its importance in translating information about the spectrum into usable form, the diagnostic process is included as the chapter's final section.

It is not the purpose of this chapter to exhaustively catalog all the known presentations, methods of fabrication and diagnostic tests in MBP. Rather, the reader should regard this chapter as the scaffolding upon which to fasten the information learned in the remainder of this book. Traveling through the spectrum of deceivers and their deceptions, the spectrum of harm, and the spectrum of risk will equip the reader with a framework for comprehending the range of this extraordinary disorder. In this excursion, the limits upon our understanding of MBP will also become manifest.

Defining any spectrum intimately involves the techniques of classification. So that the reader will understand what classification can do for us and what it can't, and how far we have progressed in defining the spectrum of MBP, this will be addressed first.

To ease reading, throughout this chapter the perpetrator will be referred to as the mother, with the recognition that perpetrators with another relationship to the child—father, grandmother, day care worker, and others—have occasionally been described. What is written applies equally to them.

On the Benefits and Limitations of Classification

Classification is the process of naming and grouping. It is the formalization of patterns. Though we rarely think of it as such, pattern recognition is fundamental to every aspect of our lives: we recognize *friends*, eat *vegetables*, sit on *chairs*, sense *danger*, seek *safety*. We could not function, even for an hour, without recognizing the patterns in our physical and emotional world. In everyday life, furthermore, highly refined pattern recognition is useful and goes by various names: intuition, educated guessing, a sixth sense.

Pattern recognition, as formal classification, also has a fundamental role in the practice of medicine. In medicine, we classify disorders according to their observed, like, and defining characteristics. We similarly classify drugs, therapeutic effects, and other aspects of disease. The great benefit of classification is that it enables us to *cluster* problems. This clustering, in turn, allows us to pursue research, thereby enlarging our knowledge of those disorders that afflict humans: their causes, presentations, treatments, prognoses, and ultimately, their prevention.

Classification of those medical and psychological disorders that assail our species is admirable and necessary, but always imperfect. Classification lumps together individuals who share some important characteristics, but not all. No two cardiac patients are precisely the same, even if both have had the same extent of heart damage. Inevitably, there are differences, for example, in age, weight, diet, immunity, or family medical history. Those differences may affect how sick each patient becomes and the outcome. The doctor's ability to prognosticate, therefore, may be excellent but is never exact. Doctors operate on the basis of conclusions drawn from group trends but the inferences drawn may not apply precisely to an individual. In a real sense, each patient creates his or her own classification.

But we cannot practice medicine if we treat each patient as *entirely* different from every other patient. When possible, it is to the patient's benefit if the physician can say, "I know of other cases *similar enough* to yours, so that I can intervene in your behalf, to your benefit." In saying this, we also implicitly say: "I will pay attention to how you, as an individual, differ from the group classification." In short, group information gleaned from reliable literature and one's own clinical experience, and then adjusted for individual differences, is the best method we have of judging a patient's situation.

As medical disorders are increasingly understood, classification schemes are revised. In our time, the most vivid example of this is the constantly refining classification scheme for Acquired Immune Deficiency Syndrome (AIDS), but the histories of such disorders as pneumonia or cancer vividly tell the story of how classifications evolve. The best classification schemes come from a combination of methodologically sound research, long experience, and level-headedness. Serendipity and brilliance also figure in the equation, though less mathematically.

We are in the earliest stages of this classification endeavor for MBP. As we define the spectra of falsified illnesses, perpetrators, harm, and risk, we are simultaneously aware of our relatively limited data. The syndrome has been recognized only a few years—compare it to tuberculosis. As far as we know, the prevalence rate is quite low—compare it to more common disorders such as colds or headaches. We have little experience in understanding the psychological problems in the perpetrators—historically, understanding of psychological disorders tends to proceed slowly. (Regrettably this "understanding" is sometimes a matter of prevailing psychological fashion rather than scientific scrutiny.) Finally, no large studies of comparative interventions have been published.

No classification scheme, however refined, can capture every case precisely. The line of distinction between MBP and other conditions may be unclear. For example, a mother claims that her children all have Environmental Sickness Syndrome and keeps them home from school. Is this MBP, parental anxiety, or some other condition? Though her children appear normal, another mother claims that they are developmentally delayed or psychiatrically disturbed, and has insisted upon—and obtained—treatment for them. Is this Vulnerable Child Syndrome, MBP, or some other problem? A hospital discovers that one mother called the radiology department and, impersonating her pediatrician's receptionist, ordered a CAT scan of her child's head: "Doctor wants it done. With contrast." What does this situation represent? One must bear in mind: Cases that fall around the diagnostic edges of the spectrum have the pivotal matters of risk and harm in common with MBP.

MBP is a complex disorder, involving features unusual among medical conditions. From case and series reports, we have a substantial and enlarging body of information about the spectrum of deceptions. On the other hand, because the perpetrators are elusive and skilled at avoiding assessment, we do not know a great deal about them. We have a reasonable measure of the short-term harm that may be done to children, but know relatively little about the long-term physical and emotional harm. The spectrum of risk is reasonably well defined on a population basis, but not as it pertains to an individual child. We currently have no valid way of deciding which children are at low risk, that is, which children are likely to be sufficiently cared for if returned home. This is obviously a crucial matter, but one is not reassured that such a means of deciding will be designed, or is indeed designable, judging by the well-documented difficulties in creating such a tool for use with other types of child maltreatment.[2]

As we learn more about MBP, classification will evolve. A 1987 study showed that the average time between initial presentation to a doctor and diagnosis of MBP was 15 months.[3] As awareness of Munchausen Syndrome by Proxy spreads throughout the medical community, and diagnostic strategies are used earlier and more efficiently, the time from initial presentation to diagnosis presumably will decrease. Also, as health care systems are revised over time, here and abroad, mandatory case scrutiny by health care overseers or insurance company specialists may hasten diagnosis. Even today, MBP might first be considered by a nurse specialist evaluating claims for a child's insurance carrier. Given that the definition of MBP emphasizes *chronic* fabrication, it will be interesting to see how this accelerated diagnostic tempo will affect definition. Will a mother need three events of fabrication over at least a week to qualify? Will one episode do it? What if a nurse walks into the hospital room as the mother is loading her first syringe-full of insulin?

THE SPECTRUM OF DECEPTION

1. *The hallmark of MBP is fabrication of medical illness with persistence.*

Fabrication means falsifying illness in some way. The persistence may be short-lived (days to weeks) to long-lived (months to years). MBP means *any* fabrication of medical problems over some period of time.

2. *Fabricated illness may be either simulated or produced, or both.*

Some children have been victims of mothers who *simulate* illness only (faking or lying, without doing something to the child). For example, a mother may present the child to the doctor, claiming that he has recurrent, high nightly fevers, although this claim has no basis in fact.

Other children are the victims of mothers who *produce* illness (actually do something to the child). For example, a mother may repeatedly suffocate her child and claims that the child suffers from apneic (stopping breathing) episodes.

Some mothers both simulate and produce illness.

3. *Perpetrators of MBP do not necessarily stick to type.*

Simulators sometimes evolve into producers. Producers weave lies into their productions, sometimes lying exclusively. That a mother has hitherto only simulated illness does not mean she is incapable of later producing illness. This makes sense: simulation itself requires a substantial degree of psychopathology, however well concealed. Clinical experience indicates that, in general, the psychological problems of simulators and producers overlap. In other words, one should not feel reassured about the safety of a child because the mother is today a simulator but not a producer. One has no way of knowing what she may be tomorrow.

4. *The variety of means by which mothers may simulate or produce illness is truly astounding.*

MBP may present with any of a huge array of problems—cardiovascular, respiratory, neurologic, dermatologic, hematologic, neoplastic, allergic, immunologic, infectious, gastrointestinal, endocrine, renal, reproductive, metabolic, musculoskeletal, psychiatric, or behavioral. The problems may occur at any time during childhood, including the perinatal period (surrounding the time of birth). Most commonly, they occur in infants and toddlers, but school-age children and adolescents may also be victims.

In one series, the symptoms seen most commonly were neurologic (seizures), hematologic (various types of bleeding), respiratory (apnea), gastrointestinal (vomiting, diarrhea), fever, and rash.[4] All of these presentations will be reviewed in the chapters that follow. Only two—behavioral/developmental/psychiatric presentations and false abuse complaints—will be taken up briefly in this chapter as well as later in this book.

Although lists of these presentations are periodically compiled in the medical literature[5] no list of presentations should ever be considered comprehensive. Since MBP was first described, one has amply seen that the presentations are almost limitlessly diverse, and every year new ones are described.

Not only are there hundreds of presentations of MBP, but each of them may have multiple methods of simulation or production. For example, there are several ways to fabricate vomiting. A mother may simply lie about it or she may poison the child with a medication that induces vomiting. Seizures may be fabricated by lying, by poisoning with various drugs, or by suffocation. Bleeding may be produced by administering rat poison to cause true bleeding or by draining blood from an existing intravenous line, or it may be simulated by applying exogenous blood, paint, cocoa, or dye to the child's skin.

Within this syndrome that doctors, nurses, social workers, judges, and juries already find on the margins of believability, there are yet presentations that further astonish. Even if one is able to comprehend the possibility that a normal-appearing mother might submit her child to this peculiar form of torture, it is still hard to fathom that cystic fibrosis, diabetes, or immune deficiencies, among other complex illnesses, can be fabricated. Dr. Meadow's original reference to MBP as "the hinterland of child abuse" has an eerie fidelity.[6] Despite one's sympathy for the mother's underlying troubles and psychopathology, one should not underestimate her capacity for deception, or for the complexity of that deception. However perversely, the mother has invested herself utterly in this child, making a career for herself from his false illnesses. She is able to devote to her fiction what most professionals only wish for their careers: almost unlimited time.

5. MBP may include deliberate withholding of medication or treatment from a child who is genuinely ill.

This type of occurrence is most likely to be seen in a child who has a chronic illness, such as asthma or allergies. Medication or treatment is surreptitiously withheld with the purpose of exaggerating the condition. In other words, MBP may be perpetrated not through fabricating illness, but through fabricating compliance. The mother says she is tending to the child as directed, but she is not, and the child thereby becomes more ill, more frequently.

How does one distinguish deliberate omission, calculated to exacerbate the child's problems, from the more common situation of medical care neglect? If there is evidence of *calculation in the omission*, it is MBP. For example, a mother comes for medical visits, fills the prescriptions and the medicine bottle is empty on schedule, but the child becomes sicker and serum drug levels are subtherapeutic. The child does not improve with home help for the mother, but improves on the prescribed regimen in the hospital or a foster home.

By contrast, mothers who medically neglect their children, without the purpose of making the child sicker, are more likely to miss appointments, leave prescriptions unfilled or not refilled, and have full or partially full medicine bottles. The medically neglected child often does better when home help or transportation assistance is made available to the mother. Sometimes, these children are neglected in other obvious ways, in contrast to victims of Munchausen Syndrome by Proxy.

When other causes of inexplicably persistent illness in a child have been eliminated, and the only two remaining possibilities are MBP and medical care neglect, differentiating the two is, to some extent, an exercise in inferring the mother's intent. However, the mother's intent may be very difficult to assess. (See more on this under Diagnosis, in this chapter.)

It is possible that the doctor or authorities will not be able to determine whether the child's ill health is the result of medical care neglect, noncompliance for another reason, or MBP. *For whatever reason*, if not receiving vital medical care, the child must be protected. It is not necessary to show the civil court which of these problems is causing the child to be unnecessarily ill. It is sufficient to show that the recommended treatment would significantly improve the child's state without causing undue harm, that the mother has been repeatedly apprised of the situation, that she has received the necessary assistance to tend to the child, and that the child remains hazardously untreated and at significant risk of harm.

Occasionally an exhausted mother, who needs temporary respite from a truly chronically ill child, brings her child for medical care, claiming the child has symptoms that would require hospitalization. The symptoms, however, do not exist and it is determined that the mother did not misinterpret the child's problems, but instead either lied or exaggerated. How is this situation distinguished from MBP? In general, since *chronicity of fabrication* is the hallmark of MBP, one must consider the possibility that a single event is more likely to be a the result of desperate maternal fatigue. If one can sit in a quiet place with the mother and sympathetically ask her about her home situation, the mother is most likely to divulge her problem and her ill-conceived solution. In such a way, one is most likely to speedily come to a correct diagnosis, thereby insuring that both mother and child receive the help they need.

6. *MBP and real illness may occur together.*

In some instances, the child does have a genuine medical problem which is acute, should resolve with treatment, but inexplicably continues with congruent or incongruent symptoms. For example, a child with straightforward appendicitis, apparently cured by surgery, develops chronic (fabricated) vomiting. Another child with a treated bone infection develops (fabricated) apnea.

Victims of MBP are not protected from other illnesses that intrude into childhood. Like other children, they catch colds, have skin rashes, or develop other real illnesses. Some may in fact be excessively prone to intercurrent illnesses because of exposures during frequent and prolonged hospitalizations or because of an immune system compromised by chronic fabricated illness. Other children may be at heightened risk of serious childhood disease because of fabricated contraindications to vaccines, which prevented their being immunized.

7. *MBP may present with complaints of behavioral, developmental, or psychiatric abnormalities.*

Extraordinary as it seems, such disorders as cerebral palsy, developmental retardation, and deafness, among others, have been reported.[7] There are also reports of child victims of MBP who present with fabricated psychiatric problems.[8] Surely, if a mother were intent upon fabrication, she might lie about psychiatric symptoms, produce them with various drugs, or "brainwash" a growing child, over time, to believe that he is disturbed. Given the fluidity of psychodiagnosis and the subjectivity of many symptoms, this would appear to be a fertile field. It is not far-fetched to observe that this process could itself create a genuine psychiatric disturbance, in childhood or later.

8. *MBP may present as falsified complaints of abuse.*

There are a number of reports of MBP presenting as falsified complaints of sexual or physical assault.[9,10] Apart from the context of MBP, there are other contexts, such as custody disputes and revenge, in which a parent makes a false allegation of sexual or other child maltreatment. A battered mother might allege that her husband abuses the child because she hopes that such allegation will strengthen her request for a restraining order. Another mother might be psychotic, out of touch with reality. Such situations, of course, must be differentiated from MBP.

Highlighted by these troubling cases is the fact that not all fabrication is MBP. Nor, from a practical point of view, is it always necessary to establish whether a given situation is or is not MBP. Though relying on a fabricator to divulge the reason for fabrication is not necessarily productive, one must at least ask, "I know you made this up. Why?" It is possible that there is a plausible explanation for the fabrication, one that can be verified factually. For example, a mother may admit fabricating a history of sexual abuse to her 3 year old, because she had recently discovered that her husband previously molested a daughter by a prior marriage. The girl, now a teenager, refused to discuss it with any authority, and told the mother that, if asked, she would deny it. The mother, fearing for her own daughter, thought the fabrication would ensure protection. When the teenager was interviewed, she corroborated the mother's story. In this example, the fabrication has involved lying, but not production of findings. If the mother had gone to the extent of sexually or physically injuring the infant, it would have been necessary to protect the baby from her.

9. *Children who agree they have all the symptoms which their mothers falsely claim they have, whether those are physical or psychiatric, should not be thought of as liars.*

This is the result of chronic implantation in the child's mind of false information. One 11-year-old girl told me that, every night while sleeping, she had seizures and very high fevers "to a hundred and six." This is really no more remarkable than a normal child with a normal mother who believes that she snores, because her mother tells her so. Children generally believe what they are told by the adults who care for them. This is how they learn. We should not expect a child victim of MBP to be better able to distinguish fact from fiction than a nonabused child.

10. *MBP should be distinguished from other disorders that feature parental persistence.*

Obviously, not all parental persistence is MBP. In fact, most parental persistence is the result of the child's having a genuine illness.[11]

A differential diagnosis is a list of possible medical explanations. Parental persistence must generate a differential diagnosis by the pediatrician, one which amply takes into account the possibilities of

FIGURE 2-1

The persistence algorithm. The most common pathway is depicted with arrowheads.

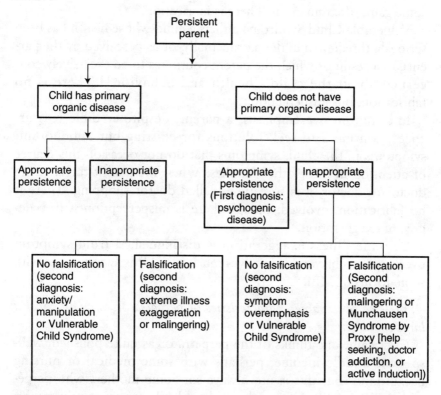

Reprinted with permission from Waring, 1992. Note: First diagnosis = What is wrong with the child, if anything? Second diagnosis = Why is the child being brought at this time?

genuine illness, psychogenic illness in the child, parental anxiety, malingering, Vulnerable Child Syndrome, symptom overemphasis, extreme illness exaggeration and MBP (see Figure 2–1).

Psychogenic illness in the child is an illness whose origins are emotional. A child may have intermittent abdominal pain, not because of a disease, but because the child doesn't want to go to visit her grandmother. Parental anxiety is seen in pediatric practice when a child has a symptom (complains of something) or sign (observable abnormality) and the distressed parent brings the child for medical care. There is no fabrication. It is not science that distinguishes among concern, worry, and anxiety. Rather, they are defined by personal, local, or vernacular use.

Malingering involves genuine illness which is elaborated for some gain, often financial. There is fabrication.

Vulnerable Child Syndrome afflicts a child whose health has been seriously threatened in the past (actually, or as perceived by the parent), as a result of which the parent continues to be excessively concerned about the child's health and behavior.[12] There is no fabrication, but misperception.

In symptom overemphasis, a parent, despite credible reassurances, continues to seek solutions for existing but unimportant symptoms in the child, symptoms that do not occasion this degree of attention in most other families. When the parent travels from doctor to doctor, it is sometimes called doctor shopping. There is no fabrication involved, though there is misperception with a degree of exaggeration.

Extreme illness exaggeration is distinguished from symptom overemphasis because it involves fabrication. It is synonymous with some forms of MBP.

11. *The observable characteristics of perpetrators of MBP cover a large spectrum.*

Classically, one thinks of the perpetrator as quite polished, well-spoken, middle income, perhaps with some medical or nursing background. But this is not always so. Some mothers who perpetrate MBP are poor, or uneducated, or labile, or constantly cranky. In fact, there is no profile of these mothers that is infallible. One looks forward to increasingly helpful information from one's psychiatric colleagues.

One characteristic of mothers who perpetrate MBP has not received much attention elsewhere, but bears mention. An occasional mother invests her energies in harassing a doctor, generally the one who reported the abuse to the authorities. She may do this in many ways, among them communicating with other parents in the practice to solicit information about their possible dissatisfaction with the doctor, making odd telephone calls, writing letters or causing unusual events around the office building or the doctor's home. The mother may constantly threaten to litigate, but not take action. Doctors are well advised to notify their malpractice carrier, the practice or hospital attorney, a private attorney, or several of these. At the first suggestion of a mother's criminal behavior or intent, the police and the district attorney's office should be notified immediately.

12. *Mothers who perpetrate MBP may profit.*

Some mothers have injured or killed their children and have then sued the hospital or treating physician for malpractice. Other mothers have sued for malicious reporting of child abuse. The single-mindedness with which some mothers pursue litigation is reminiscent in quality of the determination with which they pursued the fabrication in the first place. When it is no longer possible for them to continue their avocation of perpetrating false illness, some mothers turn their pathological energies to making misery for the doctor, and money for themselves. Unfortunately, insurance companies that represent the hospital or doctor may make decisions about case disposition not upon the merits of the case, but solely according to costs. An insurance carrier may surmise that, in the long run, it will cost a great deal more to defend a doctor, however sturdy the doctor's position, than to simply give the mother a cash settlement that closes the case.

There are other possible sources of income for mothers who fabricate illness. The National Vaccine Injury Compensation Program was established as a result of the 1986 National Childhood Vaccine Injury Act (Public Law 99-660). Its purpose is to compensate victims and families for vaccine-related injury while decreasing the number of civil suits filed against doctors and pharmaceutical companies. It was designed to decrease manufacturers' liability concerns, thereby decreasing vaccine costs and increasing research and development. Some believe that the program, while laudatory, may have a hidden down-side as a financially attractive invitation to child abuse.

Other possible benefits to mothers who perpetrate MBP include funds from private and governmental programs for families with chronically ill children; the adulation and local fame associated with self-sacrificing maternal care; special parking privileges; access to respite, transport, nutrition and other community programs; access to organizations that offer wish fulfillment events to severely ill children; and more. One mother who perpetrated MBP was convicted of embezzling funds from the municipal government office in which she had worked. She asked the prosecutor for leniency; having a chronically ill child (the prosecutor was unaware of the Munchausen Syndrome by Proxy) had so distressed her that, in her grief, she had uncharacteristically committed a crime!

THE SPECTRUM OF HARM

1. *Harm is a function of the mother's deeds and of the ill that befell the child as a result of those deeds.*

Harm is what has already occurred to the child. It may also be called *damage* or *degree of intrusion*. Assessing harm is a retrospective process.

The deeds of the mother that harm the child are those that invite unnecessary medical examinations, testing, or intervention. In this regard, lying is no less a deed than actually producing illness, but simply a way of producing illness through an employee who has been unwittingly seduced into the ghastly charade. Naturally, the production of illness is also a deed.

But the deeds of the mother are not only those of commission. Deeds of omission may seriously affect the child too. The time that a normal mother devotes to nurturing, protecting, and teaching her child is instead committed to harming the child. The benefits to the child from having a loving, attentive mother, including normal physical and emotional development, may simultaneously be lost. This loss may have a profound effect upon the child, and is occasionally catastrophic. The spectrum of harm is elaborated in Table 2–1.

2. *The severity of the MBP must be based upon the harm to the child.*

Harm, rather than maternal behavior, is used to assess severity because only from the victim's perspective can harm be properly assessed.

3. *Produced illness is generally more harmful to the child than simulated illness.*

As the perpetration of MBP increasingly or exclusively involves producing illness, the child is more likely to be harmed. It is obviously more dangerous for a child to have his mother actually suffocate him and cause him to stop breathing, than it is for his mother to do nothing to him but to lie to the doctor.

Table 2–1
The Spectrum of Harm*

Fear	Complications of surgery
Pain	Temporary disfigurement: physical effects
Suffering	
Loss of attachment	Temporary disfigurement: psychosocial effects
Loss of development	
Loss of growth	Temporary impairment: physical effects
Loss of normal sibling and peer interaction	Temporary impairment: psychosocial effects
Loss of school time	Permanent disfigurement: physical effects
Effects of drugs	
Side-effects of drugs	Permanent disfigurement: psychosocial effects
Complications of drugs	
Effects of medical tests	Permanent impairment: physical effects
Side effects of medical tests	Permanent impairment: psychosocial effects
Complications of medical tests	
Effects of surgery	Other psychological problems
Side effects of surgery	Death

*With the exception of death, not in increasing order of severity.

4. *Simulated illness, however, may sometimes be very harmful, and is sometimes more harmful to the child than produced illness.*
Children whose mothers simulate illness have usually been subjected to medical testing. Some of them have had a minimal amount, while others have undergone extensive procedures and intervention. The discomfort, fear, or pain of the child during this process is a form of harm.

Intrusive investigations or treatment for the child may also precipitate a cascade of damage to the child. For example, a mother contaminates a sample of her child's urine with her own menstrual blood and brings the girl to the doctor, with the sample, saying that the child has bloody urine. A series of medical tests is begun, but no diagnosis is made. Eventually, a kidney biopsy of the child is ordered, and when performed, is complicated by internal bleeding, which in turn causes other genuine illnesses.

5. *Harm to the child is not always a function of persistence.*

Although harm to the child may increase as time goes on, this is not inevitably the case. Mild fabrication may persist for a long time; occasionally one sees cases that do not escalate and remain undiagnosed.

On the other hand, very serious harm may persist for only a short time; prompt diagnosis, the advent of a new victim, or death of the child may decrease the time period.

6. *Child victims of MBP may have unnecessary surgery.*

Nationwide, most children who are operated on need the surgery, but some do not. The reasons for unnecessary surgery vary. Medical error or worse, incompetence or avarice, are some of the possibilities. There are also dozens of reports in the pediatric literature of victims of MBP who receive unnecessary surgery. How does this happen?

What is repeated throughout the literature is consonant with one's own experience. Typically, a well-meaning surgeon receives a consultation from another doctor, often a pediatrician. The referring physician asks the surgeon to evaluate the child for the possibility of performing surgery, most often an elective procedure (i.e., necessary but not emergent). The pediatrician describes the child as suffering from a disorder such as chronic vomiting or diarrhea, and therefore requiring frequent venous access for rehydration. Would the child be a suitable candidate for a central venous catheter? Or perhaps the child is described by the pediatrician as having severe failure to thrive, and it is hoped that a permanent feeding tube would facilitate growth. Would the surgeon consider placing a gastrostomy tube in the child? (These examples are not accidentally chosen. Central venous catheters and gastrostomy operations are dismayingly common types of surgery associated with Munchausen Syndrome by Proxy).

The child is examined by the surgeon, not primarily for the purpose of corroborating the pediatrician's diagnosis, but more for the purpose of assessing the patient's state and suitability for surgery. In other words, the surgeon considers not *why* the patient has failure to thrive, but only *if* the patient has failure to thrive, and whether there are unacceptable risks for surgery.

More often than not, if the referring pediatrician tells the surgeon that the surgery is necessary, barring contraindications, it will be done. Unfortunately, if the pediatrician has been utterly deceived by the mother, the deception is propagated down the line to the surgeon.

One might argue that, before operating, a surgeon has an absolute obligation to review all medical records from a completely fresh perspective. In reality, surgeons are no more or less likely to do this than the many other subspecialty consultants. Regrettably, the volumes of medical records and the excellent reputations of the referring physician and prior consultants combine to discourage a complete case re-examination.

7. Child victims of MBP may die as a result of the maltreatment.

When death occurs, the children have usually been killed by the perpetrator. However, a child may also die because of complications of a medical test or treatment ordered to diagnose or treat the fabrication. Most practitioners would consider this homicide, with the parent as perpetrator. It is analogous to the situation when a murderer shoots his victim and the victim dies during the course of medical intervention, even if the intervention is not optimal.

If there was chronic illness fabrication prior to death, serial homicides may also be cases of MBP. In other words, single or serial homicide and Munchausen Syndrome by Proxy are not mutually exclusive.

Whether the perpetrator meant to kill the child, or inadvertently went "too far" during the course of "routine" fabrication is a matter for the prosecutor's office to allege and the triers of fact to decide. Even if it existed, convincingly showing premortem fabrication is often problematic because, almost always, it is diagnosed in retrospect. Judges and juries may find these retrospective diagnoses troubling. When there has been serial homicide, unless the premortem fabrication is explicit and there is credible expert testimony to support that contention, it is sometimes better not to invoke the term MBP. On the other hand, when these cases are before civil courts to protect surviving children, or when day-care licensure is involved, the burden of proof is less and testimony pertaining to MBP may be useful.

8. The mother is solely responsible for the harm.

Sometimes those who review cases of MBP see clearly that a diagnosis could conceivably have been made earlier in the child's course, thus saving the child some harm. Viewed so clearly through the retrospectoscope, this is actually true in every case. Although, in a macabre way, the deceived doctor is the conduit through which harm is amplified, if ignorant of the deception the doctor is not culpable for the harm. As the underlying instigator, the mother is culpable.

   9. Harm is not the same as risk.
Just as the type of fabrication does not necessarily predict the harm to the child, the harm does not necessarily predict the risk. For example, a child is fed rat poison by his mother who then brings him to the hospital, saying that he is bleeding. The resident who sees the child happens to have just finished a doctoral degree on the subject of rat poison, and makes the diagnosis. The child recovers quickly, with no permanent damage. The fabrication in this example, though extremely intrusive, is fortunately not accompanied by severe harm. Although the harm was mild, the risk was high.

THE SPECTRUM OF RISK

   1. Once MBP is uncovered, the first order of business is protection of the child. This involves estimating risk.
   Risk is the hazard or peril to the child. It is in the present and future. It may also be called *threatened harm* or *danger.*

   2. Assessing risk to a child victim of MBP may be done only in a general way.
   Assessing risk involves predicting the future. Risk is largely a function of the mother's capabilities and the likelihood of her carrying out those capabilities. One may also take into account characteristics of the child—age, developmental stage, health, for example—and other factors such as who is available to help this mother, how helpful that person or agency can be, or how the presence of other children in the home may alter any of these variables.
   Assessing risk is a projective process involving poor data.[13] It is therefore problematic, both concerning MBP and indeed concerning other forms of child abuse. The only way to know absolutely if someone could maim, disable, or murder is if she has already done

so.[14] In reality, we do not know how to predict the behavior of unpredictable people.

3. *Despite this, risk must still be estimated. The damage that has already occurred is an estimate of the least possible risk.*

Because all state statutes mandate that any *suspicion* of child abuse must be reported, it is a curious fact of clinical life that one is often called upon to first enunciate the degree of risk to the child at the same time a one has just made a provisional diagnosis. The necessity to protect the child from imminent danger is paramount. Thus the opportunity to collect evidence may be lost because doing so would unacceptably compromise the child's safety.

It is prudent to place the child victim of MBP outside the home. No test can tell us which children are at low risk if they return home to an untreated mother. Few extensive case series have been published to guide this decision, and none that prospectively compare different types of intervention. The best that can be said for returning the child home is that it is wishful. In one series, 20% of child victims of Munchausen Syndrome by Proxy who were killed died after the mother had been "confronted", and the child discharged to her.[15] Putting aside the obvious problem that "confrontation" has no universal meaning, MBP is not a disorder that is repaired by confrontation. To understand the depth of pain that normal parents suffer when their children suffer is to understand the vacancy in mothers who perpetrate MBP.

If no damage or little damage has occurred, one estimates the risk to the child based upon similar cases in the literature and, if there has been any, upon one's own professional experience. This is the same process as that used with children who have been physically abused, sexually abused, or neglected.

4. *A mother's merely desisting from simulating or producing illness in the child is not sufficient evidence that the child is safe with her.*

MBP is, at least in part, a profound disorder of empathy. It is a serious form of psychopathology, probably with its roots in early, profound neglect, with or without physical or sexual abuse. It is entirely possible that the reason a mother stops her abusive behavior is not because her emotional problems have vanished, but simply because once the fabrication has been discovered, she is no longer logistically able to deceive and no longer able to gain whatever it is she gained from the deception.

5. Risk may also be estimated in those cases which fall around the cloudier edges of the diagnostic spectrum.

One should not become too tangled up in definitions, and in so doing, lose sight of the more important question: what is the threatened harm to the child? There is no oracle (nor should there be) to pronounce which of the cases that fall around these imprecise edges of the spectrum should or should not qualify as MBP. Again, the risk to the child is at least the harm that has already occurred.

The Diagnostic Process in Medicine and Munchausen Syndrome by Proxy

Though the term is in almost universal use, one does not so much *make* a diagnosis as discern one. One formulates possible explanations for the known information about a patient. The diagnostic process differs from the simple accumulation of facts because it *uses* facts to generate and test hypotheses.

Facts: I see something grey. It is very big. I am at the zoo.
Hypotheses: It is an elephant. It is a building. It is a cloud.
Tests: Can I touch it? Does it eat?

A diagnosis of MBP is arrived at in the same way as other diagnoses: taken into account are the patient's history, physical findings, and laboratory results. Normal findings (pertinent negatives) are as important as abnormal findings (pertinent positives). A list of possible explanations for this constellation of findings is then generated and tested.

Oski[16] has distilled the diagnostic process into straightforward guidelines:*

1. Always think of a number of diagnostic possibilities that are compatible with the chief complaint or the initial physical findings. Always consider the most common diagnosis first, but always include among your diagnoses those conditions no matter how rare, for which treatment is available, and, if missed and untreated, would produce irreparable harm or even death to your patient.

---

*Reprinted by permission of the author and J. P. Lippincott Co.

2. Form a reasoned plan for testing your hypothesis. Sequence laboratory tests to establish, or rule out, the most common diseases first as well as the diseases requiring urgent treatment.
3. Don't rush to make a diagnosis for which no treatment is available.
4. Never perform a diagnostic procedure that is not related to any of your diagnostic possibilities (e.g., a urinalysis in a patient being evaluated for inspiratory stridor).
5. Do not pursue a differential among diagnoses that will not alter your course of action.
6. Always consider the harm that tests might do as well as their costs. Balance the harm and the costs against the information that may be gained.
7. Be constantly aware of the natural tendency to discount, or even disregard, evidence likely to eliminate your favored diagnosis.
8. Don't ever dismiss the possibility that a patient with multiple complaints or problems may have more than one disease. The chances of having two common diseases simultaneously is greater than the chance of having one rare disease.
9. When you can't rule out the possibility of the presence of a disease which would result in serious harm to the patient if left untreated, treat the patient as if the disease was present.

Remember that probability and utility should always guide your actions.

The diagnostic process must be as rigorously pursued in instances of suspected MBP as it is with any other medical diagnosis. Six points deserve special emphasis.

1. Failure to consider the possibility of MBP as part of the differential diagnosis is the single largest impediment to making the diagnosis. Once the diagnosis is considered, it is usually confirmed or rejected quickly.

2. Occasionally a suspected case of MBP is something else entirely, perhaps a missed organic problem. It does not behoove physicians to marry themselves to *any* diagnosis in the face of solid medical evidence which, if regarded objectively, would exclude it.

3. MBP is a pediatric, not a psychiatric, diagnosis. There is no psychiatric or psychological test, no interview technique, that can exclude it. Similarly, in the absence of a confession, there is no test or technique that can confirm the diagnosis. Different psychological tests may highlight a perpetrator's personality or psychopathologi-

cal traits, but this must not be confused with making or excluding the diagnosis. One has heard mental health professionals report that a certain individual "is not capable of perpetrating MBP," or "does not have the traits of someone who would victimize a child in this way," or "does not have a character disorder, therefore could not have done this." None of these statements is plausible. In each of them, conjecture has been mistaken for medical diagnosis.

4. From a pediatric point of view, the intent of the perpetrator is diagnostically immaterial. Realistically, the pediatrician has no way to measure intent, either quantitatively or qualitatively. The perpetrator, who would be the only reliable source of information concerning intent is, by definition, unreliable. She generally lacks insight, is severely psychologically disturbed, and has a vested interest in clouding, rather than clarifying, matters. Therefore, intent cannot be added into the diagnostic equation.

For example, cases of MBP have occurred in which the perpetrator says that she never *intended* to harm the child. She smothered the child *only that once* to convince the doctors of the severity of the child's actual problem. She *only intended* to get the attention of her husband. She *did not intend* to kill the child, but simply to cause a little diarrhea. How is a pediatrician supposed to weigh these remarks in the diagnostic process or in the estimation of risk to the child? In fact, there is no good way. Later on, if the mother is seeing a mental health professional, the invocation of the recently popular psychiatric diagnoses of multiple personality disorder or other dissociative phenomena does not illuminate the path. How does one weigh intent when the mother (or her psychiatrist) says that she "dissociated" or that "the abuse was done by one of her alternative personas"? The remarks about intent in this chapter reflect the pediatric viewpoint. The matter of intent figures differently for other professionals.

Intent is of concern to the civil court, responsible as it is for protecting the child and treating the family. In civil court, intent will be important to explore, especially when a family treatment program is being recommended or ordered. However, earlier on in the proceedings, when the matter of protecting the child from imminent harm is before the court, intent is less salient. The court should view the assault from the child's point of view: the complicated, perhaps impenetrable labyrinths of intent hardly matter when your mother's hand is closing off your airway.

In criminal court, the apparent intent of the perpetrator reckons in the degree of culpability, and will be weighed in such matters as criminal charges. The matter of intent may be explored much more thoroughly in a court of law than on a hospital ward.

From a psychiatric point of view, true intent will be an important (but probably difficult) issue in therapy. A mother's acknowledgment of her assaults and her probing the matter of her intent during those assaults perhaps has some prognostic value for the likelihood of a psychotherapeutic success.

5. When MBP is strongly suspected and a final diagnosis must be determined, the separation of the child from the suspected perpetrator may be the least deleterious diagnostic test available.

In medicine, most diagnostic tests and intervention strategies have potential liabilities. For example, a simple blood test may diagnose a serious and treatable illness but may also cause a skin infection. Placement of a child in a foster home may prevent a child from being raped by her father but also cause emotional trauma because of separation from siblings. In both examples, the emotional and financial costs of the strategy are worth the result.

Similarly, as one makes a provisional diagnosis of MBP, one is also legally obliged to report the case and protect the child. As the mother is notified, the opportunity to collect evidence of commission (videotapes, tests on vomitus for poisons) is jettisoned. Therefore, separation from the suspected perpetrator to demonstrate whether the child improves dramatically may be the best diagnostic test available. This is not to say that separation is without problems, but simply that when compared to the cost of either allowing MBP to continue or failing to exclude the diagnosis, separation from the suspected perpetrator may be the most benign diagnostic strategy.

6. The pediatric practitioner must make certain that all the facts are available before making a final diagnosis of MBP. However, a preliminary diagnosis is often necessary, based upon the currently available facts, so that the protection of the child is assured while all the data are being collected and reviewed. One generally needs the civil court's ruling to protect the child and also to secure court-ordered discovery of medical records and other documents.

In cases of suspected MBP, reviewing all records may be an enormously time-consuming endeavor. For example, the occasional victim of MBP has had over 100 hospitalizations. The practitioner must take the time to review these records in as timely a way as possible, recognizing that simultaneous responsibilities may also demand attention. There is no substitute for careful, exhaustive records review, and the court must allow the doctor enough time for it. Although the records to be reviewed may be voluminous, the questions before the doctor may be simply stated.

1. What are the facts?
2. Is there a discrepancy between the facts and the history provided by the mother? If so, is that discrepancy the result of misunderstanding, incapacity, or fabrication? Show why.
3. Is there a discrepancy between the various histories that the mother may have provided? If so, is that discrepancy the result of misunderstanding, incapacity, or fabrication? Show why.
4. Is there a discrepancy between the set of medical facts and known medical entities? If so, show how.
5. What is the differential diagnosis for the child's condition, in order of likelihood?

Conclusion

In the panorama of pediatric disorders, MBP is an oddity. Unlike virtually any other problem, a *defining* feature of the syndrome integrally involves the response of the medical system. MBP, like a tango, cannot be done alone.

Those who minister to children are perhaps peculiarly uncomfortable in making the diagnosis. As a pediatric practitioner, one learns to listen carefully to a parent's history and to rely upon her information. Of course, with experience, one learns to weigh histories, but, by dint of disposition and education, one is not inclined to contemplate that an entire presentation is an elaborate fiction.

Involvement with even one perpetrator of MBP may profoundly anger, frustrate, or disillusion a doctor or nurse. Doctors testifying to diametrically opposite interpretations of a set of facts usually find it a miserable experience. It is useful to bear in mind that one must bring to a court not only the content of one's medical thinking, but just as important, the balance and logic. With civility, one may agree to disagree with one's colleagues, as occurs in other cases. Physicians have a different job from lawyers, and it is best not to become involved in the adversarial tone or spirit of the legal process. Medical practitioners no more "belong" to the defense or the prosecution than they belong to the legal profession altogether.

Finally, one must put the matter into perspective. Only the very occasional mother is an absolute liar. It remains the pediatrician's lucky work to harken carefully to a parent's concerns.

References

1. Meadow R. Munchausen syndrome by proxy: the hinterland of child abuse. *Lancet.* 1977; 2:343–5.
2. Wald M. and Woolverton M. Risk assessment: the emperor's new clothes. *Child Welfare.* 1990; 69:483–511.
3. Rosenberg DA. Web of deceit: a literature review of Munchausen syndrome by proxy. *Child Abuse Negl.* 1987; 11:547–563.
4. Rosenberg, Web.
5. Rosenberg DA. Munchausen syndrome by proxy. In: Reece R, ed. *Child Abuse: Medical Diagnosis and Management.* 1993; Philadelphia: Lea & Febiger:266–278.
6. Meadow, MBP.
7. Stevenson RD and Alexander R. Munchausen syndrome by proxy presenting as a developmental disability. *J Dev Behavior Peds.* 1990; 11:262–4.
8. Fisher GC, Mitchell I, and Murdoch D. Munchausen's syndrome by proxy. The question of psychiatric illness in a child. *Br J Psychiatr.* 1993; 162:701–703.
9. Libow JA and Schreier HA. Three forms of factitious illness in children: when is it munchausen syndrome by proxy? *Am J Orthopsychiat.* 1986; 56:602–11.
10. Meadow R. False allegations of abuse and munchausen syndrome by proxy. *Arch Dis Child.* 1993; 68:444–447.
11. Waring WW. The persistent parent. *Am J Dis Child.* 1992; 146:753–6.
12. The concept of vulnerable child syndrome is reviewed and updated in: Boyce WT. The vulnerable child: new evidence, new approaches. *Adv Peds.* 1992; 39:1–33.
13. Wald and Woolverton, Risk assessment.
14. This is analogous to the advice, given by the Canadian Department of Agriculture in 1962, that the only way to know whether a mushroom is poisonous is to eat it. (*Edible and Poisonous Mushrooms of Canada.* Ottawa: Information Canada: 1.)
15. Rosenberg, Web.
16. Oski FA. The diagnostic process. In: Oski FA, DeAngelis CD, Feigin RD, Warshaw JB, eds. *Principles and Practices of Pediatrics.* Philadelphia: Lippincott; 1990; 50–2. Reprinted by permission.

3

Etiological Speculations

Geoffrey C. Fisher

One of the advantages of writing a chapter in a book, unlike writing a formal research article, is that there is greater latitude for speculation, discussion, even musing. I do not have any explanations for why the perpetrators of Munchausen Syndrome by Proxy (MBP) do what they do. A book could be written on this single question, but, partly because of space the following is an essay, not a fully referenced research paper, nor a fully comprehensive one, outlining some of my personal reflections on possible etiological aspects of this alluring human behavior.

Since MBP was initially recognized, many professionals have been intrigued by what may lie behind the perpetrations involved in the deliberate and at times long lasting and life threatening harm toward the children. Those of us who work in the field of child abuse can, at times, understand how a parent frustrated by life's problems and in a state of rage can perpetrate an episode of physical harm toward a child. It is very difficult, however, to imagine how a person can deliberately plot the deception involved in some cases of MBP. It is unlikely that any form of etiological theory can be proposed that will encompass all the behaviors of all the perpetrators so far described in the literature or encountered clinically.

I suppose some analogies can be made with the perpetration of some types of sexual abuse. It is very difficult for most persons to imagine and understand the plotting, coercion, and "grooming" of young victims that is necessary for many incest perpetrators to maintain their victims in states of psychological captivity so that they can be used to satisfy facets of the perpetrator's psychodynamic functioning. We do know that in most cases of adult-child incest the offenders' behavior is well planned and they are experts at deception. We also know that in most cases sexual offenders come from highly dysfunctional backgrounds and use their victims to satisfy both conscious and unconscious desires for control, power, and sexual gratification. Although we may be able to track their behavior to various familial, societal, and sometimes biological factors and provide complex psychiatric formulations and explanations, we cannot empathize with the behavior or personally understand why they have chosen this pathway of dealing with their psychodynamic dysfunction. Nearly every society has incest taboos that are culturally and biologically based, recognizing that incest works against evolutionary principles. In psychological terms incest destroys the group and family matrix necessary for the healthy rearing of children. From a biologic evolutionary perspective incest constricts the pool of genetic material. Incest taboos have very deep roots in cultural, societal, and biological history; those who break these taboos are breaking something fundamental to human nature. Our sophisticated psychological formulations, though pragmatically useful for case planning and legal dispositions for example, are insufficient to fully understand the primitive nature of their transgressions.

The care and rearing of children also has very deep evolutionary, cultural, societal, and biological roots. Attachment of a caregiver to a child is not only an expected social phenomenon, but (as is often forgotten), has very deep-seated biological components. For perpetrators of MBP to consciously plot and deceive while putting their child's life deliberately at risk is breaking an evolutionary care-giving taboo. I strongly suspect that we will be able to create complex psychological formulations that superficially appear to explain the behavior of individual MBP perpetrators. But for those who perpetrate the most malignant fabrications we will probably never fully comprehend the motivations. Although it is not a particularly accurate analogy, I recall from my early psychiatric training that one of the *sine qua non* of psychosis was an inability of the assessing clinician to comprehend the patient. Of course phenomenological descriptions of their mental status were advanced, and treatment plans designed, but true understanding was impossible. In my meetings with perpetrators of MBP I have been able to provide child protection agents, pediatricians, and attorneys with phenomenological descriptions of mental states and recommendations for management and child safety, but I have nearly always been left with the feeling that I did not truly understand the person. I have regularly been impressed by the consummate aloneness (not loneliness) and desperation in the lives of these women that they were unable to articulate. I have sometimes wondered whether the perpetrators of the more serious forms of fabrication were indeed psychotic, but not in the way we understand psychosis today in terms of DSM IV diagnoses[1] or neuroanatomy and physiology. Rather, they have broken primitive evolutionary-based taboos of child rearing, and as their psychodynamic functioning is likely equally primitive, perhaps prelinguistic, we do not have the language to grasp an understanding of their individual experiences.

I have suggested that perpetrator behavior is based in a unique psychodynamic makeup and that in the more malignant and lethal forms of MBP we are probably dealing with very primitive psychopathology. However it must be understood that MBP is not a unitary phenomena. Libow and Schreier have categorized perpetrators into *active inducers, help seekers,* and *doctor addicts* and propose that each of these groups have differing motivations.[2] Eminson and Postlethwaite advance the idea that MBP behaviors are the extreme of a dimension ranging from child neglect through normal illness-seeking behaviors to MBP itself.[3] Although coming from different theoretical backgrounds, one a proposed categorical classification, and the other a dimensional approach, both groups make the very important point that there is variation in the types of perpetration and presentation of the children, and that different motivations operate at the various levels or points on the continuum. This has far-reaching implications. Although the very malignant forms of the fabrications may be impossible to comprehend, the less severe presentations (such as exaggeration without fabrication, single episodes of fabrication, or fabrications that do not endanger life) may be more amenable to understanding in context of the better known types of child abuse and psychopathological explanations.

In Chapter 29 I describe some of the diagnoses that have been applied to perpetrators. For example, many of the perpetrators appear to be depressed and some may have diagnosable major affective disorders. However most persons who are depressed direct their suffering against themselves, not others. The critical question is why do some people resort to fabricating illness in their children while others, who may have been exposed to the same experiences and stressors, do not. It is absurd to think that there is an illness that perpetrators have called MBP that is directly causative. It is equally ridiculous to assume that all perpetrators have Munchausen syndrome (factitious disorder) or that MBP is simply a variation of Munchausen syndrome.

Nearly all adults with Munchausen syndrome perpetrate against themselves, not others. Clearly there must be a mix of specific influences and variables that interacts with abnormal individual psychodynamic functioning and various triggers that results in the subsequent situations of fabrication referred to as MBP (Figure 3–1).

We do know some things about perpetrators' attributes from the extensive case report literature. We find numerous examples of perpetrator personality disorder, psychiatric illness, past histories of abuse, parent-child symbiosis, social disadvantage, and absent spouses. Many perpetrators have worked in the health care professions. These are characteristics described from diverse fields of knowledge. As a result, simple cause-effect models and theories are inadequate as explanations for the perpetrators' behavior. Almost all complex human behaviors are determined by multifactorial agents. Single-factor theories or classification systems based on categorization are unhelpful. We require a fluid dynamic conceptualization of the myriad interacting components. Unfortunately at the present time we lack coherent philosophical and epistemological models that enable us to comprehend complex diverse interactional behavioral human systems. About the best we can invoke at the moment are "clumsy eclectic formulations"[4] and biopsychosocial theories of interpretation. Biopsychosocial formulations, although appearing to offer so-

FIGURE 3–1
Cultural and societal context.

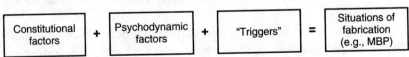

lutions which integrate findings from various theoretical inclinations, in fact, only provide us with "illusions of integration"[5] but we have little else.

A further supposition is that it is unlikely that significant disturbance of any single factor in Figure 3–1, on its own, would be sufficient cause for behavior as complex as MBP. It is, however, likely that there are probably one or more distinctive mixes of these factors that result in individuals, over the years, developing certain personality distortions and abnormal psychodynamic functioning. They may function relatively normally until confronted by particular "triggers" that are threatening to them in context of their unique psychodynamic functioning (their *weltanschauung* or in crude translation, their "world view"). At this point their defensive structure crumbles and previously covert psychodynamics become overt with resulting personal dysfunction and perpetration. In other cases the individual may be so disordered, and the defensive structure so precarious, that abnormal patterns and behaviors may be life-long with the perpetration of fabrication being only one more facet of this life-long turmoil. In still other circumstances the development of overt psychiatric illness, such as depression, may precipitate or uncover the abnormal personality organization and dynamics. Clearly, then, the task of simply applying a DSM-IV psychiatric diagnosis to a perpetrator is insufficient explanation for the events. Most perpetrators will probably have axis 1 and/or axis 2 DSM diagnoses, but those descriptive categories convey little true understanding of the perpetrator's motivations.

Figure 3–2 is an attempt once again to depict these ideas in schematic form. The constitutional factors can be thought of as a combination of biological vulnerabilities. For example, there may be genetic or biological predispositions for affective or anxiety disorders or a particular personality style that interacts with the individual's experiences during the formative years. Abuse or being exposed to abnormal illness behaviors could result in such a specific personality development. In turn this process occurs in a context of cultural, societal, and family influences. These influences include how society views physicians and medical services (the "benevolent father" as it has been sometimes described), women being the identified nurturers and child caretakers in society, the malevolent effects of poverty, and how society treats our single parent (usually

FIGURE 3–2

Factors and triggers leading to fabrication or induction of illness.

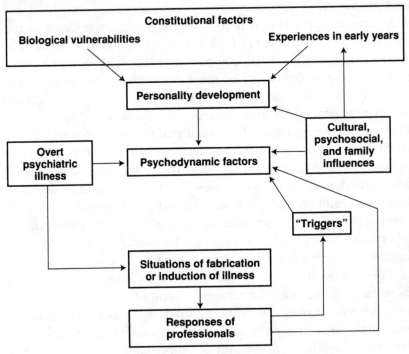

mother-headed) families. In the setting of these variables the future perpetrators (usually women) develop their unique world view. It may initially be unconscious and expressed (as many other motivations are expressed) by working as a nurse or other health care professional, "caring for self by caring for others," or by overly identifying as the nurturer (as society dictates). It may express itself through a symbiotic attachment to a child, thus obtaining the needed psychodynamic validation.

Up to this point the perpetrator's psychopathology may be relatively harmless to others and the motivations for these behaviors remain unconscious. The future perpetrators may be overly dedicated to caring for others, overly close to their own children, overly worried about physical illnesses, or overly compliant and pleasing to their (usually emotionally absent) spouses. They may overprotect their children and limit natural exploratory behaviors, or take them to the doctor more often than is required. They may tell "tall stories" about other events in their lives as a means of maintaining a fragile facade towards the world. In other situations the psychopathology may be so severe that from very early years they may seek validation and recognition through lying, pretending, abnormal illness behaviors, suicide attempts, or a desperate struggle to be the perfect parent.

Whatever the mixture of variables present it is probable that personal and emotionally significant prevailing life events, triggers, complicate the picture—for example, the already fragile woman now experiences isolation, threats to self esteem, or the stressors of being a single parent. The mixture melds together and the fabrications are brought forth. Like any complex human behavior, the sequelae of the perpetrators' fabrications and the medical and social responses will positively or negatively affect the perpetrator's future actions. In other words, the perpetrators' behaviors will likely obey rules akin to operant conditioning. (In operant conditioning the result of a behavior determines the frequency and intensity of that behavior recurring.) For example, the caring responses of the physicians and nurses may reinforce help seeking. In other circumstances it is possible that the development of overt psychiatric illness may directly result in situations of fabrication. One could imagine, for example, delusional beliefs about the presence of illness in a child, part of a psychotic illness, as being directly causative of MBP. However the available literature is noteworthy in its absence of reported cases of psychosis in MBP.

Whether the foregoing suppositions are accurate or not is debatable given the present state of knowledge. But it is conceivable that something like this process is involved in the genesis of the situations where fabrication or induction of illness in a child is discovered. My sole purpose in outlining all this is to stress that simplistic single-factor explanations are to be avoided. Psychiatric DSM-IV diagnoses do not convey the complexity of the psychopathology, nor do politically motivated interpretations (such as gender role theory and feminist teaching) or naive assertions that the perpetrator is only attention seeking. The truth will be an amalgamation of all these explanations with a greater or lesser emphasis on different aspects of the individual's case history.

The astute reader may have noticed a seeming contradiction in my reasoning. At the beginning of this essay I clearly stated that those perpetrators who deliberately, deceitfully, repeatedly, and knowingly placed their children's lives at risk were breaking primitive taboos with psychopathology that was probably equally primitive and that we cannot comprehend their motivation. Yet now I appear to be providing an "understanding." There are a number of reasons for this apparent contradiction. The proposed model is not a vehicle for understanding. It is no more than a framework for organizing what we do know about MBP and placing this within the context of other realms of knowledge (a biopsychosocial formulation). The ecological models presented in Figures 3–1 and 3–2 should be very familiar to those conversant with general child abuse practice. There is a great difference between being familiar with components and how they interact and actually understanding individual motivations. In addition, it is possible that in the less serious forms of MBP we can indeed understand how the interaction of components in the model leads to a comprehension of perpetrator motivation, because, with the lesser forms, we may be able to have some degree of empathy for the perpetrator's world view. We cannot understand the malignant perpetrator because we cannot empathize with the transgression of the basic and ancient taboo of child rearing. Finally, we may be dealing with different conditions. The psychopathology of the perpetrator of lesser forms of MBP (exaggeration and lying without repeated active induction) may be dramatically different from that of the malignant offender.

Child abuse is an exceedingly complex pattern of human behavior that is the result of abnormal and maladaptive interactions between parents, caretakers and children. Society dictates that the caretakers of children should rear their children with loving care, tending to their needs, and respecting their individuality. In most cases this biological and cultural necessity is carried out adequately and the next generation of adults is prepared to raise their children in the same way. Unfortunately the neglect and maltreatment of children is also a human attribute. No two abusive parents are the same, yet careful study of physically, sexually, or emotionally abusive parents reveals common patterns of past histories and life experiences—and many of these histories are shared with parents who fabricate or induce illnesses in their children. Unfortunately, and probably because of the dramatic and sensational reports of MBP in the literature and recently in the media, I believe there has been a tendency for MBP to be considered radically different from the better known and understood types of child abuse. The titles of such publications as Jonathan Kellerman's novel, *Devil's Waltz*[6] or the professional texts *Hurting for Love*[7] and *Patient or Pretender: Inside the Strange World of Factitious Disorders*,[8] in my opinion, only heighten the furor this sad variant of childhood suffering is attracting. In those professional journal reports that describe in detail the examinations, assessments, speculations, and explanations of perpetrator motivations, the discussions are sometimes restricted to the particular case without reference to the wider field of child abuse. This, I believe, is a mistake. The reader familiar with the general child abuse literature and practice will have noticed that many of the perpetrator characteristics, past histories of abuse, and family factors described in Chapter 29 are also those of the perpetrators of physical, sexual, and emotional abuse. Some of the specific experiences and psychodynamics may be unique to MBP. But the underlying mechanisms and parental vulnerabilities, particularly in relation to attachment theory, are probably similar to other forms of child abuse—particularly for the milder variants of MBP. If we can stand back from the sensationalism as well as our revulsion at the seemingly well-contrived, deliberate, and often expertly executed fabrications and inductions of illness, we could learn much about the etiological influences.

It is common for perpetrators of childhood physical and sexual abuse and neglect to give histories of abuse themselves. In my encounters with women who have induced or fabricated illness in their children, all report significant emotional, sexual, or physical abuse. The literature also suggests that the majority of MBP perpetrators have been abused in some fashion. Often they readily disclose this abuse, although others describe abusive experiences but do not consider their histories to have been abusive. Still others maintain, even in the face of ample evidence, that they were not abused and desperately grasp constructed images that their parents were loving and kind. This suggests that the histories are genuine and not simply further deception. Perhaps recognizing that they were uncared for would be too threatening. It is very common for parents who have perpetrated abuse to disclose that they felt uncared for, not close to their parents, never good enough, left out, or unwanted. The same appears to be true for MBP parents.

Episodes of childhood physical and sexual abuse may be painful and the recollection of such events may be the focus of much later suffering during adult life. However the most destructive and long lasting component of any abuse is the emotional injury that accompanies it. Ney[9,10] has clearly demonstrated the worst combinations of child abuse and neglect from the child's perspective, and notes that the earlier the onset of emotional and verbal abuse the more severe the maltreatment and long term outcome. In other words abusive ordeals in early life leave the victim with long-lasting feelings of inadequacy and deprivation, fragile self concept, poor self esteem, aloneness, and an inability to trust others. Given the frequency of past abusive episodes in MBP parents we can safely assume that many, if not most, share these long-lasting sequelae.

One of the well-documented mediating factors in physical abuse is societies' legitimatization of physical violence as a solution to interpersonal difficulties. Whether in the movie theater or the home environment, the physical punishment of those who transgress rules is condoned and often passed from generation to generation as an acceptable response. In North American and Western society in general some form of physical coercion or punishment in families is widespread, often beginning in infancy. Physical punishment has a number of sequelae in addition to the "teaching" of childhood self control. The child comes to learn that hitting others is acceptable, but more important, the child also learns that those who do the hitting, usually the parents, are also the ones who love and care. An equivalent mediating factor in some MBP families may be an unconscious or unvoiced expectation or observation that sickness is associated with love and caring. In the same way that physical punishment may be an implicit and normal facet of some families' functioning, the obtaining of nurturance via abnormal sick role behavior may be implicit in other families and subtly reinforced by Western societies' trust in the imposing edifice of the all-caring physician. Society has imbued health care professions, and physicians in particular, with images of healing, nurturing, and caring. One of the basic premises of society's expectations of medicine is the sanctity of the doctor-patient relationship. The message of absolute confidentiality is indeed legitimate, but for those who may have been exposed to abnormal illness behaviors during their formative years, it may imply something "special" in terms of meeting needs for security and nurturance.

An early and classic paper on "The Concept of Illness Behavior," by David Mechanic in 1961[11] proposed a definition of illness behavior and used the term to refer to "the ways in which given symptoms may be differentially perceived, evaluated, and acted (or not acted) upon by different kinds of persons." There are those who will make light of symptoms and others who will respond to the slightest discomfort by seeking medical care. The author makes the very important, and obvious, point that "illness behavior even determines whether diagnosis and treatment will begin at all," clearly hinting at the interactional nature of the patient, symptoms, and the socially prescribed role of the physician. We know nothing of these interactional processes between the MBP perpetrator and the physician. Mechanic also described the cultural differences in illness behavior and commented on the person's learned behaviors for coping with symptoms, asking the question "what are the factors affecting the appearance or nonappearance of persons for medical diagnosis?" As part of these considerations other early work by Talcott Parsons is important; "when a person's illness has been legitimized by medical sanction, or that of intimates and/or persons having influence over him, the person occupies a special role in society" [as quoted in Mechanic]. I need not describe the special and heroic roles many MBP perpetrators play in our offices and wards. Suffice to say there is a complex matrix of ingredients operating between the way we sanction the practice of medicine and the unique experiences and world view of the MBP perpetrator.

Complicating matters further is the social role that has been traditionally ascribed to women: that they are the nurturers in a paternal society. Some women, whether we like it or not, have come to associate self worth with caring for others, and children in particular. Leeder[12] notes that women at risk of fabricating illnesses "have adopted, without question, their socially prescribed roles as nurturers and caretakers of others." Gender role theory highlights the chronic powerlessness many of these women experience in their families. Combining this with their often physically or psychologically absent spouses, abuse within their families of origin, poor self worth (especially in relation to parenting), possible early exposure to abnormal sick role behaviors, and the edifice of the male-dominated nurturing health care system, we have a rich cultural medium for the emergence of MBP perpetrator behaviors. I believe that social and cultural variables such as these are a large component in the etiology of MBP, but do not believe they are directly causative influences, as many other women are exposed to the same environments and do not go on to fabricate illness in themselves or others. Shreier and Libow have thoroughly reviewed these psychosocial variables in their book *Hurting for Love*.[13]

Complicating women's roles even more is the way we treat our single parent families. To be a single mother in North America today may often be sentenced to poverty, poor employment or social welfare, and isolation, with little chance of the family breaking out. We all are aware of the associations of poverty, subsidized housing, poor antenatal care, and inadequate infant nutrition with all varieties of child abuse. Nearly all of my MBP parents have been single struggling mothers, and I can empathize with those who have perpetrated a single desperate episode of non–life-threatening fabrication or who have exaggerated their children's symptoms as a bid to obtain something for themselves. Libow and Shreier's help seekers may be in this category that is more open to intervention. "Medical confrontation with these patients often helps a mother communicate such problems as her anxiety, exhaustion, or depression."[14] However, MBP perpetrators may also come from more affluent backgrounds, once again illustrating how a mix of individual factors (Figures 3–1 and 3–2) come together uniquely to result in a particular case.

To be recognized and validated as a person of worth in our society is highly valued. How often do we tell our children to study hard at school least they fail or be unable to meet the demands of society? The pressure to be successful is pervasive; success is almost a religion in North America. But there are those for whom life dictates otherwise. They have to play games of "let's pretend," often with school friends and sometimes as adults. I have met two MBP mothers who constructed elaborate facades, somewhat akin to *pseudologica fantastica*. One said she was the leader of a well-known bike gang, and the other said she dated wealthy government leaders. I did not know where truth ended and lies began. They were sad impostors in life. Lloyd Wells defines imposture as the attempt to make others believe that one is someone other than him or herself or fill a role for which he is not in fact qualified.[15] He quotes Karush and Ovesey who believe that "becoming someone else, however briefly, probably is an early coping mechanism which, in children, can be reparative" and that adult failures, or the perception of them, can reactivate these fantasies of being another. Given what I have said about the social pressures on women's' roles it is perhaps not surprising that the MBP mother often plays the character of the "supermom".

Lurking behind all these cultural and societal pressures is something even more insidious and covert that has relevance to our speculations. In 1980 Rothenberg wrote a paper entitled "Is There an Unconscious National Conspiracy Against Children in the United States?"[16] He asserts that the child abuse, legislative, justice and economic systems, with the mass media, view children as "appendages to the adult world." His arguments are persuasive and unsettling. He quotes DeMause, who believes that when a child requires something from an adult, the adult responds in one of three ways: (1) the child may be used as a vessel for projection of adult needs (projective reaction), (2) the child may become a substitute for images of adults from the their own childhood (reversal reaction), or (3) the adult may empathize with the child. Rothenberg believes that the "national conspiracy" against children is largely unconscious and maintained by the projective and reversal reactions. I find this concept intriguing. Could something like this also be part of cultural mediating factors in MBP?

We live in an era in which it is fashionable to cite psychosocial causes for many of the psychological and psychiatric disorders. We may look upon biological explanations with suspicion and distrust. *Homo sapiens* is a biological entity whose infants enter this world, not with the *tabula rasa* of the behavioral psychologist, but with a rich genetic and (if one has Jungian sympathies, as I do) cultural and racial heritage. Not only do we enter the world with our endowed strengths but also with our weaknesses. In some, the genetic personality inheritance may lead towards serious adult personality disorder. In others, biological vulnerabilities to affective, psychotic, anxiety disorders, or substance abuse may be present. We know from life events research, attachment theory, and neurophysiology that some individuals may progress through life without meeting the triggers to precipitate overt illness, while others meet all the traumas and biological illness is brought forth. Others still may have such potent genetic and biological vulnerabilities that the emergence of disease is inevitable. In general, psychosocial disadvantage and biological vulnerabilities tend to cluster in families with significant psychiatric illnesses, particularly those with depressive illnesses. Blending the significant cultural pressures, abuse histories, and abnormal family environments so many of our MBP perpetrators appear to have, it is therefore not surprising that Bools, Neale, and Meadow[17] found such a high prevalence of overt personality disorder and psychiatric illness in their population of MBP mothers. In this first systematic and important study of the psychopathology of MBP mothers they found that of 47 mothers, 34 had a history of factitious or somatoform disorders, 26 had attempted self harm, and 10 had problems with substance abuse. They noted that the most significant psychopathology was the presence of borderline and histrionic personality disorder in 17 of 19 interviewed mothers. I find this study fascinating for two reasons: first, the high incidence of significant illness, and second, speculations on what may lie behind the diagnostic labels. We should also keep in mind the nonsystematic case literature that also essentially reports a high incidence of depressive illness, personality disorder, and episodes of self harm. In this, the "decade of the brain," extensive evidence, clues, and associations are being found between clinical conditions such as depressive illness and some forms of personality disorder and neurophysiological and neuropsychological abnormalities. The weight of this evidence is impressive, and I do not think it can be ignored in our considerations of MBP. There will never be a "pill" to treat MBP, but to disregard the biological perspective is negligent.

While discussing psychiatric factors it is theoretically possible, though as yet not reported in the literature, that illnesses such as psychosis and psychotic depressions could be directly causative of MBP in some cases. In cases of infant homicide by starvation or neglect, the appalling appearances of the children suggest the abuse occurred over a lengthy period of time. Fortunately these cases are rare and the caregivers were likely acting under the influence of delusional beliefs, depressive or otherwise. Untreated maternal postnatal depressive illness is a known cause of infant homicide and of great personal suffering to the mother. Cases have been reported of mothers who became convinced that their infant was possessed by the devil. Likewise, one could imagine a seriously depressed mother developing abnormal delusional ideas about illness in her child. I have met a number of schizophrenic adults who have had delusional beliefs about various illnesses and infestations in themselves (often of a bizarre nature) and who have acted upon these. However I have not come across any such individuals who have delusionally thought relatives or their children have illnesses, though I suspect these cases do occur.

Generalized anxiety disorders are also a potential cause of overreacting to or misinterpreting symptoms in a child. The overly anxious person is in a state of pathological hypervigilance to environmental cues and events, and tends to ruminate and exaggerate minor stressors. If psychiatric illnesses were the direct causes of some cases of exaggeration or fabrication, I would suspect that the perpetrator's behavioral patterns would not follow those so well described in the literature of more typical MBP presentations. However, such behavior may be occurring but unrecognized as MBP.

Let us now return to what I called the constitutional factors. The development of a healthy self concept is laid down during the early years of childhood, and depends on healthy attachment with the parent and validation of the child. A child does not have to be beaten or sexually assaulted to end up with significant defects in self concept. Helfer[18] has described "The World of Abnormal Rearing" in which the child, on an almost daily basis is ignored, belittled, or overly controlled. He says this "is hell, no matter how it manifests itself." Children during their early years must learn how to get their needs met in acceptable ways and when it is appropriate to do so. One of the insidious effects of the World of Abnormal Rearing is, according to Helfer, that these children find themselves surrounded by unrealistic expectations.

> Their parents have little understanding of childhood and make demands that are far in excess of a child's capabilities. Babies shouldn't cry too much, should eat well, smile early, and remind mom or dad of someone the parent likes; two-year-olds should shape up, not explore the cupboards and pull down the pots, not spill anything, and eat well. "Look after me," the child is told by the parent. "To hell with your needs," he hears in a variety of ways. A child who struggles with these issues day after day learns, as the years of childhood wear on, that his needs are not being met; even worse he is not learning the necessary

skills to get these needs met. He is much too busy looking after the needs of his parents and other adults around him.

In this environment the child is doomed to fail, and cannot reach the dizzy heights of what is expected. In my conversations with MBP mothers I am continually reminded of Helfer and the World of Abnormal Rearing. I suspect that many of our perpetrators have experienced such childhoods. It is also my impression from general clinical practice that these types of family are very traditional in their male-female dominance and power patterns, with male attributes being validated and female skills being relegated to second place—yet another dynamic to be thrown into the melting pot, and one which may have later relevance to the disproportionate number of female MBP perpetrators. Combine the insidiously destructive environment described by Helfer (plus or minus more direct abusive episodes) with, for example, extensive sickness in the family or experiences of personal illness where for once the child's needs were met, and we can see the potentially very rich ingredients and culture for the emergence of significant personality disorder and, in some, MBP behaviors.

How or why do some individuals turn to fabricating illness in their children, while others who may been exposed to the same stressors and life events, do not? Unfortunately I have no answers. The narrative of each offender's story and how that person sees and interprets the world will be different. I think we can be safe in saying that most perpetrators have a terror of isolation, abandonment, aloneness, and in some maybe even an existential dread of personal dissolution. The histrionic personality presents to the world a constantly shifting tapestry of facades, yet is inwardly empty. According to dynamic theory, histrionics suffered disapproval and inadequacy in the early maternal-child relationship and later turned to their fathers (physicians?) for nurturance using all their excessively dramatic and emotional displays and facades.

Borderline personalities exist in a world of intense fear and intolerance of aloneness, which they will only sometimes talk about. More usually they will act out in a series of self-destructive acts and intense relationships replete with manipulation, dependency, and devaluation, or short-lived psychotic episodes. Psychodynamically they were frustrated in the most early of relationships with the caregiver and either interject this with later urges for self-destruction or project it in their desperate search for a new caregiver (the health care professional?). Some theorists believe the borderline personality failed, during the first year of life, to interject images that would provide comfort during periods of separation from the caregiver. In adulthood, when threatened by abandonment, borderlines exhibit a primitive rage and desperation. Some use self-destructive acts like slashing at themselves to prevent the loss. Others, when loss occurs, lapse into experiences resembling psychosis.

In the depressed person the depression itself is the ego's response to the loss of an object or internal ideal. The anxiety and anger is turned, as it were, onto the self. Could some depressed persons be attempting to replace their lost object and ideals via their children? "Normal" people do this all the time.

I have speculated and wondered what might happen if the above disorders, which seem to appear frequently in MBP parents, were associated with a symbiotic relationship between parent and child. In the classic work of Margaret Mahler,[19] the first developmental stage is the autistic phase. In this the infant is initially completely absorbed by self (primary narcissism) and only later comes to realize that needs cannot be satisfied by self alone. During primary narcissism the self and object (mother) are undifferentiated. This later merges into a primitive need-satisfying relationship with the object. In other words the mother is only perceived in terms of her ability to meet the child's needs and is an extension of the self. This stage corresponds to Mahler's symbiotic phase, and is the classical interpretation of symbiosis. I am not sure whether MBP authors who state that children are symbiotically tied to their mothers are referring to this classical use of the term or whether they really mean enmeshment or simply being too close to the child. In enmeshment the behavior of one family member affects another member in a way that transcends or oversteps boundaries.

Let us play with some of these ideas. I cannot envisage simply being too close to a child as being sufficient to cause inability to differentiate a mother's needs from a child's. I can imagine this, for example, in context of an anxious parent who overprotects her child. On the other hand, enmeshment, being almost the simultaneous experience of emotion and the clear trespassing of boundaries, may have a role to play in the milder perpetrations of fabrication. A parent experiencing personal pain or distress may need solace, and by exaggerating symptoms may achieve some benefit. But again, I cannot see this as being a substantial factor in the life-threatening and repeated inductions of illness; the couple are too differentiated in terms of dynamic functioning. I can, nonetheless, conceive of a parent who in her own infancy was unable, because of highly abnormal parenting or symbiosis with her mother or early neglect, to psychodynamically achieve Mahler's next stage of development, that of separation and individuation. This parent would have only partially negotiated the symbiotic phase herself. If this were so, then we are dealing with very early preverbal psychopathology. This is also the sort of early psychopathology that is responsible for the origins of the more severe personality disorders, such as the borderline. If such a woman goes on to have her own children, then this could activate islands of preverbal memory and distort her individuation from her child. At a very primitive level she would literally be unable to separate the selves. As these dynamics are preverbal in origin, they would be impossible to articulate.

I find it noteworthy that Eminson and Postlethwaite[20] place MBP and child neglect at opposite ends of the same dimensions. Child neglect is essentially a product of a parent being unaware of the child's individual needs or unable to respond to them. Yet, MBP is the same. Could unresolved parental symbiotic issues be responsible for the inability of MBP parents to separate their own needs from their children's? Coloring these psychodynamics with those of the borderline or the histrionic we could have a mechanism to explain in part the behavior of repeated and serious inductions of illness. Whether the foregoing is correct or not, I do not think really matters. What does matter is the recognition that in the most malevolent of perpetrations, as I indicated at the beginning of this essay, we are almost certainly dealing with extremely primitive psychodynamic functioning.

Within the context of all of the foregoing, that is evolutionary and cultural taboos, societal influences, biological vulnerabilities, experiences within the family of origin, and psychodynamic functioning, we now come once again to the role of triggers. In the general child abuse literature a common question is asked: Why do some parents respond to stressors by assaulting their children while others do not? The answer to this rests on the fact that certain mediating variables need to be present. Many of these variables have already been outlined: for example the sanction of the health care professions, the experiences of illness in early life or observation of abnormal illness-seeking behaviors, or the necessary presence of unresolved issues of symbiosis. Whatever the trigger, it will be threatening in the context of these mediating factors and the current psychodynamic and defensive structure of the individual. The physical or emotional absence of a spouse could activate threats of abandonment. The threat of marital separation or divorce could do the same. The more primitive the psychopathology, the greater the potential psychodynamic hazard for the individual. The threat of isolation in circumstances of symbiosis could, I imagine, activate the need for self-nurturence or self-preservation. But as the perpetrator and victim are undifferentiated in the perpetrator's world view, the child becomes the vehicle for this satisfaction. Genuine sickness in the child (or during the perpetrator's own pregnancy, as Schreier and Libow believe[21]) and the subsequent contacts with the accepting health care profession could mitigate against some of the isolation of psychosocial deprivation or provide a woman with validation. If the psychopathology is mild, the perpetrator may remain at the level of exaggeration but, as I have already described, primitive dynamics may be mobilized.

In summary, I have only two certainties to offer the reader. First, invoking single factor theories or politically correct dogmas alone is not the answer to understanding MBP. Reality will be much more intricate, absorbing, and enigmatic. Second, we may be able to devise complex models to explain the interactions of the various components, but I suspect that reasonably normal people will never truly comprehend the torment and motivations that lie within the souls of the most disturbed (and creative) perpetrators. Therein lies a challenge. We are dealing with the dynamics of complex systems. I am very attracted by the ideas of Ilya Prigogine,[22] chaos theory,[23,24] catastrophe theory,[25] and fractal geometry,[26] but as I do not understand the mathematics I cannot comment further. Could some explanations be prowling these realms of knowledge, and could anyone apply these constructs to MBP?

4

The Munchausen Syndrome by Proxy Family

Randell Alexander

Children do not grow up in a vacuum. They are part of families. The behaviors that constitute Munchausen Syndrome by Proxy (MBP) have family consequences, even though there is little evidence that they result directly from family dysfunctions. Because an individual calculated choice is made to commit MBP, it is important that personal responsibility be assigned to the perpetrator, rather than explained away as a social or environmental imperative. Nevertheless a focus solely upon the parent and the targeted child ignores the important contributions of others who catalyze or fail to prevent MBP behaviors, the effect upon the family and community, and the natural history of unchecked MBP.

The Concept of Family

The term *family* derives from the Latin *familia* describing a household, and is related to *famulus*, a servant.[1] When described as the body of persons who live in one house and under one head, the definition appears too narrow (and probably sexist). A family can also be described as a kindred, lineage, tribe, or race; still incomplete definitions. Part of the difficulty in defining family is that biological commonalities obviously are important, but are not sufficient or necessary. Traditional concepts of family structure may no longer be true. Thus a family might be defined as: Individuals with common biological (or adoptive) backgrounds and/or interpersonal relationships banded together as a small group for mutual interests including personal growth, protection, nurturance, stability, and stimulation.

Although no commonly agreed-upon definition is likely, or would describe all contingencies, the concept of mutual interests is important in describing what is dysfunctional about families with child abuse. By its nature, MBP is both physical abuse (e.g., with the first unnecessary needle poke) and neglect (denial of proper medical and parental care). The protection parents owe to children breaks down. Nurturance and stability are denied. MBP strikes against personal growth for the child victim and the perpetrator. Thus exploitation by the perpetrator, for secondary gain at the expense of the child, endangers the very meaning of family. As a chronic condition, MBP often results in a grouping of individuals that is the shell of a family, with little left to be rehabilitated.

Viewed as a series of outwardly expanding concentric relationships, there is a blurring of relationships between nuclear family, extended family, and the community. For example, in some cases of MBP, the apparent adoption of the hospital staff into a family relationship is a central feature.

Parent–Child Relationship

The first ingredients in creating MBP must be a caregiver and a child. A parent, usually the mother, is nearly always the perpetrator of MBP. To date, too few fathers have been reported as perpetrators of MBP to make meaningful comparisons of their individual characteristics and possible motivations, although Meadow has found them similar to MBP mothers.[2] Identifying MBP before it first occurs is not yet possible. Thus retrospective analysis of the mothers must be used to identify how they may create MBP. However, attempts to use a profile to confirm or deny that a particular individual may have committed MBP are not justified by scientific data nor do they have a good theoretical basis. With these limitations in mind, a considerable number of case reports have attempted to describe the mother. Several aspects pertain to interactional relationships.

What might the mother be like without the child, before MBP is committed? Observations usually suggest a fairly normal and well-socialized woman. Yet the nature of MBP often elicits a search to provide a rational and understandable reason for her behavior. Frequently, psychiatric evaluation of the mother is sought to somehow confirm whether MBP occurred (it usually cannot answer this) or helping to understand why it was done (often this is also unsuccessful). Although most writers feel that the mother is usually psychiatrically normal,[3,4] others feel that some sort of personality disorder must be present even if it does not show up on standard psychological tests.[5-7] The possibility of a dissociative disorder has also been raised.[8] In cases where the mother has committed MBP on more than one child, psychiatric problems and suicide attempts may be more common.[9-12] The observation that MBP occurs mostly with mothers is not well explained, but there is no particular reason to suspect a sex-linked genetic basis. Thus MBP must be a product of environmental factors primarily impacting women.

The difficulty in finding an explanation by examining the individual's psychiatric profile may lie in the manner in which psychiatric testing is performed. By themselves, many of the mothers may be relatively normal. It is the interaction with the child that is abnormal. This is rarely tested, and it would be difficult to do so. These interactional problems also manifest themselves with others such as fathers, doctors, and even lawyers. That they predate the birth of the child is evidenced by the high proportion of mothers with histories of Munchausen's Syndrome themselves and/or have suicide attempts.[13] Schreier and Libow believe that many women who commit MBP felt abandoned or unrecognized by their own parents, particularly their fathers.[14]

The interactional problems of the mothers may be related to abuse that they often encountered as children.[15,16] Meadow[17] found emotional abuse and neglect in "at least 70%" of 27 mothers who had suffocated one or more children, with childhood physical or sexual abuse in about one-quarter of the mothers." Because most physical abuse victims later are unwilling to use this label in self report[18] and MBP mothers are very deceptive about presenting themselves as other than normal, their actual incidence of child abuse may be higher. However, the incidence of child abuse is high in the general population and yet MBP is rare. Thus child abuse per se does not explain the dysfunctional interactional style or motivations of MBP.

The frequency of maternal medical care backgrounds has several possible explanations, none of which may be mutually exclusive.

Who better to fool a doctor than someone who knows how to fake the history or symptoms? Interestingly, no reports of female doctors as perpetrators exist, an unexpected finding even taking into account the differences in numbers between female physicians and other female health personnel. Perhaps the dynamics of MBP require a different relationship between the perpetrator and the social context than that which a woman physician encounters.

Unlike many other abusive parent-child interactions, MBP is calculated. The willingness to exploit the child is especially dehumanizing,[19] and in forms of child abuse resembles only the seduction of children by pedophiles in terms of intent. Not surprisingly, some observers consider pedophilia and MBP to be among the least treatable types of child abuse.

Other Family Relationships

FATHERS

Fathers may be perpetrators,[20,21] or co-participants at some level.[22] However, they are usually uninvolved and apparently unknowledgeable about the commission of the MBP. Perhaps the most remarkable feature about the father's involvement is one that is rarely acknowledged: MBP nearly always occurs in a two-parent household.[23] In 1991 in the United States, approximately 72% of children under 18 years of age lived with 2 parents.[24] About 22% lived with the mother only, 3% only with a father, and 3% with neither. Although the percentage of parents living together may be slightly higher for younger children (the age range most vulnerable to MBP), it is rare for MBP to occur when a father has been entirely absent. Although a father is necessary at the point of conception, this suggests that his presence may be part of the necessary psychosocial dynamic in many MBP cases. This is illustrated in the following case:

> A 1-year-old female was seen approximately 11 times in the emergency room for apparent apneic episodes. On several of these occasions she was hospitalized and had extensive evaluations for near-miss SIDS. All findings were normal. On the final visit to the emergency room the mother apparently was distressed when hospital personnel told her that

they could find nothing wrong, would not admit the child, and that she and her child should go home and resume the apnea monitoring. As the paperwork was being completed for discharge, the mother ran out of the examination room announcing that her child had vaginal bleeding. Close inspection of the diaper by the female pediatric resident revealed the substance on the diaper to be cosmetic rouge. MBP was diagnosed and a timeline made of all the episodes. The father had a job which periodically required him to be out of town for several days at a time. The timeline showed that each time one of the "apneic" episodes occurred, he had recently left. The effect of hospitalization was that he would have to rush back to be with the mother and child. Failure to hospitalize the child when he was out of town on the last occasion apparently precipitated the mother's uncharacteristically clumsy attempt at deception.

Several cases of MBP have been brought to my attention in which the father has been in the military (e.g., Operation Desert Storm in the Middle East) and he has been summoned back on an emergency basis for medical concerns of his child. Although a variety of other motivations must exist for MBP, the exploitation of the child to elicit something from the father (e.g., his presence or attention) deserves further research. For this subset of MBP, events that separate fathers from their families may pose an increased risk. Conversely, cases have been reported and observed[25] in which the motive of the mother was to escape an alcoholic and/or abusive spouse.

The father is often described as passive or peripheral,[26–28] although this is not always the case.[29] This characterization may be partly unfair. When the mother has a medical background, the father may justifiably defer many of the medical details to his more sophisticated spouse. In North American families in which MBP is not present and neither parent has a background in the health care field, the mother is often the person who brings the child to the hospital or clinic for regular appointments or acute care. Because the mother is typically the only one to "observe" the alleged symptoms, the father may have little to contribute even when present with the physician. Thus it is possible that in some chronic cases, the father learns to be passive regardless of his initial attitude.

However, it is often the impression that the passivity of the fathers transcends these understandable dynamics. A strong father figure might question his spouse's claims and/or monitor the child, thereby averting the development of MBP. Marital dysfunction is often present at some point[30] although it may be worsened or precipitated once the diagnosis of MBP is made. Further study is needed to determine when and whether the passivity of some fathers contributes to the inception of MBP for certain predisposed mothers, whether it is a conditioned response to a chronic situation, or whether it indicates a marital problem that some mothers attempt to resolve through the MBP.

SIBLINGS AND SERIAL MBP

Siblings may be overlooked, but are often entangled in MBP in one form or another. MBP involving siblings other than the index child is a frequent finding when specifically investigated.[31-33] Rosenberg[34] found 8.6% of children in published reports to be victims of multiple-child MBP. Alexander and co-workers.[35] estimated that 25–35% of MBP cases had siblings who were also victims of MBP. However, many of the children in both of these studies had no siblings. In families identified as having 2 or more children, both of whom had MBP, 72% of all the children were known to be victims.[36] These serial MBP statistics may be underestimates in that the medical history of the siblings is often furnished by the mother (i.e., it is not objective) In other cases the perpetrator might have extended the MBP victimization to subsequent children, had medical or social intervention not occurred first. The natural history of unchecked MBP may never be fully known.

There are important social, medical, and legal ramifications when serial MBP is discovered. Serious, long-term psychological morbidity may also be seen in the siblings,[37] and the full impact of MBP on the emotions of siblings who witness it remains to be researched. In serial MBP cases, the mother may be even more likely to have Munchausen's Syndrome herself, to have a psychiatric history including suicide attempts, and to have overt changes in marital status once the diagnosis is made.[38] It is not clear whether these are consequences of long term MBP behavior itself (because several children are affected, these mothers are necessarily older at time of discovery) or whether there are even greater initial problems in mothers who would continue these behaviors with more than one child. Psychiatric referral for assistance in addressing mental health concerns is important in all MBP cases, but especially in serial MBP cases since the risk of maternal suicide is high.

Curiously, it appears that only one child is the target of MBP at any given time.[39] Removal from the home of only the target child ignores the strong probability that subsequent children will become victimized, even if they are not currently involved. Thus the most reasonable policy is to separate all children from the perpetrator if evidence is strong enough that the removal of one child is planned.

OTHER FAMILY MEMBERS

Other family members (e.g., aunts, grandmothers, stepmothers) who serve as primary caregivers may be the perpetrators of MBP.[40] It is not uncommon for other family members to have concerns about the truth of the perpetrator's claims or even to express these concerns to others. However, it is uncommon for family members to report possible MBP to authorities, even though family members often report other forms of child abuse. Perhaps the medical nature of the cases may introduce sufficient doubt to inhibit such reports, since the perpetrator can nearly always argue that a physician has made a diagnosis of a true medical problem. The lack of knowledge about MBP, and confusion over whether claims about a child are mere exaggerations, are obstacles to professionals and nonprofessionals alike. It will be interesting to see whether this situation changes and more reports of MBP are received from the public as the disorder becomes better known.

Because the perpetrators often are child abuse victims and because they have a high frequency of Munchausen's Syndrome, the possibility exists that they may also have been victims of MBP. The hypothesis of intergenerational transmission of MBP would be difficult to prove, but impressions are that it might have occurred in some cases.

As in other forms of child abuse, family members may be supportive of the perpetrator or the child, or seek some accommodation between the two. In some instances when the child has been placed outside the home with a family member and the mother is allowed visitations, some elements of MBP may persist. Expecting a family member to completely supervise the visit may not always be realistic. The risk to the child and the possibility that persistence of "symptoms" will be used as an argument against the diagnosis of MBP should be carefully considered in making such placement and visitation arrangements. If the child is returned to the family with the father to supervise, these risks are magnified.

THE COMMUNITY

Although this concept is missing from most definitions of MBP, the deceptions cannot be sustained unless a professional is duped into the charade.[41,42] For example, a mother complaining that her child has seizures will not usually get very far with school officials unless a physician agrees that seizure disorder is the diagnosis. The community representatives who help to sustain MBP can be divided roughly into two groups: health care and legal professionals.

The health care team consists of physicians, nurses, social workers, and other professionals. The perpetrator may engage in "doctor shopping"[43] in an attempt to avoid suspicion or to find the person who will unconsciously collude in the deceit. Once enlisted, that doctor or other health care professional may become an aggressive advocate on the caregiver's behalf. This advocacy may transcend the bounds of professional support and resemble or become a personal attachment. Such advocacy can subvert legal efforts if the professional continues to argue for organic disease even while others diagnose MBP. Little research has been done to explain the vulnerabilities of physicians and the seduction process to which they are exposed. Clearly individual differences exist that make some professionals more trusting than others, but it is possible that under the proper circumstances any professional may be fooled. The long term effects upon physicians, whether or not they agree with the MBP diagnosis, have also not been adequately evaluated. Without the winning over of these enablers, the perpetrator could not obtain the desired outcome.

The perpetrator's deceptive efforts do not necessarily stop once MBP has been medically identified. Child protective service workers and lawyers may become convinced that the doctors misunderstand the parent or are missing some rare medical condition. It is difficult to distinguish between legal advocacy on behalf of a client (a professional responsibility) and unswerving belief in their point of view. Again, there has been no research on the involvement of the legal community in MBP or the effect of different legal sanctions upon the child and family's long-term outcomes.

Summary

MBP not only has an impact on the child and perpetrator, but also has secondary effects upon siblings, spouses, other family members, and the community personnel who become involved in these cases. MBP is a chronic form of child abuse with the potential for serious injury or death. While all other forms of child abuse can exist with only one child and one caretaker, MBP requires at least three players (child, caretaker, and physician or other health care professional). The effects are necessarily both intra- and extrafamilial. Perhaps more than other forms of child abuse, the entire community is interlinked and suffers when MBP is committed.

References

1. *Webster's New Collegiate Dictionary*. Springfield, Mass.: Merriam, 1981.
2. See Chapter 1.
3. Meadow R. Management of munchausen syndrome by proxy. *Arch Dis Child* 1985; 60:385–393.
4. Rosenberg DA. Web of deceit: a literature review of munchausen syndrome by proxy. *Child Abuse Negl* 1987; 11:547–563.
5. Samuels MP, McClaughlin W, Jacobson RR, et al. Fourteen cases of imposed upper airway obstruction. *Arch Dis Child* 1992; 67:162–170.
6. Schreier HA. The perversion of mothering: munchausen syndrome by proxy. *Bull Menninger Clinic* 1992; 36:421–437.
7. Sigal M, Gelkopf M, and Meadow RS. Munchausen syndrome by proxy: the triad of abuse, self-abuse, and deception. *Comp Psychiatr* 1989; 30:527–533.
8. Rosenberg DA. Munchausen syndrome by proxy. *Child Abuse: Medical Diagnosis and Management*. Philadelphia: Lea & Febiger; 1994:266–278.
9. Alexander R, Smith W, and Stevenson R. Serial Munchausen by proxy. *Pediatrics* 1990; 86:581–585.
10. Black D. The extended munchausen syndrome: a family case. *Br J Psychiat* 1981; 138:466–469.
11. McGuire TL and Feldman KW. Psychologic morbidity of children subjected to munchausen syndrome by proxy. *Pediatrics* 1989; 83:289–292.
12. Samuels et al. Fourteen cases.
13. Meadow, Management. Rosenberg, Web. Alexander et al., Serial.
14. Schreier HA and Libow JA. *Hurting for Love: Munchausen by Proxy Syndrome*. NY: Guilford Press; 1993: particularly chapters 5–6.

15. McGuire and Feldman, Morbidity. Samuels et al, Fourteen cases. Sigal et al., Triad.
16. Lesnik-Oberstein M. Munchausen syndrome by proxy. *Child Abuse Negl* 1986; 10:133. (Letter)
17. Meadow R. Suffocation, recurrent apnea and sudden infant death. *J Pediatr* 1990; 117:351–357.
18. Berger AM, Knutson JF, Mehm JG, et al. The self-support of punitive childhood experiences of young adults and adolescents. *Child Abuse Negl* 1988; 12:251–262.
19. Schreier, The Perversion.
20. Makar AF, Squier PJ. Munchausen syndrome by proxy: father as a perpetrator. *Pediatrics* 1990; 85:370–373.
21. Samuels et al., Fourteen.
22. Rosenberg, Web.
23. Alexander et al. Serial MBP.
24. U.S. Department of Commerce. *Statistical Abstract of the United States.* Washington, DC: U.S. Government Printing Office. 1992.
25. Alex Levin, personal communication.
26. Libow JA and Schreier HA. Three forms of factitious illness in children: when is it munchausen syndrome by proxy? *Am J Orthopsychiatr* 1986; 56:602–611.
27. Guandolo VL. Munchausen syndrome by proxy: an outpatient challenge. *Pediatrics* 1985; 75:526–530.
28. Sigal et al., Triad. Schreier and Libow, Hurting.
29. Rosenberg, MBP.
30. Alexander et al., Serial. McGuire and Feldman, Morbidity. Samuels et al., Fourteen cases.
31. McGuire and Feldman, Morbidity. Samuels et al., Fourteen cases. Meadow, Suffocation.
32. Burman D. Stevens D. Munchausen family. *Lancet* 1977; 2:456.
33. Pickford E, Buchanan N, McLaughlan S. Munchausen syndrome by proxy: a family anthology. *Med J Australia* 1988; 148:646–650.
34. Rosenberg, Web.
35. Alexander et al., Serial.
36. Alexander et al., Serial.
37. McGuire and Feldman, Morbidity.
38. Alexander et al., Serial.
39. Alexander et al., Serial.
40. Rosenberg, Web.
41. Sigal et al., Triad
42. Zitelli BJ, Seltman MG, and Shannon RM. Munchausen syndrome by proxy and its professional participants. *Am J Dis Child* 1987; 141:1099–1102.
43. Libow and Schreier, Three forms.

5

Munchausen Syndrome by Proxy in Context I

Deception in Society

Mary S. Sheridan

You shall not repeat a false report.
—Exodus 23:1

And none is false, and none is wholly true.
—Steven Vincent Benet
John Brown's Body

The most basic element of Munchausen Syndrome by Proxy (MBP) is deception. One reason MBP attracts attention is the horrifying novelty of its deception. We like to believe that dishonesty is rare, and that most people are honest most of the time. We also like to think that people in positions of special trust—such as parents—deceive to keep their children's faith, not to break it. But deception, like child abuse, is common. Feldman and Ford write:

> The universal identification of factitious disorders is that almost everyone can admit either to having played sick to get sympathy (instead of asking directly for attention, nurturing, and/or lenience) or to having fantasized about how people would react to their serious illness and possible imminent death. . . .
>
> Factitious disorders are an exaggerated outgrowth of a relatively

69

harmless, normal behavior—"playing sick." And that's what makes it at once frightening and familiar. The primary distinction, however, between most people and those with full-blown factitious disorders is that factitial patients take playing sick to *pathological extremes*, profoundly affecting their lives, as well as the lives of others who support them.[1]

Ann Jones commented,

> Dangerous people ... may not be so very extraordinary as we think. ... Florence Monahan, who knew many murderers during her career as warden of various women's prisons, wrote that "they are just average, everyday sort of women. ... in most instances they are futile, ineffectual women who couldn't think of a better solution than to shoot their way out of a bad situation."[2]

This chapter is an attempt to place MBP in larger contexts. It will consider how deception occurs in society and in health care. Chapter 6 will consider other forms of deception analogous to MBP.

Deception in Society

Deception might be thought of as a simple, personal matter: an individual making a decision whether to be honest. Yet there are many reasons for concealing the truth, and society has decided that some of these are honorable and some not. In writing about the multiple forces, conscious and unconscious, which bring people to deceive, Lerner says, "We can never know for sure where a lie begins, with whom it originates, or the many factors that sustain it."[3] Bok comments:

> Individuals, without a doubt, have the power to influence the amount of duplicity in their lives and to shape their speech and action. They can decide to rule out deception wherever honest alternatives exist, and become much more adept at thinking up honest ways to deal with problems. ...
>
> The social incentives to deceit are at present very powerful; the controls, often weak. Many individuals feel caught up in practices they cannot change. It would be wishful thinking, therefore, to expect individuals to bring about major changes in the collective practices of deceit by themselves. Public and private institutions, with their enormous

power to affect personal choice, must help alter the existing pressures and incentives.[4]

Although exhortations to tell the truth are at least as ancient as the book of Exodus, deception is inextricably woven into society. Much of it comes from greed or desperation. These deceptions are so common that they don't interest us unless the scheme is particularly novel or the circumstances are unique, poignant, or form a syndrome.

There are many levels of deceit. Germaine Greer wrote of her father's hidden life:

> Some people like secrets; they love knowing things that other people don't know. They specially like knowing things that other people need to know and not telling them. They like to lead people on in their ignorance, sniggering at them inside. . . . Our whole lives are lived in a tangle of telling, not telling, misleading, allowing to know, concealing, eavesdropping, and collusion. When Washington said he could not tell a lie, his father must have answered, "You had better learn."[5]

Some forms of deception, in some circumstances, are considered acceptable, even praiseworthy. A person who always said and did "the truth, the whole truth, and nothing but the truth" would be at significant disadvantage in business and social life. Richard Nixon, for example, explained, "You can't say what you think about this individual or that individual because you may have to use him."[6] From a more kindly perspective, Lerner recalls, "When I was younger, I believed that timing and tact were the opposites of honesty. Now I believe instead that timing and tact are what make truth-telling possible . . ."[7] And later she observes, "Much of what we call 'telling the truth' involves an unproductive effort to change, convince, or convert another person, rather than an attempt to clarify our own selves."[8] Society makes a complex dance of when and whether to tell the truth, even while professing that truth-telling is good and deception is bad. Bowyer says, "To be is to be cheated. The process of discovering how one is to be cheated, how one is being cheated, how one will be cheated . . . may be one small step toward reality.[9]

Deception usually suggests the transmission of deliberate misinformation, but there are exceptions. Ekman differentiates falsification from concealment,[10] which some people do not consider deceptive. Omitting to tell the truth somehow seems less reprehensible than lying, and it is certainly easier. People may also be mistaken and thus inadvertently misinform others. Perception and memory are active, integrative processes, and often in error.[11] Paranoids routinely relate disproportionately to those parts of the environment that confirm their fears or suspicions; in these areas they can be extremely alert and perceptive, accurate as to transactions while distorting the context.

Although deception connotes an interpersonal process, we deceive ourselves, a paradox because we simultaneously know and do not know.[12] The psychological defense mechanisms are also efforts to avoid recognizing the truth, and it is uncomfortably easy to talk ourselves into or out of opinions and deeds. In a classic annual cartoon, each fall we watch Lucy pull the football away from Charlie Brown. She deceives him, but he also deceives himself by choosing yet again to trust her. We laugh because we recognize the dilemma. Society depends upon a certain level of trust. Ethics teaches that it is right to forget the past and think the best of others. Experience contradicts both, but does not determine the future. Hope wars with common sense, and society scorns the fool. We love Charlie Brown, but we may not respect him. We don't necessarily like Lucy very much, but we think she is smarter than Charlie Brown because she can manipulate him. If we can understand this, perhaps we can understand how a mother's anger at health care professionals could be gratified by deceiving them, or her dependency needs could find an opportunity in a sick child. She "shoots her way out of a bad situation" with a needle or a lie.

Deception usually connotes the distortion of information in a disapproved direction, although distorting in the opposite direction is equally deceptive. The terms "faking good" and "faking bad" can be used to describe these deceptive possibilities.[13] Underplaying illness is an American norm.[14] Sick people who struggle out of bed to go to work are greeted with admiration by their now-infected colleagues. Workers who take sick days when not ill are considered minor league liars and cheats.

Society usually does not punish deception when it is harmless to others, and particularly when it is skillfully done to enhance the deceiver. Those who color their hair and dress to give an illusion of slimness or success are usually not considered deceitful. We smile with understanding at a study that compared volunteers' driver's licenses with measures of their actual height, and found that the licenses often exaggerated.[15] A pastor in Washington State was found to have exaggerated the story of his sinful past; yes, he was a murderer, but had never been a Mafia hit man.[16] Such failures in deception seem more humorous than culpable. We have also learned that it is often wise to tell others, particularly those in power, what they want to hear.

Much of our reality perception is based upon convention and partial truth.[17] Sometimes language is primarily symbolic and disinformation is a legitimate part of strategy. Predictions of the future as fact—both political parties, for example, speaking of their candidate as the next president—are not considered deceptive. In business, diplomacy, and games, deception is one means to a socially approved end. Proponents of positive thinking encourage denial in the belief that it turns hope into deeds, and there is some evidence that it may do so. Depression may be a failure of adaptive denial, not an overly pessimistic view of the world.[18] It can be difficult to discern the truth; some starlets who pose nude may, after all, truly care about freedom and artistic expression. There is often no way to know for sure, particularly when the rules about deception change over time. Once, for example, cosmetics were used only by loose women, but the ingredients in patent medicines were not part of the public's right to know.

Some forms of deception, like pretending, are understood as deliberate and rewarded by society. The arts deceive, yet they do so in the search for truth. Without "suspension of disbelief," there is no theater. The fun of trompe l'oeil, magic, and optical illusions is in their playing with reality. We ask to be fooled, enjoy the success of illusions, and are disenchanted when they fail.

The ethics of some situations in which lying and deception occur are not clear cut. They depend heavily on interpretation—and an absence of self-deception. One author wrote the following introduction to ways businesspeople could better keep secrets:

> There is a tremendous difference between deceiving and lying. From a professional point of view, a deception is carried out to protect information from those with no legitimate reason to have access to it. Lying,

on the other hand, is a compromise of integrity. It should be avoided. . . . Deception is carried out when a group of individuals conspire to ensure that the sanctity of their mission is protected. A liar generally acts as a lone individual and his or her lies are self-serving with an illegal or immoral intent. Quite frequently in government and industry it is a perfectly normal and accepted practice to carry out deception. The intent of a deception is to keep the enemy or adversary in the dark to protect and safeguard vital information.[19]

Deception is more serious when it harms others or confers an unfair advantage. In Maeve Binchy's *The Lilac Bus*, a young woman talks with her father about the lover who proved false.

> "He's a liar and nothing else. . . . Why do people do that?"
>
> "Because they see themselves as having lost out and they want some of everything, and society doesn't let us have that, so we have to tell lies. And in a funny way the secrecy keeps it all going and makes it more exciting at the start."[20]

But "a liar and nothing else" oversimplifies. In a popular romantic novel, Jenny has met David, a childhood friend, by chance after many years. Thinking she will see him only once, she tells him that she fulfilled her teenage goal and became an artist. David hints that he has been successful, but understates the true extent of his success. The trouble comes when they fall in love, and David—who hates lying—learns that Jenny is only an illustrator of greeting cards. Jenny muses:

> We tell polite lies, like the lie she had told the hairdresser [that she liked the new style]. And we tell it's-good-for-you lies, like the one she'd told Rhonda [her daughter] about the clarinet lesson. And we tell protective lies, like the pride-based lies she had told David.
>
> There were white lies and black lies, egregious lies and innocent lies. Polite lies, helpful lies, the lies you told friends because you didn't want to hurt their feelings. And there was the silent lie. David hadn't lied outright, but he'd let Jenny believe a false assumption and had done nothing to correct her impression.
>
> Then there was the worst lie of all. Self-deception.
>
> "He's lying, too," she whispered, feeling the anger begin again. . . . By trying to live as if money wasn't important, he was deceiving himself. . . .

Furious and hurt, Jenny pressed her face into the pillow and wished life weren't so complicated.[21]

Jackson[22] says that truth is valued because people must depend on each other. Although human interaction is replete with opportunities for misunderstanding, and although a certain degree of skepticism is a necessity for survival, it is difficult to imagine how a society would work if no information exchange were trustworthy. (Followers of some popular psychological movements, however, posit such a world when they hold individuals completely responsible for what happens to them.) Jackson suggests that deception is prohibited only for the important aspects of life. In areas such as personal appearance and social conversation, deception is harmless and contributes to other important goals. Truth for its own sake is not always the highest value to be served, Jackson and situation ethicists believe. Kindness, loyalty, or self-preservation may be more important. Yet there is significant danger here. Henderson sums up the quandry of these conflicting values: "You can do harm by the process that is quaintly called telling the truth. You can do harm by lying. . . . try to do as little harm as possible."[23]

Given the right combination of motive or advantage, many people choose to deceive, particularly when the victim is an impersonal bureaucracy or "deserves it." Twenty-three percent of people surveyed in 1991 saw nothing wrong with inflating an insurance claim after an accident. Twenty-one percent felt it was not wrong to hide income from the Internal Revenue Service. Thirty-two percent believed it was not immoral to bargain for a better salary in a job interview by lying about current income.[24] In a more recent survey, 80% of teenagers said that cheating was common at their schools, and 78% admitted that they cheated.[25] When dishonesty becomes prevalent, that very fact contributes to its growth, since people perceive that honesty puts them at a disadvantage.

Society's concern with deception is shown in persistent, though often unavailing, efforts to discover and regulate it. People may question the effectiveness of polygraphs and other "honesty tests,"[26] but seldom question their desirability. Various methods are used to correlate facial expressions with deception,[27] yet "in general, no reliable and valid method or procedure exists within the mental [health] or criminal justice systems that by itself adequately measures distortion [lying]."[28] Society often seems to care more about discovering and punishing deception than about changing the intense pressures toward individualism and achievement that provoke it. Our efforts to value, honor, teach, and reward honesty in any meaningful fashion are inconsistent at best.[29]

Deception is not unique to human society. Some insects have colors or patterns that enable them to blend into their surroundings or appear larger and fiercer. There are deep water fishes with lights in their mouths to attract the smaller fishes on which they feed. Some animals appear to deceive deliberately: Cuckoos lay their eggs in other birds' nests; the host birds raise cuckoo young as their own. Rhesus monkeys are punished if they are found with food but have not called others in their group. Despite this, they apparently choose whether to alert others to the presence of food, and do so only about 45% of the time.[30] One theologian argues that deception is adaptive, and that what modern society really needs is more deception in the form of a unifying religion or mythology. In reporting this speech, Suplee comments, "Genetically speaking, good guys finish last when treachery increases the likelihood of eating better and breeding more often. . . . If species as diverse as bacteria, bugs, birds, and baboons frequently deceive others—or even their own kind—is it 'unnatural' or 'aberrant' for humans to lie and cheat?"[31]

Humans learn about deception early in life. Children must separate reality from imagination, a task made harder by enticing toy commercials, sports heros who become actors, actors who become politicians, and politicians who promise chickens for every pot and honest government. By the age of three, children can deceive in simple games,[32] and most parents are telling stories of Santa Claus or the Tooth Fairy. Some psychologists believe that lying is part of children's individuation. When they can have secrets from their parents, they recognize that they are separate beings. When they make things happen through lies, they test their power.[33] Conforming to certain socially accepted or expected lies is also part of socialization. Traditionally boys have been taught to deny their fears while girls have been taught to minimize their strength. Such hiding of emotion continues into adulthood, when many adults feel fraudulent, although they may be objectively competent and holding positions of responsibility.[34]

Deception in Health Care

As a complex part of a complex society, health care generates its own issues of deception. Professional training and ethics should ensure a higher standard of truth-telling, but lying to patients or families is common, while telling unpleasant truths can be punished. One physician commented on the situation of a young colleague who "made a mistake and told the truth about it," and was dismissed from his residency program:

> Where are our medical societies and organizations that should be a source of support for this truth-telling physician? He should be a hero for upholding the highest standards of the profession. Every human being makes mistakes, but it takes a person of exceptional courage to take responsibility . . . and accept the consequences. . . . By standing by and doing nothing . . . we are boldly making the statement that forgiveness is not acceptable. . . . We will create a professional atmosphere where rewards come from lying.[35]

Of course, such an atmosphere already exists. Fifty-two percent of 407 physicians surveyed in 1989 were willing to misrepresent the purpose of a laboratory test so that insurance would pay for it, or deceive the wife of a man with gonorrhea so that she could receive treatment without threatening the marriage.[36] Some practitioners administer placebos to silence or placate difficult patients.[37] In scientific research, "blinded" study designs are necessary because of the natural human tendency to find what one seeks, reinforced by the potential rewards to the researcher who gets the "right" results. Chop and Silva discuss the rewards of plagiarism and data falsification in nursing research: promotions, status, tenure, grants, and—that most American of accomplishments—"success."[38] Medical fads characterize various times and regions.[39] While most clinicians do the best they can, deliberate quackery also exists, and can be rewarded very generously. Petersdorf believes that cheating in scientific research and medical practice is a logical progression from cheating to get into medical school.[40] To counter temptation, Chop and Silva recommend a climate that stresses integrity, mentoring that includes discussions of fraud, and rewarding research quality over quantity. Such organizations as the American College of Obstetricians and Gynecologists have declared that deception by ex-

plicit lies, implication, or omission are unethical,[41] but such statements did not begin appearing until 1980.[42] They still meet opposition from those who believe that the ancient precept, "first do no
harm," is sometimes at war with the truth.

In America, lying to patients about diagnosis has decreased. In
1961, for example, 90% of physicians preferred not to tell patients
that they had cancer. By 1979, 97% would share the diagnosis.[43]
However, practitioners may distort prognosis either because they believe it will help the patient or as part of their own self-deception.[44]
One third of physicians surveyed by Novack admitted that they
would mislead a family about a patient's death if a mistake contributed to it.[45] The county hospital staff that Sudnow observed in
the 1960s presented death to survivors as painless and inevitable.
Families rarely challenged these statements, even when they had witnessed the patient's suffering.[46]

Caregivers must know the facts, even the dangerous and em-
barrassing ones, if they are to cure patients. This underlies the
strict confidentiality and its privileges that are basic to health
care.[47] Yet few practitioners believe that their patients always tell
them the truth. This author recalls, for example, a facetious
memo on an emergency room wall implying that no patient's report on sexual or chemical history should ever be trusted. Too
often, health care professionals consider the honest expression
of pain to be exaggerated and discourage it.[48] Or they believe
that it is kinder to understate the amount of pain which will be
associated with a procedure, least the patient expect and unconsciously create discomfort. Thus deception in health care is, indeed, a two-way street. There has been little research on the
extent to which patients report symptoms honestly and how
they make decisions about seeking care. The social conditions
that encourage patients to tell the truth to their health care
providers were detailed by Talcott Parsons.[49] He saw the role of
the seriously ill person as a contract with society containing four
key elements:

1. The illness, at least initially, is not held to be the sick person's
   fault.
2. The sick person is exempted from normal responsibilities such
   as work as long as the illness is judged to be real.

3. The sick person is expected to get well as soon as possible, and not take advantage of the exemption from work.
4. The sick person is expected to seek out and cooperate with competent sources of help, however those may be defined by the culture.

Deception, of course, violates the entire spirit of this contract. The presence of such tacit agreements with society explains why we react so strongly to "faking bad," but not to "faking good." Factitious illness is not just a personal matter, but a breaking of faith with all those who work. Society "forgives" illness when it is truly "bad luck." It does not expect illness to be induced for the benefit of the inducer. Illness, or perhaps "getting better," becomes a work substitute; factitious illness is evading work. "The pride of a doctor who has caught a malingerer" Asher wrote.[50] "is akin to that of a fisherman who has landed an enormous fish."

Going for treatment and describing symptoms depend upon the patient's sophistication, age, personality, experience with and beliefs about medical treatment, the nature of the symptoms themselves, level of psychological and physical distress, and other factors.[51] The availability of health care also influences frequency and type of utilization.[52] I undertook an informal survey of 116 adults attending a hospital "health fair" in suburban Honolulu, and found that ten admitted telling a "serious lie" (undefined) to a health care provider. Of these, seven had exaggerated illness or said that they were sick when, in fact, they were not. Three had denied illness or minimized symptoms.[53]

Health care professionals have a strong definitional role in all of this: they are the ones who decide whether illness is real, and if not, whether the presentation of illness occurred in good faith. Part of this latter process may result in the redefinition of the deception itself as an illness. This is, of course, at the base of the debate over whether MBP is a behavior or a disorder, and if the latter, who "has" it. Pseudologia fantastica, or pathological lying, was initially described in 1891.[54] It may include words, behavior, and even deceptive unconscious processes, but excludes delusions and hallucinations that the subject believes to be true and the confabulation that is an attempt to cover memory defects. Pseudologues may feel compelled to lie. The lies they tell are plausible, persistent, and enhancing to the liar. In their review of the literature on pseudologia fantastica, King and Ford found few reliable demographics except that 40% of reported cases (50% of those with Munchausen Syndrome) had some history of central nervous system abnormality. Thirty-five percent came from families in which another member had neuropsychiatric illness or was alcoholic. Hoyer[55] considers pathological lying to be an expression of unresolved Oedipal conflicts, castration anxiety, and a primitive desire to bolster self-esteem at the expense of adults. King and Ford suggest that adult Munchausen Syndrome is but one manifestation of the more general condition of pseudologia fantastica, and of course suggest that further research is needed.

Conclusions

This brief survey is only intended to show how pervasive and complex deception is. The practitioner who hopes to understand MBP can usefully consider its commonalities with other forms of deception as well as its differences. It is said that student asked Stanislavsky, the famous teacher of method acting, how to portray a contract killer, since the student had never murdered anyone. The teacher answered with a question: "Have you ever swatted a fly?" "Of course," the student replied. "Then," said Stanislavsky, "you know what it is to be a cold-blooded killer." We may never have been tempted to MBP, but we cannot deny knowing what deceit is, or how easy it is to lie to ourselves or others.

References

1. Feldman MD and Ford CV. *Patient or Pretender: Inside the Strange World of Factitious Disorders.* New York: John Wiley; 1994: vi.
2. Jones A. *Women Who Kill.* New York: Holt, Rinehart Winston; 1980: 14.
3. Lerner HG. *The Dance of Deception: Pretending and Truth-Telling in Women's Lives.* New York: HarperCollins; 1993: 7.
4. Bok S. *Lying: Moral Choice in Public and Private Life.* New York: Pantheon; 1978: 243–4.
5. Greer G. *Daddy, We Hardly Knew You.* New York: Knopf; 1990: 172.
6. Quoted in: Ekman P. *Telling Lies: Clues to Deceit in the Marketplace, Politics, and Marriage.* New York: Norton; 1985: 25.
7. Lerner. *Dance.* 103.
8. Lerner. *Dance.* 115.

9. Bowyer JB. *Cheating.* NY: St. Martin's.; 1982: 428.

10. Ekman: 28.

11. This has been well known in the field of social psychology for many years, but has recently come to the fore again in the sudden "recollections" of childhood abuse. See, for example, Bower B. Sudden recall: adult memories of child abuse spark a heated debate. *Science News.* 1993; 144:184.

12. For an extended discussion, see Lockard JS and Paulhus DL, eds. *Self Deception: An Adaptive Mechanism?* Englewood Cliffs, NJ: Prentice Hall; 1988.

13. I have seen these terms most often used in reference to the Minnesota Multiphasic Personality Inventory. "Faking good," of course, refers to denying symptoms which truly exist, while "faking bad" is the false claim of having symptoms. See, for example: Graham JR, Watts D, and Timbrook RD. Detecting fake good and fake bad MMPI-2 Profiles. *J Pers Assessment.* 1991; 57:264–13.77. I am indebted to Harold Hall, Ph.D., for originally pointing out this concept to me.

14. Sheridan MS. *Pain in America.* Tuscaloosa: Univ of Ala Press; 1992.

15. Willey P and Falsetti T. Inaccuracy of height information on driver's licenses. *J Forensic Sci.* 1991; 36:813.

16. Hendrickson P. Lives of the killer preacher. *The Washington Post* Feb. 22, 1992: C1.

17. Gergen KJ and Gergen MM. The social negotiation of reality. *Social Psychology, 2nd ed.* New York: Springer Verlag; 1986: 56–59.

18. Lazarus RS interviewed by D Goleman. Positive denial: the case for not facing reality. *Psychology Today.* 1979; 13: 44–60.

19. Genva RL. *Managing Your Mouth: An Owner's Manual for Your Most Important Business Asset.* New York: Amacom; 1992: 106.

20. New York: Dell; 1992: 50.

21. St. George M. *Castles and Fairy Tales.* Toronto: Harlequin; 1986; 184.

22. Jackson J. Telling the Truth. *J Med Ethics.* 1991; 17:5.

23. Quoted in: Helm A. Truth telling, placebos, and deception: ethical and legal issues in practice. *Aviation Space Environmental Med.* 1985; 56:69.

24. Reich K. Survey finds many condone lying to insurers. *Los Angeles Times.* Nov. 19, 1991:A26.

25. USA Today. Cheating Poll. In: *The Honolulu Advertiser.* October 21, 1993: B1.

26. For a thorough discussion of issues related to polygraphs and honesty tests, see: Lykken DT. *A Tremor in the Blood: Uses and Abuses of the Lie Detector.* New York:McGraw Hill; 1981. Lykken suggests that deception surrounding such tests—i.e., the creation in the subject of trust in the instrument—often influences confessions and revelations of the truth, which are then taken as measures of the instrument's effectiveness. See also Lilienfield SO. Do 'honesty' tests really measure honesty? *Skeptical Inquirer.* 1993; 18:21–41. In evaluating such tests, Lilienfield notes, "The blatantly overblown and sometimes deceitful assertions of a number of honesty-test publishers might lead an impartial observer to wonder whether such publishers would succeed in passing their own tests." (p.37)

27. Ekman's book is largely concerned with this topic.
28. Hall H. The forensic distortion analysis: proposed decision tree and report format. *Am J Forensic Psychology.* 1986; 4:31–59. Quote p. 37.
29. Bok. *Lying.*
30. Hauser MD. Costs of deception: cheaters are punished in rhesus monkeys. *Proc Natl Acad Sci USA.* 1992; 89:12137.
31. Maugh TH. The lies that bind: nearly all species deceive. *Los Angeles Times.* April 1, 1991: B3. Also Suplee C. Nature's hidden agenda: from molecules to mankind, deception seems a part of life. *Washington Post.* February 24, 1991; B3.
32. Chandler M, Fritz AS, and Hala S. Small scale deceit: deception as a marker of two-, three- and four-year-olds' early theories of mind. *Child Dev.* 1989; 60:1263–77. Also:, Bower B. Deceptive successes in young children. *Science News.* 1989; 135:343.
33. Ford CV, King BH, and Hollender MH. Lies and liars: psychiatric aspects of prevarication. *Am J Psychiat.* 1988; 145:554.
34. Kolligan J Jr and Sternberg RJ. Perceived fraudulence in young adults: is there an 'imposter syndrome?' *J Pers Assessment.* 1991; 56:308–26. Lerner (*Dance*, pp. 74–78) suggests that feelings of fraudulance are not always dysfunctional, but rather may reflect the inherent fraudulance in certain roles people are asked to play.
35. Greenberg MA. The consequences of truth telling. *JAMA.* 1991; 266:66.
36. Novack DH, Detering BJ, and Arnold R, et al. Physicians' attitudes toward using deception to resolve difficult ethical problems. *JAMA.* 1989; 261:2980–5.
37. For a fuller discussion of the ethical dimensions of placebos, see: Helm A. Truth telling, placebos, and deception: ethics and legal issues in practice. *Aviation Space & Environ Med.* 1985; 69–72 and Sheridan. *Pain*; 25–26.
38. Chop RM and Silva MC. Scientific fraud: definitions, policies, and implications for nursing research. *J Prof Nursing.* 1991; 7:166–71.
39. Stiehm ER, in The psychologic fallout from Chernobyl (*Am J Dis Child.* 1992; 146:761–2.) describes "an epidemic of monumental proportions" affecting Russian children. The disease of "vegetative dystonia," similar to chronic fatigue syndrome, he writes, is unrelated to known patterns of radiation exposure, and is more a creation of physicians' and parents' anxiety than of any pathology on the part of the children. He concludes, "it is the psychological fallout of the accident, occurring at a unique period of social unrest. . . . The medical response to date is not part of the solution, but it is a good part of the problem." (quote p. 762)
40. Petersdorf RG. A matter of integrity. *Acad Med.* 1969; 64:119–23.
41. ACOG Committee on Ethics. Deception. *Int J Gynecol Obs.* 1992; 37:63–4.
42. Jackson J. Telling the Truth. *J Medical Ethics.* 1991; 17:5–9.
43. Helm. This change may also reflect realistic changes in the prognosis of cancer.
44. This author, for example, was recently involved in a case where a physician would not tell a teenage patient that the boy's cancer was terminal because

the young man "would give up hope." It is also my observation that specialists in high acuity areas sometimes exaggerate the efficacy of proposed treatments, perhaps to deny their own frequent failures. For further discussion of denial in health care, see Sheridan, *Pain*; 129–133. For a profile of transplant surgeons and denial, see Fox R, Swazey JP. *Courage to Fail*. Chicago: University of Chicago Press; 1974.

45. Novack et al. Physicians attitudes, 1989.

46. Sudnow D. *Passing On: The Social Organization of Dying*. Englewood Cliffs, New Jersey: Prentice-Hall. 1967: 146. The implicit denial to other patients that a death has occurred is discussed in Chapter 3.

47. The Latin roots of "confidentiality," are "with faith," stressing the implied contract between patient and caregiver.

48. See Sheridan, *Pain*, for a discussion of how health care professionals deny chronic pain, particularly in women and children. Also: Cunien AJ. Psychiatric and medical syndromes associated with deception (In: Rogers R., ed. *Clinical Assessment of Malingering and Deception*. 1988; NY: Guilford Press: 13–24) discusses compensation neurosis as a questionable concept.

49. Parsons T. *The Social System*. 1951; NY: MacMillan: 436–7.

50. Quoted in Cunnien: 22.

51. See: Berkanovic E, Hurwicz M-L, and Landsverk J. Psychological distress and the decision to seek medical care. *Soc Sci Med*. 1988; 27:1215–21, Calnan M. Managing "minor" disorders: pathways to a hospital accident and emergency department. *Sociology of Health and Illness*. 1983; 5:149–167, Egan KJ and Beaton R. Response to symptoms in healthy, low utilizers of the health care system. *J Psychosomatic Research*. 1987; 31:11–21, Kolitz SL, Antoni MH, and Green CJ. Personality style and immediate help-seeking responses following the onset of myocardial infarction. *Psychology and Health*. 1988; 2:259–89, Turk DC, Litt MD, and Salovey P. Seeking urgent pediatric treatment: factors contributing to frequency, delay, and appropriateness. *Health Psychology*. 1985; 4:43–59, and Wagner PJ and Curran P. Health beliefs and physician identified 'worried well. *Health Psychology*. 1984; 3:459–74.

52. Schneider KC and Dove HG. High users of VA emergency room facilities: are outpatients abusing the system or is the system abusing them? *Inquiry*. 1983; 20:57–64.

53. Sheridan MS. Response to symptoms and use of medications by adults. *Proc Straub Pacific Health Fdn*. 1994; 58:10–12.

54. This discussion is based on Cunnien and on King BH and Ford CV. Pseudologia Fantastica. *Acta Psychiatr Scand*. 1988; 77:1–6.

55. Cited in Cunnien.

6

Munchausen Syndrome by Proxy in Context II

Professional Proxy and Other Analogs

Mary S. Sheridan

This chapter began as a search for analogs of Munchausen Syndrome by Proxy (MBP), in the hope that they would shed light on its inner workings. That did not occur; fewer of these analogs have been recognized than cases of conventional MBP. Until they are sufficiently studied, one can only generalize that certain behaviors are not unique to parents and children, and guess that some psychodynamics of MBP also underlie the phenomena reported here.

When deception is rewarded, perhaps we should not be surprised that deception occurs. If parents sometimes betray their obligations to children, perhaps it is natural that others in less sacred positions of trust betray their obligations. If a society advocates self-promotion and makes demigods of celebrities, perhaps it should not surprise us that those who are desperate for approval sometimes will do anything to be noticed.

Munchausen by Professional Proxy: Looking Good at "Codes"

Health care is occasionally as glamorous and dramatic as portrayed in the media, but most of the time it is a matter of detail and routine. One can be a hero, but such opportunities, as in the rest of life, are usually rare and depend on circumstance as much as skill. I did not begin with a search for *nurses* who abuse patients. Rather, I raised a wide-ranging question as to whether any health care professionals might make themselves look good at patients' expense. To date, all cases that I have encountered involved nursing personnel—a situation that has sometimes been of concern to nurses, who wonder if they are being scapegoated. That is possible; but it is also possible that they, more than other health care workers, have the means, opportunity, and motive. Nurses' knowledge of and access to drugs, syringes, and other supplies, combined with their routine role in bedside care probably makes it easier for them to induce, then "discover" a cardiorespiratory arrest ("code"). One can only speculate that other members of the health care team with similar knowledge and access might have different consequences should they induce codes. (Perhaps physicians are more likely to be blamed or lose status if a patient "crashes.") Perhaps other professionals have behaved similarly but have not yet been discovered. Or deception in other professions may simply take other forms.

Before describing specific cases, it should be said that these are probably only the "tip of an iceberg." One frustration in doing this research has been the frequency with which nurses and others are accused and even convicted of murder or attempted murder without any motive being advanced. One also has to suspect that not all cases are discovered. What follows is a listing of situations in which it has been alleged at some point that hospital personnel assaulted and/or killed patients for some form of attention.

In 1975, two nurses[1] were accused of injecting Pavulon into as many as 9 victims at a Detroit Veteran's hospital. This was an unclear case in which only vague motives were offered. At one point investigators suggested that the nurses might have been trying to call attention to staff shortages at the hospital. Another writer said that they seemed exhilarated during codes. Both of the nurses were immigrants from the Philippines and commentators believed that they were naive about the American judicial system. The nurses may have thought that only the guilty hired lawyers to defend themselves. Supporters suggested that they were doubly vulnerable because they were aliens and women. Their original convictions were overturned on appeal. It is probable that a series of murders occurred at the Veterans' hospital, but these two nurses may or may not have been the culprits.[2-6]

In 1980, wide publicity was given to the allegation that a Las Vegas nurse had tampered with life support equipment on up to 6 intensive care (ICU) patients. According to the story, the ICU nurses bet on which patient was to die next, and one nurse wanted to ensure her chances of winning. Dubbed "death's angel" by the popular press, she was arrested for the murder of a single patient who, in fact, had died of septicemia. Her boyfriend, a respiratory therapist, was briefly suspected, but never arrested. There was no evidence to support the charges, and the indictment was dismissed.[7–10]

In a 1981 case that is still controversial, several nurses at the Hospital for Sick Children, Toronto, were suspected of administering digoxin to as many as 25 victims. Investigations conducted by Canadian authorities and, at their invitation, the U. S. Centers for Disease Control (CDC) disagreed on which nurses were suspect. One nurse was indicted, but charges were later dropped. Another was suspected but not indicted. Some observers speculated that the murders had been committed to support the need for a pediatric intensive care unit. Most recently, questions have been raised as to whether murders actually occurred.[11] The case and its extended controversy had a traumatic effect on the nurses involved.[12–16]

In perhaps the best-known of these cases, Genene Jones, a Texas practical nurse, was convicted and jailed in 1983 for inducing codes with succinylcholine. At the time of her discovery she was working for a private pediatrician. A review of her career suggests that she probably also induced codes at one or more hospitals where she had previously worked. She may have assaulted as many as 67 patients. Her biographers suggest that she wanted to justify the need for pediatric intensive care units and prove that practical nurses could function appropriately in them. However, she also seemed to enjoy performing well at codes and being at the center of action. She became a controversial figure at the hospital where she practiced before moving to the pediatrician's office. Accounts vary, but PICU staff probably suspected her involvement in a series of codes, but were unable for personal and institutional reasons to confront the problem directly.[17–19]

The following year, Robert Diaz, a California nurse, was convicted and jailed for injecting patients with lidocaine. Some accounts credit him with up to 27 victims in several hospitals. No motive for his actions was given during his trial. However, newspaper accounts suggested (based on comments from colleagues) that he was exhilarated during codes and "liked to play doctor." One account also says that he liked to predict deaths.[20-22]

In 1987, Richard Angelo, a New York nurse, volunteer emergency medical technician (EMT), and EMT instructor, was convicted of murder for injecting patients with pancuronium. He may have assaulted up to 25 victims. One woman who later died asked her family to keep the "nurse with the beard" away from her, and a patient who survived saw Angelo inject something into his intravenous tubing just before he went into distress. Angelo told interviewers that he wanted to be a hero, "felt inadequate in general," and needed to prove himself.[23]

In 1990, Florida nurse Jeffrey Feltner received a sentence of life in prison for smothering one nursing home patient. He may have assaulted up to 7 victims, and supposedly wished to call attention to poor nursing home conditions. His case is complicated by the fact that he confessed repeatedly, then recanted, and finally pleaded guilty.[24-26]

A Georgia intensive care nurse, Joseph Dewey Akin, was charged in 1991 with murdering a ventilator-dependent quadriplegic by injection of lidocaine. He was suspected in up to 16 other patient deaths and several assaults which patients survived. He specifically denied police hypotheses that he had induced codes to appear heroic. When he was sentenced to life in prison for murder in 1992, the prosecutor described him as someone who "simply likes to kill people."[27-29]

In 1993, British nurse Beverly Allitt was convicted of murdering 4 children, attempting to murder 3, and harming 6, primarily by injecting various drugs into their IV lines.[30] Three of the children suffered permanent impairments. MBP was discussed explicitly during the trial as the reason for her actions. A book about Allitt details the circumstances of her assaults, but little of her internal motivations.[31] Allitt had a long history of medical complaints, confabulated tales, and playing tricks on others. Her assaults on children took place in an understaffed, bureaucratically and politically compromised hospital.

Looking Good at Fires

Nurses are not the only professionals who want to excel in dramatic situations. Fires can allow the responding firefighters to receive attention, and fires have been set to enhance that opportunity. As with nurses involved in patient deaths, the motives of arsonist-firefighters are often missing from newspaper accounts. Following, however, are cases in which fires were apparently set to help the responders "look good."

In 1990, 11 men, ages 17–21, all volunteer firefighters at two separate fire companies in Prince George's County, Maryland, were charged with torching 10 vacant houses over a 14-month period. According to one volunteer, starting the fires was inspired by their perception that the fire chief did not respect them. They wanted to prove themselves at the next fire, and that led to the idea of creating their own opportunities. Arson investigators also suggested that the young men thought it was fun to put out the fires. Apparently the two groups of men came up with the idea independently. An 18-year-old high school dropout who had wanted to be a firefighter since the age of 10 commented, "It isn't like we wanted to go out and burn down houses to hurt people. . . . The firehouse was like our second home, and we were just tired of getting hassled and never having anybody say nothing good about what we did."[32]

In 1991, two former New Jersey volunteer firefighters were jailed for setting fires in abandoned homes. One, age 20, "told the court he . . . wanted to demonstrate his leadership when he returned later to fight the blaze." He and his accomplice were both reportedly depressed and in counseling before setting the fires.[33]

The same year, a Long Island store detective confessed to setting three separate fires. According to an arson investigator, he didn't want to appear heroic, just "on the spot and effective in his job." The third fire killed two people, injured twenty-eight, and leveled the store.[34]

In 1992, a 19-year-old volunteer firefighter, also from New Jersey, was charged with setting two fires in a storage area at the discount store where he worked as assistant manager. Arriving firefighters found the man already suited up in his fire gear. He led them to the fire.[35]

Most flagrant and dramatic of the firefighter-arsonists was John Orr. A California fire captain and chief arson investigator, he was convicted in 1992 of torching three stores after attending an arson investigators' convention. Two years previously he had written a novel or movie manuscript (accounts differ, but it was apparently never published/produced) describing an arson investigator who set fires. He was also suspected in a string of Los Angeles–area blazes.[36,37]

Commenting on Orr's arrest, *Los Angeles Times* reporter Dean Murphy[38] wrote that arson by firefighters is more common than most people realize. He cited a "decades old" finding that 4% of firefighters fit an attention-seeking pattern.[39] In some areas they are routinely included as suspects by arson investigators, although fire professionals are reluctant to confront the problem. Occasionally arsonists seek jobs with fire departments, much as pedophiles seek jobs in child care. Where fire services depend on volunteers or have lax screening of potential employees, both arsonists and those who want to be heros have easier access.

Murphy's sources said that "ego"—the desire to be regarded as a hero or an exemplary firefighter—is the most common motive for arson by firefighters. Like the nurses who discover or lead the way to a code, these firefighters often arrive first at the scene and help to pinpoint the origin of the blaze. They are often young men who cannot match the veterans' "war stories" or who want to prove themselves and receive the more glamorous assignments. Some firefighter-arsonists have grudges against their departments, and perhaps some simply enjoy the camaraderie that goes with fighting fires.

Most recently, two volunteer firefighters have been accused of starting fires in Malibu, California in the fall of 1993, perhaps with the motive of being "hailed as heroes." The men claim that they were "merely driving by . . . and jumped from [their] truck to put [the fire] out with a garden hose." As this chapter is written, the case is still under investigation.[40]

Veterinary MBP

I know of only two references in the MBP literature to symptoms induced in animals by their owners. Meadow refers to it in passing as an observation made to him by veterinarians (see Chapter 1). Sigal and Altmark's case of "the old man with his companion lady and her pet dog" also suggests veterinary MBP (see Chapter 21). The dynamics would appear to be the same as those in MBP between parents and children: the symptom reporter's need for attention and, possibly, for a relationship with a nurturing figure[41] which overwhelms empathy, plus an available victim who is at the mercy of the inducer and unable to counter the inducer's statements.

I had previously surveyed Honolulu County pediatricians and family practitioners to determine how accurately they believed parents report symptoms in children under 5 years of age.[42] I sent the same survey, modified only by substituting "animal" for "child" and "owner" for "parent" to Honolulu County veterinarians. The results, in the form of averaged responses, are shown in Table 6–1.

In discussing the reasons why animal owners might report problems with their animals inaccurately, the veterinarians felt that owners might underreport out of ignorance, particularly because they

Table 6–1
Symptom Reporting by Parents and Animal Owners*

	Pediatricians and Family Practitioners	Veterinarians
Number of responses received	43	24
Response rate	33%	34%
"Please estimate about what percent of parents/owners, for any reason:		
do not report/conceal symptoms that you feel are important	5%	17%
minimize or "play down" symptoms	8%	16%
report accurately	80%	62%
exaggerate or overinterpret	10%	15%
falsely report or induce symptoms"	1%	5%
"Do you have any children/animals under your care with recurrent or prolonged symptoms of illness which, after extensive testing or appropriate treatment, remain puzzling?"		
Yes	37%	92%

*Numbers do not total 100% because some respondents' answers did not total 100%

do not understand what behaviors are normal for their animal or what symptoms should raise concern. They also speculated that some owners do not want to show the strength of their emotional attachment to the animal, feel guilty for neglecting a problem, or are trying to deny that the problem is serious. The cost of veterinary care, which is not reimbursed by insurance, may also cause owners to understate their animals' problems. Exaggeration of symptoms, they felt, might stem from overidentification with the pet or the desire for a quick appointment. Several admitted the possibility of MBP only indirectly; for example, "I *seldom* see knowing misrepresentation," "the few who create symptoms . . ." One veterinary subspecialist commented,

> Rarely I find clients who exaggerate or invent problems . . . due to a hypochondriac-type personality but applied toward their pets which are 'surrogate children.' Usually it is quickly apparent such [that] individuals have other psychological or emotional disorders. In such cases we are treating for the owners rather than the patient.

It was my subjective impression in doing these surveys that the veterinarians were more open than the physicians to the abstract possibility of MBP, but perhaps less aware of its seriousness. This is an area for further study.

The Law: False Confessions and "Vexatious Complaints"

I have been unable to find any analog to MBP among police, perhaps because it is harder to imagine how they could profit from feigning solved crimes without implicating themselves.[43] Police sometimes tamper with evidence or construct false hypotheses to solve cases that have not yielded to standard investigative methods.[44] The motives, however, are usually to "clean up" pending and troublesome cases or to divert suspicion in a desired direction. To stage a crime or emergency, guarantee that one would be dispatched to investigate it personally, and successfully resolve it without being contradicted by other participants appears far more cumbersome than inducing a code or setting a fire.

More analogous to MBP is the area of false confessions. It is well known that some people come forward to accuse themselves of crimes that they have not committed. This is a different phenomenon from people who are coerced into confessing, or who make a genuine confession that they later retract. After the Lindberg kidnapping, for example, more than 200 people confessed.[45] False confessions have not received much study, but Gudjonsson states that there are three motives: a "morbid desire for notoriety," underlying feelings of guilt that are expiated by confessing to *anything*, and psychotic hallucinations that one has committed a crime. The desire for notoriety generally poses little problem for the police, as it is usually quickly apparent that the suspect was not involved. (On occasion, however, such confessions do lead to false convictions.) Gudjonsson believes that many of these false confessions are "irrational," and that those who confess do not think through the possible consequences of their publicity-seeking.

There are also people with litigious personalities, generally paranoids, who devote their lives to carrying through the legal system or public administrative channels hopeless, trivial, or exaggerated complaints.[46] Little is known about these "vexatious complainers," who are genuinely—if wrongfully—convinced of the rightness of their claims. Many appear plausible at first. They may be analogous to the parent, identified with a subtype of MBP, who has a delusion that the child is genuinely ill.

It should be noted that falsely confessing is not limited to crimes. In a Honolulu case, two modest bypassers rescued a man from a burning house. They left the scene before police and fire fighters arrived, and that night while watching television they saw someone else take credit for the rescue.[47]

Other Syndromes Reminiscent of MBP

Probably killer nurses, firesetting firefighters, and false confessers are only a fraction of those who make factitious reports and stage self-aggrandizing deeds. Goodwin, and co-workers, describe three unrelated girls, ages 9 and 10, all adopted into troubled homes. They factitiously complained that their parents dressed them in rags, forced them to do all the chores, and favored their siblings. The reports were sufficiently convincing that child protective authorities were called. The authors named this "Cinderella Syndrome" and speculated that it was a cry for help in genuine emotional—and probably impending physical—abuse.[48] *USA Today* reported that a 9-year-old Chicago girl falsely accused a substitute teacher, whom she did not like, of molesting her. She offered ten classmates $1.00 each to support her story. One educator commented, "It's not hard for kids in this day and age to know that accusations of sexual abuse get adults' attention. Kids know it's . . . a real bell ringer."[49] Marc Feldman even describes[50] a fabricated literature report of Munchausen's Syndrome. The physicians who published the article later stated that they never meant for it to be taken seriously, but hoped to illustrate "the paradox of different levels of fabricated symptoms and disease."[51] This is not even hinted at in the original text.[52]

Little is known about package and product tampering, but there are frequent "copy cat" incidents after an initial incident.[53] During the summer of 1993, a single report of a hypodermic syringe found in a soft drink can was followed by multiple similar reports from around the United States, although this was inconsistent with the product's manufacture and distribution. According to the literature, there are three causes of product contamination: processing accidents, attempted extortion, and malicious tampering unrelated to a desire for financial gain.[54] The motives for this last type are unclear, but manufacturers have been advised to avoid sensational publicity when tampering occurs,[55] perhaps in an implicit acknowledgement that attention-seeking may be a motive for product adulteration. At least one person, a woman on welfare with a collapsing and abusive marriage, admitted making a false claim against the soft drink manufacturer as a means of seeking sympathy. Commenting on the soft drink tamperings, some mental health professionals cited greed as a major motive. However, lonely people crying for attention and a public appetite for lurid spectacles were also probable motives in some of the cases. "It may seem fun at first to jump on the bandwagon, to get on TV rather than just watch it, and even get money from this big, rich corporation," said one. "But the fun goes away fast once you see those 'poor victims' . . . being led away in handcuffs by the police."[56]

Understanding and Countering

As with MBP, the primary clue to the nursing cases, about which most is known, was statistical: too many incidents on one unit, often on night shift, and—ultimately—in the presence of a single person.[57] This must have been true for at least some of the cases involving firefighters: an unusual number of fires in a particular district brought attention. Many prosecutions of nurses succeeded or failed on the willingness of judges and juries to make the leap from numbers to guilt. "Statistical analysis," said one investigator, "cannot answer whether intentional acts were committed against patients."[58] But it can suggest the need for further scrutiny. This suggests that institutions, whether health care, public government, or manufacturers, ought to be aware of when and in whose presence incidents occur. They ought to make such surveillance a routine part of their risk management, particularly if they have building designs that reduce staff visibility. Care must be taken to avoid the appearance or reality of scapegoating, and of course surveillance should not be limited to any one group. Nor should naive staff or those who know and assert their rights be penalized. Because life is random, clusters of incidents will occur, and the names of those who work many shifts in high acuity areas will appear on lists more frequently, but proper statistical technique should correct for this. Almost nothing is known about preventing Munchausen Syndrome by Professional Proxy (MBPP), but such a policy, routinely communicated to all staff, might deter the rare employee who would be tempted. The possibility of a professionals with MBPP propensities working for temporary placement agencies, particularly those with national or international scope, is horrifying but logical. Requiring contracting institutions to report all incidents on units where an agency's personnel are present might reduce this risk.

The total number of verified MBPP cases involving nurses and firefighters is so small as to make any speculation risky. The perpetrators reported here may be only the most florid or least lucky. However, there are some commonalities that deserve consideration. For example, many hospital incidents are reported on the night shift, a time when nurses are less likely to be observed by visitors, extra staff members, or patients themselves. Finally, the two nurses on whom most is known, Bev Allitt and Genene Jones, had long and troubled personal and work histories. One hesitates to recommend that troubled and troublesome workers never be given another chance, but they should be carefully screened to separate the troublemaker from the maligned, and second chances should be carefully supervised probation periods. The number of these chances should not be unlimited, and institutions should be wary when their need for personnel is so pressing that they can no longer be selective in the staff they recruit and retain. One gains a sense that perhaps these nurses were desperate for the kind of acceptance, work achievement, and friendship that most people take for granted. Perhaps they lacked the normal skills to achieve these goals and turned to a bizarre parody of heroic behavior. Some business circles would have applauded a comparable lack of conscience and willingness to turn situations to their own advantage.

Two other themes emerge as these cases are considered: marginality and anger toward the employing institution. Stonequist[59] used the term "marginal man" to describe immigrants who always stand on a metaphorical boundary line, never perfectly fitting into their culture of origin or their culture of residence. Two accused nurses were literally immigrants. Genene Jones, as a practical nurse, was not fully qualified for work in an intensive care unit. Many of the firefighters were young, or volunteers who might not be screened as thoroughly as civil service employees. Compared to their proportion in nursing as a whole, males are overrepresented among MBPP nurse-perpetrators. Could it be that male nurses, like the young firemen, have a stronger need to prove themselves? Perhaps the marginal nurse or firefighter who has a particular underlying personality structure (type unknown) is at higher risk to commit MBPP.

Anger has been offered as a possible motive for product tampering[60], as well as for MBP. Speculation that nurses kill patients to point out institutional deficiencies is reminiscent of some MBP parents' defense that they only induced symptoms "this once" to "prove to the doctor that there was a real problem." It may be rationalization, but it also has its own logic, built upon smoldering anger and the inability to get what one wants. "They'll be sorry," one can imagine the nurse thinking: sorry they didn't listen, sorry they treated staff or patients like this, sorry they didn't do things my way. "I warned them that something could happen." Who has not had such fleeting thoughts? If suicide is a cry for help, so, sometimes, is murder or arson.

It is easier to see the remedies than to implement them. Good management to produce a facility of high quality is a first step in preventing this sort of MBPP, just as listening to parents and taking their concerns seriously (as well as setting limits) is probably basic to preventing MBP. Thorough screening of potential employees, whether paid or volunteer, is a second defense. Open, accessible management that works to help all staff feel included and important is a third: staff who are concerned about facility conditions should be able to talk rather than act out. For most staff, these and the routine surveillance already discussed should be sufficient. Approval for those who do well in emergencies should be balanced with meaningful recognition of those who contribute in quieter ways. There will always be disagreements over what should be done—whether, for example, practical nurses should be allowed to work in critical care units or volunteers in fire companies. Most professionals will accept a management decision they don't like, particularly if their ideas have been considered. However, for potential vexatious complainers the decision will become an obstacle and a source of long-term resentment. Management that stays close to its staff can spot these few and attempt to work with them. If they remain seriously disaffected, they may need encouragement to explore other job possibilities and not remain where they are unhappy.

The ambiguity of these cases, with their circumstantial and statistical evidence, leaves many professionals feeling vulnerable. Must nurses work in pairs, as was proposed after the Detroit cases? Should they hesitate to call a code? Will a lone nurse on night duty in a nursing home face false accusations when several of his patients slip away? MBPP is not the only instance of such concerns, and sometimes innocent people are accused. But the Beverley Allitt and Genene Jones cases bring to life the meaning of statistical improbability. Time after time Allitt went into a room with a syringe in her hand and came running out to report a patient in distress. Time after time in an ordinary pediatrician's office Jones was momentarily alone with an infant who went limp and stopped breathing. These cases went far beyond coincidence and bad luck. Rather than engaging in witch hunts, management closed their eyes and ears to what was being reported. Colleagues, direct supervisors, and upper level administration must consider the possibility of MBPP just as they consider the possibility that their employees might steal drugs or sleep on duty. They must take appropriate steps to guard against it and pursue it when it occurs.

Most people sublimate their fascination with fire, death, and crime into socially acceptable channels. They become well-functioning emergency personnel, police, or firefighters. "Professional drug study patients" who enjoy attention for their illness move from clinical trial to clinical trial, ask to be included in studies, and know when their protocols expire so they can enroll again.[61] Those who do well at parenting sick children become special needs foster parents or hospital volunteers. But not everyone has the ego strength to do this: Levin and Fox wrote:[62]

> Ironically, the need to control may get played out in courageous, benevolent behavior. . . . Saving a life is a way of controlling someone's fate, just as is taking a life. In 1969, long before his rampage of death and mutilation had begun, [serial killer] Ted Bundy received a commendation from the Seattle Police Department for capturing a purse snatcher. . . . During the summer of 1970, he plunged into Seattle's Green Lake to save a drowning 3-year-old child. And while an undergraduate psychology major, Bundy worked on Seattle's Crisis Clinic hotline. . . .
>
> The psychological need to control is often evident in the idiosyncratic lifestyles and aspirations of serial slayers. Some are infatuated with powerful automobiles; others dream of careers in law enforcement; still others collect the symbols of power—such as police and military uniforms. . . .

Perhaps emergency work seduces the needy, marginal person described above as well as the altruist. Martin Orne, a professor of psychiatry, speculated that Richard Angelo might have been praised at some point for saving a life, then later "stepped over the line" to save "someone who wasn't really dying."[63] Most health care professionals, and perhaps people in general, have probably imagined the praise they would receive from doing well in an emergency. No doubt many kind and helpful professionals have had fleeting wishes that an emergency would occur so that they could "show their stuff." For those who can tolerate personal awareness of these feelings—the very ones with the ego strength to best guard against acting them out—it is only a very small step to empathize with a nurse who induces a code or a firefighter who starts a fire.

References

1. In order to avoid unfairly stigmatizing those who may have been unfairly accused, this chapter will name only professionals who have been convicted and whose convictions have not been overturned.
2. Darbyshire P. Licensed to Kill? *Nursing Times.* 1986; 82:22–25.
3. Wiley L. Liability for Death: Nine Nurses' Legal Ordeals. *Nursing 81.* 1981; 7:34–43.
4. Yorker BC. Nurses Accused of Murder. *Am J Nursing.* 1988:1327–32.
5. MNA Board Urges Further Investigation In Case of Two Convicted VA Nurses. *Am J Nursing.* 1977:1381 ff.
6. Jones A. Nurse Hunting in Michigan. *Nation.* December 3, 1977:584–588.
7. Darbyshire, Licensed.
8. Wiley, Liability.
9. Yorker, Nurses.
10. An extensive analysis of the case, press coverage, and implications for nursing can be found in Kalish PA, Kalisch BJ, and Livesay E. The 'angel of death': the anatomy of 1980's major news story about nursing. *Nursing Forum* 1980; 19:212–241.
11. Alex Levin, personal communications.
12. Darbyshire, Licensed.
13. Yorker, Nurses.
14. Charbonneau L. The Grange report: nurses criticize commission's report for lack of answers. *Canadian Nurse.* 1985; March: 14–18.
15. Johnson A. The baby murders. *MacLean's* April 9, 1984:36–42.
16. Edwards P. Sick Kids' nurses suffered casualties after eight babies died in the hospital. *Toronto Star,* September 3, 1987:A1, A14.
17. Darbyshire, Licensed.
18. Elkind P. *The Death Shift: The True Story of Nurse Genene Jones and the Texas Baby Murders.* 1989; NY: Viking.
19. Moore K, Reed D. *Deadly Medicine.* 1988; NY: St. Martin's.
20. Wiley, Liability.
21. Yorker, Nurses.
22. Long Island's Angel of Death. *Newsweek,* November 30, 1987:35.
23. Long Island's Angel of Death.
24. A nursing aide admits killing elderly patient. *NY Times.* January 10, 1990: A24.
25. L. I. Nurse Gets 50-Year Term in Four Killings. *NY Times.* January 24, 1990: B4.
26. Schmitt E. Nurse Known as Dedicated Worker. *NY Times.* November 17, 1987; B2.
27. Georgia nurse, a focus in 16 deaths, is charged with one killing. *NY Times.* August 22, 1991: B12.
28. Yardley J. Cobb nurse charged with murder in Birmingham. *Atlanta Constitution J.* August 22, 1991: A1.

29. "Code blue nurse gets life: Akin sentenced in patient's death" *Atlanta Constitution J.* October 10, 1992: B3.

30. Manchester *Guardian Weekly*, Week Ending May 23, 1993: 1 ff.

31. Davies N. *Murder on Ward Four*. London: Chato & Windus, 1993. I am indebted to Dr. Roy Meadow for sending me this book.

32. Price DM. Firefighter says criticism drove volunteers to arson; chief's rebukes stung Prince George's men. *The Washington Post*, September 15, 1990, p. A1 f. Quote p. A11.

33. Ex-firefighters draw 5-year terms in arson. *NY Times*, August 4, 1991, 1:37.

34. Lyall S. Store detective held in blaze at Suffolk Mall; police say he set fire in order to put it out. *NY Times*, September 28, 1991, p. 22L.

35. Firefighter charged with arson at store. *NY Times*, April 10, 1992, B4.

36. On arson, convicted sleuth wrote the book. *NY Times*, August 2, 1991, A29.

37. Murphy DE. When the firebug happens to be a firefighter. *LA Times*, December 17, 1991, A1 ff.

38. Firebug.

39. I was unable to find this study.

40. 2 Firefighters are L.A. Fire Suspects. *Honolulu Advertiser*. May 5, 1994: A11.

41. Schreier HA and Libow JA. *Hurting for Love: Munchausen by Proxy Syndrome*. New York: Guilford Press; 1993.

42. unpublished data.

43. This was confirmed by my conversation with Honolulu Police Chaplain Larry Kelly, December 27, 1993. However, any information or hypotheses from readers would be appreciated.

44. After this was written, the Television program *America's Most Wanted* reported (April 8, 1995) on a Woodbury, New York policeman, Joe Harper, who blew up buildings with dynamite. He attracted suspicion because he was always "first on the scene," and had an "intuitive" knowledge of where the dynamite had been stolen from. He pleaded guilty in November, 1979, and later said that "the pressure of the job got to him."

45. This statistic and the balance of the information in this section is taken from Gisli Gudjonsson, "The Psychology of False Confessions," *Medico-Legal J.* 1989; 57:93–110.

46. Ian Freckelton. Querulent Paranoia and the Vexatious Complainant. *Intl J Law Psychiatry*. 1988; 11:127–42.

47. Ramirez T. When heroes are brave but bashful. *Honolulu Advertiser*. February 5, 1994: A1.

48. Goodwin J, Gauthorne CG, Rada RT. Cinderella syndrome: children who simulate neglect. *Am J Psychiatry*. 1980; 137:1223.

49. Johnson K. Bribes help girl, 9, frame teacher for abuse. *USA Today*. May 18, 1994: A1.

50. Feldman MD. Factitious Munchausen's syndrome: a confession. *New Engl J Med*. 1992; 327:438–9.

51. Gurwith M and Langston C. Factitious Munchausen's syndrome. *New Engl J Med*. 1992; 327:439–40.

52. That text appears in the *N Engl J Med* 302:1483, 1980.

53. Ferrell D. A chain reaction of fear. *Los Angeles Times.* June 19, 1993: A1 ff.

54. Valerie Denney, "Product Persecution," *ReActions* July, 1989, p. 23.

55. Stern W. A Common-Sense View. *Packaging.* 1989; 34 (May):37.

56. Mashberg T and Leonhardt D. FDA backs Pepsi: hoaxes revealed. *Boston Globe.* June 18, 1993: A1.

57. See Yorker, Nurses, for a list of typical events for which surveillance is done. Many of the investigations charted the movements of professionals other than nurses.

58. Quoted in Yorker, p. 1332.

59. Stonequist E. *The Marginal Man.* 1937; New York: Scribner's.

60. Ferrell, Chain.

61. Dale Reynolds, Wyeth-Ayerst Pharmaceuticals, personal communication 11/4/93.

62. Levin J and Fox JA. *Mass Murder: America's Growing Menace.* 1985; New York: Plenum: 69–70.

63. Quoted in Long Island's Angel of Death.

7

Respiratory Manifestations
Michael J. Light

Respiratory symptoms are among the most dramatic presentations of Munchausen Syndrome by Proxy (MBP), with induced suffocation an uncommon but potentially devastating conclusion. Although respiratory conditions are frequent among infants and children, the diagnosis of MBP is rare. Its most common respiratory form is apnea, which was the fourth most common presentation of MBP found by Rosenberg in her review of the literature,[1] accounting for 15% of cases. Other presentations may include asthma, bronchopulmonary dysplasia, bleeding from or attributed to the airway, cystic fibrosis, chest pain and sleep disorders.

Because breathing is so central to life itself, respiratory symptoms that are reported cannot be ignored. Equally, they can often not be documented. Objectively, respiration is difficult to assess and describe, even for the experienced professional. Thus, respiratory symptoms offer fertile ground to the parent who wishes to induce illness or its appearance. In addition, over the last ten to twenty years, increasing numbers of children are managed at home with medical technology. Palfrey[2] conducted a statewide census in Massachusetts and reported a prevalence of 0.8% of children with tracheostomies, supplemental oxygen, respirators, and other technology. Although the trend toward home care with durable medical equipment has benefited many children, their families, and the health care system, it has also provided opportunities for the occasional parents who use a child's illness to meet their own needs.

Apnea and Nonaccidental Suffocation

Home apnea monitors are prescribed for various situations during infancy. Premature babies, particularly those requiring advanced technology, infants who have experienced an apparent life-threatening episode (ALTE), subsequent siblings of Sudden Infant Death Syndrome (SIDS) victims, infants with some congenital anomalies, and occasional term babies with breathing abnormalities all may require close observation at home. For parents, each of these conditions may be associated with emotional disorders, up to and including posttraumatic stress disorder, because the parents perceive this as a potentially life-or-death situation for their infant. The immediate condition which resulted in the prescription of the monitor—especially death or apparent near-death, or a premature birth—is often experienced as a crisis.[3] Monitor alarms occur with frequency, especially in the early days when the parents are getting accustomed to the monitor. Almost always, the parents report that the infant was breathing when checked or responded to minimal stimulation. The need for cardiopulmonary resuscitation (CPR) by caregivers is rare and it is even rarer for a baby to require CPR on multiple occasions unless there is a specific underlying problem.

MBP should be suspected if a care taker reports performing CPR and/or calls the ambulance on multiple occasions, the baby appears entirely normal on physical examination, and no apnea can be documented. Apnea and bradycardia almost always resolve as the baby matures and rarely persist beyond one year of age. Most commonly, MBP with apnea is associated with apnea of infancy but Sullivan[4] reported an 8-year-old girl with multiple problems including 20–30 episodes of apnea each night requiring stimulation or resuscitation.

The incidence of MBP and apnea is unknown, but Mitchell[5] reported 11 children in 5 families who were seen during a 10-year period. They were assessed by the team at Alberta Children's Hospital which serves an area population of 1.2 million. Two strongly suspected cases in our program[6] in Honolulu led to our interest in MBP. We then surveyed apnea monitor centers[7] and found 54 probable instances reported by 51 monitor programs caring for 20,090 infants in the United States. A case from the literature[8] that illustrates both the bizarre and dramatic form that MBP with apnea often takes along with some of the normal complications of apnea is reproduced below with my editorial comments interspersed.

This infant was found apneic and cyanotic in the crib at home at two weeks of age. The pneumocardiogram (a recording of respiration and heartbeat), showed 15% periodic breathing, with 40 breathing pauses less than 15 seconds. Because of this abnormal although inconclusive pattern of short apnea, the baby was discharged home with a cardiorespiratory monitor. During the next month, the baby was seen at different facilities for multiple episodes of alarms. Since no recording device was used, it was impossible to tell whether they were true or false. At one point, the monitor was changed three times in three days. There was a report of "a 3-minute apnea alarm with bradycardia," which, if true, would have represented an infant in severe distress and danger. When baby was about 6 weeks of age, mother reported an episode of awake apnea with no detectable heart rate requiring CPR for 4 minutes. A month later, mother reported seizurelike episodes sufficiently violent that the baby was coming off the mattress, yet she refused to bring him in for evaluation. She then reported that the trailer they lived in was broken into on three occasions over a 5-day period and at the second break-in the monitor wires were cut. Another monitor was provided and, on a third occasion, the monitor was destroyed. It was not until mother reported another seizure that the Child Protection Team met to recommend placement of the child with the father. During the ensuing hospital admission mother stated that the father of the baby never believed that the episodes were occurring and that the only person who truly believed her was the apnea nurse specialist. The mother also said that ever since the baby was born, she was terrified he would die. She said that she had stopped using the monitor during naps because she would rather find him dead than have advance warning and that she might not do CPR because she knew he was going to die anyway.

These themes of not being believed[9] and of premonitions[10] certainly occur among SIDS and monitoring parents yet one can see how they added to the dramatic flair of this most unusual and symptomatically mixed picture. Although a small number of infants require resuscitation or have apnea associated with seizures, and while a small number of families lose or destroy monitors, are robbed, have premonitions, or differ among themselves over the infant's problems, the probability of these factors occurring together is remote. The authors state that MBP was considered about a month after the infant presented to them and intervention occurred one month later. It is possible that the early apnea stories were cries for help and, when they did not work in the way the mother wanted, the seizure stories were added to them. This infant had some mild apnea and the mother may have received gratification through progressively exaggerating the symptoms. It is certainly possible that if mother was inducing apnea or hypoxia, seizures resulted. If so, perhaps the infant's struggles were reported to the physicians as seizures. It is fortunate that no harm came to this child.

In the early years, when monitors were being introduced to intensive care nurseries, it became clear that there was often a discrepancy between the monitor and the reporting of apneic events by the nursing staff. This disparity between caretaker and monitor has been shown to be greater with home monitoring and applies to both apnea and bradycardia alarms.[11,12] Most parents, who misreport, however, do so from inexperience, anxiety, or as the result of having been awakened suddenly during the night. This is a very different situation from the parent who deliberately misrepresents what is occurring.

MBP presenting as apnea includes two sometimes overlapping situations. Factitious apnea implies that the caretaker is reporting symptoms that are not, in fact, occurring. Reports of 50 to 100 apnea alarms overnight or over a series of nights without obvious cause (equipment malfunction, illness, a previously documented pattern that includes multiple alarms), reports of multiple resuscitations, or life-threatening apnea in a child over 1 year of age should raise concern. This is particularly the case if the infant is asymptomatic on physical exam and appropriate diagnostic tests in the hospital reveal no abnormality.

Induced apnea occurs when the perpetrator is actually causing airway obstruction and then summoning or presenting for medical assistance. In this situation, the infant may suffer major morbidity or mortality. It is not uncommon for the infant to be presented for medical care on multiple occasions. It can be difficult to separate induced from factitious apnea and, in many cases there is probably a mix. Clinicians who receive reports of apnea see a spectrum that extends from overanxious mothers who seek care on multiple occasions for minor problems to cases in which repeated abuse occurs or the child is killed.

The literature as a whole suggests that a number of infant deaths attributed to Sudden Infant Death Syndrome (SIDS) may, in fact, have been infanticide. A case in point was recently reported in the *New York Times*.[13] The death of two infants was discussed in a 1972 article in *Pediatrics* by Dr. Alfred Steinschneider as being the result of a breathing disorder and classified as resulting from natural causes.[14] Ten years later, a district attorney reading the article became suspicious and alerted local authorities and the state police. They investigated the case and concluded that the mother had, in fact, suffocated her five children. Reece[15] has provided criteria for distinguishing SIDS from fatal child abuse and a good reference list. It is interesting that there is no mention of MBP in his article. Table 7–1 presents characteristics that help distinguish death from SIDS, child abuse and MBP.

Several authors stress the risk to other siblings. Alexander[16] reported five families in which more than one child was a victim of MBP, with a total of 13 affected children. It appears that only one sibling was involved at any time and that the symptoms were similar in siblings and index cases in each family. Apnea was the dominant presentation in three of the five families.

One of Alexander and co-workers's cases[17] made numerous ambulance calls (10 over 5 months) for apnea/seizures which triggered suspicion of MBP in a 33-month-old boy. The episodes usually occurred at 4:30 p.m. every third Tuesday and paramedics found the mother administering CPR to a nonbreathing child. After full-term birth, the baby had been reported to have had a seizure at 28 days of age with 20 subsequent hospitalizations at three major tertiary centers for seizures observed only by the mother. The symptoms ceased when the child was placed in a foster home and the mother was found guilty of child endangerment. Investigation revealed a previous child of this mother with similar unexplained apnea; that child died at 8-1/2 months of age after 20 episodes witnessed only by the mother. The autopsy reported "no evidence of child abuse" despite findings of moderate hydrocephalus suggesting repeated hypoxia and acute subdural hematoma supporting shaken baby syndrome as the cause of the fatal injury. After the child's death, the mother made weekly calls for an ambulance, stating that she

Table 7–1
Characteristics to Differentiate Diagnosis of Death of SIDS, Child Abuse and MBP

	SIDS	Child Abuse	MBP
Age	1–12 months with most occurring 2–4 months	Most after 6 months	Start at any age
History	Infant placed in crib after feeding; found several hours later to be lifeless No prior history of symptoms	May present with plausible history of trauma. May have history of prematurity Prior abuse often reported	Extensive prior medical history that may not fit the facts Months of medical problems common
Apnea history	6% have prior history of apnea	Apnea may be in history	May report multi-unconfirmed episodes of apnea
Home apnea monitor	Usually not	For premature or infant with apnea or requiring oxygen (who are at risk for abuse)	Usual with MBP with apnea
Mother	Often discovers baby. Usually upset and confused	May be perpetrator or accomplice. Affect may be inappropriate	Usual perpetrator. May have health background. May appear exemplary.
Father	Upset and may be angry	Boyfriend or stepfather often perpetrator	Absent in body or spirit
Autopsy findings	Characteristic of SIDS with intrathoracic petechiae. No other obvious cause of death.	Trauma, especially cerebral and/or abdominal hemorrhage. Evidence of prior trauma (fractures, bruises) common	Possible asphyxia; toxic screen necessary. Findings may not corroborate story.

was "passing out." When ambulance personnel would arrive, she was invariably unresponsive.

When the mother herself was 17 years old, she had reported resuscitating an infant for whom she was babysitting by herself. This infant was diagnosed with an apneic spell leading to moderate brain damage. She received community honors and publicity for her effort. It is arguable whether this should have been classified as heroics or early MBP.

Another case involving recurrent episodes of apnea and cyanosis was preceded by induced preterm labor in a 27-year-old woman.[18] At 26 weeks of gestation antepartum hemorrhage and rupture of membranes was caused by a knitting needle and resulted in delivery of a 980g male infant. The baby was discharged home at 5 months of age, and was readmitted on multiple occasions for apneic spells, febrile convulsions, and cyanotic spells. There was also significant failure to thrive from 7 months of age on, with increasing respiratory problems and significant morbidity. The father, who had never seen any of these episodes, was asked if he thought it was possible that that his wife was harming the child and he replied affirmatively. The child was removed from the mother's influence and subsequently thrived without difficulty.

At the more benign end of the continuum, it can be difficult to separate anxiety from "help seeking."[19] Clinical experience suggests that there are many cases that may be described as mild or potential MBP with apnea, that respond to early recognition and appropriate intervention. For example, good support by the apnea program in the early days of monitoring is effective in decreasing most parental anxiety. Probably the most important component of home monitoring is education in the use of the monitor and how to respond to alarms and in the naturally self-limiting nature of infantile apnea. This includes teaching the caretakers CPR according to an established protocol and routinely documenting such teaching. Parents sometimes justify injuries to the child by stating that they had been taught to perform CPR in a nonstandard fashion, and had responded as they were taught. As I evaluated one child who presented with multiple fractured ribs, the mother was asked to demonstrate her response to finding the baby apneic. She gave the doll such a thump that rib fractures were not a surprising result. She said that she had not been taught so aggressively but that in the heat of the moment she panicked. The family found an endocrinologist who stated that the child's prematurity and subsequent osteopenia resulted in fragile ribs. However, this did not explain the spiral fractures of the femur and tibia that were present and characteristic of child abuse.

It has been my clinical experience that the prompt use of recording devices or documenting monitors when questionable symptoms are reported often dramatically decreases parental reports of apnea, although I do not know of any empirical studies that have addressed this. Many clinicians have hoped that documenting monitors would become standard practice, however in many states it is difficult to get reimbursement for the additional cost of the hardware, technician time for information retrieval, or physician interpretation.

Samuels[20] reported 157 infants with ALTE, and prospectively followed them through monitoring at home. One hundred eleven (71%) had recurrent events. Of 77 (49%) in whom a diagnosis was obtained, there were 18 deliberate suffocations by a parent and seven cases of MBP with fabricated history and/or data. Meadow[21] described 27 families in which there was suffocation of at least one child with nine deaths. Twenty-four of these children were reported to have had a history of apnea, cyanosis, or seizure, with many reporting repetitive suffocation. The repetitive suffocation usually began between the ages of 1 and 3 months and continued until it was discovered or the child died, generally 6 to 12 months later. There was also a history of death among 18 siblings, most of whom had been diagnosed as SIDS.

Samuels[22] also reported imposed upper airway obstruction diagnosed by covert video surveillance in 14 patients. The episodes started between 3 weeks and 33 months of age (median 1.4 months, with 12 starting less than 4 months of age), and continued for 0.8 to 20 months with median 3.5 months. There were seven male infants and seven female. All of the babies were admitted to the hospital at least three times and one 19 times (median 5).

The use of covert video surveillance to document imposed apnea or suffocation continues to be controversial, yet is the most effective means of detection reported in the literature. It is my belief that if the history strongly suggests that a caretaker is harming a child, the use of methods to document this action should be justifiable for professionals who are acting as advocates for the child. Covert video surveillance is discussed at greater length elsewhere in this volume. The responsibility for this monitoring should be decided by hospital policy, perhaps with discussion with hospital counsel, security, and ethics committee, child protection services and local law enforcement. The burden of covert video surveillance on the hospital is not necessarily heavy; Samuels reported a mean of 24 hours from its initiation until attempted suffocation was seen. It is important to monitor the victim because if any harm came to the child while under surveillance, which is certainly a risk with suffocation, the ability to identify the perpetrator would not mitigate the responsibility of the hospital to protect a child under its care.

Rosen used two cameras[23] to uncover an instance of suffocation. The first camera was visible and the parent consented to its use. This camera was later removed, ostensibly for maintenance, and the perpetrator did not realize that she was still being observed by a second hidden camera. It could then be argued that the mother had consented to observation by camera, although deception was still involved. In order to preserve the privacy of the family, it has been suggested[24] that the camera should be focused on the bed—which obviously only works if the child is confined to the bed. The major problem, other than the obvious legal questions, is whether the circumstances surrounding the situation encourage perpetrators to "prove" to the medical team that the story they are telling is true. In some cases, mothers have justified their attempts to suffocate their children in hospital by stating that they were "desperate" to prove that the apnea was occurring. As Epstein[25] has stressed, it is also important for the medical team to have a plan of response when the perpetrator is confronted since there is potential for harm to professionals, perpetrator, and the child. Appropriate psychiatric support should be available for the perpetrator.

In an editorial in the British Medical Journal, Meadow[26] wrote:

> When the British press heard of this covert video surveillance there was criticism that a mother should be filmed without her permission: some professional organizations proclaimed that patients always should be informed if they were to be filmed. Those critics were forgetting the identity of the patient. The patient was the child (who had presented

with recurrent apnoeic [sic] spells). If that 2 year old, who had had periods when his air supply was cut off and he had had to struggle to get air, had been asked if he wanted to be filmed so that the cause of those episodes could be found he would have answered "yes."

I believe that covert video surveillance is occasionally a necessary part of the evaluation of an infant or child who is at risk for harm by an abusing parent. The perpetrator may be devious enough to produce a history that can only be contradicted by documentation. Southall[27] states that such confirmation "avoids the need for medical and nursing staff to confront the mother with a possibly incorrect suspicion."

Asthma and Bronchopulmonary Dysplasia

There are few reports of MBP and asthma, which is somewhat surprising, as asthma in childhood is very common. Perhaps 10% of children wheeze at some time and, as with any dramatic chronic illness, the potential for abuse is great. Godding[28] suggested that 1% of his asthmatic patients (17/1648 families) could be considered as victims of MBP. Ten of these families with a total of 11 children seen over a 3-year period induced symptoms by withholding medications. The children had a mean age of 7.5 years and most had severe asthma with repeated attacks. During acute wheezing, parents failed to give prescribed treatment in 7 of 11 cases and gave ineffective treatment in 6 instances. One child died of status asthmaticus, five were rehospitalized or visited the emergency room frequently, and three had chronic airway obstruction. The mean age of seven other children whose asthma was overtreated was 8 years. Their families behaved as if they wanted the children to remain chronically ill. The asthma was mild and the symptoms were falsified, leading to aggressive unnecessary treatment prescribed by physicians and administered by the parents.

Management of the child with asthma that appears to be poorly controlled despite an appropriate medical regimen begins with questions. First and foremost, has the right diagnosis been made? Wheezing is common in childhood and particularly if the onset is during infancy the label of asthma can be made because there is persistent reversible reactive airway disease. The use of a daily diary card with measurement of peak expiratory flows of children over 5 years old twice daily (generally morning and evening) establishes the individual's baseline. By reviewing the diary and the response to changes in peak flow and pulmonary function obtained in the office, the physician can evaluate the appropriateness of home management and the amount of medication to be used. For the younger child, the daily diary card is useful to correlate symptoms with treatment and again may help clarify whether the parent is over-, under-, or appropriately treating.

The differentiation of MBP from true physical illness can be difficult in complex situations when there are multiple risk factors. The association between bronchopulmonary dysplasia and sudden death has been noted.[29] In addition, the graduate from the neonatal intensive or special care nursery is clearly at risk for child abuse. I have followed cases of technologically dependent graduates of the nursery who fit all the criteria for MBP but in whom confirming the diagnosis would be very difficult. Examples include children with tracheostomies and those requiring long-term mechanical ventilation who present complex legal, ethical, and logistic problems.

Cystic Fibrosis (CF)

Orenstein[30] reported a 5-1/2-year-old boy who was seen in the Memphis Cystic Fibrosis Center in 1982 at the request of the mother who claimed to be a nurse.

> Mother reported that the child had been born prematurely with aspiration of vomitus at 6 hours of age necessitating chest tubes and mechanical ventilation for several days. She stated that a sweat chloride concentration at 5 months of age was 95 mEq/L (normal <40 mEq/L), and the patient was diagnosed as having CF by a family physician. By 5 years of age, he had coughing spells that were reportedly relieved by his mother's reaching into his throat to extract mucus plugs. Medical charts could not be obtained from other hospitals and it was later found that the mother called and rescinded her consent to provide the records. Evaluation in Memphis revealed a poorly nourished child with clubbing of the fingers and clinical and radiologic evidence of chronic pulmonary disease. The child was admitted multiple times for episodes of severe cough that responded to intravenous antibiotics. The mother

would stay at his bedside continuously and would assist the nurses in adminstering medications.

During one hospitalization, sweat chloride concentrations of 57, 116, and 75 mEq/L were obtained. The third test was performed under observation by a physician. Towards the end of the one-hour collection period, the mother announced "he has to go to the bathroom" and on returning said to a nurse "I don't know why the resident had to be with us the whole time—it's almost as if they suspected me of altering the test." Sputum tests invariably were of normal flora, except once when there was isolation of Pseudomonas aeruginosa with antibiotic sensitivity identical to that of a CF patient who was hospitalized at the same time.

After 20 months of care at Memphis, bronchoscopy revealed scarring of the right lower lobe bronchus presumably from the initial aspiration. The tracheobronchial tree was otherwise normal. Secretions from the right middle lobe were purulent and yielded *Haemophilus influenzae* sensitive to ampicillin. A woman claiming to be a medical student called the laboratory and said that she had seen the culture plates from the bronchoscopy washings. She stated that she was able to identify Haemophilus, Klebsiella, and Pseudomonas and that the real plates had been replaced. On this admission, a 72-hour stool collection was turned in by the mother containing 22 grams of fat per 24 hours (normal = 7 grams/24 hours). Previous attempts to complete stool collection had failed.

The local Cystic Fibrosis Foundation provided a tearful woman with the names of CF families in the area after she said that her infant was recently diagnosed as having CF. One of the families was contacted by a "pharmacy student" who arranged for a teenage CF patient to drive to the hospital parking lot to give a sputum sample to help with a research project. Shortly thereafter the in-patient's mother gave the floor nurses the sputum sample they had been waiting for for three days. Identification of the mother as the "student" by the CF teenager, whose sputum culture result was identical, provided proof that the mother had been fabricating the CF history. Sweat chloride concentration of the child was repeated with normal results of 13 and 14 mEq/L on two separate tests.

Medical records from another area were then obtained revealing a hospitalization one year previously with similar episodes. The mother had been confronted about her fabricating the CF story but did not follow up for counseling and eventually found her way to the Memphis CF Center. Custody of the child was awarded to the Department of

Human Services for 6 months at the end of which time the child was returned to the parents against medical advice. They have been lost to follow-up.

In their discussion, the authors point out the extremes to which perpetrators will go to make their case. This mother added salt to the sweat test, fat to the 72-hour stool collection, and provided a sputum specimen from a patient with CF on two occasions—all of this to support her need to have a child with CF.

Single[31] reported a father who presented his 11-year-old son with a plausible history of CF. In this case the diagnosis was easily refuted by a normal sweat test but the father was diagnosed as having a severe antisocial personality disorder. The son talked freely about his previous "life-threatening CF," which he claimed had now been cured. He then said that he suffered from another illness which his father had told him would soon leave him unable to walk and would result in his death.

Bleeding from the Upper Airway

Two reports of hemoptysis illustrate different methods of inducing symptoms and achieving diagnosis. Although epistaxis is common and the source usually can be found, hemoptysis is an uncommon symptom in young children and it may be more difficult to separate bleeding from the lungs and the gastrointestinal tract. A careful history is helpful but confirmation may necessitate invasive tests. As with other symptoms, if the bleeding is factitious, it may stop after separation from the perpetrator.

> An 8-week-old presented with bleeding from the upper respiratory tract.[32] Major investigations including angiography, endoscopy, radiolabelled ^{51}Cr and scanning failed to identify the source. However, radioactivity of new onset facial bleeding had no increase from background radioactivity while the infant's peripheral blood showed persistent radioactivity (left from the scan). Rhesus typing of the blood on the face revealed subtype cc, while the infant's blood was Cc, which confirmed that the blood was from an external source.

Lee[33] also described a family with twins who had multiple admissions for apparent hemoptysis. The mother was actually traumatizing the children and was found on one occasion to be causing the bleeding with a pin. One of the cases in our survey[34] was of a mother who was found to have caused superficial bleeding by placing broken glass in the baby's mouth. As with other forms of MBP involving the respiratory and associated systems, induced bleeding is a dramatic symptom that connotes (at least to the lay observer) immediate threat to life, yet which is relatively easy to fabricate either through trauma or through the use of supplied blood.

Chest Pain

Chest pain is often a difficult symptom to evaluate in children. It is a relatively uncommon presenting complaint. It may occur following trauma or with pulmonary infection. In children with a history of asthma, it may be related to pneumothorax or rib fracture.

Kahan[35] reported a 9-year-old boy who underwent bronchoscopy, endoscopy, and esophageal biopsy for chest pain that his mother stated had interfered with school attendance. No cause was found and the boy was transferred to the hospital's Medical/Psychiatric Unit. The mother reported other symptoms including behavior problems, bed-wetting, fecal soiling, and a tic. An only child, he lived with stepfather and mother who was a licensed practical nurse. Mother had a history of repeated hospitalizations for stomach and bladder problems. During the next hospitalization 6 months later, the school principal called wanting to know how the boy's recovery from "brain cancer" was progressing. The boy's parents had repeatedly told the school principal that he was in treatment for the malignancy, which was inoperable because of a severe heart condition. Fund-raising events had been arranged to pay for the cancer treatment.

Management of MBP Associated with Pulmonary Symptoms

Apnea is a common symptom and presentation of an apneic infant for care is often associated with minimal clinical findings. When the statistical probability of MBP is higher than that of the rare disorders being considered, MBP must be added to the differential diagnosis. If apnea or cyanosis have been reported as occurring in front of others, corroboration of the story is necessary. Early consideration of documented monitoring may reduce the potential for progression to harm of the infant. If there has been death of a sibling, the death summary or autopsy results should be obtained, if available, particularly if the diagnosis was SIDS. Emery[36] suggests that 10–20% of SIDS cases may be attributable to unnatural causes. He says that this "does not necessarily mean that all unexpected deaths need to come under active suspicion."

If there are excessive reports of apnea it is helpful to obtain waveform printouts of alarm events, both in the home and in the hospital. Certain patterns suggest smothering, such as excessive movement artefact or increased chest wall movement with hypoxia ensuing shortly thereafter. Referral to child protective services or the legal system may be necessary to prevent further harm.

It is important to observe closely any child with suspicious respiratory symptoms in a monitored or intensive care unit if there is suspicion that the mother may have abused the child. Watch mother's interaction with the child. Her behavior may seem very appropriate as she participates in the care of the child. It is frequent that health care professionals do not believe that a mother could be responsible for such abuse. Be wary if the mother is the only one close to the baby when the monitor alarms and symptoms ensue, or if mother is affectionate towards the baby only when she believes that she is observed. Avoid situations where the mother can harm the baby behind closed curtains, or contaminate lab samples.

Education is probably the most important preventive measure for the management of MBP. As this relates to respiratory disorders, health care professionals need to be aware of the potential for abuse especially with apnea and technologically dependent patients. Early recognition of abnormal behaviors may result in appropriate intervention. Medical professionals, child protective services and the legal profession need to be educated about the necessity of recognizing the at-risk infant or child and how to intervene appropriately.

References

1. Rosenberg DA. Web of deceit: a literature review of Munchausen syndrome by proxy. *Child Abuse Negl* 1987; 11:547–63.
2. Palfrey JS, Walker DK et al. Technology's children: report of a statewide census of children dependent on medical supports. *Pediatrics*. 1986; 87:611–18.

3. Sheridan MS. Things that go bump in the night: home monitoring for apnea. *Health Social Work.* 1985; 10:63–70.

4. Sullivan CA, Francis GL, Bain MW, et al. Munchausen syndrome by proxy: 1990: a portent for problems? *Clin Pediatr.* 1991; 30:112–16.

5. Mitchell I, Brummitt J, DeForest J, and Fisher G. Apnea and factitious illness (Munchausen's syndrome) by proxy. *Pediatrics.* 1993; 92:810–814.

6. Kapiolani Medical Center for Women and Children, Honolulu.

7. Light MJ and Sheridan MS. Munchausen syndrome by proxy and apnea (MBPA). *Clin Pediatr.* 1990; 29:162–8.

8. Kravitz RM and Wilmott RW. Munchausen syndrome by proxy presenting as factitious apnea. *Clin Pediatr.* 1990; 29:587–92.

9. Jenkins, RL. Maternal experience with apparent life-threatening events. *Adv Med Sociology.* 1991; 2:39–63.

10. Henslee JA. Personal communications and presentation to NAAP/SIDS Alliance Meeting, Pittsburgh, November, 1993.

11. Weese-Mayer DE, Silvestri JM. Documented monitoring: an alarming turn of events. *Clin Perinatol.* 1992; 19:891–906.

12. Steinschneider A and Santos V. Parental reports of apnea and bradycardia: temporal characteristics and accuracy. *Pediatrics.* 1991; 88:1100–05.

13. *NY Times.* March 25, 1994.

14. Steinschneider A. Prolonged apnea and the sudden infant death syndrome: clinical and laboratory observations. *Pediatrics.* 1972; 50–646.

15. Reece RM. Fatal child abuse and sudden infant death syndrome: a critical diagnostic decision. *Pediatrics.* 1993; 91:423–429.

16. Alexander R, Smith W, and Stevenson R. Serial Munchausen syndrome by proxy. *Pediatrics.* 1990; 86:581–5.

17. Alexander et al., Serial.

18. Goss PW and McDougall PN. Munchausen syndrome by proxy: a case of preterm delivery. *Med J Aust.* 1992; 157:814–817.

19. Libow JA and Schreier HA. Three forms of factitious illness in children: when is it Munchausen syndrome by proxy? *Am J Orthopsychiatr.* 1986; 56:602–11.

20. Samuels MP, Poets CF, et al. Diagnosis and management after life-threatening events in infants and young children who received cardiopulmonary resuscitation. *Br Med J.* 1993; 306:489–492.

21. Meadow R. Suffocation, recurrent apnea, and sudden infant death. *J Pediatrics.* 1990; 117:351–7.

22. Samuels MP, McClaughlin W, Jacobson RR, et al. Fourteen cases of imposed upper airway obstruction. *Arch Dis Child.* 1992; 67:162–70.

23. Rosen CL, Frost JD, Bricker T, et al. Two siblings with recurrent cardiorespiratory arrest: Munchausen syndrome by proxy or child abuse? *Pediatrics.* 1983; 71:715–20.

24. Epstein MA, Markowitz RL, Gallo DM, et al. Munchausen syndrome by proxy: considerations in diagnosis and confirmation by video surveillance. *Pediatrics.* 1987; 80:220–24.

25. Epstein et al, Considerations.

26. Meadow R. Video recording and child abuse. *Br Med J*. 1987; 294:1629–30.
27. Southall DP, Stebbens VA, Rees SV, et al. Apnoeic episodes induced by smothering: two cases identified by covert video surveillance. *Br Med J*. 1987; 294:1637–41.
28. Godding V and Kruth M. Compliance with treatment in asthma and Munchausen syndrome by proxy. *Arch Dis Child*. 1991; 66:956–60.
29. Werthammer J, Brown ER, Neff RK, et al. Sudden infant death syndrome in infants with bronchopulmonary dysplasia. *Pediatrics*. 1982; 69:301–4.
30. Orenstein DM and Wasserman AL. Munchausen syndrome by proxy simulating cystic fibrosis. *Pediatrics*. 1986; 78:621–4.
31. Single T, Henry LH. An unusual case of Munchausen syndrome by proxy. *Aust N Z J Psychiatr*. 1991; 25:422–5.
32. Kurlandsky L, Lukjoff JY, Zinkham WH, et al. Munchausen syndrome by proxy: definition of factitions bleeding in an infant by [51]CR labeling of erythrocytes. *Pediatrics*. 1979; 63:228–31.
33. Lee AL. Munchausen syndrome by proxy in twins. *Arch Dis Child*. 1979; 54:646–57.
34. Light and Sheridan, 1990.
35. Kahan BB, Yorker BC. Munchausen syndrome by proxy. *J School Health*. 1990; 60:108–110.
36. Emery JL. Child abuse, sudden infant death syndrome, and sudden unexpected infant death. *Am J Dis Child*. 1993; 147:1097–1100.

8

Gastrointestinal Manifestations
Emil Chuang and David A Piccoli

Gastrointestinal (GI) symptoms, together with respiratory complaints, are the most common reasons for referral to a pediatric practice. The GI problems are usually uncomplicated and therapy is straightforward, despite the high incidence of functional (rather than organic) etiologies. Sometimes the symptoms are complex and confounding. Despite extensive and often expensive investigations, there is still no explanation or diagnosis. It is usually at this time that the physician becomes alerted to the possibility of Munchausen by Proxy (MBP).

It is not uncommon for patients with MBP to present with GI complaints such as vomiting, diarrhea, weight loss, failure to thrive, hematemesis, and rectal bleeding. These presenting symptoms are generally indistinguishable from genuine organic disease. The clinician's pursuit of an etiology often results in prolonged hospitalization, expensive investigations, and invasive interventional procedures. Unnecessary morbidity to the child may be the end result. Moreover, advances in medical diagnostics and therapy have been challenged by an increased level of sophistication and cunning in the methods used by the perpetrator to feign illness in the child, thereby making the task of diagnosis even more difficult for the gastroenterologist. A careful history, physical examination, and in particular, constant vigilance are paramount for a correct diagnosis and positive outcome.

Factitious Vomiting

Vomiting is a cardinal symptom of underlying disease in children. It is nonlocalizing, and may be an indication of pathology in any of sev-

121

eral organ systems, particularly the GI tract and the central nervous system (CNS). The underlying process may be relatively benign, as in patients with gastroesophageal reflux, or life threatening as in raised intracranial pressure from brain tumor or CNS infection. Factitious vomiting is somewhat of a misnomer in most cases of MBP, since the vomiting episodes are usually real, while the underlying illness is fraudulent. Factitious vomiting can be caused by the ingestion of a number of noxious substances. These most commonly implicated are the forced ingestion of Ipecac[1-4] or table salt.[5,6]

Ipecac is a natural product derived from the dried root of *Cephaelis ipecacuanha* or *Cephalaelis acuminata* which contain the alkaloids emetine, cephaeline, and psychotrine. It is generally considered to be a safe over-the-counter emetic agent, and frequently kept in households for use in the first aid of accidental poisonings. Therefore, it is of little surprise that Ipecac has been connected with numerous cases of MBP. Recurrent or cyclic vomiting with diarrhea are the most common symptoms encountered in children poisoned with Ipecac. Short term use of Ipecac is associated with GI symptoms only. However, if MBP is not recognized early, the development of other symptoms and signs may cloud the clinical picture and further delay the diagnosis. Emetine has a long half-life and may persist in body organs for up to 60 days following usage.[7] The toxic effects are cumulative and may result in profound neurological and cardiovascular side effects. Weakness is another common side effect and it may be indistinguishable from other causes of myopathy and cardiomyopathy.[8-10] The diagnosis is sometimes difficult because commonly used methods of urine and serum drug screening may be negative even when Ipecac is suspected.[11] This is partly explained by the erratic absorption of the medication from the gut. Even the use of sensitive testing methods such as high-pressure liquid chromatography may result in undetectable blood and urine levels when the samples are taken within 2 hours of ingestion.[12]

Although unusual, it is possible for excessive salt ingestion to result in vomiting alone. More common presentations include drowsiness, seizure, coma, and hypernatremia, with or without vomiting.[13-15] The most perplexing aspect of forced salt ingestion is how mothers would be able to lure their children, most of whom are toddlers or young children, to ingest the enormous quantity of salt necessary to produce the symptoms. In at least one case report, it is believed that the mother, who was a trained nurse, dispensed table salt directly into the stomach by the use of a gastric tube.[16] The diagnosis in this setting is straightforward, providing that MBP is considered. The finding of high serum sodium and osmolality with increased urinary excretion of sodium will quickly lead the clinician to the conclusion of an increased salt intake rather than any intrinsic endocrine or renal disease.

Arsenic is a heavy metal commonly found in many insecticides, herbicides, fungicides, and wood preservatives. It is also one of the more popular poisons chosen by novelists in fictional murder mysteries. In smaller, sublethal doses, symptoms of acute toxicity are manifested in the gastrointestinal tract mainly as vomiting, diarrhea, and abdominal pain.[17] However, repeated poisoning or larger doses may result in death. Alexander reported a case of MBP where two siblings and five puppies died in a short period of time as a result of arsenic poisoning. A 9-year-old was admitted for intractable vomiting, abdominal pain, and dehydration. He died on the day of admission. His 8-year-old brother was admitted soon after with similar complaints; he also died a week after the initial presentation. It was then that heavy metal poisoning was considered and confirmed.[18] Another case presented with cyclic vomiting, anemia and intermittent diarrhea over a period of 3 months, with multiple hospital admissions before the diagnosis was finally made.[19] Diagnosis is made by measuring an elevated arsenic level in urine, serum, hair, or other tissue samples in suspected patients. If a correct early diagnosis is made, appropriate chelation therapy with dimercaprol (BAL) or penicillamine may be implemented and these patients will usually improve over time.

Probably one of the more curious cases was a previously well child who presented with feculent vomiting, reported by Meadow. It was subsequently found that the mother kept a container of soft feces in her cubicle and mixed it into her child's vomitus thus simulating an extremely rare case of gastrocolic fistula.[20]

Perhaps the most common form of MBP related to vomiting does not involve vomiting at all: the history is factitious. For example, in the report by White and co-workers of surreptitious warfarin ingestion, an 11-month-old infant presented with failure to thrive and a history of intermittent vomiting although no vomiting was ever observed during any of the child's four hospitalizations.[21] In addition, vomiting may be induced by stimulation of the posterior pharynx. This is also a not uncommon manifestation of MBP which we have seen at the Children's Hospital of Philadelphia as part of a picture of recurrent oropharyngeal ulceration (see Chapter 17).

Gastrointestinal Bleeding

Bleeding may occur from anywhere within the GI tract. Sites of bleeding away from the mouth or anal opening, and especially in the lower GI tract, can be difficult to localize. Gastrointestinal bleeding must be distinguished from bleeding elsewhere, such as swallowed blood originating from the nasal passage following a nose bleed which is then subsequently vomited. It must also be distinguished from bleeding that originates in the respiratory tract (as discussed in the previous chapter). A comprehensive discussion on the etiologies and the diagnostic approach to a child with GI bleeding can be found elsewhere.[22] Furthermore, many substances including food and food colorings, as well as some medications, may mimic blood and therefore have been diagnosed erroneously as GI bleeding.

Hematemesis is the vomiting of blood. It may be fresh bright red blood, or acid denatured in the form of "coffee grounds." Many reported cases of MBP have presented as hematemesis.[23] Methods employed to fabricate the symptoms are numerous. In most instances, no direct injury is inflicted by the perpetrator onto the child. The most common source of blood is the mother, who pricks herself or reopens existing wounds. Occasionally blood is obtained from the child by the disconnection of the intravenous canula.

In recent years, two unusual cases of MBP presenting with hematemesis were diagnosed at our hospital. Unlike previous case reports, direct injury was inflicted by the parent to produce the symptoms. The first child had a long history of feeding difficulties and vomiting. He had been seen by numerous doctors and extensively investigated. This eventually led to a fundoplication and gastrostomy tube placement. Following the surgery, he was readmitted with recurrent hematemesis and abdominal pain. Nonspecific gastritis was documented by endoscopy, but was resistant to standard ulcer therapy. Later, it was suspected that the mother was adding hydrogen peroxide into the stomach via the gastrostomy tube, thus causing an erosive gastritis. How this was achieved was never documented clearly. The mother was never confronted because of the lack of direct evidence, but once she was made aware of our suspicions, her son's symptoms resolved.

In another case, the father was the perpetrator, a phenomenon reported only rarely.[24] He induced his child to vomit by scraping the oropharynx with a blunt instrument. This caused the child to gag and induced a bloody vomitus at the same time. The hospital chart was carefully reviewed by the nursing staff. They documented the timing of each bleeding episode in relation to the presence or absence of the father. It was found that every bleeding episode occurred only in his presence.

Rectal bleeding can originate from the upper or lower GI tract. Bright blood is suggestive of lower GI bleeding or massive proximal bleeding, whereas darkened blood (melena) is more indicative of gastric or esophageal bleeding. Cases of MBP may present with rectal bleeding alone or in combination with other GI symptoms.[25,26] The blood may be mixed directly into the stool by the perpetrator, or it may have been swallowed and passed with otherwise normal stool.

Phenolphthalein is a laxative used commonly by the elderly. It is colorless in an acidic environment, but changes to a pink color on alkalinization. Sometimes it can be confused with blood, as in several reported cases of MBP with "bloody" diarrhea.[27,28] A case reported by Malatack[29] highlights the morbidity that can occur as a result of delayed or incorrect diagnosis. A central line was initially inserted into the child due to weight loss and intractable diarrhea, which in retrospect was probably induced by the mother. From this, she repeatedly drew blood and mixed it with stool in the diaper, therefore mimicking recurrent massive GI bleeding. During a 13-week admission the patient had multiple investigations performed, received 10 liters of packed red cells and several surgical procedures, including a hemicolectomy. This case clearly demonstrates how easily doctors can be unwitting participants in the perpetration and escalation of the damage.

Gastrointestinal bleeding is rarely benign and, as a rule, warrants further investigation. When MBP is suspected, the challenge is to prove the fabrication. It may require nothing more than identification of a blood type that is different from the patient's. Sometimes a careful documentation of the events in the hospital setting may lead to the correct diagnosis. More sophisticated and creative forensic testing is occasionally required. With the help of radioactive labeled red blood cells, Kurlandsky was able to demonstrate blood that was "vomited up" was not from the child.[30] In the presence of identical blood groups, human lymphocyte antigen (HLA) testing currently offers the most accurate means of identification of a source of blood, and has been used successfully to help confirm a case of MBP.[31]

Chronic Diarrhea

MBP presenting as chronic diarrhea is not uncommon. When it occurs, failure to thrive is a frequent accompaniment.[32,33] The laxatives implicated are generally those that are available over the counter, and frequently kept in the household. Phenolphthalein and other anthracene derivatives are the most common agents involved, but Epsom salts have also been described. Phenolphthalein, as discussed earlier, may be mistaken for bloody diarrhea. Chronic diarrhea may cause weight loss as well as profound electrolyte disturbance resulting in weakness, cardiac dysrrhythmias, and even death. Moreover, chronic laxative ingestion is associated with a mild colitis.[34] The symptoms and biopsy may be misinterpreted as inflammatory bowel disease, and inappropriate therapy may be started.

The differentiation between an osmotic and secretory diarrhea is fundamental to any gastroenterological workup for diarrhea. Fasting is the quickest and most reliable method to distinguish between them. The presence of an osmotic diarrhea that persists during fasting is indicative of laxative abuse. Analysis of diarrheal fluid will confirm the diagnosis. This may involve the measurement of the osmolality, anion and osmotic gap, electrolytes, or pH of the stool sample. Further specific testing such as the measurement of magnesium and sulfate levels will confirm Epsom salts abuse. A color change on alkalinization or acidification is diagnostic of the presence of phenolphthalein. Chemical analysis of stool samples will generally characterize other abused substances.

We were previously involved with a young child who was admitted for failure to thrive and chronic diarrhea. Following an extensive work-up which was negative, a colonoscopy was performed and revealed melanosis coli, a typical finding of chronic laxative abuse in the elderly. With this information, the nurses observed the mother and child closely in the hospital. The mother was quickly caught administering laxative to the child. Previously, the mother was considered to be a model parent and was always helpful and encouraging to the ward staff. She had also developed a friendship with several members of the nursing staff and commonly joined them for afternoon tea.

References

1. Jones JG, Butler HL, Hamilton B, Perdue JD, Stern HP, and Woody RC. Munchausen syndrome by proxy. *Child Abuse Negl.* 1986; 10:33–40.
2. Berkner P, Kastner T, and Skolnick L. Chronic ipecac poisoning in infancy: a case report. *Pediatrics.* 1988; 82:384–6.
3. McClung HJ, Murray R, Braden NJ, Fyda J, Myers RP, and Gutches L. Intentional ipecac poisoning in children. *Am J Dis Child.* 1988; 142:637–9.
4. Feldman KW, Christopher DM, and Opheim KB. Munchausen syndrome/bulimia by proxy: ipecac as a toxin in child abuse. *Child Abuse Negl.* 1989; 13:257–61.
5. Pickel S, Anderson C, and Holliday MA. Thirsting and hypernatremic dehydration: a form of child abuse. *Pediatrics.* 1970; 45:54–5.
6. Meadow R. Munchausen's syndrome by proxy: the hinterland of child abuse. *Lancet.* 1977; 2:343–5
7. Gimble AI, Davison C, and Smith PK. Studies on the toxicity, distribution and excretion of emetine. *J Pharmacol Exp Ther.* 1948; 94:431–8.
8. Czajka PA and Russell SL. Non-emetic effects of ipecac syrup. *Pediatrics.* 1985; 75:1101–4.
9. Mateer J, Farrell B, Chou SM, and Guttmann J. Reversible ipecac myopathy. *Neurology.* 1979; 29:596. (abs)
10. Manno BR. Toxicology of ipecac: a review. *Clin Toxicol.* 1977; 10:221–42.
11. McClung, Feldman.
12. Moran DM, Crouch DJ, and Finkle BS. Absorption of ipecac alkaloids in emergency patients. *Ann of Emergen Med.* 1984; 13:1100–2.
13. Pickel, Meadow.
14. Rogers D, Tripp J, Bentovim A, et al. Non-accidental Poisoning: An extended syndrome of child abuse. *Br Med J.* 1976; 1:793–6.
15. Feldman K and Robertson WO. Salt Poisoning: Presenting Symptom of Child Abuse. *Vet Hum Toxicol.* 1979; 21:341–3.
16. Meadow.
17. Fowler BA and Weissberg JB. Arsine poisoning. *N Engl J Med.* 1974; 291:1171–4.
18. Alexander R, Smith W, and Stevenson R. Serial Munchausen syndrome by proxy. *Pediatrics.* 1990; 86:581–5.

19. Embry CK. Toxic cyclic vomiting in an 11-year-old girl. *J Amer Acad Child Adol Psychiat.* 1987; 26:447–8.
20. Meadow R. Munchausen syndrome by proxy. *Arch Dis Child.* 1982; 57:92–8.
21. White ST, Voter K, and Perry J. Sureptitious warfarin ingestion. *Child Abuse Negl.* 1985; 9:349–52.
22. Berry R and Perrault J. Gastrointestinal bleeding. In: Walker WA, et al, ed. *Pediatric Gastrointestinal Diseases.* : B.C. Decker. 1991; 111–31.
23. Mills RW and Burke S. Gastrointestinal bleeding in a 15 month old male. A presentation of munchausen's syndrome by proxy. *Clin Pediatr.* 1990; 29:474–7.
24. Makar AF and Squier PJ. Munchausen syndrome by proxy: father as a perpetrator. *Pediatrics.* 1990; 85:370–3.
25. Meadow 1982.
26. Malatack JJ, Wiener ES, Gartner JC Jr, Zitelli BJ, and Brunetti E. Munchausen syndrome by proxy: a new complication of central venous catheterization. *Pediatrics.* 1985; 75:523–5.
27. Fleisher D and Ament ME. Diarrhea, red diapers, and child abuse. *Clin Pediatr.* 1977; 17:820–4.
28. Ackerman NB, Jr, and Strobel CT. Polle syndrome: chronic diarrhea in munchausen's child. *Gastroent.* 1981; 81:1140–2.
29. Malatack, 1985.
30. Kurlandsky L, Lukoff JY, Ziakham WH, Brody JP, and Kessler RW. Munchausen syndrome by proxy: definition of factitious bleeding in an infant by ^{51}Cr labeling of erythrocytes. *Pediatrics.* 1979; 63:228–231.
31. Maltacak, 1985.
32. Ackerman 1981, Fleisher, 1977.
33. Fenton AC, Wailoo MP, and Tanner MS. Severe failure to thrive and diarrhea caused by laxative abuse. *Arch Dis Child.* 1988; 63:978–9.
34. Read NW, Krejs GJ, Read MG, and Santa Ana CA, Morawski SG, and Fordtran JS. Chronic diarrhea of unknown origin. *Gastroent.* 1980; 78:264–71.

9

Hematologic Manifestations

Cindy Christian

Hematologic manifestations are among the most common presentations of Munchausen Syndrome by Proxy (MBP). Factitious bleeding, the production of false signs and symptoms of bleeding, is well described in the medical literature. Descriptions of factitious bleeding predate Asher's original report of Munchausen Syndrome in 1951.[1] In 1944, Salinger described a woman who presented with severe, recurring nasal hemorrhages that failed to resolve despite multiple interventions.[2] As Salinger wrote, ". . . we are convinced that the bleeding is the result of self trauma, but are unable to obtain a confession from the patient."[3] Since that time, numerous reports of factitious bleeding,[4] self-induced lead poisoning,[5] factitious aplastic anemia,[6] and other hematologic manifestations of Munchausen Syndrome (MS) have appeared in the adult medical literature. Occasionally the perpetrator of factitious bleeding is a child. Abrol and co-workers[7] report a 10 year old who simulated hematuria by pricking his finger and dipping it into his urine samples. On occasion, a parent and child work together to fabricate bleeding. Sneed and Bell[8] describe a 10 year old who presented with factitious renal stones and associated hematuria, presumably in an attempt to avoid legal action by the school because of poor attendance. Although the patient's mother never acknowledged participating with her son in creating his illness, the authors felt there was some collusion on her part.

Children with MBP can present with hematological signs and symptoms reflected by abnormalities on physical examination, in the complete blood count (CBC), or in clotting studies that suggest that a child has an inherited or acquired clotting disorder. The child may have bled to the point of anemia or, rarely, to the point that the vital signs are unstable. The first patient described in Meadow's landmark work on MBP[9] presented with hematuria. In his later review of 19 victimized children, bleeding was the presenting symptom in 12.[10] In Rosenberg's thorough review of the MBP literature, bleeding represented the most common presentation of illness, occurring in 44% of cases.[11] The site of bleeding most commonly involves the gastrointestinal or genitourinary systems (presenting as hematuria, hematochezia, melena, and/or hematemesis) but can include bleeding from any area of the body. Hemoptysis and epistaxis are well described, as is bleeding from the ears, palate, skin, and genitals. Bleeding may be the sole presentation of MBP, or may be seen in association with other fabricated signs and symptoms. Meadow[12] describes 32 children with factitious seizures, 50% of whom had other factitious illnesses, including 19% with bleeding. Children sometimes present with features of multisystem disease. Apnea, chronic diarrhea and vomiting, infections, neurologic abnormalities (ataxia, lethargy, seizures), rashes, dehydration, and vaginal discharge are some of the reported complaints described in association with factitious bleeding. As is the case with other forms of child abuse, one or more children in any given family may be victimized by the parent. Lee[13] describes 4-month-old twins who presented on consecutive days with gastrointestinal bleeding, discovered to be factitious. Hvizdala and Gellady[14] describe siblings who were intentionally poisoned with various prescription drugs, both of whom presented with bleeding at some time during their illness. The second child, whose course was dominated by a hemorrhagic diathesis, was ultimately diagnosed with warfarin poisoning.

The presenting histories, sites of bleeding, and methods used to produce factitious bleeding are quite variable. Yet as with all cases of MBP, the evaluation of children with hematologic manifestations of this disorder often results in unnecessary pain, testing, hospitalizations, and expenditure of resources before the correct diagnosis is made. Reviewing the methods used to produce and diagnose false hematologic disease will improve our ability to recognize this disorder, preventing unnecessary suffering.

Factitious Bleeding

There are generally two methods by which parents cause factitious bleeding in their children. In simulated or apparent bleeding, a parent deceitfully produces blood (or blood like products), but does not cause direct harm to the child. Alternatively, a parent may actually cause a child to bleed, referred to as produced or actual bleeding. Unlike adult cases of MS, in which the majority of factitious bleeding is genuine induced bleeding, cases of MBP far more often involve simulated blood. There are cases, however, in which both simulated and actual bleeding occur. In Lee's report, the mother used her own blood to simulate bleeding in the first infant, but stuck the second twin with a diaper pin to produce actual bleeding.

SIMULATED BLEEDING

The most common method used by parents to fabricate bleeding in a child is by inserting their own blood into a specimen that appears to have come from the child. The deception begins with a false history of bleeding which is quickly supported by the appearance of blood. Hematuria is often fabricated by adding blood to a specimen of urine when the sample is collected without supervision.[15] Gastrointestinal (GI) blood, presenting as hematemesis, hematochezia, or melena, is simulated by inserting blood in the mouth of the patient or by placing blood on the diaper or on the perioral/perineal skin of the child.[16] Bleeding from the respiratory tract is most commonly fabricated by smearing blood on the child's face and relating a history of apnea, cyanosis, or cough.[17] Simulated blood has also been discovered coming from an infant's ears.[18] Occasionally parents produce multisystem illness using their own blood, as in Waller's report of a 2 year old who presented with hemoptysis, hematuria, and hematochezia, among other symptoms.[19] Although simulated blood is almost always parental in origin, discarded blood from laboratory samples has been described as being the source of factitious blood in one case.[20]

A less common method of simulating bleeding in a child is by producing specimens that appear to contain blood, but do not. Fleisher and Ament[21] report three unrelated cases of chronic laxative poisoning. The laxatives all contained phenolphthalein, which can produce a red-pink color in urine or stool. The children presented with various combinations of chronic diarrhea, vomiting, neurologic abnormalities, and failure to thrive. The parents all reported blood in the urine or stool at some time during the evaluation. In all cases, the clue to the correct diagnosis of poisoning and MBP was the intermittent appearance of a red color to the urine or stool. Tests for blood were negative and toxicologic studies were positive for phenolphthalein. Paint and cocoa have also been used to simulate blood.[22]

ACTUAL BLEEDING

Although simulated bleeding is more common in MBP, there are various methods by which parents actually cause their children to bleed. The most common of these is pricking the child with a needle, pin or other foreign object. Infants as young as 8 weeks old have been victims of this type of abuse. In Clark's remarkable case report, the mother repeatedly pricked her infant daughter's skin causing severe anemia. The working diagnosis of "Autoerythrocyte Sensitization Syndrome" (the existence of which is questioned by some authors) was corrected to MBP only after extensive and elaborate testing.[23]

Gastrointestinal, aural and palatal bleeding have also been produced by pricking children with foreign objects. Zohar and coworkers[24] report a 5 year old with recurrent, resistant otitis externa. The presence of excoriations in the external canal led to the diagnosis of inflicted injury. The mother was confronted with the suspicion of MBP, after which the child had no further episodes of otitis externa. At The Children's Hospital of Philadelphia, we have seen two cases MBP in which the initial presentation was palatal bleeding (see Chapter 16).

A less common method of producing actual bleeding in a child is by phlebotomy. Intravenous lines have been disconnected from children by their parents to simulate gastrointestinal bleeding.[25] Malatack and co-workers[26] reported a 2-year-old child who was evaluated for fever, joint pain, and diarrhea. The child was thought to have juvenile rheumatoid arthritis. Because of chronic, severe diarrhea, a Broviac catheter was placed for hyperalimentation. Shortly after the placement of the catheter, the child developed hematochezia. An extensive workup failed to identify the source of bleeding and the child ultimately was treated by multiple transfusions, hemicolectomy, and ileostomy. The child continued to bleed into the ileostomy bag and developed upper GI bleeding as well. After the child was transferred to the intensive care unit, where he was observed continuously, all bleeding ceased. When transferred back to the general pediatric floor, he again began to bleed, leading to the suspicion that the mother might be responsible for the bleeding. Continuous nursing observation resulted in the correct diagnosis; a nurse entered a bathroom which the mother and child had occupied for an extended period of time and found blood on the walls, sink, and wastebasket. Although the mother claimed that the blood was there prior to their arrival, red cell antigen and HLA typing showed the blood had come from the child. The mother had been repeatedly withdrawing blood from the Broviac line to feign gastrointestinal bleeding.

Finally, patient bleeding can be caused by ingestion of certain drugs. Anticoagulant ingestion has been used by many adults with MS to produce bleeding,[27] and has also been reported in the MBP literature. Hvizdala and co-workers[28] described two siblings who were intentionally poisoned with prescription drugs by their mother. Multisystemic symptoms predominated in the initial child's course, including ataxia, rashes, fever, and arthralgia. Repeated toxicologic testing revealed drug ingestions. While this 4-year-old child was being evaluated for unexplained hematuria, his 7-year-old sister presented with an acute hemorrhagic diathesis, manifested by multiple petechiae, ecchymoses, and bleeding from venipuncture sites. Although she had been evaluated for multiple medical complaints in the past, including petechiae, no cause for her illnesses had been found. Coagulation screening revealed a prolonged prothrombin (PT) and partial thromboplastin time (PTT) with a normal CBC and platelet count. Correction of the PT and PTT was achieved with fresh frozen plasma and Vitamin K. Toxicologic testing of the child's admission serum confirmed the presence of warfarin. White and co-workers[29] reported an 11 month old who presented with acute hemorrhagic otitis media and purpuric nodules due to Warfarin poisoning.

Chronic Ipecac ingestion, although not commonly associated with bleeding, has been reported to cause a hemorrhagic enteropathy. Johnson and co-workers[30] describe a 2 year old who underwent extensive evaluation for chronic diarrhea and vomiting.

During the fifth hospital admission, the child developed persistent, grossly bloody stools. Biopsies obtained during colonoscopy were consistent with the diagnosis of pseudomelanosis coli, typically associated with cathartic use. Urine specimens revealed emetine, an active component in Ipecac.

Many drugs can cause bleeding, either by inducing thrombocytopenia (e.g., chloramphenicol, chemotherapeutic drugs, thiazide diuretics), interfering with the normal coagulation cascade (heparin, warfarin) or by causing platelet dysfunction (aspirin, indomethacin, valproate). There are only a few published reports of drug-induced bleeding associated with MBP. The most commonly available drugs associated with bleeding are those that inhibit platelet function. Although drug-induced platelet dysfunction can lead to bleeding, in most cases drug ingestion does not cause spontaneous hemorrhage in otherwise healthy individuals.[31] Furthermore, many of the drugs that can induce spontaneous bleeding in healthy individuals (such as the anticoagulants) are not generally available to the public. For these reasons, the use of medications to produce artificial bleeding has been limited. Unfortunately, parents continue to devise methods of feigning illnesses in their children. New schemes for producing factitious bleeding will certainly be identified in the future.

Methods of Diagnosis

A history of unexpected bleeding in an infant or young child must be taken seriously by health care professionals and the appearance of gross blood often prompts thorough searches for its cause. Given the nature of the complaint, the dynamics of the doctor-patient relationship, and the parental psychopathology associated with MBP, a delay in diagnosing factitious bleeding is predictable. The diagnosis becomes even more difficult to make in cases in which children have genuine underlying illness. Salmon and co-workers[32] describe a 2-year old whose mother contributed her own blood to the child's urine samples, simulating hematuria over a 3-year period. The child's extensive workup revealed a number of underlying renal abnormalities—urinary tract infection, vesicoureteral reflux with a duplication of the left collecting system, and hypercalcuria—that could potentially cause hematuria, further delaying the identification of the correct diagnosis of MBP. In fact, a genuine initial illness may produce signs that are later mimicked by the fabrication associated with MBP.

CLINICAL INFORMATION AND HISTORY

The evaluation of an infant or child who develops a possible bleeding disorder begins with a careful history. A history of bleeding during the neonatal period (after circumcision, from the umbilical stump), the development of deep hematomas after immunizations, easy bruising with minor trauma, prolonged bleeding with lacerations, and/or a history of epistaxis may indicate a true bleeding diathesis. A family history of bleeding disorders or a history of exposure to drugs that can interfere with normal bleeding may further reveal the etiology of the problem. It is important to obtain complete past medical information about both the child and parent, especially if the history of bleeding seems unusual or excessive. Some parents will not only fabricate details of the present illness, but of past illness and family history. Because most victims of factitious bleeding are quite young, obtaining a history directly from the patient is typically impossible. It is important, however, to do so if the patient is capable. On more than one occasion a child has confirmed the diagnosis of MBP after being interviewed.[33] In one case, mother's threat of corporal punishment kept the child from disclosing the source of her hematuria.[34]

The physical examination of a child with a history of abnormal bleeding should be thorough, with an emphasis on the vital signs (especially if the patient presents with acute, active bleeding) and abnormalities that may indicate an underlying disease. The liver, spleen, and lymph node examination should be carefully done. One should carefully look for icterus and the presence of rashes (e.g., purpura, petechiae). The sites and approximate ages of bruises should be recorded. The presence of bruises in various stages of healing may be a result either of child abuse (including MBP) or organic disease, but close examination may reveal a pattern to the bleeding episodes. Finally, the orifice from which the bleeding has occurred should be evaluated carefully. The identification of oral, genital, or skin trauma may be the first clue to the correct diagnosis of inflicted bleeding.

Rapid, dramatic changes in the characteristics of specimens are one clue to fabricated bleeding. For example, in cases of factitious hematuria, grossly bloody urine may clear then recur within minutes or hours. Significant, active bleeding, the source of which cannot be found, may be another clue to factitious bleeding. In one case report, a child had such significant gastrointestinal bleeding that daily transfusions were required for 2 weeks.[35] Despite the rapidity of the bleeding, an extensive evaluation including surgical intervention failed to reveal any source of blood. Acute, seemingly severe bleeding without corresponding signs or symptoms in the patient may also indicate fabricated bleeding. In one reported case, a child with hematuria suddenly dropped her hemoglobin by half, without any changes in her vital signs.[36] This resulted in the suspicion and ultimate diagnosis of MBP, and the confession by the mother that she both used her own blood to feign hematuria and diluted the child's blood sample to simulate anemia.

Bleeding that occurs only after the patient is left alone with the parent is also well described in the MBP literature. A transfer to the intensive care unit or the initiation of constant supervision results in sudden improvement. Likewise, abnormal specimens may appear only when the parent is involved with some aspect of the collection process. When any of these clues are present and the suspicion of MBP is raised, there needs to be structured supervision of the family and meticulous documentation of observations, including careful recording of the time, persons involved, handling of specimens and results of specimen collections.

LABORATORY DIAGNOSIS

Standard screening tests should include a platelet count, PT, PTT, and bleeding time. Normal platelet count and bleeding time indicate normal platelet number and function respectively. The PT and PTT are sensitive indicators of deficiencies in the coagulation factors. If all of these tests are normal, the presence of a bleeding disorder is unlikely. (Von Willebrand's disease can be an exception, because in mild cases, the PTT and bleeding time can be normal.) If a laboratory result is abnormal or unexplained, the test should be repeated using a fresh sample of blood to eliminate errors in collection, processing, or storage. The collection and interpretation of these tests in the neonate is more complicated. Venous access is often limited, blood drawn through indwelling umbilical lines can be contaminated with small amounts of heparin, and high hematocrit values can lead to falsely abnormal PT and PTT values. In addition, there is a wide range of normal values for the PT and PTT in the neonate, especially if premature.[37] The use of reputable laboratories and careful interpretation of results will limit the need for further, unnecessary testing.

When the diagnosis of MBP is considered, the initial step in the laboratory evaluation is to ask whether or not the specimen in question actually contains blood. The ingestion of red foods (beets) or beverages (red fruit drinks), medications (phenolphthalein), rare diseases (some forms of porphyria, ochronosis), and the presence of urinary urates or overgrowth of Serratia in the stool may all give the false appearance of blood. Red stools have also been reported in a child who sucked on a checker that was stained red with eosin.[38] As a general rule, these substances will not test positive for occult blood. A number of substances will give false positive results to urine dipstick tests for blood. Iodine solutions, either in the urine or from the patient's skin, bleach that may be present in the collection vessel, and microbial peroxidase in association with urinary tract infections may all produce false positive urinary screens. False positive stool guaiac tests may result from diets that are high in red meats or peroxidase-rich vegetables such as horseradish, turnips, artichokes, or broccoli. In addition, the stool of normal individuals may sometimes contain occult blood. A Wright stained smear of stool mucus can differentiate true blood from false, since actual blood will be identified by abundant red blood cells.[39]

Assuming the specimen in question contains blood, the next question is whether the blood is coming from the child. In some reports, major blood group typing established the correct diagnosis of MBP.[40] Some parents and children will share major blood group types. Minor blood group typing has been particularly valuable in these cases and is being used with more frequency. Urinary blood, fresh and old blood samples, and dried blood can all be tested using a variety of techniques. Local blood banks are often capable of performing such tests. Other reports have relied on erythrocyte acid phosphatase determination of urinary red blood cells[41] and the use of radioactive chromium-labeled red cells[42] to differentiate the patient's blood from the parent's. Forensic laboratories are a good resource for more complicated situations. Chain of evidence procedures and careful documentation are important when multiple specimens are tested.

A more difficult situation arises if MBP is suspected but the source of the bleeding proves to be the child. In these cases, ingestion, phlebotomy, or trauma to the child's body may be the cause. Toxicologic evaluation can be used to diagnose poisoning. Careful monitoring of intravenous sites or central venous lines may reveal tampering. Repeated examinations for evidence of trauma may be necessary.

Other Hematologic Manifestations of MBP

Johnson and co-workers[43] describe a 25-year-old man who developed lead poisoning because of a faulty exhaust system in the oxidation/reduction furnaces at his work place. He underwent successful chelation, only to develop chronic, recurring lead toxicity. Eventually a hidden bottle of lead acetate was found in his possession and the diagnosis of MS was made. The correct diagnosis was delayed in this case because the patient's initial illness was not fabricated. While there are no reports of factitious lead poisoning in the MBP literature, iron deficiency anemia has been deliberately induced by a parent.[44] An otherwise healthy and thriving 14-month-old child who was known to have iron deficiency anemia since 6 months of age required hospitalization because of the severity of her anemia (hemoglobin 5.7 gm/dl). The child had supposedly been given iron replacement throughout the 8 previous months and the mother reported feeding the child iron-fortified foods and formula. She was able to correctly describe the preparation of the formula and the dose of iron the child was taking. Hospital evaluation revealed severe iron deficiency anemia with no source of blood loss and the child was started on ferrous sulfate. The patient's reticulocyte count and hematocrit improved and she had no further episodes of anemia. In this unusual case, dietary and medicinal iron was covertly withheld from the child, yet her caloric intake was adequate to ensuring proper growth and development.

Other reports of MBP have described anemia as a part of the presentation. More commonly, victims of MBP develop iatrogenic anemia. An infant who was the victim of salt poisoning required 2 blood transfusions, likely due to the 83 venopunctures she underwent during her evaluation.[45]

Finally, abnormalities of hematologic values may play a secondary role in the presentation of MBP. Children who develop sepsis as a result of "bacteriologic battering" may develop disseminated intravascular coagulation. An increase in the white blood cell (WBC) count has been reported in an infant who presented with seizures and cyanosis.[46] The elevation in the WBC was attributed to severe anoxic stress.

Conclusions

The long-term morbidity of MBP is not known. It is clear that the diagnosis is often made only after enormous energy, resources, and money have been used and there has been significant suffering on the part of the victim. Avoiding transfusions by recognizing victims of MBP before they are severely anemic has now become more important because of possible compromises and limits to the community blood supply. We will need to remain alert to the possibility of factitious hematologic illness in our patients as parents devise new methods of fabricating disease.

References

1. Asher R. Munchausen's syndrome. *Lancet*. 1959; 1:339–341.
2. Salinger S. A case of malignant recurring nasal hemorrhage of undetermined etiology. *Ann Oto Rhinol Laryngol*. 1941; 53:583–588.
3. Salinger, p. 586.
4. Tucker LE, Hayes JR, Viteri AL, et al. Factitial bleeding: successful management with psychotherapy. *Dig Dis Sci*. 1979; 24:570–572 and Abram HS and Hollender MH. Factitious blood disease. *South Med J*. 1974; 67:691–695.
5. Johnson G, Mullan B, and Rich G. A case of factitious disorder presenting as plumbism. *Med J Australia*. 1987; 146:264–266.
6. Ford CV, Stein R, Kelly MP, and Adelson LM. Factitial aplastic anemia. *J Nerv Mental Dis*. 1984; 172:369–372.
7. Abrol RP, Heck A, Gleckel L, and Rosner F. Self-induced hematuria. *J Natl Med Assoc*. 1990; 82:127–128.
8. Sneed RC and Bell RF. The dauphin of munchausen: factitious passage of renal stones in a child. *Pediatrics*. 1976; 58:127–129.
9. Meadow R. Munchausen syndrome by proxy: the hinterland of child abuse. *Lancet*. 1977; 2:343–345.
10. Meadow R. Munchausen syndrome by proxy. *Arch Dis Child*. 1982; 57:92–98.
11. Rosenberg DA. Web of deceit: a literature review of munchausen syndrome by proxy. *Child Abuse Negl*. 1987; 11:547–563.

12. Meadow R. Fictitious epilepsy. *Lancet*. 1984; 1:25–28.
13. Lee AL. Munchausen syndrome by proxy in twins. *Arch Dis Child*. 1979; 54:646–647.
14. Hvizdala EV, Gellady AM. Intentional poisoning of two siblings by prescription drugs. *Clin Pediatr*. 1978; 17:480–482.
15. Clayton PT, Counahan R, Chantler C. Munchausen syndrome by proxy. *Lancet*. 1978; 1:102 [letter] and Outwater KM, Lipnick RN, and Luban NLC. Factitious hematuria: diagnosis by minor blood group typing. *J Pediatr*. 1981: 98:95–97.
16. Mills RW and Burke S. Gastrointestinal bleeding in a 15 month old male: a presentation of munchausen syndrome by proxy. *Clin Pediatr*. 1990; 29:474–477, Amegavie L, Marzouk O, Mullen J et al. Munchausen syndrome by proxy: a warning for health professionals. *Br Med J*. 1986; 293:855–856, and Lee, MBP in twins.
17. Kurlandsky L, Lukjoff JY, Zindham WH, et al. Munchausen syndrome by proxy: definition of factitious bleeding in an infant by CR 51 labeling of erythrocytes. *Pediatrics*. 1979; 63:228–231.
18. Bourchier D. Bleeding ears: case report of munchausen syndrome by proxy. *Austr Paediatr J*. 1983; 19:256–257.
19. Waller DA. Obstacles to the treatment of munchausen by proxy syndrome. *J Amer Acad Child Psychiatr*. 1983; 22:80–85.
20. Yomtovian R and Swanger R. Munchausen syndrome by proxy documented by discrepant blood typing. *Am J Clin Pathol*. 1991; 95:232–233.
21. Fleisher D and Ament ME. Diarrhea, red diapers, and child abuse. *Clin Pediatr*. 1977; 17:820–824.
22. Meadow, 1982.
23. Clark GD, Key JD, Rutherford P, et al. Munchausen syndrome by proxy (child abuse) presenting as apparent autoerythrocyte sensitization syndrome: an unusual presentation of Polle syndrome. *Pediatrics* 1984; 74: 1100–1102.
24. Zohar Y, Avidan G, Shivelli Y, et al. Otolaryngologic cases of munchausen's syndrome. *Laryngoscope*. 1987; 97:201–203.
25. Mills and Burke, Gastrointestinal bleeding.
26. Malatack HH, Wiener ES, Gartner JC, et al. Munchausen syndrome by proxy: a new complication of central venous catheterization. *Pediatrics*. 1985; 75:523–525.
27. Angle DP, Ratnoff OD, Spring GK. The anticoagulant malingerer. *Ann Int Med*. 1970; 73:67–72 and O'Reilly R, Aggeler PM. Overt anticoagulant ingestion: study of 25 patients and review of world literature. *Medicine*. 1976; 55:389–399.
28. Hvizdala and Gellady, Intentional poisoning.
29. White ST, Voter K, and Perry J. Surreptitious warfarin ingestion. *Child Abuse Negl*. 1985; 9:349–352.
30. Johnson J, Carpenter B, Benton J, et al. Hemorrhagic colitis and pseudomelanosis coli in ipecac ingestion by proxy. *J Pediatr Gastro Nutr*. 1991; 12:501–506.

31. Beardsley DS. Platelet abnormalities in infancy and childhood. In: Nathan DG, Oski FA (eds). *Hematology of Infancy and Childhood, 3rd ed.* 1987; Philadelphia: Saunders:1591.
32. Salmon RF, Arant BS, Baum MG, et al. Factitious hematuria with underlying renal abnormalities. *Pediatrics.* 1988; 82:377–379.
33. Waller, Obstacles and Salmon et al., Factitious hematuria.
34. Salmon et al., Factitious hematuria.
35. Malatack HH, Wiener ES, Gartner JC, et al. Munchausen syndrome by proxy: a new complication of central venous catheterization. *Pediatrics* 1985; 75:523–525.
36. Clayton et al., MBP.
37. Andrew M. The hemostatic system in the infant. In: Nathan and Oski, *Hematology*.
38. Fleisher and Ament, Diarrhea.
39. Fleisher and Ament, Diarrhea.
40. Bourchier, Bleeding ears and Clayton et al., MBP.
41. Meadow, 1982.
42. Kurlandsky et al., Definition.
43. Johnson et al., A case of factitious disorder.
44. Ernst TN and Philip M. Severe iron deficiency anemia. An example of covert child abuse (munchausen syndrome by proxy). *West J Med.* 1986; 144:358–359.
45. Nicol AR and Eccles M. Psychotherapy for munchausen syndrome by proxy. *Arch Dis Child.* 1985; 60:344–348.
46. Geelhoed GC and Pemberton PJ. SIDS, seizures, or 'sophogeal reflux? *Med J Australia.* 1985; 143:357–358.

10

The Deliberately Poisoned Child

Fred Henretig

In his seminal paper, Meadow defined the uncommon but clinically significant phenomenon of parents who deliberately falsified their child's medical history, altered laboratory specimens and/or brought specific injuries to bear over time, so as to necessitate numerous medical diagnostic and therapeutic interventions.[1] One of the first two children reported by Meadow had been repetitively poisoned with table salt. This chapter will focus on the administration of exogenous poisons as a form of Munchausen Syndrome by Proxy (MBP).

It is important to distinguish the several forms of chemical child abuse.[2,3] The repeated unintentional ingestion of drugs or household substances by toddlers may represent a manifestation of poor parental supervision, and thus child neglect. At least three other categories of intentional poisoning are also recognized, including impulsive acts, unorthodox childrearing practices, and MBP.

Impulsive acts tend to occur when parents are under extreme stress and these acts may be triggered by a particularly fussy or colicky infant. Parents with severely disorganized social circumstances or overt mental illness may pose a greater long-term risk for such acts.

Families who subscribe to unorthodox child-rearing styles may utilize nontraditional diets and folk medicines. Such practices have resulted in the poisoning of their children with toxic amounts of vitamins, herbal remedies, or heavy metals. Parents who themselves are members of the drug culture may allow or encourage early drug use by young children. Unorthodox attempts at discipline around eating behavior issues may include bizarre interventions such as forcing the ingestion of water, salt, or pepper with resultant intoxication.

In contrast, families who commit MBP act in a methodical, deliberate, repetitive, and purposefully deceptive manner. These families often manifest complex and profoundly disturbed psychosocial dynamics.

The first published case of MBP via poisoning appears to be that reported by Dine in 1965[4], 12 years prior to Meadow's classic description. The patient was a 19-month-old boy with repetitive perphenazine poisoning who was hospitalized for coma and seizures five times over a 4-month period. The child's mother had been prescribed this major tranquilizer for postpartum psychosis. The first case series of nonaccidental poisoning in children was published in 1976 by Rogers and co-workers, and provided details on six cases that would now be considered MBP[5]. These authors provided an outline of several recurring diagnostic features in such patients, and described common aspects of the family dynamics. A particularly compelling anecdote in the annals of MBP poisoning was the publication of a Letter to the Editor of the *Lancet* in 1978, asking readers for help in diagnosing a puzzling case of recurrent coma in a 2-year-old boy.[6] This child became unresponsive and hypotonic on more than six occasions while hospitalized, and extensive neurologic, metabolic, infectious, and toxicologic screening tests were unremarkable. Within a month, the author wrote again to the *Lancet* with the fascinating denouement of this story,[7] and provided a detailed case report two years after, which also thanked the many *Lancet* readers who had offered suggestions.[8] It had been finally discovered on repeat toxicologic testing that the child was suffering from repetitive barbiturate poisoning. The same barbiturates were found in the mother's hospital room locker. By the time the discovery had been made, this child had suffered nine episodes of coma and two respiratory arrests requiring endotracheal intubation.

In 1981, Schnaps and co-workers described an 18-month-old girl who was poisoned with chlorpromazine, and had likely been a victim of MBP poisoning since the age of 3 months.[9] The authors were able to tally 16 additional cases of poisoning from the literature at that time, most of which would today be considered MBP. Fourteen of these 16 patients were chronically poisoned over a period of time ranging from 1.5 months to 48 months, with eight of the 16 having been poisoned in the hospital. By 1982, Dine and McGovern were able to report on seven original cases of acute intentional childhood poisoning, and to tabulate 41 additional cases that had been found on literature review.[10] Although they did not use the term MBP, and their review did not distinguish between acute, one-time overdoses and repetitive poisonings, they did note that 13 of the cases involved ongoing poisoning that occurred during hospitalization. Thus these most likely do represent MBP. To date, at least 53 cases of intentional poisoning have been reported that fit the paradigm of MBP.

Epidemiologic Aspects

Table 10–1 lists 53 cases reviewed from the literature and one patient seen by the author. The number and variety of toxins represented in cases of MBP poisoning spans a wide spectrum of common household products and both over-the-counter and prescription pharmaceutical agents. When psychoactive medications were implicated they had frequently been prescribed to the parent who was ultimately identified as the perpetrator. On occasion, the child's own medication (e.g., carbamazepine) was inappropriately dosed, and in retrospect was probably prescribed unnecessarily in response to fabricated symptoms (e.g., seizures) described by the mother.[11] The most common psychoactive medications reported in MBP poisoning include barbiturates (six cases), phenothiazines (five cases), antidepressants (two cases) and sedative-hypnotics (two cases). Another large group of reported pharmaceutical agents are those causing gastrointestinal symptoms, particularly ipecac (11 cases) and laxatives (five cases). A number of cases are reported involving household substances such as table salt. Most of these cases occur via ingestion of the toxic agent, but five cases have been reported involving ocular exposure and parenteral injection, including two cases with insulin.

The gender of the children has shown a male predominance, with 31 male victims and 23 female. The age range, 3 weeks to 10 years, is of interest in that many victims are outside the usual 1- to 4-year-old "pica-prone" age.

In all but three cases where the perpetrator was suspected with

Table 10–1
Munchausen Syndrome by Proxy Caused by Poisoning

Author	Age (mos)	Sex	Clinical Features	Toxins	Perpetrator	Outcome*
Neurologic Syndromes						
Dine[33]	14	M	fever, seizure, coma	Perphenazine	Mother	R
Lansky[34]	36	F	recurrent coma	Chloral hydrate	Mother	R
Lorber[35,36]	24	M	recurrent coma	Barbiturates	Mother	R
Lorber[37]	24	M	recurrent coma	Barbiturates	Mother	D
Watson[38]	84	M	recurrent coma	Imipramine	Mother	R
			ventricular tachycardia			
Verity[39]	60	M	lethargy, myoclonus	Phenothiazine	Mother	R
Mahesh[40]	48	M	lethargy	Carbamazepine	Mother	R
Children's Hosp. of Phila.[41]	18	M	coma, ataxia	Benzodiazepines, Cyclobenzaprine	Mother	R
Shnaps[42]	3	F	coma	Chlorpromazine	Mother	R
Rogers[43]	24	M	ataxia, confusion	Barbiturates	Mother	R
Rogers[44]	84	M	ataxia, coma	Methaqualone	Mother	R
Rogers[45]	15	F	lethargy, miosis	Dihydrocodeine	(?)	R
Rendle-Short[46]	24	?	recurring coma	Barbiturates	Mother	R
Burman[47]	60	M	"bizarre" neurologic symptoms	Promethazine	Mother	R
Simon[48]	0.6	M	lethargy, tachycardia	Amitriptyline	Mother	R

Gastrointestinal Syndromes

	Age	Sex	Symptoms	Agent	Perpetrator	Outcome
Fleisher[49]	17	M	"bloody" diarrhea	Phenolphthalein	Mother	R
Fleisher[50]	27	M	"bloody" diarrhea	Phenolphthalein	Mother	D
Fleisher[51]	3	F	"bloody" diarrhea	Phenolphthalein	Mother	R
Feldman[52]	9	F	vomiting, lethargy	Ipecac	Mother	R
Fenton[53]	7	F	FTT, diarrhea	Epsom salt	Mother	R
McClung[54]	10	F	vomiting, diarrhea, weakness	Ipecac	Mother	R
McClung[55]	1	M	vomiting, diarrhea	Ipecac	Mother	R
McClung[56]	1	M	vomiting, diarrhea, weakness	Ipecac	Mother	R
Berkener[57]	1.5	F	vomiting, weakness	Ipecac	Mother	R
Sutphen[58]	120	M	vomiting, diarrhea	Ipecac	Mother	R
Sutphen[59]	9	M	vomiting, diarrhea, weakness	Ipecac	Mother	R
Colletti[60]	10	F	vomiting, diarrhea	Ipecac	Mother	R
Day[61]	48	F	vomiting, diarrhea, CHF	Ipecac	Mother	D
Goebel[62]	29	M	vomiting, diarrhea, CHF	Ipecac	Mother	R
Goebel[63]	60	M	vomiting, diarrhea, weakness, CHF	Ipecac	Mother	R

Metabolic Disturbances

	Age	Sex	Symptoms	Agent	Perpetrator	Outcome
Friedman[64]	12	M	vomiting, lethargy	Salt	Mother	D
Bauman[65]	13	M	lethargy, hypoglycemia	Insulin (parenteral)	Mother	R
Bauman[66]	3	F	hypoglycemia, diarrhea	Insulin (parenteral)	Mother	R
Rogers[67]	2	F	anorexia, dehydration	Salt	Mother	D
Rogers[68]	48	M	dizziness, diaphoresis	Furosemide, Chlorothalidone	Mother	R

Table 10-1 (continued)
Munchausen Syndrome by Proxy Caused by Poisoning

Author	Age (mos)	Sex	Clinical Features	Toxins	Perpetrator	Outcome*
Rogers[69]	24	F	seizure, coma, hypoglycemia	Phenformin	(?)	D
Meadow[70]	1.5-41	6M, 6F	vomiting, lethargy, coma, hyperreflexia, seizures	Salt	9 mothers 1 father 1(?)	2D 10R
Hemorrhagic diathesis						
Hvizdala[71]	24	M	ataxia, hematuria	Barbiturates, Phenothiazines, Warfarin	Mother	R
Hvizdala[72]	48	F	syncope, hematuria, petechiae	Barbiturates, Warfarin	Mother	R
White[73]	11	F	hematomas, hemorrhagic otitis	Warfarin	Mother	R
Miscellaneous						
Taylor[74]	72	F	recurrent conjunctivitis, keratitis	(?)chemical(ocular)	Father	R
Taylor[75]	6	M	conjunctivitis	(?)chemical(ocular)	(?)	R
Saulsbury[76]	9	M	apnea, seizures, respiratory arrest, pneumonia	Naptha(parenteral)	Mother	R

* R = recovered, D = died.
CHF = Congestive heart failure

some certainty, the mother was identified. In two children in whom the father was suspected, a caustic chemical was applied to the victims' eyes;[12] the third was a case of salt poisoning.[13] The mothers who perpetrated had often themselves been abused as children or by their spouses. They generally fit the stereotype of perpetrators. A number were nurses and/or had some connection with the health care professions. Most were very caring and devoted to their children during hospitalization, and were typically very appreciative of the medical staff's (usually unsuccessful) diagnostic and therapeutic labors. However, in some cases the mothers were prone to odd behaviors, mood swings, and hostility. The families were notable for several common features, including significant marital discord, the child having been the product of an unwanted pregnancy, and/or a history of mental illness in the parental perpetrator.

The potential for serious morbidity and mortality in MBP by poisoning is obvious. A number of children suffered seizures, deep coma and respiratory arrest, but still survived. Nine of the 54 patients (16.67%) reviewed in Table 10–1 died as a result of their poisoning.

Specific Toxic Syndromes in MBP Poisoning

CENTRAL NERVOUS SYSTEM

Variable degrees of altered sensorium, ranging from lethargy to deep coma, have characterized the cases involving psychotropic medications and anticonvulsants. Additional findings include confusion, ataxia, myoclonus, and pupillary changes. The improvement and subsequent "relapse" into coma, often occurring in the hospital, was particularly characteristic. The usual neurologic investigations were typically unrevealing, although in several cases the electroencephalogram (EEG) demonstrated fast-wave activity that was ultimately a clue to drug intoxication. When toxicologic screens were ordered, they were often initially reported as negative. In some cases, more specific toxicologic analysis in light of clinical suspicion was eventually diagnostic. In the patient described by Lorber in 1978, repeat toxicologic testing on blood obtained at the time of admission was found to be positive for the specific barbiturates found in the mother's locker.[14,15] The original nonspecific screen had been negative. The following descriptive case illustrates several of the features of MBP poisoning:

> An 18-month-old boy presented to Children's Hospital of Philadelphia with lethargy and ataxia, and was found to have positive toxicologic screens for benzodiazepines in urine and blood at the time of admission. His mother admitted to having triazolam (Halcion, Upjohn) in the home. When the child became unresponsive in the hospital about 36 hours after admission, the initial diagnosis of acute benzodiazepine ingestion was questioned. A computed tomography scan was scheduled. Just prior to its being performed, the child was noted to have a foreign body in his mouth. This was subsequently found to be a cyclobenzaprine tablet. Further quantitative toxicologic testing suggested that diazepam (Valium, Roche) might also have been administered to the child subsequent to admission. When the mother was separated from the child, he manifested a rapid return to normal consciousness.

Most psychoactive medication overdoses follow a predictable pattern of absorption, distribution, and elimination. The clinical course parallels this, with rapid development of maximum alteration in sensorium followed by steady improvement. There are, however, two notable exceptions: glutethimide (Doriden, Rorer) and meprobamate (Equagesic, Wyeth-Ayerst; Miltown, Wallace), both of which can cause a fluctuating, prolonged coma. Neither is frequently prescribed today.

GASTROINTESTINAL TRACT

Chronic vomiting and diarrhea that remain undiagnosed after multiple investigations and hospitalizations has been the hallmark of this group of MBP cases. The predominant agents reported have been syrup of ipecac (11 cases) and phenolphthalein-containing laxatives (three cases). In many of these cases the perpetrator-mother has had a history of anorexia/bulimia.

Patients poisoned with ipecac have typically presented with recurrent vomiting which was not bilious or bloody, and intermittent diarrhea. Musculoskeletal weakness and cardiac toxicity may also complicate the course, with at least three patients reported to have developed congestive heart failure resulting in one death. A recent case report by Goebel and co-workers[16] highlights the spectrum of ipecac toxicity. A 29-month-old boy developed appendicitis and underwent appendectomy which was complicated by a small bowel obstruction 4 months after the operation. This was successfully repaired, and he began to thrive. However, over the following 18 months he was hospitalized every 2- to 4 months for recurrent dehydration caused by vomiting and diarrhea. His weight dropped from the 25th to the third percentile. He underwent exhaustive studies, and was fed by nasoduodenal tube, though it frequently dislodged "spontaneously." The tube was eventually replaced surgically by jejunostomy. Eighteen months after initial presentation, the boy developed dyspnea, weakness, and peripheral edema and was found to have congestive heart failure. His serum creatine phosphokinase (CPK) was 11,336 u/l. He was admitted to the intensive care unit and appeared to improve promptly on diuretic therapy. One night his jejunostomy tube became dislodged while his mother was in his room. Toxicologic screening for ipecac alkaloids was performed soon thereafter. The blood was negative, but the urine was positive by a high-pressure liquid chromatography (HPLC) method. The child was placed in his grandparents' custody and began to thrive, with complete resolution of cardiomyopathy over 4 weeks. His jejunostomy tube was removed and he remained asymptomatic on a regular diet.

The myopathy of ipecac is believed to result from a primary toxic effect of the alkaloid emetine on muscle fibers. The skeletal muscle effects result in a predominantly proximal muscle weakness. The serum CPK and aldolase are often elevated. Cardiomyopathy caused by emetine is manifested by tachycardia, congestive failure, and electrocardiograph (ECG) abnormalities including flattened or inverted T waves, prolonged PR interval, and dysrhythmias. Echocardiography may demonstrate decreased left ventricular function and dilated chambers.

Ipecac alkaloids are not easily detected in body fluids. The routine hospital laboratory overdose screens in common use do not test for ipecac. When specifically requested, many hospitals utilize thin-layer chromatography for blood and urine specimens. Those specimens, however, typically contain levels below this technique's limit of detection, although a few cases have reported positive tests on vomitus by this technique. HPLC is now the procedure of choice, although even with HPLC it is necessary to have both urine and blood specimens. Blood emetine levels decline within hours of a single emetic dose, while traces may be present in urine for several weeks.[17]

Intractable diarrhea was the presenting syndrome for the laxative poisoned children. As in the ipecac group, the children were typically subjected to extensive diagnostic investigations, including contrast radiography and endoscopy, which were unrevealing. The phenolphthalein patients were noted to manifest an intermittent pink-red color in urine and stool, which at times was misinterpreted as blood.[18] The correct diagnosis was established by the demonstration of phenolphthalein in diapers through the addition of dilute (1 N) acetic acid, which makes the pink color disappear. Further confirmation was noted by the addition of dilute alkali (1 N potassium hydroxide) resulting in a deepening of the pinkish color to dark red.

Another form of MBP laxative abuse has been reported using Epsom salts[19]. A 7-month-old girl presented with severe failure to thrive and persistent watery stools. On hospital admission for dehydration, her stool electrolyte analysis revealed a large solute osmolal gap, which subsequently proved to be due to a 10-times normal magnesium excretion. When confronted with this finding, the mother admitted to administering Epsom salts so that the "doctors would take her more seriously." Separation from the mother resulted in cessation of diarrhea, and resultant weight gain.

METABOLIC ABERRATIONS

This diverse group includes a number of reported MBP patients with altered electrolyte and/or glucose homeostasis. Implicated drugs and toxins include table salt with resultant hypernatremia (14 cases, four resulting in death), insulin administered parenterally (two cases), phenformin given by mouth with resultant hypoglycemia (one case), and diuretics causing hypernatremia (one case).

One of Dr. Meadow's original cases of MBP was that of a boy who first presented with recurrent attacks of vomiting and drowsiness associated with hypernatremia at the age of 6 weeks.[20] His serum sodium ranged from 160- to 175 mmol/L. He suffered attacks as often as every month, but extensive renal and endocrinologic investigations at three medical centers between attacks were always unrevealing. By 14 months of age the suspicion had been raised that his mother, a nurse, was administering salt to him. A social service investigation was initiated. During this period, he arrived at the hospital one night in extremis from severe hypernatremia and died. His mother wrote a note thanking the medical staff for their care, and then attempted suicide.

More recently, Meadow has reported as a group this infant and an additional 11 children who were studied over a 15-year period. These children were repeatedly poisoned with salt, primarily during the first 6 months of life. The perpetrator was mother in 10 cases, father in one case, and unclear (but one of the parents) in the final case. Among 12 siblings in this cohort, two had been poisoned with salt and three had been victims of other fabricated illnesses. Most commonly, salt had been put into the child's mouth or into food or drink, which had often been flavored to disguise the salty taste. In one case, the salt was introduced through a nasogastric tube, and in another case concentrated saline solution was introduced through an intravenous line.[21]

Unexplained hypoglycemia caused by surreptitious insulin administration has been reported in two patients.[22] Another was cared for at the Children's Hospital of Philadelphia.[23] One of the reported cases was a 13-month-old boy with lethargy, found to have blood glucose of 23 mg/dl on hospital admission. The hypoglycemia was initially quite resistant to treatment with hypertonic glucose. Though eventually stabilized after 8 hours of therapy, at 35 hours after admission he relapsed into listlessness and was found to have blood glucose of 27 mg/dl. Subsequently, blood drawn from the initial hypoglycemic episode proved to have elevated insulin but low C-peptide levels, which proved that the insulin was exogenous in origin.[24] The child's brother was a diabetic with a history of difficult control and repeated hypoglycemic episodes. Bauman and Yalow's second patient was an 18-month-old girl who had suffered recurrent bouts of hypoglycemia since the age of 3 months, necessitating 4 months of diazoxide therapy. She also was found to have high insulin levels and unmeasurable C-peptide during one episode. Both children were found to have porcine insulin in the blood by testing with species specific antisera.

One additional patient poisoned with phenformin was found to be hypoglycemic on several occasions. Her father was a diabetic, and her brother had died in hypoglycemic coma. She presented at the age of 2 years, having been found unconscious. She suffered cardiac arrest and ultimately died.[25]

HEMORRHAGIC DIATHESIS

At least three patients have been reported with chronic anticoagulant poisoning and have presented to medical attention with a hemorrhagic diathesis. A 4-year-old boy was admitted to the hospital for ataxia and hyperactivity, and urine toxicologic screening revealed phenothiazine and phentermine.[26] After an overnight pass home, he returned to the hospital with urine positive for methaqualone. Social service investigation and psychiatric counseling for the mother were undertaken. However, over the next several months he developed unexplained, persistent hematuria such that he was scheduled for renal biopsy. At that time his 7-year-old sister presented with multiple petechiae, ecchymoses and bleeding from puncture points. She gave a 15-month history of hematuria and petechiae with prolonged prothrombin time (PT) and partial thromboplastin time (PTT). Putting together the information from both children, the medical staff suspected deliberate warfarin administration. The mother denied this possibility when questioned. However, it was learned that she had been treated with warfarin for thrombophlebitis, and subsequent testing of the girl's serum was positive for warfarin. After the children were placed in the custody of their grandparents, the mother admitted to administering Warfarin.

Similarly, an 11-month-old girl presented with acute hemorrhagic otitis media and multiple hematomas.[27] Her PT was 53 sec (control 12) and PTT greater than 180 (control 34). Her mother, a nurse's aide, had herself been treated with warfarin for a deep vein thrombosis. The child's blood was found to contain a pharmacologically active level of warfarin. Note that both the PT and PTT are typically prolonged in warfarin overdosing, and large doses of vitamin K1 replacement are usually necessary to correct the resultant coagulopathy.

MISCELLANEOUS

Two children were apparently administered caustic agents repeatedly to their eyes, causing a severe chemical conjunctivitis.[28] In a separate case, an 11-month-old boy with a several-month history of recurrent, unexplained apneic spells was admitted for coma and generalized seizures.[29] On his seventh hospital day he suffered a sudden respiratory arrest, and a strong odor of volatile hydrocarbon was noted on his breath. Oily droplets were visible in his intravenous tubing. Subsequent to resuscitation, he developed a typical clinical and radiographic picture of hydrocarbon pneumonitis. The mother later admitted that she had injected her son's intravenous line with a hydrocarbon, found to be of the naptha variety by gas chromatography. The infant survived but was left with developmental delay, cortical blindness, and cerebral palsy.

Diagnostic Evaluation

CLINICAL FEATURES

Poisoned children often present as diagnostic dilemmas, with alterations in sensorium, multiorgan system dysfunction, and peculiar electrolyte or acid-base disturbances. This is probably even more the case with MBP patients, in whom the history from the parents is not only unreliable but often deliberately misleading. Certain clinical features should alert the practitioner to this uncommon situation:[30,31]

1. Symptoms, signs, or laboratory values that are baffling to an experienced clinician
2. altered neurologic status (especially recurrent coma, seizures, or ataxia with seemingly normal intervals)
3. medications in use by other family members that might cause a similar syndrome
4. history of parental drug abuse, psychiatric illness, or overt psychosocial stress
5. suspicious illness or death of a sibling
6. illness recurrence after being at home or parental visiting
7. parental medical/nursing background
8. parental access to drugs
9. any suggestions in a child who is clinically suspected of having been poisoned, either by the presence of a recognizable toxic syndrome or proven laboratory testing, that the poisoning is not accidental

LABORATORY CONSIDERATIONS

The laboratory evaluation of children with suspected MBP is crucial to diagnosis and to the institution of specific medical therapy.
Most MBP victims will require a comprehensive battery of clinical
chemistries (e.g., serum glucose, electrolytes, BUN, creatinine and
at times osmolarity, calcium, liver function tests, and CPK), hematologic studies (e.g., complete blood count and at times evaluation
for carboxyhemoglobin and methemoglobin), consideration of arte-
rial blood gas analysis and standardized toxicologic testing. As
noted in several of the cases detailed above, routine toxicologic
testing (e.g., the rapid overdose "tox screen" utilized by most hospitals) is frequently negative in suspected MBP. Most hospitals currently utilize enzyme multiplied immunoassay testing (EMIT) in
rapid screening for commonly abused illicit drugs and intentionally
overdosed psychoactive medications. These screens typically determine the presence of barbiturates, benzodiazepines, and tricyclic
antidepressants in blood, and amphetamines, barbiturates, benzodiazepines, cocaine metabolites, cannabinoids, and opiates in urine.
Some hospitals may also include phencyclidine in their EMIT
screens. Separate testing is usually done for alcohol, acetaminophen, and salicylates. Practitioners should be familiar with
their hospital's standard panel. Most hospitals have reference toxicologic laboratory testing available when a specific drug or toxin is
suspected. This type of analysis can be crucial in MBP cases. Many
psychoactive medications, as well as a host of other common and
exotic poisons, are detectable with modern HPLC or mass spec-
trophotometry. Consultation with the director of the reference toxicology lab or regional poison control center may be very helpful.
Pharmacokinetic studies may also be useful.[32]

Certain patterns on routine chemistry evaluation are also frequently suggestive of specific toxic syndromes. As noted in the case
discussions above, hypoglycemia is the hallmark of insulin and oral
hypoglycemic intoxication. Hypernatremia and excess stool magnesium are found in poisoning with these salts, respectively. Metabolic acidosis with an increased anion gap is characteristic of poisoning
with methanol, paraldehyde, iron, isoniazid, ethanol, ethylene glycol, and salicylates (adding the clinical states of uremia and diabetic
ketoacidosis gives the mnemonic: *mudpies*). A measured serum osmolarity in excess of the calculated osmolarity, based on the formu-

la 2 x serum Na + BUN/2.8 + glucose/18 (usually in the 290 mosm/kg range) should suggest the presence of unmeasured compounds of high osmolarity, such as ethanol, methanol, or ethylene glycol. Specific comments regarding the toxicologic testing for certain psychoactive drugs, ipecac, phenolphthalein, exogenous insulin, and warfarin were made above in the respective sections discussing these agents.

Additional laboratory tests are often necessary in MBP in order to evaluate for other medical problems in the differential diagnosis. Such tests may include routine radiologic studies, computed tomography, electroencephalography, and electrocardiography as indicated by the child's clinical presentation.

In the event a child is brought to the hospital in extremis caused by an encephalopathy of obscure origin, liver failure, hemorrhagic diathesis, severe dehydration as a result of vomiting or diarrhea, and/or extreme serum chemistry or acid-base disturbances, it is essential to save samples of blood and urine for later definitive toxicologic testing. If the child dies, it is vital to discuss the possibility of occult poisoning with the medical examiner and to insure that appropriate tissue samples undergo toxicologic analysis.

Summary

The occurrence of deliberate, repetitive occult poisoning of children by their parents, usually the mother, with other MBP characteristics, is an uncommon but clinically significant subset of nonaccidental poisoning. The mother typically attempts to hinder the diagnostic process, and the poisoning not infrequently continues while the child is hospitalized. Several forms have been recognized, including neurologic, gastrointestinal, metabolic, and hematologic disturbances. This form of MBP carries a serious prognosis for morbidity and mortality. The clinician must have a high index of suspicion for MBP especially when confronted with a poisoned child whose exposure is not easily explained as an accident. The possibility of MBP should also be entertained when a pediatric illness does not fit a recognizable pattern and is marked by multiple recurrences associated with contact alone with the parent, or when a parent's reaction to their child's illness does not seem appropriate to the clinical situation.

References

1. Meadow R. Munchausen syndrome by proxy: the hinterland of child abuse. *Lancet.* 1977; 2:343–345.
2. Fischler RS. Poisoning: a syndrome of child abuse. *Am Fam Physician.* 1983; 28:103–108.
3. Meadow R. Poisoning. *Br Med J.* 1989; 298:1445–1446.
4. Dine MS. Tranquilizer poisoning: an example of child abuse. *Pediatrics.* 1965; 36:782–785.
5. Rogers D, Tripp J, Bentovin A, et al. Non-accidental poisoning: an extended syndrome of child abuse. *Br Med J.* 1976; 1:793–796.
6. Lorber J. Unexplained episodes of coma in a two-year-old. *Lancet.* 1978; 2:472–473.
7. Lorber J. Unexplained coma in a 2 year old. *Lancet.* 1978; II: 680.
8. Lorber J, Reckless JPD, and Watson JBG. Nonaccidental poisoning: the elusive diagnosis. *Arch Dis Child.* 1980; 55:643–647.
9. Shnaps Y, Frand M, Rotem Y, et al. The chemically abused child. *Pediatrics.* 1981; 68:119–121.
10. Dine MS and McGovern ME. Intentional poisoning of children—an overlooked category of child abuse: report of seven cases and review of the literature. *Pediatrics.* 1982; 70:32–35.
11. Mahesh VK, Stern HP, Kearns GL, et al. Application of pharmacokinetics in the diagnosis of chemical abuse in Munchausen syndrome by proxy. *Clin Pediatr.* 1988; 27:243–246.
12. Taylor D and Bentovim A. Recurrent nonaccidentally inflicted chemical eye injuries to siblings. *Pediatr Ophthalmol.* 1976; 13:238–242.
13. Meadow R. Non-accidental salt poisoning. *Arch Dis Child.* 1993; 68:448–452.
14. Lorber, Unexplained.
15. Lorber, Reckless, and Watson, Nonaccidental.
16. Goebel J, Gremse DA, and Artman M. Cardiomyopathy from ipecac administration in munchausen syndrome by proxy. *Pediatrics.* 1993; 92:601–603.
17. Sutphen JL and Saulsbury FT. Intentional ipecac poisoning: munchausen syndrome by proxy. *Pediatrics.* 1988; 82:453–455.
18. Fleisher D and Ament ME. Diarrhea, red diapers, and child abuse. *Clin Pediatr.* 1977; 16:820–824.
19. Fenton AC, Wailoo MP, and Tanner MS. Severe failure to thrive and diarrhea caused by laxative abuse. *Arch Dis Child.* 1988; 63:978–979.
20. Meadow, Hinterland.
21. Meadow, Non-accidental.
22. Bauman WA and Yalow RS. Child abuse: parenteral insulin administration. *J Pediatr.* 1981; 99:588–591.
23. Levin, personal communication.
24. C-peptide is a molecule cleaved off the insulin precursor (proinsulin) as insulin is made naturally by normal human beings. High levels of insulin without high levels of C-protein prove that the insulin was not made in the body.

25. Rogers, Tripp, Bentovin, et al. Non-accidental.
26. Hvizdala EV and Gellady AM. Intentional poisoning of two siblings by prescription drugs. *Clin Pediatr.* 1978; 17:480–482.
27. White ST, Voter K, and Perry J. Surreptitious warfarin ingestion. *Child Abuse Negl.* 1985; 9:349–352.
28. Taylor and Bentovim, Recurrent.
29. Saulsbury FT, Chobanian MC, and Wilson WG. Child abuse: parenteral hydrocarbon administration. *Pediatrics.* 1984; 73:719–722.
30. Rogers, Tripp, Bentovin, et al. Non-accidental.
31. Meadow R. Munchausen syndrome by proxy. *Arch Dis Child.* 1982; 57:92–98.
32. Mahesh, Stern, Kearns, et al. Application.
33. Dine, Tranquilizer.
34. Lansky LL. An unusual case of childhood chloral hydrate poisoning. *Am J Dis Child.* 1974; 127:275–276.
35. Lorber, Unexplained.
36. Lorber, Reckless, and Watson, Nonaccidental.
37. Lorber, Reckless, and Watson, Nonaccidental.
38. Watson JBG, Davies JM, and Hunter JLP. Nonaccidental poisoning in childhood. *Arch Dis Child.* 1979; 54:143–144.
39. Verity CM, Winckworth C, Burman D, et al. Polle syndrome: children of Munchausen. *Br Med J.* 1979; 2:422–423.
40. Mahesh, Stern, Kearns, et al., Application.
41. Personal communication, Alex Levin.
42. Shnaps, Frand, Rotem, et al., Chemically.
43. Rogers, Tripp, Bentovin, et al., Non-accidental.
44. Rogers, Tripp, Bentovim, et al., Non-accidental.
45. Rogers, Tripp, Bentovim, et al., Non-accidental.
46. Rendle-Short J: Non-accidental barbiturate poisoning of children. *Lancet.* 1978; 2:1212.
47. Burman D, Stevens D. Munchausen family. *Lancet.* 1977; 2:456.
48. Simon FA. Uncommon type of child abuse. *J Pediatr.* 1980; 96:785.
49. Fleisher and Ament, Diarrhea.
50. Fleisher and Ament, Diarrhea.
51. Fleisher and Ament, Diarrhea.
52. Feldman KW, Christropher DM, and Opheim KB. Munchausen Syndrome/bulimia by proxy: ipecac as a toxin in child abuse. *Child Abuse Negl.* 1989; 13:257–264.
53. Fenton, Wailoo, and Tanner, Severe.
54. McClung HJ, Murray R, Braden NJ, et al. Intentional ipecac poisoning in children. *Am J Dis Child.* 1988; 142:637–639.
55. McClung, Murray, Braden, et al., Intentional.
56. McClung, Murray, Braden, et al., Intentional.
57. Berkner P, Kastner T, Skolnick L.: Chronic ipecac poisoning in infancy: a case report. *Pediatrics.* 1988; 82:384–386.
58. Sutphen and Saulsbury, Intentional.

59. Sutphen and Saulsbury, Intentional.
60. Colletti RB, Wasserman RC. Recurrent infantile vomiting due to intentional ipecac poisoning. *J Pediatr Gastro Nutr.* 1989; 8:394–396.
61. Day L, Kelly C, Reed G, et al. Fatal cardiomyopathy: suspected child abuse by chronic ipecac administration. *Vet Hum Toxicol.* 1989; 31:255–257.
62. Goebel, Gremse, and Artman, Cardiomyopathy.
63. Goebel, Gremse, and Artman, Cardiomyopathy.
64. Friedman EM: Caustic ingestions and foreign body aspirations: an overlooked form of child abuse. *Ann Otol Rhinol Laryngol.* 1987; 96:709–712.
65. Bauman and Yalow, Child abuse.
66. Bauman and Yalow, Child abuse.
67. Rogers, Tripp, Bentovim, et al., Non-accidental.
68. Rogers, Tripp, Bentovim, et al., Non-accidental.
69. Rogers, Tripp, Bentovim, et al., Non-accidental.
70. Meadow, Non-accidental. The cases were grouped in this article, and individual details are not available. The case previously reported in Munchausen syndrome by proxy: the hinterland of child abuse was included in the grouping (per personal communication with Dr. Meadow, 9/1994).
71. Hvizdala and Gellady, Intentional.
72. Hvizdala and Gellady, Intentional.
73. White, Voter, and Perry, Surreptitious.
74. Taylor and Bentovim, Recurrent.
75. Taylor and Bentovim, Recurrent.
76. Saulsbury, Chobanian, and Wilson, Child abuse.

11

Infection and Fever

Marcellina Mian and Dirk Huyer

Fever is a common manifestation of childhood illness. It is a symptom that must be taken seriously, and it is relatively easy to feign.[1] Infections are the most common cause of illness in children.[2] It is not surprising, therefore, that infection and fever are part of the constellation of signs and symptoms manifested by Munchausen Syndrome by Proxy (MBP) patients. In Rosenberg's review, the presentation in 10% of 117 cases of MBP was fever.[3] Approximately 9% of patients, both adults and children, with fevers of unknown origin of greater than one year's duration have been found to have factitious fever or self-induced infection.[4]

As with other manifestations of MBP, fever can be simulated or produced. The latter is usually the result of an induced infection. The following are case examples of each, drawn from the literature.[5,6]

A 7-year-old girl was admitted for placement of myringotomy tubes. She had a chronically draining right ear despite 7 months' treatment with many different antibiotics. In the past she had been treated for multiple episodes of otitis media beginning at 4 months, and required tubes at age 14 months. Her mother, a 30-year-old who was trained as an emergency medical technician, reported admissions for bacterial meningitis and for pneumonia in the first year of life. In the 5 years prior to the current admission the child had been seen at least 126 times in different clinics and by a private doctor and was treated for several disorders. At 1 year of age she was admitted to hospital for evaluation of fever. Soon after admission the patient began to have spiking fevers with peaks occurring once or twice daily with subnormal temperatures in between. Cultures of blood, urine, stool, cerebrospinal fluid, and bone marrow were negative and several sedimentation rates were normal. Numerous diagnostic tests including various X-rays and nuclear medicine procedures were normal. The patient was discharged on aspirin for presumed systemic-onset juvenile rheumatoid arthritis.

Between 12–18 months of age the patient did not grow well. Her mother reported daily fevers to 39°C, diarrhea, vomiting, and hematemesis. The patient was usually afebrile when seen in the clinic. At 4 years of age, based on historical information supplied by mother, the child was begun on medications for asthma and allergic rhinitis. By the age of 6 she was using five different asthma medications. Her diet was limited to 10 foods based upon a history of food intolerance.

On examination the child was a healthy afebrile girl. The physical examination was normal except for granulation tissue in the right ear. After placement of the myringotomy tubes the patient developed a fever. Radiographs showed mastoiditis. The patient underwent a right mastoidectomy but continued to be febrile while on intravenous antibiotics. Cultures were negative. Testing suggested the presence of a right sigmoid sinus thrombosis. No clot was discovered on subsequent exploration. She was taken to the intensive care unit for 24 hours where she remained afebrile. After returning to the floor she developed a fever of 39°C orally. Efforts to obtain reliable temperature recordings were hampered by mother's reluctance to give up an active role in vital sign monitoring and medication administration. She stated that she was the only person who could get her child to take her medications.

Despite persistent fever the child was otherwise asymptomatic. Planning for discharge was begun. Soon after the child developed severe diarrhea and vomiting with toxic theophylline levels. The patient was transferred to the intensive care unit and once again became afebrile. A protective custody order was obtained. Thereafter the child was asymptomatic and well.

A female born at home to a 25-year-old mother was evaluated for multiple problems over the first few months of life. The first major problem was episodes of cyanosis and apnea, the evaluation of which showed no definite abnormalities during three admissions. The second problem was unexplained infections and recurrent sepsis caused by gram-negative organisms which prompted an evaluation for immune deficiency. Although the child had profound neutropenia on two occasions, within 8 to 24 hours the total neutrophil counts were above normal. Immunoglobin levels were normal. The level of complement C3 was elevated, with decreased C4 level and a minimally decreased CH50 level. Despite adequate dosing of intravenous antibiotics the child had two further episodes of bacteremia without any obvious primary or secondary site. All organisms were sensitive to at least one of the two antibiotics with which the child was being treated. Nurses recalled spraying leaks from the intravenous tubing that were temporally related to episodes of illness.

The Child Protective Services was notified, who accompanied the police when talking with the child's mother. She admitted injecting contaminated water into the child's intravenous tubing. Cultures of the contents of syringes in her purse revealed the three organisms isolated from the latest blood sample all having the same antibiotic sensitivity profiles, as well as Enterococcus which was not cultured from the child. The child recovered uneventfully, was placed in foster care, and continued to thrive without evidence of infectious disease

In these examples, fever and/or infection were the salient features of the child's illness. In other reported cases of MBP, and in our own experience with many such cases, fever is a common symptom for the child's frequent presentations for medical care prior to a diagnosis of MBP made on the basis of some other major component. Further, factitious fever may complicate an existing or resolving organic illness.[7]

Factitious Fever

Factitious or simulated fever exists when a health care professional is deceived into believing a truly afebrile patient has a fever. It has been aptly termed by some "hyperthermia of trickery".[8,9]

EXTENT OF THE PROBLEM

Factitious fever is said to be an uncommon occurrence in childhood and few cases are reported even when series of children with prolonged fevers of unknown origin are reviewed.[10–15] However, review of the information provided suggests that some of the children listed did, in fact, have factitious fever, which was ascribed to parental misunderstanding or psychoneurosis.[16] In light of more recent knowledge, some children with factitious fever might well fit the diagnosis of MBP. Several reports of factitious fever in children over 10 years old and adolescents are available.[17-20] Some of these were felt to fit the diagnosis of Munchausen Syndrome in that their fever involved purposeful deception by the youth.[21]

Our review of Rosenberg's original references reveals that five of the 117 cases or approximately 4% involved factitious fever.[22-28] These and additional articles (Table 11–1) revealed 53 cases which we considered to fit the definition of factitious/fraudulent fever or induced infections in children and adolescents. Factitious fever was definitely present in 28 patients or approximately 53% of cases, though not necessarily as the presenting complaint.[29-37] Of these 28 cases, 20 or about 71% were simulated by the youths themselves and 8, or about 29%, represented cases of MBP with the deception carried out by the parent. Reports of seven additional cases of diagnosed or probable factitious fever did not provide sufficient information for inclusion in the above figures.[38-40]

METHODS OF SIMULATING FEVER

The three methods described in the literature for simulating fever in both adults and children are

1. Thermometer manipulation, including
    a. Use of external heat sources applied to the thermometer, such as a hot water warmer, a heating pad, or immersion in hot water
    b. Mechanical friction such as rubbing the thermometer
    c. Tampering with the thermometer, manually by displacing the column of mercury upwards, or electronically
    d. Increasing heat at the site of temperature measurement, by anal irritation with erythema and repeated anal sphincter contractions
2. Switching thermometers
3. Altering temperature charts

Aduan states that, "True factitious fever probably does not occur in children less than 10 years of age because they do not yet know how to systematically manipulate the thermometer."[41] This lack of sophistication probably applies also to the other methods of simulating fever. However, in victims of MBP, factitious fever is simulated by the parent or guardian.

INDICATORS OF FACTITIOUS FEVER

"Pediatricians by nature and clinical experience are unlikely to consider self-induced fever as a plausible diagnosis in their patients."[42] The following indicators will assist health care providers in considering the diagnosis of factitious fever when appropriate.

1. Fever with no evidence of active disease either by physical examination or diagnostic testing.[43]
2. Prolonged duration of fever without any progression of an underlying disorder.[44] These patients do not deteriorate, improve, or develop more overt symptoms of their suspected underlying disease.
3. Temperature of 41°C is rare and should be accepted "as valid only after very careful scrutiny of the evidence."[45,46] Temperatures of 108°F and above are incompatible with life and these measurements should arouse the suspicion of fraud.
4. Discrepancy between the patient's high temperature and physical findings, such as temperature elevation unaccompanied by skin warmth or tachycardia.[47-51]
5. Absence of diurnal variation in temperature, reversal of the diurnal pattern, or any unusual pattern.[52-54]
6. Strikingly rapid defervescence unaccompanied by diaphoresis.[55-57]
7. Marked difference between oral and rectal temperatures taken at the same time.[58,59]
8. No fever recorded in the presence of a trained observer.[60]
9. Other associated factitious symptoms.[61,62]

METHODS OF DETECTION

When the possibility exists that the correct diagnosis is MBP with factitious fever, the following approach will assist in either confirming or denying that possibility:

1. A low index of suspicion.
2. Close supervision of the temperature measurement by a health

Table 11-1
Summary of Cases of Factitious and Fradulent Fever and Produced Infections Reported in Children under 18 Years of Age

Author	Patient Age (yrs)	Sex	Symptoms and signs	Final Diagnosis	Method of simulating or inducing fever	Perpetrator
Ackerman 1966	15	F	Fever, nodular skin lesions	Fraudulent fever	Subcutaneous injection of homogenized milk	Self
Aduan 1979	11	M	Fever	Factitious fever	Thermometer manipulation	Self
	17	F	Recurrent abscesses	Factitious fever, self-induced abscesses	Switching thermometers	Self
	15	M	Fever	Factitious fever	Switching thermometers	Self
	15	F	Fever	Probable factitious fever	Thermometer manipulation	Self
	14	F	Fever	Probable factitious fever	Thermometer manipulation	Self
	17	F	Fever	Factitious fever	Switching thermometers	Self
	17	F	Fever	Factitious fever	Thermometer manipulation	Self
	14	F	Fever	Probable factitious fever	Thermometer manipulation	Self
	13	M	Fever	Factitious fever	Thermometer manipulation	Self
	15	F	Fever	Probable factitious fever	Thermometer manipulation	Self
	11	M	Fever	Factitious fever	Thermometer manipulation	Self
Clayton 1978	3	F	Hematuria, fever	Factitious fever	Altering temperature charts	Mother
Dine 1965	1.5	M	Prolonged sleep, fever	Drug poisoning	Perphenazine administration	Mother

Reference	Age	Sex	Presenting symptoms	Diagnosis	Method	Perpetrator
Edwards 1987	15	F	Recurrent fevers	Factitious fever	Thermometer manipulation	Self
Fleischer 1977	3	M	Recurrent fever, rashes, gastrointesinal and neurologic symptoms.	Unkown	Brother of next case—overdose of Phenolphthalein suspected	Mother
	1	F	same	Drug poisoning	Phenolphthalein administration proven	Mother
Frederick 1990	1.5	M	Recurrent central catheter sepsis	Induced mono– and polymicrobial bacteremia	Catheter contamination	Foster mother
Halsey 1983	8	M	Recurrent fever, bacteremia	Induced polymicrobial bacteremia	Contamination of intravenous infusion	Mother
Hawkings 1956	17	F	Fever, skin lesions, neurologic symptoms	Factitious fever	Unknown	Self
	17	F	Fever, hemorrhagic anemia, epistaxis, septic spots	Factitious fever and induced infection	Switching thermometer and pricking with a dirty needle	Self
Herzberg 1972	17	F	Recurrent fever and gingival ulcers	Factitious fever	Switching thermometer and self-induced ulcers	Self
	15	M	Recurrent fever	Factitious fever	Switching thermometer	Self
	13	F	Recurrent fever	Factitious fever	Falsifying temperature reports	Mother
	11	F	Recurrent fever	Factitious fever	Falsifying temperature reports	Self
	11	M	Recurrent fever and headache	Factitious fever	Unknown	Unknown
Hodge 1982	Teen	F	Recurrent infections	Self-induced infections	Unknown	Self
	1	M	Recurrent infections, fever	Induced polymicrobial bacteremia	Contamination of intravenous sites	Mother

Table 11-1 (continued)
Summary of Cases of Factitious and Fradulent Fever and Produced Infections Reported in Children under 18 Years of Age

Author	Patient Age (yrs)	Sex	Symptoms and signs	Final Diagnosis	Method of simulating or inducing fever	Perpetrator
Hvizdala 1978	4	M	Fever, rash, neurologic and joint symptoms	Drug poisoning	Unknown—fever part of medical history	Mother
	7	F	Hemorrhagic diathesis, urinary tract infection, seizure, fever, and ataxia	Drug poisoning	Unknown—fever part of medical history	Mother
Koch 1988	7.5	M	Recurrent fever, otitis	Induced polymicrobial bacteremia	Injection of foreign fluid into the blood stream	Mother
Kohl 1978	4.75	F	Fever, recurrent skin infections	Induced polymicrobial bacteremia	Injection into the skin and and intravenous infusions	Mother
Liston 1983	0.3	F	Recurrent sepsis	Induced polymicrobial bacteremia	Admitted injection of contaminants into the intravenous tubing	Mother
Malatack 1985	2	M	Fever, joint pain, diarrhea, bloddy stools	Induced blood loss	Unknown—fever part of medical history	Mother
McClung 1972	6	?	Fevers	Psychoneurotic mother	Unknown	Mother
	10	?	Fever	Psychoneurotic mother	Unknown—some misrepresentation	Mother
	2	?	Diarrhea and fevers	Exaggerated parental parental concern	Unknown	Unknown
	8	?	"Brucellosis & typhoid fever"	Neurotic misunderstanding of child's illness	Unknown—some misrepresentation	Parents

Study	Age	Sex	Symptoms	Diagnosis	Method	Perpetrator
Meadow 1977	12	?	Fever & joint pain	Factitious fever	Purposeful misrepresentation	Self
	13	?	Fevers	Factitious fever	Purposeful misrepresentation	Self
Meadow 1982	6	F	Fever and urinary infections	MBP	Tampering with urine specimens, Iatrogenic fevers	Mother, Physicians
	4 children (0.3 to 7 yrs)		Fevers	MBP	Thermometer manipulation	Mother
Palmer 1984	9	F	Recurrent fever and infection	Induced polymicrobial bacteremia	Unknown	Mother
Rogers 1976	1	F	Electrolyte imbalance, recurrent abscesses	Poisoning and possible induced infections	Unknown—infection part of medical history	Mother
Rosenberg 1987	4	M	Chronic fever, osteomyelitis, intermittent bacteremia	MBP	Spitting into intravenous line	Mother
Rubin 1986	11	F	Gastrointestinal ulceration, recurrent polymicrobial bacteremia	Induced polymicrobial bacteremia	Tampering with intravenous catheter	Mother
Rumans 1978	16	F	Fever	Factitious fever	Thermometer manipulation	Self
	5.5	M	Fever	? Factitious fever	Unknown	Mother
	0.75	F	Fever	? Factitious fever	Unknown	Mother
Wood 1989	7	F	Fever, recurrent infections, gastrointestinal symptoms, hematemesis, asthma, allergic rhinitis	Factitious fever and drug poisoning	False recording	Mother

Bold: included in Fever category in Rosenberg 1987
? or unknown: information not available in report

care professional is essential. Experience with adults has shown that manipulation of the thermometer is most likely to occur while the thermometer is *in situ*.[63] The supervision must continue throughout the temperature measurement as the thermometer equilibrates.

3. The medical caretaker must not be aligned with the patient, either personally or professionally, or have any ulterior motive or secondary gains to achieve as a result of the patient's elevated temperature.[64] This may become quite difficult in cases of MBP when the perpetrator has befriended the hospital staff to such a degree that they may actually become very hesitant to accuse or even consider the parent as an MBP perpetrator.

4. Rectal measurement is preferable to the oral since manipulation of the oral thermometer is easier.[65–67]

5. Although they are not foolproof, electronic thermometers are preferable to mercury ones since it is more difficult to tamper with them.[68]

6. If it is suspected that a reading is fraudulent the following methods should resolve the issue:

    a. A second reading with a different thermometer will eliminate technical error and document any discrepancy.[69]

    b. Simultaneous measurement of oral, axillary, and rectal temperatures will reveal any discrepancy.[70]

    c. Measurement of the temperature of freshly voided urine or stool, which is closely related to oral and rectal temperature, will give an indication of core temperature.[71,72]

    d. Temperature flowcharts for the child should be kept away from the bedside, preferably in a secure place to which the parent has no access.

7. The temperature measurement must be recorded in ink immediately upon removal of the thermometer by the professional in whose presence it was obtained.[73,74] The entry should be initialed by the medical caretaker who took and entered the reading.

Fraudulent Fever

Fraudulent or produced fever is a genuine temperature elevation in response to a noxious stimulus, usually infectious, which is purposely self-administered or administered by someone else.[75]

EXTENT OF THE PROBLEM

The overall rate of polymicrobial bacteremia in children with positive blood cultures is 0.6% with a mortality rate in these children of 32%.[76] In 97% of cases these infections occurred in children with an underlying condition that was considered a predisposing factor. In approximately one third of them, this condition was the presence of an indwelling central venous catheter. Yet no mention was made of child abuse as a possible cause of the bacteremia, particularly in the presence of intravenous lines.[77]

Rosenberg's review of the MBP literature includes 4 cases (3%) of 117 reported cases with the presentation of fever caused by an adult care giver.[78-83] In an additional three cases it is also likely that fever was produced, but the original references are not explicit on this point.[84,85] Of the 53 patients reported in the literature which we considered to fit the definition of factitious or fraudulent fever or produced infections in children and adolescents (Table 11–1), 15 (28%) had definite evidence of fraudulent fever. MBP was the diagnosis in 11 (73%) while the illness was self-induced in four (27%), all adolescents. In another five cases, fraudulent fever was likely but the information in the original reports was not definitive.

METHODS OF PRODUCING FEVER

Fever may be produced by the inoculation or administration of substances in the following categories:[86]

1. Material contaminated with bacteria, including dirt, water,[87] fecal matter (the literature reports both human[88,89] and parrot[90]), oral secretions,[91-93] vaginal material[94]
2. Pure bacterial cultures[95]
3. Foreign proteins, such as milk[96,97]
4. Pyrogenic substances, such as tetanus toxoid or other immunizing substance[98,99] and drugs.[100]

There is some overlap in these categories, since a foreign protein such as milk may also be bacterially contaminated. Substances in the first three categories result in infection usually caused by multiple organisms (polymicrobial bacteremia). The route of inoculation has been reported to be of several types:

1. Intravenous via central or peripheral line injections or contami-

nation.[101-105] These injections have resulted in unexplained infections and recurrent sepsis. Some of them were accompanied by phlebitis and purulent drainage at the catheter site.[106] Skin abscesses and pyogenic arthritis have been described.[107-109] Severe manifestations included shock, acidosis, disseminated intravascular coagulation, and renal failure.[110] Secondary immune deficiency has been described as a result of the recurrent infections although the clinical presentation seemed to support the diagnosis of a primary immune deficiency.[111-113] These children have been described as pale, ill-looking, and thin.

2. Subcutaneous injection.[114] Extravasation of contaminated intravenous fluid into the surrounding subcutaneous tissue has resulted in skin abscesses or purulent drainage at the catheter or needle site.[115-118] In addition, direct injection of contaminants as listed above into subcutaneous tissue has been reported in several patients.[119] These local infections were also associated with bacteremia and systemic signs of illness.

3. Otic contamination.[120] This may have been the cause of recurrent and chronic otitis media and externa with systemic signs of infection in twin children. The mother had insisted on keeping large bandages on the ears of the sister who had died at 4 years of age with multiple problems, the most chronic of which had been middle and outer ear infections. However, the 7 1/2-year-old boy also had an indwelling intravenous catheter and the microbiologists involved felt certain many peculiar organisms were being injected into his blood stream. His condition improved dramatically when the catheter was removed and a nurse was placed permanently at his bedside.

4. Drug-induced fevers have been reported to result from the administration of perphenazine, which causes pyrexia as an idiosyncratic reaction,[121] and phenolphthalein.[122,123] Drug-induced fevers are accompanied by the other symptoms produced by the drug. For perphenazine this includes prolonged sleep with depressed neurologic function and convulsions, all of which resolve promptly after drug ingestion ceases. For phenolphthalein this includes diarrhea, the passage of "bloody" stools which test negative for occult blood, dehydration, and in one case death. In some children with drug ingestions, fever was an associated finding during the course of their various presentations.[124]

INDICATORS OF FRAUDULENT FEVER AND INFECTIONS

All of the indicators of MBP in general are applicable to cases of fraudulent fever and infection. In addition, the following list of indicators are specific to raising the level of suspicion regarding fraudulent fever and infections.

1. Multisystem, prolonged, unusual, unexplained, or bizarre illness without an apparent pathologic explanation.[125–128]
2. Polymicrobial bacteremia, since the condition itself is rare even in children with underlying causes.[129,130]
3. Absence of an underlying condition or source of infection to explain polymicrobial bacteremia.
4. The presence of an indwelling intravenous catheter. Although this is a predisponent to polymicrobial bacteremia,[131] most of the reported cases of induced bacteremia have occurred in patients with intravenous lines that provide the access for willful contamination.
5. Recurrence of polymicrobial bacteremia and other symptoms, even after successful treatment.[132,133]
6. Recurrent skin infections at intravenous infusion sites.[134]
7. Recovery of unusual organisms, including those that are not commonly pathogens,[135] anaerobes not usually found in nosocomial infections,[136] organisms susceptible to an antibiotic the child is already receiving,[137,138] organisms not found in the child's bowel or other suspected source of seeding,[139] or different organisms from different culture sites obtained simultaneously.[140]
8. Treatments that are ineffective or poorly tolerated.[141–143]
9. Association of symptoms with the presence of the parent or caretaker. A review of cases indicates some bizarre occurrences having been noted between parent and child, such as a mother found after having disconnected her daughter's intravenous set and pouring fluid on the floor.[144–147] Therapeutic concentrations of antibiotics may not be achievable in the mother's presence.[148]
10. Disappearance of symptoms when the parent or caretaker is absent: The child becomes afebrile, lesions heal, and general recovery is achieved.[149–152]
11. Typical profile of the MBP parent,[153,154] including a close but

atypical relationship with the child and denial of any responsibility for the illness when presented with the staff's suspicions.

12. History of similar or unusual illnesses or early deaths in siblings.

13. Immunologic deficiencies, such as transient neutropenia, that are secondary to the infection.[155,156]

METHODS OF DETECTION

When MBP with induced or produced fever is present, the following approach will assist in either confirming or denying that suspicion.

1. A low index of suspicion and isolation of the child from the parents may be the key to early recognition.

2. Since some children have died of infections or drug overdoses while under medical surveillance,[157,158] the child's immediate safety should be the primary concern while decisions are made regarding further evaluation and treatment. Supervision should be provided by someone who is medically trained and fully aware of the potential threat posed by the perpetrator and her ability to manipulate health care providers to suit her ends.

3. It is equally important to rule out underlying pathology, allowing some latitude for variants of a disease without invoking explanations that are implausible.

4. Comparison of organisms from the laboratory culture and the suspected source of infection.[159]

5. Careful documentation of parental contact and correlation with the child's symptoms are also critical.

6. Culture of intravenous infusion simultaneously at different sites, including the container[160]

7. Toxicologic and pharmacokinetic analysis, which will will identify the presence of noxious drugs and interference with the therapeutic regimen. Because routine toxicology screens are often ineffective in detecting offending agents, undue reliance should not be placed on them, and specific assays should be obtained as the case warrants.[161]

8. Consultation with microbiologists and toxicologists will assist in identifying possible etiologies and developing a diagnostic plan that will ensure accurate results with minimum morbidity for the child.[162]

References

1. Feldman MD and Ford CV. *Patient or Pretender: Inside the Strange World of Factitious Disorders.* New York: Wiley; 1994:75–76.
2. Dingle JH, Badger GF, and Jordan WS. *Illness in the Home.* Cleveland: Press of Western Reserve Univ.; 1964: Ch. V.
3. Rosenberg DA. Web of deceit: a literature review of Munchausen syndrome by proxy. *Child Abuse Negl* 1987; 11:547–563.
4. Aduan RP, Fauci AS, Dale DC, et al. Factitious fever and self-induced infection: a report of 32 cases and review of the literature. *Ann Intern Med* 1979; 90:230–242.
5. Wood PR, Fowkles J, Holden P, and Casto D. Fever of unknown origin for six years: Munchausen syndrome by proxy. *J Fam Pract* 1989; 28:391–395.
6. Liston TE, Levine PL, and Anderson C. Polymycrobial bacteremia due to Polle syndrome: the child abuse variant of munchausen syndrome by proxy. *Pediatrics* 1983; 72:211–213.
7. Aduan et al., Factitious fever.
8. Edwards MS and Butler KM. "Hyperthermia or trickery" in an adolescent. *Pediatr Inf Dis.* 1987; 6:411–414.
9. MacNeal WJ. Hyperthermia, genuine and spurious. *Arch Int Med.* 1939; 64:800–808.
10. Hale V and Evseichick O. Fraudulent fever. *Am J Nurs.* 1943; 43:992–994.
11. Feigin Rd and Shearer WT. Fever of unknown origin in children. *Curr Prob Pediatr.* 1976; 6:1–65.
12. Lohr JA and Hendley JO. Prolonged fever of unknown origin. *Clin Pediatr.* 1977; 16:768–773.
13. McClung HJ. Prolonged fever of unknown origin in children. *Am J Dis Child.* 1972; 124:544–550.
14. Pizzo PA, Lovejoy FH, and Smith DH. Prolonged fever in children: review of 100 cases. *Pediatrics.* 1975; 55:468–473.
15. Sneed RC and Bell RF. The dauphin of munchausen: factitious passage of renal stones in a child. *Pediatrics.* 1976; 58:127–129.
16. McClung, Prolonged fever.
17. Aduan et al., Factitious fever.
18. Herzberg JH and Wolff SM. Chronic factitious fever in puberty and adolescence: a disgnostic challenge to the family physician. *Psychiatr in Med.* 1972; 3:205–212.
19. Rumans LW and Vosti KL. Factitious and fraudulent fever. *Am J Med.* 1978; 65:745–755.
20. McClung, Prolonged fever.
21. Aduan et al., Factitious fever.
22. Dine MS. Tranquilizer poisoning: an example of child abuse. *Pediatrics.* 1965; 36:782–785.
23. Fleischer D and Ament ME. Diarrhea, red diapers, and child abuse. *Clin Pediatr.* 1977; 16:820–824.
24. Herzberg and Wolff, Chronic factitious fever.

25. Hvizdala EV and Gellady AM. Intentional poisoning of two siblings by prescription drugs. *Clin Pediatr.* 1978; 17:480–482.
26. Kohl S, Pickering LK, and Dupree E. Child abuse presenting as immunodeficiency disease. *J Pediatr.* 1978; 95:466–468.
27. Liston et al., Polymicrobial bacteremia.
28. Meadow R. Munchausen syndrome by proxy. *Arch Dis Child.* 1982; 57:92–98.
29. Aduan et al., Factitious fever.
30. Edwards and Butler, Hyperthermia.
31. Herzberg and Wolff, Chronic factitious fever.
32. McClung, Prolonged fever.
33. Meadow, MBP.
34. Rumans and Vosti, Factitious.
35. Hawkings JR, Jones KS, Sim M, et al. Deliberate disability. *Br Med J.* 1956; 1:361–367.
36. Wood et al., Fever.
37. Meadow R. Munchausen syndrome by proxy: the hinterland of child abuse. *Lancet.* 1977; 2:343–345.
38. Herzberg and Wolff, Chronic factitous fever.
39. McClung, Prolonged fever.
40. Rumans and Vosti, Factitious.
41. Aduan et al., Factitious fever, p. 234.
42. Edwards and Butler, Hyperthermia, p. 411.
43. Aduan, Factitious fever. Herzberg, Chronic factitious fever.
44. Edwards and Butler, Hyperthermia.
45. Edwards and Butler, Hyperthermia.
46. MacNeal, Hyperthermia, p. 808.
47. Aduan et al., Factitious fever.
48. Feigin and Shearer, Fever.
49. Hale and Evseichick, Fraudulant fever.
50. Herzberg and Wolff, Chronic factitious fever.
51. Schnur S. Malingering responsible for long-continued, unexplained fever. *South Med J.* 1940; 33:768–769.
52. Aduan et al., Factitious fever.
53. Feigin and Shearer, Fever.
54. Herzberg and Wolff, Chronic factitious fever.
55. Aduan et al., Factitious fever.
56. Edwards and Butler, Hyperthermia.
57. Feigin and Shearer, Fever.
58. Aduan et al., Factitious fever.
59. MacNeal, Hyperthermia.
60. Aduan et al., Factitious fever.
61. Aduan et al., Factitious fever.
62. Herzberg and Wolff, Chronic factitious fever.
63. Schnurr, Malingering.

64. Aduan et al., Factitious fever.

65. Edwards and Butler, Hyperthermia.

66. Feigin and Shearer, Fever.

67. Schnurr, Malingering.

68. Edwards and Butler, Hyperthermia.

69. Edwards and Butler, Hyperthermia.

70. MacNeal, Hyperthermia.

71. Feigin and Shearer, Fever.

72. MacNeal, Hyperthermia.

73. Edwards and Butler, Hyperthermia.

74. Schnur, Malingering.

75. Rumans and Vosti, Factitious.

76. Bonadio WA. Polymicrobial bacteremia in children. *Am J Dis Child*. 1988; 142:1158–1160.

77. Amir J. Polymiucrobial bacteremia and child abuse. *Am J Dis Child*. 1989; 143:444 (letter).

78. Rosenberg, Web.

79. Dine, Tranquilizer poisoning.

80. Herzberg and Wolff, Chronic factitious fever.

81. Kohl et al., Child abuse.

82. Liston et al., Polymicrobial bacteremia.

83. Meadow, 1982.

84. Fleixcher and Ament, Diarrhea.

85. Hvizdala and Gellady, Intentional poisoning.

86. Aduan et al., Factitious fever.

87. Liston et al., Polymicrobial bacteremia.

88. Halsey N, Tucker TW, Redding J., et al. Recurrent nosocomial polymicrobial sepsis secondary to child abuse. *Lancet*. 1983; 2:558.

89. Kohl et al., Child abuse.

90. Raff MJ, Stodghill WB, and Roy TM. Fraudulent feculent fever in a female fabulist. *South Med J*. 1975; 68:360–362.

91. Aduan et al., Factitious fever.

92. Kohl et al., Child abuse.

93. Rosenberg, Web.

94. Halsey et al., Recurrent.

95. Aduan et al., Factitious fever.

96. Ackerman AB, Mosher DT, and Schwamm HA. Factitial Weber-Christian syndrome. *JAMA*. 1966; 198:155–160.

97. Duff A. Pyrexia of unusual origin. *Br Med J*. 1951; 2:549 (letter).

98. Laws JW. Pyrexia of unusual origin. *Br Med J*. 1951; 2:157–158.

99. Sigal M, Gelkopf M, and Meadow R. Munchausen by proxy syndrome: the triad of abuse, self-abuse, and deception. *Comp Psychiatr*. 1989; 30:527–533.

100. Aduan et al., Factitious fever.

101. Aduan et al., Factitious fever.

102. Kohl et al., Child abuse.

103. Hodge D, Schwartz W, Sargent J, et al. The bacteriologically battered baby: another case of munchausen syndrome by proxy. *Ann Emerg Med.* 1982; 11:205/77–207/79.
104. Liston et al., Polymicrobial bacteremia.
105. Samuels MP and Southall DP. Munchausen syndrome by proxy. *Br J Hosp Med.* 1992; 47:759–762.
106. Rubin LG, Angelides A, Davidson M, et al. Recurrent sepsis and gastrointestinal ulceration due to child abuse. *Arch Dis Child.* 1986; 61:903–905.
107. Halsey et al., Recurrent.
108. Kohl et al., Child abuse.
109. Rubin et al., Recurrent sepsis.
110. Halsey et al., Recurrent.
111. Koch C and Hoiby N. Severe child abuse presenting as polymicrobial bacteremia. *Acta Pediatr Scan.* 1988; 77:940–943.
112. Kohl et al., Child abuse.
113. Liston et al., Polymicrobial bacteremia.
114. Aduan et al., Factitious fever.
115. Aduan et al., Factitious fever.
116. Halsey et al., Recurrent.
117. Kohl et al., Child abuse.
118. Rubin et al., Recurrent sepsis.
119. Aduan et al., Factitious fever.
120. Koch and Hoiby, Severe.
121. Dine, Tranquilizer poisoning.
122. Aduan et al., Factitious fever.
123. Fleischer and Ament, Diarrhea.
124. Hvizdala and Gellady, Intentional poisoning.
125. Frederick et al., MBP.
126. Halsey et al., Recurrent.
127. Rogers et al., Non-accidental.
128. Wood et al., Fever.
129. Bonadio, Polymicrobial.
130. Hodge et al., Battered baby.
131. Bonadio, Polymicrobial.
132. Amir, Polymicrobial.
133. Hvizdala and Gellady, Intentional poisoning.
134. Amir, Polymicrobial.
135. Amir, Polymicrobial.
136. Halsey et al., Recurrent.
137. Halsey et al., Recurrent.
138. Palmer AJ and Yoshimura GJ. Munchausen syndrome by proxy. *J Am Acad Child Psychiatr.* 1984; 23:503–508.
139. Halsey et al., Recurrent.
140. Halsey et al., Recurrent.
141. Hodge et al., Battered baby.

142. Kohl et al., Child abuse.
143. Liston et al., Polymicrobial bacteremia.
144. Kohl et al., Child abuse.
145. Liston et al., Polymicrobial bacteremia.
146. Rubin et al., Recurrent sepsis.
147. Malatack JJ, Wiener ES, Gartner JC, et al. Munchausen syndrome by proxy: a new complication of central venous catheterization. *Pediatrics* 1985; 75:523–525.
148. Kohl et al. Child abuse.
149. Frederick V, Luedtke GS, Barrett FF, et al. Munchausen syndrome by proxy: recurrent central catheter sepsis. *Pediatr Infect Dis J.* 1990; 9:440–442.
150. Halsey et al., Recurrent.
151. Rubin et al., Recurrent sepsis.
152. Rogers D, Tripp J, Bentovim A, et al. Non-accidental poisoning: an extended syndrome of child abuse. *Br Med J.* 1976; 1:793–796.
153. Meadow R. MBP.
154. Rosenberg, Web.
155. Kohl et al., Child abuse.
156. Liston et al., Polymicrobial bacteremia.
157. Fleischer and Ament, Diarrhea.
158. Koch and Hoiby, Severe.
159. Halsey et al., Recurrent.
160. Halsey et al., Recurrent.
161. Rosenberg, Web.
162. Rogers et al., Non-accidental.

12

Alteration of Laboratory
Specimens and Test Results

Joseph M. Campos

Munchausen's Syndrome by Proxy (MBP) has attracted attention since its original description by Meadow in 1977.[1] His initial characterization of the syndrome referred to "parents who by falsification caused their children innumerable hospital procedures." One of the falsification techniques used frequently by such parents is the manipulation of their children and/or their children's laboratory specimens to generate abnormal test results. Such an approach has been favored because of its relative ease and likelihood of escaping detection. When coupled with a false medical history, abnormal laboratory results are generally sufficient to gain patients entry into the medical care system.

Simulated illnesses stem from deliberate parental misinformation and/or tampering with laboratory specimens to yield abnormal results. Deliberate poisoning, willful administration of inappropriate medications, and injection of infection-producing microorganisms are examples of illness-inducing measures which can transiently or permanently harm MBP victims. Approximately 75% of published cases of MBP describe induced illnesses. The reporting of simulated illnesses may be limited to those that are unusual or sensational in nature. Accordingly, literature surveys of MBP likely underestimate the overall magnitude of the problem. In her review of the MBP literature published between 1966 and 1987, Rosenberg concluded that alteration of laboratory test results, either before or after specimen collection, was a commonly used ploy to misdirect the efforts of medical personnel.[2]

Those who alter specimen or test results tend to exhibit predictable characteristics. They usually possess some level of medical knowledge or have access to medical expertise in order for the ruse to be successful. Altered test results cannot be so outlandish that they are physiologically unachievable. The victim typically is incapable of resisting, passively accepts the manipulation, or is completely unaware of the exploitation. Not surprisingly, victims tend to be younger than 6 years of age or mentally handicapped.

Laboratory results have been rendered abnormal by MBP perpetrators in very resourceful ways. The two most common approaches entail (1) surreptitious administration of result-altering medications prior to specimen collection, and (2) physical alteration of specimens after collection but before laboratory testing. The remainder of this chapter describes alteration techniques that have led to unnecessary, expensive, and sometimes dangerous workups of MBP patients.

Factitious Bleeding

The addition of blood to urine, feces, vomitus and other materials has been the most common specimen-alteration technique used by MBP perpetrators.[3] They usually obtain their own blood via finger stick or from menstrual flow and mix it with the child's specimen to feign hematuria, hematemesis, hemoptysis, or hematochezia/melena. In at least one instance, blood was removed from the victim's own indwelling subclavian intravenous catheter and used to simulate gastrointestinal and nasogastric bleeding.[4] Blood has even been smeared on the child's person or clothing to enhance the perception of a bleeding illness.

Outwater and co-workers presented the case of a 5-year-old girl with a history of persistent hematuria.[5] Initial workup yielded negative findings. When the child presented 2 months later with the same complaint and the workup was once again negative, the possibility of factitious hematuria was considered. The child was hospitalized and specimens collected by the mother continued to contain numerous erythrocytes and leukocytes but no casts. Conversely, specimens collected by medical personnel were all normal. A fresh specimen collected by the mother was centrifuged and the erythrocytes were antigen typed. The blood type matched that of the mother but not that of the child. The mother eventually admitted to adding her own blood, obtained by fingerstick, to her child's urine.

Discovery of similar scenarios reported by others has been achieved by detecting blood group/type antigens unique to the MBP perpetrator in the child's specimens.[6-8] Transfusion of a child victim with ^{51}Cr-labeled erythrocytes was a fortuitous approach used successfully by Kurlandsky and co-workers.[9] The absence of radioactivity in the child's bloody specimens confirmed the exogenous source of blood.

Factitious Coagulopathy

Related to the simulated bleeding disorders described above are induced hemorrhagic disorders caused by nontherapeutic administration of the anticoagulant warfarin, a problem that is well described in the adult Munchausen's Syndrome literature.[10] Similar cases in children, however, have been recognized only occasionally.

One childhood case was that of a 1-month-old female who presented with an acute left hemorrhagic otitis media and multiple hematomas.[11] Coagulation studies revealed elevated prothrombin time (PT) and partial thromboplastin time (PTT) results and the patient was given vitamin K1 intramuscularly. When the bleeding persisted she was given additional vitamin K1 and fresh frozen plasma intravenously. Because of a suspicion of warfarin ingestion, a serum sample from the child was tested and found positive at a pharmacologically active level. The authors recommended that the possibility of involuntary warfarin ingestion be entertained in children with unexplained, repetitive episodes of bleeding.

Factitious Diarrhea

Laxative abuse and deliberate manipulation of the diet are well established means of inducing diarrhea in MBP children.[12-14] Ex Lax (yellow phenolphthalein) is the laxative most commonly chosen, and its presence can be detected readily by red color development in alkalinized stools. The presence of other laxative compounds is more difficult to confirm, although assays for elevated concentrations of osmotic purgatives (e.g., magnesium sulfate), or anthracene derivatives (e.g., seena, cascara, and aloes) in stool have proved suc-

184 · *Munchausen Syndrome by Proxy*

cessful.[15] Induced diarrhea following ingestion of foods with high fiber content or high osmolality (e.g., apple juice) is very difficult to document by means other than direct continuous observation of the patient and parents.

An instance of MBP laxative abuse by a 34-month-old girl was chronicled by Ackerman and Strobel.[16] The patient had experienced a total of 186 outpatient visits at 6 different medical centers and 12 hospitalizations after the age of 19 months for dehydration and chronic intermittent diarrhea. Multiple workups had yielded normal findings. During the final admission the child had no diarrhea while receiving a one-quarter strength-infused elemental diet, but developed copious, watery diarrhea when the infusate was advanced to one-half strength. Alkalization of the stool water revealed a pink color change at pH 8.5. The mother later admitted giving laxatives to the child.

Factitious Hypoglycemia

Parents or family members with diabetes mellitus, medical personnel, and those who live in regions where they are sold over-the-counter have ready access to insulin and the syringes necessary for its injection. Accordingly, reports of children with exogenous insulin-induced hypoglycemia can be found in the MBP literature.[17,18] Confirmation of MBP was facilitated in one instance via use of species-specific insulin antibodies.[19] The presence of bovine rather than human insulin in the "diabetic" patient's blood stream proved the exogenous source of the insulin.

Probable substitution of a diabetic mother's urine for that of her 3-year-old child was recounted in a case report by Nading and Duval-Arnould.[20] The authors demonstrated that a series of glucose/ketone-positive specimens could not have come from a child being evaluated for diabetes because they were unable to detect ascorbic acid in her urine despite dietary supplementation with vitamin C (100 mg/kg).

Simulated Cystic Fibrosis

In an elaborate hoax to convince medical personnel that her son had cystic fibrosis, a mother falsified his history, withheld nutrition to make him appear chronically ill, added small quantities of salt to his sweat test specimens, added fat to his stools, and obtained sputum for culture (ostensibly for "research") from a true cystic fibrosis patient.[21] This case illustrates that even a complicated, multisystem disease can be imitated in a convincing fashion by a cunning mother with a background in nursing.

Induced Infection

One of the more hazardous forms of MBP is causation of infections via tampering with intravenous medications, manipulation of intravenous catheters, or direct injection of microorganisms into the blood stream. Not surprisingly, many victims of these manipulations present with polymicrobial bacteremia, an uncommon observation in pediatric patients and thus a warning sign for the possibility of MBP. Clinical findings suggestive of induced infection include recurrent episodes with multiple organisms, cellulitis/phlebitis in a patient who has had intravenous catheter insertion, lack of underlying immunodeficiency, and cessation of infections when the child is separated from a suspected perpetrator.

Multiple cases of induced infection are detailed in the literature. Those with particular significance for laboratory personnel are detailed here.

Kohl and co-workers described a 4-year-old child with recurrent severe infections secondary to repeated skin and intravenous fluid injection with oral and fecal microorganisms.[22] As a consequence, the child underwent a series of expensive immunologic workups to detect the cause of her "primary immunodeficiency." The perpetrator mother was eventually identified by a house officer who witnessed her administering an unauthorized injection.

Halsey and co-workers recounted the saga of an 8-year-old boy's 6-year history of polymicrobial sepsis that was eventually attributed to intravenous line contamination with vaginal and fecal flora from his mother.[23] As in many cases of this type, an extensive immunodeficiency workup was conducted to identify the cause of the child's medical problems, which resulted in 27 hospitalizations. As suspicion of child abuse accumulated, a court order was obtained to drastically limit visits to the boy's room. The child experienced a rapid recovery.

From the Scandinavian literature came a report of a 7-year-old boy with a history of chronic otitis media since the age of 5.[24] During the diagnostic episode he required hospital admission for *Pro-*

teus mirabilis otitis and bacteremia. His hospitalization was notable for 14 positive blood cultures in 20 days yielding growth of more than 10 different microorganisms. Permanent placement of a nurse at the patient's bedside eliminated any further episodes of bacteremia. Because his twin sister had suffered constant ear infections from the age of 5 months until her death at age 4, the mother was tried and convicted of criminal child abuse.

Frederick and co-workers[25] described MBP caused by the actions of a foster parent. The victim was a 22-month-old boy born with jejunal atresia which required surgical repair and insertion of an indwelling subclavian catheter for nutritional support. A series of 13 hospitalizations for catheter-related sepsis began at age 8 months and continued for the next 14 months. Recovery of a wide variety of microorganisms suggested either intentional contamination of the catheter or very poor technique. Permission was obtained to remove the child temporarily from the foster home. During that period the boy remained infection-free and he was subsequently placed in a permanent adoptive home.

Conclusion

The crucial components on the part of both clinicians and lab personnel in making a diagnosis of MBP are (1) being aware of the entity, (2) having a high index of suspicion, and (3) possessing the expertise necessary to reveal the deception. When the deception may involve alteration of specimens and test results, or when a suspected victim of MBP has test results inconsistent with the rest of the clinical picture, advice should be sought from knowledgeable individuals within the laboratory to reinforce the clinician's suspicion and devise strategies to confirm the diagnosis. Identification of MBP patients eliminates further unnecessary and expensive diagnostic workups, as well as protecting these patients from further abuse. Failure to act in a reasonable time frame can have devastating consequences to the victim.

References

1. Meadow R. Munchausen syndrome by proxy: the hinterland of child abuse. *Lancet*. 1977; 2:343–345.
2. Rosenberg DA. Web of deceit: a literature review of Munchausen syndrome

by proxy. *Child Abuse Negl.* 1987; 11:547–563.

3. Rosenberg, Web.

4. Malatack JJ, Wiener ES, Gartner JC, et al. Munchausen syndrome by proxy: a new complication of central venous catheterization. *Pediatrics.* 1985; 75:523–525.; 9:349–352.

5. Outwater KM, Lipnick RN, Luban NLC, et al. Factitious hematuria: diagnosis by minor blood group typing. *J Pediatr.* 1981; 98:95–97.

6. Salmon RF, Arant Jr BS, and Baum MG. Factitious hematuria with underlying renal abnormalities. *Pediatrics.* 1988; 82:377–379.

7. Yomtovian R and Swanger R. Munchausen syndrome by proxy documented by discrepant blood typing. *Am J Clin Pathol.* 1991; 95:232–233.

8. Bourchier D. Bleeding ears: case report of munchausen syndrome by proxy. *Aust Paediatr J.* 1983; 19:256–257.

9. Kurlandsky L, Lukoff JY, Zinkman WH, et al. Munchausen syndrome by proxy: definition of factitious bleeding in an infant by ^{51}Cr labeling of erythrocytes. *Pediatrics.* 1979; 63:228–231.

10. O'Reilly R and Aggeler PM. Overt anticoagulant ingestion: study of 25 patients and review of world literature. *Medicine.* 1976; 55:389–399.

11. White ST, Voter K, and Perry J. Surreptitious warfarin ingestion. *Child Abuse Negl.* 1985; 9:349–352.

12. Fleisher D and Ament ME: Diarrhea, red diapers, and child abuse. *Clin Pediatr.* 1977; 17:820–824.

13. Ackerman NB and Strobel CT: Polle syndrome: chronic diarrhea in munchausen's child. *Gastroenterology.* 1981; 81:1140–1142.

14. Volk D. Factitious diarrhea in two children. *Am J Dis Child.* 1982; 136:1027–1028.

15. Volk, Factitious.

16. Ackerman and Strobel, Polle syndrome.

17. Bauman WA and Yalow RS. Child abuse: parental insulin administration. *J Pediatr.* 1981; 99:588–591.

18. Mayefsky JH, Sarnik AP, and Postellon DC. Factitious hypoglycemia. *Pediatrics.* 1982; 69:804–805.

19. Bauman WA and Ualow RS. Child abuse: parenteral insulin administraton. *J Pediatr.* 1981; 99:588–591.

20. Nading JH and Duval-Arnould B. Factitious diabetes mellitus confirmed by ascorbic acid. *Arch Dis Child.* 1984; 59:166–179.

21. Orenstein DM and Wasserman AL. Munchausen syndrome by proxy simulating cystic fibrosis. *Pediatrics.* 1986; 78:621–624.

22. Kohl S, Pickering LK, and Dupree E. Child abuse presenting as immunodeficiency disease. *J Pediatr.* 1978; 95:466–468.

23. Halsey NA, Tucker TW, Redding J, et al. Recurrent nosocomial polymicrobial sepsis secondary to child abuse. *Lancet.* 1983; 2:558.

24. Koch C and Heiby N. Severe child abuse presenting as polymicrobial bacteremia. *Acta Paediatr Scand.* 1988; 77:940–943.

25. Frederick V, Ludetke GS, Barrett FF, et al. Munchausen syndrome by proxy: recurrent central catheter sepsis. *Pediatr Inf Dis.* 1990; 9:440.

13

Dermatologic Manifestations
Charles F. Johnson

Because of its accessibility, the skin provides the potential perpetrator of Munchausen Syndrome by Proxy (MBP) with a ready canvas upon which to create or simulate chronic illness. Although not all series of reviewed MBP cases show dermatologic manifestations, in a review of 19 children with MBP, "rashes" were among the symptoms in six (31%) children.[1] These were caused by rubbing the skin with a fingernail or object to create bullae, applying caustics, or painting the skin with a dye. Included in another review of 117 MBP cases were four (3.4%) reports of rash and 11 (9.4%) cases of easy bruising.[2] In addition, fabricated symptoms, with no physical findings, may be reported by perpetrators of MBP. It is unlikely that a report of MBP for chronic skin disease would be made unless lesions were actually seen by an examiner.

The skin has a broad repertoire of reactions to trauma (see Fig. 13–1). It can be bruised, lacerated, punctured, tattooed, or banded by a variety of objects. It can be burned with hot objects and liquids or with caustics,[3] or intentionally frozen.[4] Lesions may also be produced by the perpetrator's hands by pinching, scratching, or twisting, or by the perpetrator's mouth through suction marks or biting. Instruments such as combs or brushes can also be used to create skin lesions. The variety of potential traumatic agents and reactions may result in a panoply of skin conditions that can be mistaken for a disease (see Table 13–1). As with MBP of other systems, the creativity of technically sophisticated perpetrators may confound the most astute clinician. Balancing the potential for a perpetrator to create a variety of conditions, however, is the limited number of chronic skin conditions that can be accurately duplicated by trauma.

FIGURE 13–1

Methods of intentional trauma and their consequences. Mechanical trauma can be inflicted by abrading, accelerating into an object, banding, biting, impacting, lacerating, pinching, puncturing, injecting, scratching, sucking, tattooing, and traction. Burns may be inflicted with caustics, electricity, hot liquids, or hot objects. Infection may be introduced by a contaminated object or by inoculation from an infection on the host. Painting, though nontraumatic, may be used to create a variety of pigmented lesions.

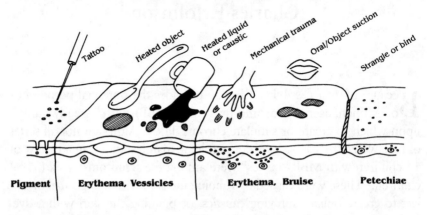

Table 13–1

Diseases that May Be Mimicked by Intentional Actions to the Skin

Action	Consequence	Disease Mimicked
Abrading	Erythema, vesiculation	Impetigo, atopic dermatitis, dermatitis herpetiformis
Accelerating into object	Bruises	Bleeding disorder
Banding	Scarring, amputation Lymphedema	Ainhum, frostbite pseudo ainhum Milroy's disease, filariasis, other lymphatic obstructions
Biting	Bruise, erythema	Tinea corporis, scabies
Burn from liquid or caustic	Erythema, vesicles	Impetigo, erysipelas, epidermolysis bullosa, drug reaction, shingles, bullous pyoderma, viral exanthem, tinea, chronic herpes

Table 13–1 (continued)

Action	Consequence	Disease Mimicked
		simplex, diaper dermatitis, atopic dermatitis, contact dermatitis, candida
Burn from object: car cigarette lighter, cigarette	Patterned burn	Tinea corporis erythema multiforme impetigo
Impacting	Bruise, erythema	Allergic skin reaction, bleeding disorder
Injecting: victim's blood, petroleum jelly, feces, milk, saliva, urine	Bleeding, eschars nodules, sinuses	Autoerythrocyte sensitization panniculitis, adenopathy
air	crepitation	infection, clostridium
Lacerating	Cut, scratch	Scratch marks from impetigo, sepsis, insect bites
Painting	Pigmentation	Burn, cyanosis, jaundice, rash
Pinching	Bruises	Bleeding disorder
Puncturing	Punctures, eschars	Insect bites, impetigo, sepsis, animal bites
Scratching or gouging	Cut, linear abrasion, gouge	Scratch marks from insect bites, impetigo, eczema, creeping eruption
Sucking	Erythema, ecchymosis	Bleeding problem
Tattooing	Pigment in patterns	Melanoma, Peutz-Jeghers Syndrome, hemangioma mastocytosis neurofibromatosis
Traction on hair	Hair loss	Tinea capitis, trichotillomania, alopecia areata, ectodermal dysplasia

If a child with an unusual, undiagnosed, or consternating skin disease were hospitalized for a diagnostic workup the perpetrator would need to either recreate the disease during hospitalization or take the discharged child home and generate the disease away from inquiring or observing eyes. Depending upon how the lesions were produced it might or might not be possible to recreate the disease in the hospital. The task of the clinician evaluating skin lesions in a child is to determine whether a particular pattern has been intentionally inflicted, and the purpose of that infliction. This chapter considers the more common skin presentations which raise the suspicion of child abuse, with special attention to the potential for mimicking typical or atypical diseases.

Ecchymosis

Accidental trauma or disease rarely results in symmetrical, paired, patterned, or geometric lesions (see Fig. 13–2). Such lesions should suggest the use of an instrument to cause intentional trauma.[5] The shape of the offending instrument may be silhouetted or outlined on the skin. Curved surfaces or surfaces overlying superficial bones, such as on the back, chest, or back of the hand[6] may affect the impact pattern and make recognition of the instrument more difficult. Bruises of various colors suggest injuries of various ages. They are not in keeping with a single injury incident and suggest nonaccidental trauma; however, extensive bruises of irregular shapes and different colors or petechiae may be mistaken for temporary or chronic defects in clotting mechanisms (Table 13–1). The possibility that recurrent bruises caused by mechanical trauma may be caused by a bleeding disorder can be ruled out by completing appropriate bleeding and clotting studies. Bleeding problems which manifest themselves on the skin may also be caused by poisoning the child with drugs, some readily available such as aspirin or warfarin-based rat poison,[7] or prescription drugs that increase the clotting time. Because a child's symptoms may be a result of intentional poisoning, a toxin and drug screen should be part of the diagnostic repertoire for any child with an unusual, persistent, or confusing skin condition.

Children with an existing bleeding disorder may also be traumatized, perhaps with the purpose of exaggerating the disease, and the resulting injuries then mistakenly attributed to the underlying condition.[8] The diagnosis of a genuine coagulopathy does not make a child immune from

MBP. It is not uncommon for the symptoms and signs generated by the MBP perpetrator to have their foundation in the symptoms and signs of a genuine illness. The location of induced bruises in children with bleeding disorders may not be on surfaces that are readily traumatized by accidental impacts such as the skin overlying the tibias, ulna, or brow. Bruises on other surfaces may suggest induced trauma.

Erythema and Vesiculation from Burns

By rubbing the skin the perpetrator can induce erythema or vesicles that may be mistaken for a burn or a bullous skin condition.[9]

FIGURE 13–2
Petechiae in a pattern. This child, admitted after becoming unconscious from a fall from a high chair, had 15–20 1-mm bruises in a pattern on the left cheek and in front of the left ear. The marks matched the pattern on the sole of the father's slipper. A similar mark could result from pressure from a styling brush. A comb would produce a similar series of marks in a line.

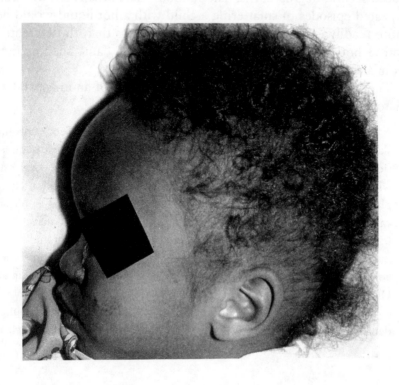

Contact with flames, heated objects, or caustic substances can result in first-, second-, or third-degree burns. As with a bruise, the shape of the burn from a heated object may mimic the shape of the instrument used. The pattern may be varied or indistinct because the instrument was unevenly heated, variously shaped surfaces of an instrument were applied to the skin, or different instruments were used. Burns from hot liquid poured onto a child or from immersion are unlikely to be repeated or mistaken for a chronic skin disease, although this has occurred. Ingestion of a liquid or granular caustic may result in severe burns to the mouth, throat, and esophagus.[10,11] Liquid caustics, such as acids, alkalies, phenol, and silver nitrate applied to the skin should cause burn patterns similar to those from noncaustic liquids. The depth of the tissue injury would reflect the length of contact with and concentration of the caustic. Granular caustics or droplets of liquid caustics might create unique burn patterns that are more likely to be confused with an unusual skin condition.[12] First-degree burns could be confused with infectious or allergic processes. There are few chronic bullous skin conditions which could be confused with intentionally produced second-degree burns. The random size burns resulting from repeated episodes of splattering a child with a hot liquid would be more readily confused with an organic process than those created with a hot object such as a cigarette or small flame such as that from a cigarette lighter.[13]

The following is a previously unreported case of an unusual dermatologic manifestation of MBP.

A 1-year-old child was admitted to hospital for evaluation of "chronic skin vesicles." The lesions had first appeared 2 months prior to admission. The child had been seen in pediatric clinic on several occasions with crops of vesicles. A cause for the skin problem had eluded clinic physicians. The child was well nourished and in no distress. The physical examination was normal except for skin lesions that consisted of 0.5 cm round vesicles in pairs. Each pair of lesions was separated by an intervening 1.5 cm of normal skin (see Fig. 13–3). The lesions were confined to the ventral surface of the abdomen, chest, and thighs. Older lesions on the chest and abdomen were healing as hyperpigmented scars (see Fig. 13–3). The mother, who had no medical background, denied that the child had any other chronic illness. Cultures of clear vesicle fluid were negative as were basic laboratory tests. A dermatologist was unable to associate this "chronic vesiculating dermatitis" with any known skin condition.

Over a 4-day period the vesicles resolved. No new lesions appeared during hospitalization. The uniform shape of the paired lesions and the separation by the same distance suggested burning with a hot object with two points or prongs. The mother was confronted with the staff conclusion that the child had been intentionally burned. She admitted creating the lesions by heating a cooking fork and applying it to the child's skin.

FIGURE 13–3

Chronic paired vesicular eruption. There are two "crops" of round, paired vesicles on the infant's thigh. Similar lesions that appeared on the chest are in various stages of healing. The lesions were created by application of a heated cooking fork to the child's skin by the mother.

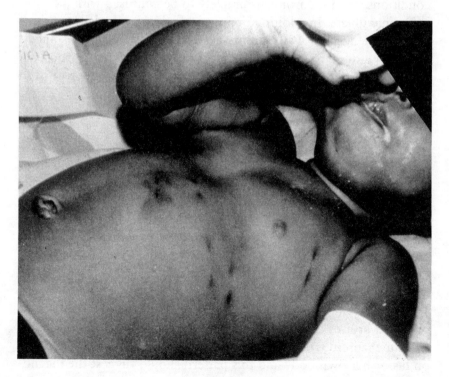

Treatments that Injure the Skin

Scratching the skin with cold or warm objects, a folk medicine practice referred to as Cai Gao[14-16] may result in parallel abrasions or burns on the front or back of the chest. In this condition, the parents are not trying to mimic or create a disease. Rather they are trying to cure or mollify an existing genuine illness. The unsophisticated observer may confuse these marks with child abuse. Cupping, coining, and moxibustion are other folk medicine practices that result in temporary or permanent lesions. Cupping can cause raised erythematous lesions with petechiae that are circular and the same size as the opening of the heated container which was applied to the skin. Coining may result in multiple small curvilinear bruises. In moxibustion the skin is burned with a heated object. Garlic, if applied to the skin over a prolonged period, may cause second-degree burns which, if severe, heal with scarring.[17]

All of these techniques could be used to simulate a chronic skin condition; however, the type and pattern of injury in these folk conditions, even if chronic, is unlikely to be confused with a chronic organic illness. In addition, if approached in a culturally sensitive and knowledgeable way, parents using the practices as folk medicine may admit to causing the lesions. The parents' purpose in using these folk remedies is, of course, quite different from the quest to simulate illness which characterizes MBP.

Scratches, Lacerations, Punctures, and Pigments

Depending upon the location and pattern, lesions which result from scratching or digging the skin could mimic chronic skin conditions such as eczema, scabies, or flea bites (see Table 13–1) in which the child scratches in response to a genuine stimulus. In self-mutilation the "distinctive, clean cut" lesions would be limited to accessible areas of the body, and do not generally involve the dominant hand or wrist.[18] The mother and her child or children may present with the same fictitious skin condition in various stages of healing.[19,20]

The skin can be sucked by mouth (see Fig. 13–4) to create oval or round bruises commonly referred to as hickeys or monkey bites. In Munchausen Syndrome, the individual sucks accessible surfaces on his or her own body and this pattern should suggest the diagnosis. In MBP any surface can be traumatized. The regularity of size and shape should preclude mistaking the lesions for a chronic organic skin condition or skin manifestation of a bleeding disorder. Human bites, because of their distinct pattern, are unlikely to be mistaken for a disease process. The reader is referred elsewhere in the child abuse literature for discussions of this important manifestation of child abuse which to our knowledge has not been reported as a manifestation of MBP.

The skin can be traumatized by pinching or twisting. Like marks from oral suction, the resulting bruises would be of uniform size and shape and not be confused with an organic disease. Appendages can be intentionally banded with resulting erythema, swelling, and eventual amputation.[21] The results can be mistaken for rare conditions, such as ainhum or lymphedema due to filariasis, Milroy's disease, or other conditions.[22,23]

Topical infection may be induced by abrading, puncturing, or

FIGURE 13–4

Series of blue oval bruises resulting from oral suction along the upper back and shoulder of an adolescent female were placed there by her father. This was reported as sexual abuse.

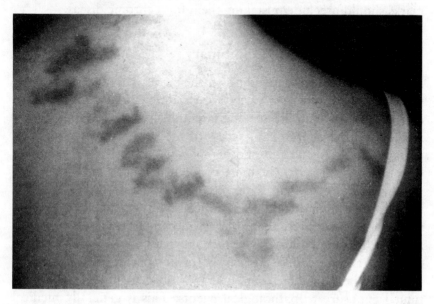

cutting the surface of the skin with a contaminated object or by introducing infected material such as stool or saliva into a wound.[24] Bleeding from cuts or punctures to the mouth and nose may simulate bleeding disorders.[25] Pharmacologically active materials injected into the body may have no effect on the skin other than the minute injury at the injection site. Other agents, such as petroleum jelly, feces, milk, saliva, and urine injected subcutaneously may cause sterile or infected nodules or sinuses that simulate panniculitis.[26] An infant with autoerythrocyte sensitization syndrome, apparently the result of intentional injection of blood into the skin, was reported to have episodes of "a pink flush followed by droplets of blood which oozed through the skin." These areas became small, raised and crusted lesions which appeared in a "longitudinal direction" over the child's chest, back, abdomen, and arms.[27]

The skin may be punctured with a pencil or other object that has been dipped into pigment with a resultant tattoo.[28] Intentional coloring of the skin for cosmetic or cultural reasons may be mistaken for child abuse.[29] The surface of the skin can be stained or painted with a variety of pigments. A bath or solvent may remove applied coloring and, without sophisticated, expensive, and unnecessary laboratory analysis, reveal the etiology of hyperpigmentation. The shape, distribution, and permanence or lack of permanence of the marks should preclude mistaking them for a chronic disease.

Summary

Perpetrators of MBP, depending on their creativity and medical sophistication, can create a variety of conditions that mimic organic disease. Parents who are seeking attention for a medical condition in their child can even gain access to the same dermatology texts used by physicians to find photographs of skin diseases. It is possible that a physician may be more concerned about a skin condition, which can be seen, than symptoms or processes that are reported by a parent and not observed clinically. Physicians must be cognizant of the possibility that a variety of common, as well as unusual or bizarre skin conditions, can be created purposely. In addition, existing genuine conditions can be prolonged or exaggerated by failure of the caretaker to provide prescribed treatment or by continued exposure to pathological agents. This is generally medical neglect; however, it may be a variant of MBP when secondary gain is obtained from the disease.

If a skin condition (1) has a varying history of causation, (2) appears unusual in pattern or location, (3) persists despite appropriate treatment, (4) appears only in the presence of a particular caretaker, (5) resolves under observation by professionals (especially when a specific caretaker is denied access to the child or in areas where the skin is securely protected by a dressing),[30] or (6) resembles an unusual skin condition in the mother, then MBP should be suspected.

References

1. Meadow R. Munchausen syndrome by proxy. *Arch Dis Child.* 1982; 59:92–98.
2. Rosenberg DA. Web of deceit: a literature review of Munchausen syndrome by proxy. *Child Abuse Negl.* 1987; 547–563.
3. Johnson CF and Showers J. Injury variables in child abuse. *Child Abuse Negl.* 1985; 9:207–215.
4. Shafer N and Shafer R. Factitious diseases including munchausen's syndrome. *NY State J Med.* 1985; 80:594–604.
5. Johnson CF. Inflicted injury vs. accidental injury. *Ped Clin N Am.* 1990; 37:791–814.
6. Johnson CF, Kaufman KL, and Callendar C. The hand as a target organ in child abuse. *Clin Pediatr.* 1990; 29:66–72.
7. White ST, Voter K, and Perry J. Surreptitious warfarin ingestion. *Child Abuse Negl.* 1985; 9:349–352.
8. Johnson CF and Coury DL. Bruising and hemophilia: accident or child abuse? *Child Abuse Negl.* 1988; 12:409–415.
9. Meadow, MBP.
10. Dine MS and McGovern ME. Intentional poisoning of children—an overlooked category of child abuse: Report of seven cases and a review of the literature. *Pediatrics.* 1982; 70:32–35.
11. Friedman EM. Caustic ingestion and foreign body aspirations: an overlooked form of child abuse. *Ann Oto Rhinol Laryngol.* 1987; 96:709–712.
12. Meadow, MBP.
13. Johnson, Inflicted.
14. Yeatman GW. Pseudobattering in Vietnamese children. *Pediatrics.* 1976; 58:617–618.
15. Gellis S and Feingold M. Cao gio: pseudobattering in Vietnamese children. *Am J Dis Child.* 1976; 130:837–858.
16. Yeatman GW. Cao Gio (coin rubbing): Vietnamese attitudes toward health care. *JAMA.* 1980; 244:2748–2749.
17. Garty B. Garlic burns. *Pediatrics.* 1993; 91:658–659.
18. Shafer and Shafer, Factitious.

19. Jones DPH. Dermatitis artefacta in mother and baby as child abuse. *Br J Psychiatr*. 1983; 143;199–200.
20. Stankler L. Factitious skin lesions in a mother and two sons. *Br J Derm*. 1977; 97:219–219.
21. Johnson CF. Constricting bands; manifestations of possible child abuse. *Clin Pediatr*. 1988; 27:439–444.
22. Shafer and Shafer, Factitious.
23. Johnson, Bands.
24. Kohl S, Pickering LK, and Dupree E. Child abuse presenting as immunodeficiency disease. *J Pediatr*. 1978; 93:466–468.
25. Kurlandsky L, Lukoff JY, Zinkham Wh, et al. Munchausen syndrome by proxy: definition of factitious bleeding in an infant by Cr labeling of erythrocytes. *Pediatrics*. 1979; 63:228–231.
26. Shafer and Shafer, Factitious.
27. Clark GD, Key JD, Rutherford P. et al. Munchausen's syndrome by proxy (child abuse) presenting as apparent autoerythrocyte sensitization syndrome: an unusual presentation of Polle syndrome. *Pediatrics*. 1984; 74:1100–1102.
28. Johnson CF. Symbolic scarring and tattooing: unusual manifestations of child abuse. *Clin Pediatr*. 1994; 33:46–49.
29. Meadow, MBP.
30. Jones, Dermatitis.

14

Allergic Manifestations
Dirk Huyer

One of the warning signals cited to alert physicians to the possible diagnosis of Munchausen Syndrome by Proxy (MBP) is the parental report that a child is allergic to a great variety of foods and drugs.[1] Allergy has been frequently reported in case presentations of MBP, occasionally as the main illness[2] but more frequently as an associated feature.[3-12] The following case examples are illustrative.

CASE ONE[13]

Two children, aged 7 and 10, were presented to an allergy clinic by their single mother with complaints of asthma and hyperactivity. Mother stated that the conditions resulted from allergies to six foods, house dust mites, and feathers. Mother had instituted dietary restrictions and insisted that the children sleep on the back of an upturned wardrobe, wrapped in toilet paper and silver foil rather than blankets. Evaluation included prick skin testing and food challenges. These revealed sensitivity to house dust mites in both children. No abnormalities were found though food challenges. Frequent school absences were reported resulting in a brief period in foster care. When mother was confronted with the evidence that the children did not have food allergy, she created havoc in the hospital waiting area. She subsequently threatened legal action for negligence in making her son very ill in hospital although he was observed to be healthy throughout his stay.

CASE TWO

An 8-year-old boy was admitted to the gastroenterology department with a history of recurrent abdominal pain for which he was taking four gastrointestinal medications. His mother was a registered nurse. His medical history was complicated by reported diabetes insipidus, malignant hyperthermia, and a seizure disorder. Numerous medications had been prescribed by the numerous physicians involved. Optimal drug levels and seizure control were difficult to obtain. Development of numerous medication allergies was reported by mother. The allergic symptoms included skin rash, mouth ulcers, and behavior disturbances. The symptoms were delayed in onset, appearing after days to weeks of treatment. Examination revealed a well-nourished and well-developed healthy boy. Gradual removal of all medications including anticonvulsants was completed without any observed abdominal pain or seizures. Review of the child's past medical record revealed clear evidence of fabrication. Three other siblings also were diagnosed as victims of MBP. Mother denied the allegations and continued to fabricate illness. The child has thrived without illness in foster care.

Allergic disorders are adverse physiologic reactions that result from immunological mechanisms involving interactions of antigens with antibodies or lymphocytes.[14] These interactions typically cause a hypersensitivity state demonstrated by various symptoms ranging in severity from mild to severe. Possible symptoms include itchy eyes, rhinitis, hives, exacerbations of asthma, and anaphylactic shock. Food and drug reactions that may not demonstrate specific immunological mechanisms are often included in allergy discussions because the reactions resemble typical allergic reactions. The most important method of diagnosis in allergic diseases is careful historical inquiry. Physical examination and laboratory testing may be contributory but often will be normal or reveal nonspecific findings. For this reason, ruling out the presence of allergy or food intolerance can be particularly difficult especially when the history is convincing.[15] Because of the lack of objective findings, especially in cases of food intolerance, physicians tend to accept the parental description when diagnosing these disorders. Fabrication of allergic disorders is therefore not difficult. In the second case example above, the described allergic reactions may have been true reactions demonstrating the consequence of unnecessary treatment or part of a fabricated pattern of ineffective treatments. Yet multiple difficulties with drug levels and seizure control were observed prior to the development of proposed allergic reactions.

One of Meadow's warning signals for MBP is the finding that multiple treatments are ineffective or poorly tolerated.[16] Paradoxically, because perpetrators of MBP typically know that prescribed medication is not actually required, they may not give the drugs to the child. The perpetrators may then claim or fabricate allergic reactions to eliminate use of the medication. Drug reactions that are unusual and without previous documentation either by a medical caretaker's observation or by prior report in the medical literature warrant consideration of fabrication. This is especially true when the reactions are included in the picture of a child who presents as a medical enigma displaying many of the other warning signals that have been identified for MBP.[17]

Food Allergy

Food allergy or intolerance is felt by many people to be a potential cause of disease even in the absence of objective evidence, and such beliefs about food may be induced by media reports or temporal relationships between food consumption and appearance of symptoms. Many symptoms are proposed to result from different foods. Elimination diets may be prescribed and followed to prevent such reactions. Occasionally such beliefs are irrationally fixed or are manipulated to produce the false appearance of a sick child. Sixteen children seen at an allergy clinic for behavior problems attributed to food intolerance were felt to be the victims of MBP.[18] Food intolerance was the presenting feature. In each of the cases evaluation failed to demonstrate clinical correlation between the behavior and the proposed food intolerance. The maternal obsession with avoidance of the implicated substances resulted in bizarre diets and lifestyles. Many of the allergy concerns had been initiated by physicians involved in the child's prior care. When presented with information that allergic disease was unlikely, the mothers refused to accept the opinion and maintained diets against advice.

Victims of MBP may demonstrate failure to thrive when food is withheld because of described food intolerance. A case example illustrating illness production coupled with fabrication follows.

An 18-month-old girl was admitted because of prolonged diarrhea and vomiting attributed by her mother to a reaction to tobramycin injections. A bizarre neurologic reaction to a Hemophilus immunization was also described along with a history of recurrent urinary tract infections and hematuria. Both parents described the child as a good eater without food intolerance. The child had gained weight well for the first 6 months of life but her weight had dropped well below the third percentile by admission. No physical abnormality was discovered through extensive urological testing. The mother, a registered nurse, went on to describe significant unexplained illness in her own past including seizures, "tunnel vision," renal failure, and gynecological problems. While in hospital the child had a period of unresponsiveness secondary to toxic ingestion of Lorazepam. Review of the past medical records revealed evidence of illness fabrication. Family members provided information that the child's mother was knowingly withholding food, citing food intolerance. Despite mother's requests to the contrary, the family members provided the child with the described food without incident. The child was placed in foster care where she thrived, returning to the tenth percentile for weight within 3 weeks.

Parental Anxiety and MBP

Increased public awareness has developed about substances present in the environment. Possible adverse effects are frequently discussed in the media, captivating the public imagination. Parents may perceive their children as suffering various ailments resulting from adverse or allergic reactions to such substances. Children may be presented with symptoms ranging from minor illness to the rare "Twentieth Century Disease" where the sufferer is thought to be allergic to many or all environmental substances. Parents may become exceedingly anxious about minor symptoms that they observe in their child and may seek out medical evaluations. Physicians, in an effort to reassure parents, may request laboratory testing. This additional step of evaluation is often perceived by the parent as validation for their concern. Anxiety may then be magnified by the lack of objective findings and definitive answers following medical evaluation. The resultant anxiety and uncertainty may lead parents to perceive symptoms in their child that others cannot observe.[19]

Because of concern for the well-being of the child, further medical evaluations may be sought from different doctors.

Parental anxiety that appears to be greater than expected in view of the presenting complaint is not uncommon when children are seen by physicians.[20] It is important for the physician to recognize and explore the underlying reason for the anxiety displayed. There are frequently unverbalized fears that the symptoms represent something more serious than the presenting picture. These fears may result from a variety of sources, some of which include past history of similar disease, fear of such dread diseases as cancer, fear of illness of vital organs, and from suggestions of illness by authority figures.[21] Allowing parents to verbalize these fears permits discussion that may help to resolve the anxiety and eliminate the need for unnecessary testing. Such parents have been previously labeled as "help seekers."[22] It may be difficult to draw a clear line between overanxious help seekers and a mild form of MBP.

Persistence in presentation of a child for diagnosis and treatment can be examined by exploring whether it is congruent with the child's morbidity.[23] The primary concerns as well as those underlying the persistence should be evaluated for congruence. If incongruent persistence is suspected, then the possibility of parental fabrication must be considered.

Management

A careful history, physical examination, and the minimum laboratory testing possible should be done in cases of suspected MBP presenting with allergy as the primary complaint. An allergist should be consulted for advice and assistance. Documentation of previously reported reactions should be reviewed and compared with the present picture. Information should be gathered from other witnesses who observed the reaction(s). If the parent is persistently presenting the child, complete past medical records should be reviewed for evidence of illness fabrication or production.

Allergy must be remembered as a possible feature in many cases of MBP. Because objective testing is not always available, absolute proof of allergy fabrication may not be achieved. Review of the allergy history must always be included in evaluations of suspected cases.

References

1. Meadow R. Management of Munchausen syndrome by proxy. *Arch Dis Child.* 1985; 60:385–393.
2. Warner JO and Hathaway MJ. Allergic form of Meadow's syndrome (munchausen by proxy). *Arch Dis Child.* 1984; 59:151–156.
3. Meadow R. Munchausen syndrome by proxy. *Arch Dis Child.* 1982; 57:92–98.
4. Meadow R. Fictitious epilepsy. *Lancet.* 1984; 2:25–28.
5. Meadow, Management.
6. Guandolo VL. Munchausen syndrome by proxy: an outpatient challenge. *Pediatrics.* 1985; 75:526–530.
7. Nichol AR, Eccles M. Psychotherapy for Munchausen syndrome by proxy. *Arch Dis Child.* 1985; 60:344–348.
8. Rosenberg DA. Web of deceit: a literature review of Munchausen syndrome by proxy. *Child Abuse Negl.* 1987; 11:547–563.
9. Sullivan CA, Francis GL, Bain MW, et al. Munchausen syndrome by proxy: 1990 a portent for problems? *Clin Pediatr.* 1991; 30:112–116.
10. Bools CN, Neale BA, and Meadow SR. Co-morbidity associated with fabricated illness (Munchausen syndrome by proxy). *Arch Dis Child.* 1992; 142:1158–1160.
11. Gray J and Bentovim A. Identification and management of cases of induced illness within a pediatric setting. (Paper presentation at Ninth National Conference on Child Abuse and Neglect, Denver, 1991.
12. Samuels MP and Southall DP. Munchausen syndrome by proxy. *Br J Hosp Med.* 1992; 47:759–762.
13. Warner and Hathaway, Allergic form.
14. Behrman RE and Vaughan VC. *Nelsons Textbook of Pediatrics.* Philadelphia: Saunders; 1987:480–513.
15. Warner and Hathaway, Allergic form.
16. Meadow, Management.
17. Meadow, Management.
18. Warner and Hathaway, Allergic form.
19. Meadow R. Commentary. *Arch Dis Child.* 1991; 66:960.
20. Bass LW and Cohen RL. Ostensible vs. actual reasons for seeking pediatric attention: another look at the parental ticket of admission. *Pediatrics.* 1982; 70:870–874.
21. Bass and Cohen, Ostensible.
22. Libow JA and Schreier HA. Three forms of factitious illness in children: when is it munchausen syndrome by proxy? *Am J Orthopsychiat.* 1986; 56:602–611.
23. Waring WW. The persistent parent. *Am J Dis Child.* 1992; 146:753–756.

15

Ophthalmic Manifestations

Alex V. Levin

Ocular signs and symptoms are a rare and often nonspecific manifestation of Munchausen Syndrome by Proxy (MBP). In fact, there are only three reported cases in which the most prominent feature of the clinical scenario was an induced ocular abnormality.[1-3] More often, the ocular manifestation is an indirect effect that appears secondary to another systemic event, usually poisoning, that is the main mode by which MBP is being perpetrated. In her MBP literature review, Rosenberg cited only nystagmus as an ocular sign, with just two references.[4] The rarity of primary ocular injury in MBP as compared to secondary involvement may be related to the inaccessibility of intraocular structures, the relative ease with which certain ophthalmic manifestations may be revealed as factitious (e.g., feigned visual loss is often quite easy to recognize), and the prominent link between certain neurophthalmic signs and the causative systemic problem.

Ocular Surface Abnormalities

Taylor and Bentovim unknowingly published in 1976 (before Meadow's 1977 classic description of MBP), what would today clearly be considered a case of MBP.[5] Two siblings were victims of presumed instillation of a noxious substance into their eyes by their father. Extensive systemic and ocular evaluations revealed no other explanation for the episodes of recurrent painful hemorrhagic conjunctivitis with associated keratitis and lid swelling which eventually rendered at least one of the children permanently legally blind.

Excepting the fact that the father was the perpetrator, the parents showed many features consistent with a diagnosis of MBP. The inflammation only occurred when the children were under paternal supervision, including one occasion when a nurse responded to the baby's screams from the hospital playroom, where the male infant was in the father's arms. The daughter required psychiatric intervention at 7 years of age as she was acting in a provocative manner and expressing "fantasies of a baby digging a knife into" its eyes. The recurring acute ocular problems disappeared after placement of the children in foster care.

It is noteworthy in these two children that the ocular damage was largely confined to the inferior half of the cornea, with extensive scarring of the inferior conjunctival sac. This may be characteristic of forced instillation of a noxious substance into the eyes, as the natural protective mechanism of the body would usually be to rotate the eyeballs into extreme upgaze (Bell phenomenon). In addition, one of the children also had periocular (glabellar) excoriations associated with one episode, and one child also showed a pupillary membrane consistent with secondary iritis.

Pupillary Abnormalities

In the absence of other signs suggestive of a third cranial nerve palsy, central nervous system disease, ocular disease, orbital disease, or blunt ocular trauma, one must consider pharmacologic manipulation of the pupils in any case of unequal pupil size.[6] One must remember, however, that a small amount of anisocoria with normally reactive pupils and with maintenance of the relative difference in pupil size in both dim and bright illumination is a not uncommon normal variant (physiologic anisocoria).

In only one reported case was a pupillary disturbance directly induced as one of the major manifestations of MBP.[7] After her mother had successfully obtained an atropine nebulizer for the treatment of what later proved to be factitious asthma, the 4-year-old patient began having episodes of unequal pupil size, presumably caused by covert instillation of atropine into one eye. More often, the pupils are involved as a secondary effect of accidental systemic poisoning. Deonna and co-workers reported a child with recurrent coma and seizures from presumed poisoning based on the child's history (toxicology screen was not revealing) in which there were miotic (constricted) nonreactive pupils on seven different admissions and midposition pupils on an eight.[8] Bilateral constricted pupils have been reported in MBP poisoning with dihydrocodeine.[9] Bilateral miosis may be induced by topical or systemic sympatholytics or parasympathomimetics including narcotics. Likewise, bilateral mydriasis (dilated pupils) can be caused by topical or systemic sympathomimetics or parasympatholytics.

Oculomotor Abnormalities

Oculomotor abnormalities including nystagmus and strabismus have been reported in MBP as a secondary manifestation of systemic neurologic events or poisoning. In their review, Fisher and Mitchell[10] state that nystagmus has previously been reported as a neurologic manifestation of MBP, but this statement is not supported by case material or a referenced citation. Nystagmus has been reported in MBP poisoning in association with ataxia and altered mental status caused by barbiturates[11] and with "writhing" movements, twitching, hypotension, and ventricular tachycardia caused by imipramine.[12] Nystagmus can be induced by various pharmacologic agents, some of which have been reported in the perpetration of MBP. (see Table 15–1)

Strabismus may be induced by the central nervous system or neuromuscular effect of many drugs.[13,14] Otherwise, it is difficult to

Table 15–1
Drugs That May Cause Nystagmus[22, 23]

Alcohol
Anticonvulsants*
Barbiturates*
Lithium carbonate
Monoamine Oxidase Inhibitors
Phenothiazines*
Tricyclic Antidepressants*

*Reported in MBP

imagine how strabismus might be simulated. One mother gave a history that her child, who was being evaluated for fabricated hearing loss, had previously had "pseudobulbar palsy."[15] This could not be confirmed by a review of the child's medical records. The case reported by Deonna and co-workers, discussed above, also presented with strabismus, although no further details were given and the presumed drug was never identified. It is interesting that the strabismus was only noted once, yet pupillary abnormalities were noted on eight of nine admissions. This may suggest that the perpetrator used more than one drug.

Periorbital Cellulitis and Other Injuries

Feenstra and co-workers reported an unusual case in which the maternal grandmother, serving as foster mother, was the perpetrator.[3] She repeatedly injected the parotid gland of her 1-year-old granddaughter with a metallic substance that caused unilateral chronic parotitis.[16] The diagnosis was made at the time of partial parotid excision for treatment of a secondary abscess. On another occasion, the child developed unexplained periorbital and secondary severe orbital cellulitis, presumably from another injection, although needle marks were never found. Pickford and co-workers reported a family in which there were multiple complex factitious signs and symptoms resulting from a combination of poisoning, direct trauma, and falsified histories.[17] On one occasion the affected infant daughter presented with periocular bruising which was attributed to an accidental injury sustained in sibling play. On another occasion the mother reported a history of "blindness" in her son.

Petechiae of the eyelids may be a sign of covert smothering.[18] I have observed subconjunctival hemorrhages in several cases of attempted suffocation, although these cases were always acute events with severe neurologic compromise, other signs of nonaccidental injury, and no history consistent with MBP.

Visual Disturbances

In any child with unexplained visual loss, a formal consultation by a pediatric ophthalmologist can be instrumental in elucidating the cause. Drugs that cause true visual compromise do so in most cases by clinically observable changes in the ocular structures such as corneal deposits, retinal pigmentary changes, or optic neuropathy. Children with functional visual loss can be "tricked" into seeing normally by a number of specialized tests and benign manipulations using ophthalmic refracting devices and optical tools. Functional visual loss is a well-recognized entity in childhood which may also be the presenting complaint in cases of covert child abuse, in particular sexual abuse.[19] However, it is difficult to understand how a perpetrator of MBP might induce a visual disturbance in a child without having any direct physical effect on the brain or eyeball. The mother reported by Kahn gave a history of "cortical blindness" in her child, but subsequent review of the child's old medical records failed to confirm this diagnosis or even reveal it as a previous complaint.[20]

The multitude of drugs that could cause a reduction in visual acuity by virtue of their effect on the cornea, retina, or optic nerve is beyond the scope of this discussion.[21] Any of these drugs, if given covertly, might cause an unexplained loss of vision. Fisher and Mitchell describe "defects of vision" as a type of chronic illness seen in MBP, but no clinical material, further explanation, or cited references are given. Perhaps MBP, in the form of falsification of historical symptoms, should be considered in cases of chronic visual complaints without organic cause that persist despite normal eye examinations.

References

1. Taylor D and Bentovim A. Recurrent nonaccidentally inflicted chemical eye injuries to siblings. *J Pediatr Ophthalmol.* 1976; 13:238–242.
2. Wood PR, Fowlkes J, Holden P, et al. Fever of unknown origin for six years: Munchausen syndrome by proxy. *J Fam Pract.* 1989; 28:391–395.
3. Feenstra J, Merth IT, and Treffers PD. A case of Munchausen syndrome by proxy. *Tijdschrift Voor Kindergeneeskunde.* 1988; 56:148–53.
4. Rosenberg DA. Web of deceit: A literature review of Munchausen syndrome by proxy. *Child Abuse Negl.* 1987; 11:547–563.
5. Taylor and Bentovim, Recurrent.
6. For a complete discussion of the diagnostic approach to pupillary abnormalities, see: Levin AV. Unequal pupils. In: Fleisher G and Ludwig S. *Textbook of Pediatric Emergency Medicine* (3rd ed.) 1993; Baltimore: Williams and Wilkins.
7. Wood, Foulkes, Holden, et al. Fever.

8. Deonna T, Marcoz JP, Meyer HU, et al. Epilepsie factice: syndrome de münchhausen par procuration. Une aytre facette de l'enfant maltraité: comas à répétition chez un enfant de 4 ans par intoxication non accidentelle. *Rev Méd Suisse Romande* 1985; 105:995–1002.
9. Rogers D, Tripp J, Bentovim A, et al. Non-accidental poisoning: an extended syndrome of child abuse. *Br Med J.* 1976; 1:793–796.
10. Fisher GC, Mitchell I. Munchausen's syndrome by proxy (factitious illness by proxy). *Curr Opin Psychiatry.* 1992; 5:224–227.
11. Rogers D, et al. Non-accidental poisoning.
12. Watson JBG, Davies JM, and Hunter JLP. Nonaccidental poisoning in childhood. *Arch Dis Child.* 1979; 54:143–144.
13. Leigh RJ and Zee DS. *The Neurology of Eye Movements* (2nd ed.). 1991; Philadelphia: Davis, pp. 467–469.
14. Mindel JS: Ocular side effects and toxicities from systemic therapy. In: Tasman W, Jaeger EA (eds.). *Duane's Foundations of Clinical Ophthalmology* (vol. 3). 1991; Philadelphia: Lippincott, pp. 42/1–6.
15. Kahn G and Goldman E. Munchausen syndrome by proxy: mother fabricates infant's hearing impairment. *J Speech Hearing Res.* 1991; 34:957–959.
16. Feenstra J and Merth IT, Treffers PD. Case.
17. Pickford E, Buchanan N, McLaughlan S. Munchausen syndrome by proxy: a family anthology. *Med J Aust.* 1988; 148:646–650.
18. Meadow R: Suffocation. *Br Med J.* 1989; 298:1572–1573.
19. Catalano RA, Simon JW, Krohel GB, Rosenberg PN. Functional visual loss in children. *Ophthalmology.* 1986; 93:385–390.
20. Kahn and Goldman, MBP.
21. Mindel, Ocular side effects.
22. Leigh and Zee. *Neurology.*
23. Mindel, Ocular side effects.

16

Renal Manifestations

Roy Meadow

R enal and urinary tract presentations of factitious illness feature prominently in the literature. This is partly because, at the time that Munchausen Syndrome by Proxy (MBP) was being defined, the index cases had presented as complex renal problems.[1] My first presentations about the syndrome were made to fellow pediatric nephrologists; they were quick to detect similar cases. Thus the early collected reports of Munchausen Syndrome by Proxy abuse overrepresented false renal illness.[2,3] More recent sequential studies of children presenting with false renal illness show that it is not the most common form of MBP *abuse*. However, it is one of the more common factitious illness stories to be associated with false *signs*, because it is so easy for a parent to tamper with a urine sample.

Nearly one-third of the children with factitious renal illness also have false symptoms and signs relating to another system; central nervous system, gastrointestinal, and allergic features are common. As with other parentally induced factitious illness the mother is the usual perpetrator, though there are rare examples of fathers as perpetrators.[4] This chapter describes the renal presentations I have encountered during my involvement with more than 300 children who have suffered MBP abuse, or which have been described in the literature. Where appropriate, information is given about specific investigations that may be helpful in identifying the deception.

Hematuria

The first report of MBP in 1977 included one child who presented with recurrent hematuria.[5] For that child, the mother was adding her own blood-stained urine to the child's urine, or sometimes substituting her own urine for the child's. There have been many cases identified subsequently.[6-8] Most commonly the mother adds blood to the child's urine after it has been passed into a container. The blood is obtained from an open wound, sometimes after the mother has pricked herself, or by stirring a vaginal tampon during menstruation into the urine.[9,10] Other parents have dipped meat into the urine or used coloring agents.[11,12] Sometimes hematuria has been caused by the parent inserting instruments into the child's urethra.[13-15] The apparent recurrent hematuria leads the pediatrician to incorrect diagnoses such as urinary tract infection or nephritis.

The investigator needs to ensure that any urine sample is collected from the child under direct supervision, and that the sample of urine is not left in the parent's presence unattended. An immediate investigation of great usefulness is microscopy of the urine. Blood that has been added at a late stage to the child's urine, after it has been passed, retains the characteristic form of the red cells to a much greater extent than that which has been present in the bladder for some time, or which has been passed through the kidneys. Genuine hematuria is almost always associated with considerable deformation of the red cells, particularly when it originates from the kidneys.

Vitamin C can be given orally as a marker to identify that a sample has come from a given child, rather than someone else.[16] Hematological and forensic laboratories can be helpful in identifying the source of blood in the urine by analysis of blood groups and red cell enzymes.[17,18] Red cells may be tagged with radioisotope to see if the red cells in the urine are the same as those in the child.[19]

Proteinuria

This is a less common presentation, possibly because it requires more scientific and medical knowledge, and also because it is less dramatic. Egg albumin has been used as the false protein.[20] As with hematuria, there have been examples of parents with proteinuria substituting their own urine for the child's.

Bacteriuria

Infection is often suspected because of false hematuria but, apart from that, some parents have deliberately fouled their child's urine to create bacteriuria. Feces and dirty water from drains and puddles have been used. [Instrumentation of the child's urethra has also caused subsequent infection.[21]]

Calculi

False renal stones have been reported from many countries.[22-24] Characteristically the parent relates a story of the child having abdominal pain, passing discolored urine, and then passing gravel. Usually the gravel or stone has been picked up from the ground. Occasionally parents have used a stone which they themselves have passed. One mother gave her child a small stone to swallow, within a toffee, an hour or so before taking the child to the hospital emergency department where she related a factitious story of renal colic. The doctors performed an abdominal radiograph and identified what might be misconstrued as a renal stone.

Chemical analysis of an alleged stone is mandatory, but will not always define a false stone because of the variable composition of genuine renal stones. Analysis of the urine in which the stone is alleged to have been passed, or which is passed shortly after passage of the stone, is important because genuine urinary tract stones cause increased cellular sediment in the urine, with or without hematuria, and are almost never found in urine which is otherwise normal on chemical dipstick testing and microscopy.

One of the youngest children alleged to have Munchausen Syndrome himself was described by Sneed and Bell in 1976.[25] There seems little doubt that this boy was inventing false illness (urinary stones) himself, but the authors point out that there may have been an element of collusion by the parents (i.e., an element of MBP).

Renal Tubular Disorders

Frequently the biochemical abnormalities caused by repetitive nonaccidental poisoning by the parent lead the clinicians to suspect complicated renal disorder.[26-29] Alternatively, such a disorder is suspected because the parent has added chemicals to the child's urine after it has been passed; sodium bicarbonate, yeast, and other baking ingredients have been used.[30] One of the substances parents commonly use to repetitively poison children is table salt (sodium chloride). The child presents with recurrent hypernatremia, vomiting, thirst, and lethargy. If the hypernatremia is marked, there will be neurological manifestations: seizures and drowsiness. Whenever extreme hypernatremia is identified it is imperative to obtain a concurrent sample of the child's urine. If the hypernatremia is associated with a high urinary sodium excretion rate, there can be confidence that the cause of the hypernatremia is excessive intake of salt. Once accidental ingestion of excess salt has been eliminated, nonaccidental administration remains the only alternative. It is difficult to give children large quantities of salt orally, and some parents have resorted to administration per rectum or by nasogastric tube. My review of 12 children who incurred repetitive nonaccidental salt poisoning contains helpful information about its detection and management.[31]

Renal Insufficiency

Genuine renal insufficiency may be encountered as a consequence of MBP. For instance, a child incurred end-stage renal failure as a result of the mother injecting diphtheria/pertussis/tetanus (DPT) vaccine three times a week for several months in order to induce fever. Not only fever was caused, but also an immune complex glomerulonephritis which led to renal failure.[32] Severe renal failure has also been caused by drugs, including acute renal failure induced by repeated doses of the analgesic Glafenine (an anthranilic acid derivative).[33]

Genuine hypertension may be a consequence of induced renal failure. False hypertension is usually the result of the mother deliberately altering the chart on which the nurse or doctor records the child's blood pressure while in hospital. Some mothers, having been asked to measure the child's blood pressure at home, deliberately record incorrectly high values, or cause others to measure the blood pressure with an inappropriately small sphygmomanometer cuff which leads to falsely high blood pressure readings.

References

1. Meadow R. Munchausen syndrome by proxy. *Lancet.* 1977; 2:343–345.
2. Meadow R. Munchausen syndrome by proxy. *Arch Dis Child.* 1982; 57:92–98.
3. Rosenberg DA. Web of deceit: a literature review of munchausen syndrome by proxy. *Chilc Abuse Negl* 1987; 11:547–563.
4. Prakken AB, den-Hartog L, and Weelkens JJ. A new variant of munchausen's syndrome by proxy: the father in an active role. *Tijdschr-Kindergeneeskd* 1991; 59:91–94.
5. Meadow, MBP, 1977.
6. Al-Mugeiren M and Ganelin RS. A suspected case of munchausen's syndrome by proxy in a Saudi child. *Ann Saudi Med* 1990; 10:662.
7. Meadow, MBP, 1982.
8. Rosenberg, Web.
9. Meadow, MBP, 1982.
10. Salmon RF, Arang BS, Barm MG, et al. Factitious haematuria with underlying renal abnormalities. *Pediatrics* 1988; 82:377–379.
11. Fleisher D and Ament ME. Diarrhea, red diapers, and child abuse. *Clin Pediatr* 1977; 17:820–824.
12. Prakken et al., New variant.
13. Clayton PT, Counahan R, and Chantler C. Munchausen syndrome by proxy. *Lancet* 1978; 1:102. (Letter)
14. Kempe CH. Uncommon manifestations of the battered child syndrome. *Am J Dis Child.* 1975; 1265.
15. Labbe J. Self-induced urinary tract infection in boys. *Pediatrics* 1984; 74:1136 (Letter).
16. Nading JH and Duval-Arnould B. Factitious diabetes mellitus confirmed by ascorbid acid. *Arch Dis Child* 1984; 59:166.
17. Meadow R. Management of Munchausen syndrome by proxy. *Arch Dis Child* 1985; 60:385–393.
18. Outwater KM, Lipnick RN, Luban NLC et al. Factitious hematuria: diagnosis by minor blood group typing. *J Pediatr* 1981; 98:95–97.
19. Kurlandsky L, Lukjoff JY, Zinkham WH et al. Munchausen syndrome by proxy: definition of factitious bleeding in an infant by CR 51 labelling of erythrocytes. *Pediatrics* 1979; 63:228–231.
20. Tojo A, Nanba S, Kimura K, et al. Factitious proteinuria in a young girl. *Clin Nephrol* 1990; 33:299.
21. Labbe, Self-Induced.
22. Douchain F. Lithiase urinaire 'factice': syndrome de munchausen par procuration? [Factitious urinary lithiasis: munchausen syndrome by proxy?] *Presse Med* 1987; 6:179.
23. Meadow, MBP, 1982.
24. Rosenberg, Web.
25. Sneed RC and Bell RF. The dauphin of munchausen: factitious passage of renal stones in a child. *Pediatrics* 1976; 58:127–129.

26. Meadow, MBP, 1977.
27. Meadow, MBP, 1982.
28. Prosemans W, Kyele A, Sina J, et al. Recurrent acute renal failure due to non-accidental poisoning with glafenin in a child. *Clin Nephrol* 1981; 16:207.
29. Rogers D, Tripp J, Bentovim A, et al. Non-accidental poisoning: an extended syndrome of child abuse. *Br Med J* 1976; 1:793–796.
30. Meadow, MBP, 1982.
31. Meadow R. Non-accidental salt poisoning. *Arch Dis Child* 1993; 68:448–452.
32. Meadow R. Factitious illness—the hinterland of child abuse. In Meadow R, ed. *Recent Advances in Pediatrics* (No. 7). Edinburgh: Churchill Livingstone, 1984; 217–232.
33. Proesmans et al. Recurrent.

17

Otorhinolaryngologic Manifestations

Alex V. Levin

Child abuse involving the ears, nose, and throat was noted at least as early as 1869 when a father and mother were successfully prosecuted for probing a hot poker into the ears, nose, and throat of their son.[1] The head and neck are involved in approximately one-third to one-half of nonaccidental injuries.[2-4] Although one review of child abuse involving the face and otorhinolaryngologic (ORL) organs did not find any cases of Munchausen Syndrome by Proxy (MBP),[5] several cases of MBP involving the ears, nose, mouth, and throat have been reported, perhaps because these organs offer orifices within which the perpetrator might assume that signs of trauma will be well hidden and from which the effects of covert trauma can be quiet dramatic. In addition, symptoms referable to the ORL organs make up a large part of the common illnesses in normal childhood, so they may be more likely to be taken at face value.

This is well illustrated by Guandolo's case of a 5-year-old boy with 250 visits to a pediatric practice.[6] On many of these visits it was the mother's complaints about ear pain, severe nasal congestion, ear infections, croup, or wheezing—all very common childhood problems—for which she was offered the appointment to be seen. At one point the child was sent to an otorhinolaryngologist for consultation. His report read, "Diagnosis: normal ear, nose and throat examination. Treatment: with the history of recurrent otitis media and normal ear examination today, I suggested adenoidectomy as an adjunct. . . ." Fialkov reported a child whose multiple visits to the doctor included concerns about a rash in the mouth, ear pain, cough, intraoral lacerations, foreign body ingestion, and sand in the eyes, mixed with real episodes of pharyngitis and otitis media that required treatment.[7] Ackerman and Strobel reported a child with factitious diarrhea who also had chronic otitis media unresponsive to antibiotics, which of course may have been a true childhood illness.[8] This mixture of factitious signs and symptoms with possible real accidental injuries and ingestions as well as genuine common childhood illnesses can make the diagnosis of MBP particularly difficult. Sometimes, the knowledge gained from the original real illness provides the perpetrator with a template for future MBP. This is illustrated by the development of recurrent ear bleeding, ear drum laceration, and acquired scar tissue of the eardrum and ear canal caused by covert trauma in a 2-year-old boy. He had previously received treatment for cleft palate and associated chronic otitis media which had necessitated myringotomy tubes.[9]

This chapter deals with the otorhinolaryngologic manifestations of MBP in which the perpetrator has directly manipulated or fabricated the appearance of a symptom or sign related to the ears, nose, mouth and throat. It should not be forgotten that these body areas can also be affected indirectly through other MBP acts. Perioral and gum bruising, facial petechiae, intraoral abrasions, cyanosis of the lips, or bleeding from the nose may occur during covert suffocation.[10,11] Hematemesis, hemoptysis, and recurrent vomiting may result from poisoning or direct stimulation of the gag reflex.[12,13] The appearance of bleeding in the ORL organs may also be created by the placement of blood or simulated blood into an orifice.[14] In addition, the throat and airways may be traumatized by the nonaccidental ingestion of caustic substances (e.g., lye) or foreign bodies (e.g., glass).[15,16] Many of these "secondary" signs and symptoms are discussed elsewhere in this book. As in all forms of MBP, the diversity of the manifestations seems to be limited only by the imagination of the perpetrator.

Ears

In MBP, the ears may be affected by direct manipulation, falsification of history, or by the secondary effects of systemic parental interventions. Most commonly, direct manipulation causes the signs and symptoms.

The most common otic manifestation of MBP involves allegations of or actual bleeding from the ear canals. Rosenberg found that 2% of all MBP cases in which bleeding was the primary manifestation involved the ears; this represented less than 1% of all MBP.[17] White and co-workers reported a case of hemorrhagic otitis media due to warfarin poisoning in an 11-month-old infant.[18] The child was initially hospitalized for gastroenteritis and dehydration followed by hospitalizations for failure to thrive. An acute unilateral hemorrhagic otitis unresponsive to multiple oral antibiotics over 3 weeks eventually led to a bloody discharge from one ear at the same time that the child presented with multiple nontraumatic skin hematomas over various areas of the body. The diagnosis of MBP poisoning was eventually made after coagulation studies were found to be dramatically above the normal range.

More commonly, MBP otic bleeding results from direct trauma to the external ear canal. Grace and co-workers reported three cases: a mother traumatizing the ear canals of her 2-year-old daughter with an "orange stick"; a 16-month-old boy who developed anemia from the bleeding inflicted by his allegedly deaf mother; and a girl who, at 10 months of age, had recurrent new eardrum tears and eventually developed cerebrospinal fluid otorrhea (spinal fluid leaking out of the ear).[19] This last child was left with an internally severely damaged, deaf ear. Two of these children also had other ORL signs (vide infra). The recognition of lacerations in the ear canal allowed Grace to attribute the lacerated eardrums to trauma. In one of the cases, the bleeding only stopped when a tamper-proof dressing was applied. Grace later reported a child with chronic bleeding from a mastoid cavity due to chronic instrumentation with a bobby pin.[20]

Bleeding from the ears in the absence of a coagulopathy, known organic ear disease or known accidental trauma should raise the suspicion of nonaccidental injury.[21] Spontaneous rupture of the eardrum can occur as a result of otitis media. However, purulent drainage is almost always present. The presence of pus or blood in the ear canal may make the recognition of external ear canal pathology, including telltale lacerations, difficult to see. Examination under anesthesia may be required for proper diagnosis.[22] With compliant patients, irrigation or manual cleaning of the canal can be achieved.[23] Other common causes of eardrum perforation include the introduction of a foreign body into the ear canal by a child exhibiting normal exploratory behavior, or overly aggressive or accidental deep insertion of an implement used for cleaning of the canal by a well-meaning caretaker.[24] Other accidental injuries include overaggressive irrigation by a caretaker, blast injuries, basilar skull fracture, or injuries sustained by fluid pressure waves generated during swimming or water skiing.[25] The latter often causes stellate tears in the anterior aspect of the tympanic membrane along with significant hearing loss.[26] Of course these events should be one-time occurrences with obvious historical explanations. A well-recognized child abuse injury, which can also be sustained by children at play (sometimes referred to colloquially as a "bell ringer"), occurs when one or both ears are slapped with open hands. A compression wave is created when the hands are applied and a suction force occurs within the ear canal when the hands are withdrawn. The result is a unilateral or bilateral eardrum rupture which is usually confined to the pars tensa area, with a ragged or stellate configuration. This is usually not associated with severe hearing loss.[27,28] In fact, this is the most common cause of eardrum perforation in Nigeria.[29] I am not aware of this injury being reported as a manifestation of MBP.

The case presented by Pickford and co-workers demonstrates how a bleeding ear may be part of a much broader picture of factitious disease.[30] A child presented at different times with vomiting, gastroesophageal reflux, recurrent cyanosis and apnea, seizures, failure to thrive, speech delay, clumsiness, polydipsia, head trauma, and epistaxis for a total of 18 hospital admissions in 18 months. The multiple symptoms and signs were produced by a combination of history falsification, poisoning, manipulation of records and tests, and direct trauma. Examination under anesthesia by an otorhinolaryngologist revealed bilateral chronic otitis media with a "subtotal perforation" of the left tympanic membrane. Chronic antibiotics were prescribed and bilateral myringotomy tube surgery performed. The nursing staff noted that episodes of acute bleeding from the left ear always disappeared in the mother's absence, during which time only old blood would be present in the left ear canal. Both the patient's mother and sister also had complex histories of factitious illnesses including the ORL organs: the mother had a history of deafness in her left ear, myringotomy, tonsillectomy, and nasal septoplasty; the sister with an undocumented history of repeated "ear infections." Eventually the mother was caught choking her daughter and subsequently pleaded guilty in court to shaking both children by the throat until they went limp. She was sentenced to 6 years in jail.

Excoriations produced by trauma to the external ear canal can simulate otitis externa.[31] Zohar and co-workers report the case of a child who had been under extensive treatment for chronic otitis media, with multiple tympanic paracenteses and mastoidectomies prior to the diagnosis of MBP. The induced otitis externa and excoriations resolved without recurrence following confrontation with the mother. These authors also report MBP manifesting as recurrent foreign bodies in the ear canal.[32] The diagnosis of MBP was made when the father (the perpetrator) was recognized as a former Munchausen Syndrome patient with symptoms mimicking sinus disease.

One particularly creative manifestation of MBP was a mother's fabrication of hearing impairment in her infant daughter.[33] Despite multiple normal brainstem auditory evoked response tests (BAER) starting at the age of 1 week, the mother used falsification of history, the involvement of multiple institutions and caretakers, and excuses designed to prevent access to her child's old medical records, to successfully obtain hearing aids for her child. She also gave false histories of multiple other medical problems including spasticity, hemiparesis, and blindness which were no longer present at the child's last medical contact when MBP was recognized. The child was eventually removed from her mother's care by the court.

In a case from The Hospital for Sick Children in Toronto which combined MBP with the mother as the perpetrator and a son who was both a victim and a participant (pediatric Munchausen Syndrome), a 13-year-old boy underwent extensive investigations for unilateral ear pain. Procedures performed on him included tonsillectomy, adenoidectomy, mastoidectomy, and mastoidectomy revision.[34] A nurse eventually discovered a vial of pink fluid at the bedside which was found on forensic analysis to be beet juice. The child was putting the juice in his ear to simulate bloody cerebrospinal fluid drainage. In another case, a mother placed her own blood, as recognized by comparative ABO blood typing, in the ear of her 2 year old to simulate bleeding.[35] This child had previous fabricated symptoms including failure to thrive, hematemesis, melena, and hematuria. Blood typing had not been done and the diagnosis of MBP had not been considered until the blood emanating from the ears allowed for definitive diagnosis.[36]

Nose

The most common nasal manifestation of MBP is nasal bleeding (epistaxis) produced either by direct trauma to the intranasal passageways, factitious simulation of bleeding, or systemic induced coagulopathy. In reviewing 19 cases of MBP, Meadow found that one (5%) had epistaxis. A total of 12 (63%) had some form of bleeding, suggesting that epistaxis is one of the less common forms of factitious bleeding.[37] Likewise, Rosenberg found that epistaxis was one of the least frequent sites (1%) of MBP bleeding, and represented less than 0.5% of all MBP.[38]

An unusual case of progressive destruction of the columella and nasal septum in two siblings was caused by an "obsessive" cleaning ritual in which the mother would use a bobby pin. This may qualify as a form of MBP, although the author of the report neither recognized it as such nor provided enough additional information for independent diagnosis.[39] Foreign bodies can also be introduced into the nose covertly by parents.[40] Although children may introduce objects into the nose as part of normal behavior, repeated occurrences should raise the suspicion of MBP.

"Frequent rhinorrhea" was one of the many complaints for which a 17-year-old boy with the "doctor shopping" variant of MBP received multiple investigations.[41] Likewise, Waring reported a case in which persistent complaints of staphyloccal rhinitis may have represented either the "doctor addict" form of MBP[42] or, as the author describes, an entity without falsification which is given the term "symptom overemphasis."[43]

Mouth and Throat

At Children's Hospital of Philadelphia, we cared for three patients in whom the perpetrators covertly caused potentially life-threatening palatal and posterior pharyngeal trauma.* In the first two cases, the presence of recurrent palatal and pharyngeal ulcerations led to extensive investigations including laryngoscopy, bronchoscopy, biopsies, and extensive infectious disease testing. The children had previously been seen by multiple physicians as well. Two of the children developed life-threatening retropharyngeal abscess. In one, a tract communicating between a posterior pharyngeal lesion and the retropharyngeal space was demonstrated on barium swallow. Two of the children also had episodes of recurrent apnea while in the care of the parent. In one case, the father was the perpetrator.

Unfortunately, placement through social service agencies was difficult in all cases in part because of the agencies' unfamiliarity with the genuineness and seriousness of the MBP diagnosis. In the first case, a 1 month old had recurrent bleeding and ulcerative lesions of his palate. The child was allowed to remain in the care of his parents, and was eventually suffocated with a stuffed toy, sustaining severe brain damage. He later died from complications of his secondary neurologic disability. At that time a skeletal survey revealed healing rib fractures. His father later admitted to prodding the child's palate with a medicine dropper. The second case was similar. A 2-week-old infant presented with recurrent oral bleeding and palatal erosions. The suggestion of trauma was finally made by the otorhinolaryngologist, who noted findings "consistent with" trauma at the time of laryngoscopic biopsy. Although the parents were adamant in their denial of inflicted trauma, the mother confessed to accidentally scratching the infant's mouth on one occasion. The infant was placed in foster care for a short time. After eventually being returned to the parents' care, the infant presented with a nonaccidental fracture of the right humerus, confirming child abuse. The third infant presented when we were more aware of this form of MBP, and the medical team suspected the diagnosis much earlier. The overprotective and overenmeshed single mother of this adopted girl demonstrated unusual feeding patterns in which the food was delivered into the baby's mouth on a spoon with rapid thrusting movements so that no food ever touched the baby's lips. The mother was obsessively fastidious about maintaining cleanliness during feeding. As the child protection agency would not agree to foster placement, home visitation by a child abuse team social worker was arranged. During this time, attempts were made to retrain the mother in normal feeding behaviors including purposely allowing the infant to play with her food. The benefit of tactile and textural stimulation that is part of normal infant development was explained. Eventually, the mother's borderline compliance caused the agency to close the case, although the mother continued to demonstrate an openly punitive and abnormal relationship with her daughter. At last contact, she was allegedly observed castigating her daughter for staining one of her dresses because it would bring less value at a local resale store.

McDowell and Fielding reported two infants with posterior pharyngeal perforations associated with fever, retropharyngeal abscess and interstitial emphysema, although these were single abusive occurrences rather than MBP.[44] One child had an associated linear abrasion of the palate. Laryngoscopy was required for diagnosis, and both children exhibited either overlying hemorrhagic sloughing or purulent material at the area of pharyngeal trauma.

Palatal and pharyngeal trauma have been occasionally been reported as manifestations of MBP. Manning and co-workers discussed a 4 month old who presented with oral bleeding. This was first attributed to a tracheitis. Later, however, the child returned with a bleeding uvula. Over time abrasions and lacerations of the gingiva, palate, and floor of the mouth associated with a retropharyngeal abscess were observed.[45] In their report of three children with MBP presenting as bleeding from the ears, Grace and co-workers noted that one child also sustained a palatal tear when his mother was observed to "ram a feeding bottle into his mouth." Another child had three deep lacerations in the posterior pharyngeal wall noted at endoscopy performed following an episode of hematemesis. These were felt to be consistent with injury inflicted by an adult fingernail.[46] An open pin lodged in the esophagus was retrieved. By the time Grace discussed the same cases again in another journal three years later, the child with palatal injury, like our case, had been the victim of several nonaccidental ingestions of foreign bodies and had a bead lodged in one ear canal.[47] Thus, covert injury to the oropharynx may be a associated with retropharyngeal abscess and nonaccidental foreign body ingestion. Perhaps radiographic imaging of the neck and gastrointestinal tract is warranted in these cases, particularly when there are systemic signs of abscess, such as fever.

In Grace's second paper, another child was reported with a 1 cm deep pharyngeal wound that was first seen at the time of resuscitation for a nonaccidental brain injury associated with a torn frenulum.[48] An unexplained torn frenulum is virtually pathognomonic for trauma.[49]

It is also noteworthy that a case reported by Morris and Reay in 1971, before Meadow's 1977 classic delineation of MBP,[50] may have been an early case of oropharyngeal MBP. The authors even raised the possibility of covert trauma, although they could not rule out a congenital abnormality.[51] They reported a 7-month-old girl with multiple fractures whose sister had died suddenly with multiple fractures. The index child presented with chronic respiratory and feeding difficulties, including vomiting and progressive stridor. Symptoms started at 6 weeks of age. She also had a split superior alveolar ridge and upper lid mucosa, frothy blood in and "mucopurulent sloughing" of the oropharynx, and adhesions involving the soft palate, uvula, and epiglottis. Surgical intervention was necessary.

Lee reported twin victims in whom hematemesis was simulated by traumatization of the mouth with a diaper pin.[52] This was not discovered until an astute nurse, responding to the infant's cries, noted a "small bleeding point" on the child's lip shortly after she was left alone with the mother. The nurse saw a diaper pin partially hidden in the mother's hand, yet the child always wore disposable diapers which have adhesive tabs. The mother admitted the single act, denied a role in all previous events, but was successfully prosecuted for assault. Both children were placed in protective custody.

One of the more notable cases of factitious bleeding involving the ORL systems was reported by Kurlandsky and co-workers.[53] The presenting complaint for the 3-week-old victim was bleeding from the nose and mouth, observed in the hospital on 14 occasions. Four of the episodes were associated with respiratory arrests requiring resuscitation. The child also received unilateral nasal cautery. On one occasion, a 2 mm flat pink lesion that blanched under pressure was noted on the upper anterior gum. No comment was offered as to the possible etiology. An extensive diagnostic workup was performed, including a laryngoscopy which showed blood below the vocal chords and hemosiderin laden macrophages in pulmonary aspirates. A diagnosis of hemosiderosis was considered.

MBP was confirmed by use of comparative Rh blood typing and radioactive assays, which demonstrated that the blood on the child was the mother's. The infant had previously been given radioactively labeled ^{51}Cr red blood cells as part of a study trying to determine the source of his bleeding. It was simply fortuitous that this test had been done before the suspicion of MBP had been raised. Perhaps earlier suspicion of factitious bleeding would have made such invasive studies unnecessary.

Complaints referable to the mouth and throat, such as bad breath, may be part of a larger chronic pattern of the more mild doctor shopping variant of MBP.[54]

The many variations of oropharyngeal child abuse are well reviewed by Grace and Grace.[55] They suggest that intraoral bruising, usually caused by forcible insertion of a spoon into the mouth, is frequently associated with other nontraumatic injuries and should therefore raise enough suspicion in the child's medical caretaker that a search for other signs of trauma is initiated. They suggest that a skeletal survey be performed in these cases. Other cases, including my own experience, have confirmed the notion that oropharyngeal abuse is a marker for severe injury and morbidity. Rubin and co-workers reported an 11-year-old victim of MBP complicated by polybacterial sepsis, recurrent gastric ulceration, intestinal perforation, and esophageal stricture in which the early signs and symptoms included sore throat, erythema of the pharynx, and a tongue ulcer.[56] Early recognition of MBP in the presence of oropharyngeal signs can be critical for preventing serious injury and death.

*NOTE: The author acknowledges the valuable assistance of Toni Seidl in the preparation of these case histories.

References

1. Grace A and Grace MA. Child abuse within the ear, nose and throat. *J Otolaryngol*. 1987; 16:108–111.
2. Leavitt EB, Pincus RL, and Bukachevsky R. Otolaryngologic manifestations of child abuse. *Arch Otolaryngol Head Neck Surg*. 1992; 118:629–631.
3. Grace and Grace, Child abuse.
4. Needleman HL. Orofacial trauma in child abuse: types, prevalence, management, and the dental profession's involvement. *J Am Acad Pediatr Dent*. 1986; 8(special issue 1):71–80.
5. Leavitt et al., Otolaryngologic.

6. Guandolo VL. Munchausen syndrome by proxy: An outpatient challenge. *Pediatrics.* 1985; 75:526–530.
7. Fialkov MJ. Peregrination in the problem pediatric patient. *Clin Pediatr.* 1984; 23:571–575.
8. Ackerman NB and Strobel CT. Polle Syndrome: chronic diarrhea in a Munchausen child. *Gastroenterology.* 1981; 81:1140–1142.
9. Manning SC, Casselbrant M and Lammers D. Otolaryngologic manifestations of child abuse. *Int J Pediatr Otorhinlaryngol.* 1990; 20:7–16.
10. Minford AMB. Child abuse presenting as apparent "near miss" sudden infant death syndrome. *Br Med J.* 1981; 282:521.
11. Meadow R. Suffocation. *Br Med J.* 1989; 298:1572–1573.
12. Rosenberg DA. Web of deceit: A literature review of Munchausen syndrome by proxy. *Child Abuse Neg.* 1987; 11:547–563.
13. Meadow R. Munchausen syndrome by proxy. *Arch Dis Child.* 1982; 57:92–98.
14. Mills RW and Burke S. Gastrointestinal bleeding in a 15 month old male: a presentation of Munchausen's syndrome by proxy. *Clin Pediatr.* 1990; 29:474–477.
15. Friedman EM. Caustic ingestions and foreign body aspirations: an overlooked form of child abuse. *Ann Otol Rhinol Laryngol.*
16. Grace and Grace, Child abuse.
17. Rosenberg, Web.
18. White ST, Voter K, and Perry J. Surreptitious warfarin ingestion. *Child Abuse Negl.* 1985; 9:349–352.
19. Grace A, Kalinkiewicz M, and Drake-Lee AB. Covert manifestations of child abuse. *Br Med J.* 1984; 289:1041–1042.
20. Grace and Grace, Child abuse.
21. Grace et al., Covert.
22. Grace et al., Covert.
23. Obiako MN. Eardrum perforation as evidence of child abuse. *Child Abuse Neglect.* 1987; 11:149–151.
24. Obiako, Eardrum.
25. Obiako, Eardrum.
26. Obiako, Eardrum.
27. Obiako, Eardrum.
28. Grace and Grace, Child abuse.
29. Obiako, Eardrum.
30. Pickford E, Buchanan N, and McLaughlan S. Munchausen syndrome by proxy: a family anthology. *Med J Aust.* 1988; 148:646–650.
31. Zohar Y, Avidan G, Shvili Y, and Laurian N. Otolaryngologic cases of Munchausen's syndrome. *Laryngoscope.* 1987; 97:201–203.
32. Zohar et al., Otolaryngologic cases.
33. Kahn G and Goldman E. Munchausen syndrome by proxy: mother fabricates infant's hearing impairment. *J Speech Hearing Res.* 1991; 34:957–959.
34. Gilbert RW, Pierse PM, and Mitchell DP. Cryptic otalgia: a case of Munchausen syndrome in a pediatric patient. *J Otolaryngol.* 1987; 16:231–233.

35. Bourchier D. Bleeding ears: case report of Munchausen syndrome by proxy. *Austr Paediatr J*. 1983; 19:256–257.
36. It should be noted that ABO blood typing may not be revealing in many cases. More sophisticated typing antigens should be considered if the suspicion of MBP exists and the blood is not obviously coming from a source on the patient.
37. Meadow, MBP.
38. Rosenberg, Web.
39. Orton CI. Loss of columella and septum from an unusual form of child abuse. *Plast Reconstr Surg*. 1975; 56:345–346.
40. Grace and Grace, Child abuse.
41. Woollcott P, Aceto T, Rutt C, Bloom M, and Glick R. Doctor shopping with the child as proxy patient: a variant of child abuse. *J Pediatr*. 1982; 101:297–301.
42. Libow JA and Schreier HA. Three forms of factitious illness in children: when is it Munchausen syndrome by proxy? *Am J Orthopsychiat*. 1986; 56:602–611.
43. Waring WW. The persistent parent. *Am J Dis Child*. 1992; 146:753–756.
44. McDowell HP and Fielding DW. Traumatic perforation of the hypopharynx-an unusual form of abuse. *Arch Dis Child*. 1984; 59:888–889.
45. Manning et al., Otolaryngologic manifestations.
46. Grace et al., Covert.
47. Grace and Grace, Child abuse.
48. Grace and Grace, Child abuse.
49. Needelman, Orofacial trauma.
50. Meadow R. Munchausen syndrome by proxy: the hinterland of child abuse. *Lancet*. 1977; 2:343–345.
51. Morris TMO and Reay HAJ. A battered baby with pharyngeal atresia. *J Laryngol Otol*. 1971; 85:729–731.
52. Lee AL. Munchausen syndrome by proxy in twins. *Arch Dis Child*. 1979; 54:646–647.
53. Kurlandsky L, Lukjoff JY, Zinkham WH, et al. Munchausen syndrome by proxy: definition of factitious bleeding in an infant by CR 51 labeling of erythrocytes. *Pediatrics*. 1979; 63:228–231.
54. Woolcott et al., Doctor shopping.
55. Grace and Grace, Child abuse.
56. Rubin LG, Angelides A, Davidson M, and Lanzkowsky P. Recurrent sepsis and gastrointestinal ulceration due to child abuse. *Arch Dis Child*. 1986; 61:903–905.

18

Munchausen Syndrome by Proxy and Sexual Abuse

Common Ground?

Martin A. Finkel

As clinicians we struggle to understand how caretakers could fabricate symptoms and create factitious illness resulting in unnecessary and at times invasive procedures performed on dependent children. We find it equally distasteful that children are engaged in sexually inappropriate activities. However, there is no doubt that both of these problems occur. Munchausen Syndrome by Proxy (MBP) is an unusual but not prevalent form of child maltreatment. Although once "society's secret," sexual abuse is now recognized as a frequent occurrence. Both require that evaluating clinicians understand specific dynamics and posess investigatory skills.

A prerequisite to addressing these conditions is overcoming the denial that they exist. MBP and child sexual abuse cases are both complex puzzles. When someone alleges MBP or sexual abuse, a considerable number of investigative challenges arise. As in all puzzles, only when each of the pieces are placed together is a full picture obtained. This is one common ground on which MBP and allegations of sexual abuse stand. Both conditions place clinicians in the uncomfortable position of attempting to determine the truthfulness of parents' observations and/or children's statements. Health care professionals must be prepared to consider that they may be lied to by parents and/or children. To obtain the most complete picture of what has occurred, physicians must share information with those in child protection, law enforcement, and mental health. All must be willing to alter diagnostic impressions as a result of new information.

Neither MBP nor allegations of sexual abuse can be expeditiously diagnosed without a confession. Neither group of perpetrators is likely to make such a confession in the early stages of the investigation. Both require psychological assessments and interviews of children and caretakers in addition to physical examinations.

Munchausen Syndrome by Proxy

MBP parents construct a history or symptoms specifically designed to result in a variety of actions on the part of doctors. They garner significant secondary gain as a result of their premediated deceit and its associated attention. The parents, rather than being distraught over the event precipitated by their own action, appear concerned about the children and may readily "assist" in the problem solving. They respond to the attention brought on by their own observations and then return to the drawing board to create additional factitious symptoms to maintain the fervor of the physicians and nursing staff who attempt to understand the diagnostic dilemma before them. However, the investigation is not actually child-driven, as few children possess the abstract thinking and knowledge necessary to willfully deceive their doctors. In MBP the impetus for continued medical intervention is the presence of historical or demonstrable, albeit factitious, illness. It is often the absence of confirmatory laboratory tests or expected response to treatment, in light of the history, that impels further action. MBP unfolds and thrives in the milieu of attention from helping professionals. This most commonly occurs under the watchful eyes of medical professionals in a hospital environment.

Perpetrators of MBP are almost always primary caretakers, most often mothers. The psychological profiles of MBP parents, although diverse, may include a history of mental illness.[1]

Sexual Abuse

The context in which sexual abuse allegations arise, unfold, and are investigated differs from MBP in several ways. Although 85% of all sexual abuse occurs at the hands of those the children know, love, and trust, only 25% of perpetrators of intrafamilial sexual abuse are parents and rarely are they mothers.[2] Child sexual abuse allegations are the result of either a purposeful disclosure on the part of the children or inferential disclosure on the part of others; for example, by observation of sexually stylized behaviors, gastrointestinal/genitourinary signs or symptoms or as a result of questioning of the children. Child sexual abuse allegations are child-driven, with nonoffending parents generally responding to protect even though most are at first unprepared to believe or address the problem. Invariably such a discovery precipitates a crisis for nonoffending parents. Nonoffending parents may want very much to minimize the observations which suggested sexual abuse and would prefer that this "nightmare" not be true.

The occurrence of child sexual abuse is greatly dependent on a shroud of secrecy that protects perpetrators and facilitates future repetition of the acts. Children are coerced into maintaining secrecy in either subtle or overtly threatening ways. Sexually abused children are frequently embarrassed, stigmatized, and frightened by their experiences. Both sexually abused children and nonoffending parents are generally reluctant to talk about the abuse.

Nonoffending parents and children want to both suppress the experience and deny the potential for psychological sequelae. An emotionally supportive and nurturing environment is critical for facilitating children's disclosures. The children's ability to provide details of their experiences depends upon many factors including age, emotional maturity, fears, severity of abuse, and the responses to the allegation by the nonoffending parents, child protective service workers, and investigators.

In sexual abuse cases few children will have physical evidence to confirm their abuse. Here, too, there is a discrepancy between history and physical findings. When residual is present it is generally nonspecific. The most common nonspecific finding, erythema, is short-lived. Acute superficial injuries heal with no residual. Even more significant injuries will heal by the formation of granulation tissue, often with surprisingly little residual.[3] Most perpetrators of sexual abuse do not have a desire to injure their victim in the process of sexually inappropriate contact. As with MBP, injury may be a byproduct of pursuing other goals. If there is no injury, residual is not observed and the covert act remains undiscovered. In contrast to MBP, lack of findings may terminate rather than impel investigation. Residual which can be stated with medical certainty to be the result of sexual abuse is uncommon. It would be possible for perpetrators of MBP to inflict injury to the genitalia or anal region. Such signs or symptoms might raise the specter of sexual abuse. However, such a suspicion could very well precipitate the immediate involvement of child protection and law enforcement. Thus it might be anticipated that MBP perpetrators would in general be less likely to take this route, which would bring immediate investigative attention.

Most children disclose their sexual abuse long after the last event, when they feel safe. (We have little information on subsequent disclosure by victims of MBP.) Thus, few children are examined in close proximity to the inappropriate contact and the opportunity to identify acute sequelae is limited. In contrast, many victims of MBP are examined just after the abuse has occurred, but this is often realized only in retrospect. When disclosure by a child victim occurs, clinicians must pay particular attention to presenting signs and symptoms and their temporal relationship to the specific events described by the child victims. In preverbal children this is problematic. In older children, it is their ability to provide specific details, sensations, symptoms, and observations relating each injury to specific events that lends credibility to their statements.

Parents of sexually abused children and parents who create factitious illness begin to share common ground when parents of the sexually abused children become hypervigilant and anxious in their desire to assure their child's protection. Most parents who believe their children have been sexually abused will act in a protective manner. Protecting children who are suspected of being sexually abused includes close supervision and limiting the alleged perpetrator's access. In order to limit access during the investigatory stage a court order is generally necessary. Depending upon the children's age and the duration of the sexual abuse the amount of information on which to assess an allegation will vary. If the children are preverbal and there are no physical findings, there may be insufficient information to substantiate an allegation and limit access. Parents who then view themselves as being unable to protect will experience increasing stress and may make frantic attempts to prove the abuse. They may repeatedly question the children, using video- and/or audiotaping of the children's statements, or present them for repeated psychological and medical examinations. When this effort does not result in the desired effect, nonoffending parents may appear increasingly agitated or irrational. They may then be accused of fabricating the allegation, being vindictive, possessing ulterior motives, or even viewed as mentally ill and unable to care for their children. This scenario is most likely to appear in the setting of a custody or visitation dispute.

False Allegations of Sexual Abuse

It is important to recognize that there are occasions where an allegation of the child sexual abuse may be false or a misrepresentation of the facts. Such an apparently fictitious report may be a result either of an unintentional misinterpretation or, more rarely, of intentional falsification.[4] Jones reviewed 576 consecutive cases of child sexual abuse and found that 6% of reports by custodial parents and 1% of reports by children were falsified.[5] All of the custodial parents who falsified reports were experiencing significant mental health problems. The children who made false allegations were all viewed as angry, retaliating adolescents. Many of these parents and adolescents were experiencing posttraumatic stress disorder, often caused by other forms of abuse.

More commonly, fictitious reports are unintentional distortions that may emanate from custodial parents who are experiencing extreme stress and/or mental illness that distorts their perception of reality. During a divorce, one parent may be certain that the estranged spouse is now capable of doing almost anything, including sexually abusing their child. As a result, parents may overreact to suspicious circumstances which, in an intact family, would perhaps lead the same parents to underreact, needing to be convinced that abuse has occurred.[6]

Clinicians must be cautious not to demonstrate a bias against allegations that surface in this context. Thoennes and Tjaden found that false allegations are no more frequent in custody disputes than they are in the general population of sexually abused children. In 9,000 families undergoing custody visitation disputes, less than 2% of the contested cases involved an allegation of sexual abuse.[7]

When it appears that parents are becoming increasingly stressed by an inability to substantiate an allegation, alternative strategies should be sought to maintain an objective and balanced course that will ultimately lead to the truth. This should obviate any need for desperate parents to create symptoms. By the same token, strategies should be sensitive enough to identify the occasional case in which the appearance of sexual abuse is only a pretext for other forms of abuse.

Physicians who care for children must be aware both of MBP and of child sexual abuse. The expression of both of these forms of maltreatment continues to be elucidated. Both require exceptional investigative and diagnostic skills yet both have significantly different circumstances in which they persist and unfold. Both groups of children are betrayed by their caretakers and have the potential for significant long-term psychological morbidity. There is some evidence that victims of MBP grow up to have specific deviations around illness, just as victims of child sexual abuse may as a result of their traumatic sexualization act out their victimization. MBP, however, has more potential for serious physical sequelae, including death.

The investigation of MBP usually occurs primarily in the hospital, usually with child protection and law enforcement brought in after extensive and invasive diagnostic procedures have been performed. Sexual abuse allegations are investigated with the assistance of child protection and law enforcement from the moment the possibility of sexual abuse arises. Both groups of children need protection from the perpetrators of their abuse. MBP victims are protected when removed from their primary caretakers (usually mothers). Sexually abused children's protection begins when the perpetrator, usually a male, no longer has access to the child. MBP is a more indirect distortion of power, used to obtain validation and nurturing of the perpetrator's pathology. Sexual abuse is a direct use of power to control victims for the perpetrator's gratification. The chief differentiating features of the two disorders are shown in Table 18–1.

Summary

The therapeutic needs of both groups of children, following substantiation of their abuse, are significant. The prognosis for sexually

Table 18–1
Differential Characteristics Between MBP and CSA*

Characteristics	MBP	CSA
Perpetrator	Females	Generally males
Primary historian	Mother	Child
Factitious history	Often	Seldom
History/behavior reflective of victimization	Infrequent	Frequent
Investigation conducted by	Primarily medical	Primary CPS**/law enforcement
Setting for investigation	Generally a hospital	Home or clinic
Victim Morbidity	Laboratory and/or physical examination positive or negative	Physical examination normal or demonstrates nonspecific residual
Victim Mortality	possible	infrequent
Protection of victim	Removal from mother	Remove perpetrator from home
Occurance during custody/visitation dispute	Unusual	Occasionally
Demonstrable mental illness in perpetrator	More often	Overt mental illness not apparent
Sex preference (victim)	None	Female more common

*CSA=child sexual abuse,**CPS=child protection services.

abused children removed from the home or protected from further abuse is generally better than for children who are victims of MBP. The prognosis for the rehabilitation of MBP parents and perpetrators of sexual abuse remains uncertain. Physicians can act in the best interest of the children they care for by acknowledging and understanding both of these forms of maltreatment—and their over-lap—and demonstrating a willingness to work in a multidisciplinary fashion with colleagues in mental health, law enforcement, and child protection.

References

1. Nicol AR and Eccles M. Psychotherapy for munchausen syndrome by proxy. *Arch Dis Child.* 1985; 60:344–348.
2. Finkelhor D. Perpetrators. In: *Child Sexual Abuse: New Theory and Research.* 1984; New York: Free Press: 33–53.
3. Finkel MA. Anogenital trauma in sexually abused children. *Pediatrics.* 1989; 84:317–322.
4. Goodwin J, Sahd D, and Rada RT. False allegations and false denials of incest; clinical myths and clinical realities. In: Goodwin J (ed). *Sexual Abuse: Incest Victims and Their Families.* 1982; Boston: John Wright: 17–26.
5. Jones D. Reliable and fictitious accounts of sexual abuse to children. *J Interpersonal Violence.* 1987; 2:27–45.
6. Faller KC. Possible explanations for child sexual abuse allegations in divorce. *Am J Orthopsychiatry.* 1994; 61:86–90.
7. Thoennes N. and Tjaden P. The extent, nature and validity of sexual abuse allegations in custody/visitation disputes. *Child Abuse Negl.* 1990; 14:151–163.

19

Neurological Manifestations

Daune L. MacGregor

Neurological symptoms are the most common presentation of Munchausen Syndrome by Proxy (MBP). Several extensive reviews[1,2] have noted that factitious epilepsy, altered levels of consciousness, and apnea account for more than 75% of cases, with seizures being the most frequent central nervous system (CNS) symptom. Because of the frequency of neurological symptoms and common overlap with other presentations (for example, hypoglycemia with lethargy or seizures), child neurologists are among those clinical specialists frequently sought out to assist in the evaluation of possible MBP. Neurological diagnosis, particularly of epileptic syndromes, is often based on historical information, being supplemented rather than confirmed by laboratory measures. The absence of electrophysiological, neuroimaging, or biochemical evidence does not exclude organic disease in many CNS disorders, making neurological symptoms a frequent target for parental simulation or symptom production.

Changing patterns of health care, from inpatient to ambulatory[3] and single-practitioner to multidisciplinary, might result in an altered complexity of neurological presentation. The greater availability of neurophysiological and imaging techniques and procedures coupled with increasing public knowledge and media focus on medical issues could produce increasingly sophisticated MBP symptoms. Computerized, paperless health records may or may not affect the frequency of MBP. It is even conceivable that a computer literate parent could alter a child's medical history, examination, and laboratory results.[4,5]

An extraordinary range of neurological symptoms, including ataxia, weakness, and movement disorders, has been reported as part of MBP. MBP may occur in an otherwise well child or complicate an existing neurologic or developmental syndrome (e.g., production of seizures by suffocation in a physically handicapped child). Neuropsychological morbidity, such as withdrawal or hyperactivity, in the child victim can also confuse the neurological diagnostic effort. The child may even become a participant in the process, feigning abnormal behaviors such as lethargy and epilepsy.[6] The evolution of symptoms in MBP children to an adolescent and adult conversion disorder or Munchausen Syndrome is well recognized.[7]

An illustrative case was seen at the Hospital for Sick Children (Toronto).

K.P. was a 5-1/2-year-old boy admitted to hospital by his attending neurologist for arteriography to rule out Moya Moya syndrome, a progressive vasculopathy involving the basal cerebral arteries. Two siblings were reported to have had cyclic neutropenia. The mother was a nursing assistant. Past medical history included recurrent outpatient assessment for febrile and afebrile seizures beginning at 9 months of age. The child had been treated with phenobarbital and diphenylhydantoin without improvement in seizure frequency. Despite increasing dosage of medication, therapeutic anticonvulsant drug levels were not achieved.

At the time of hospital admission, the mother described episodes of right-sided hemiparesis. The weakness would last for periods of up to 2 weeks and on some occasions there was an association with a seizure event. He had also been reported to have recurrent right-sided throbbing headaches, often accompanied by nausea and vomiting. The admitting differential diagnosis included possible Moya Moya syndrome, hemiplegic migraine, and a mitochondrial disorder. Physical and neurological examination was normal although minimal discoordination of the right leg was seen with hopping and running.

Investigations during the admission included an arteriogram, brain perfusion study, sleep deprived electroencephalogram (EEG), evoked potential studies, lumbar puncture with cerebrospinal fluid (CSF) analysis, and blood and urine testing. All results were normal.

Careful historical review then revealed inconsistencies. At the time of previous outpatient visits for neurological assessment the complaint had been of left-sided weakness and headache. The description of the hemiparetic symptom also varied, as the mother gave different details to different hospital personnel. The side varied from right to left in different accounts. The mother also described him as requiring frequent visits to local hospital emergency department to obtain a variety of medications for pain relief because of headache. Analgesics used included intravenous morphine and codeine. The mother carried with her to these visits a letter from a pediatrician supporting the administration of morphine to the child because of the severity of his headaches. Past neurological investigations had included multiple biochemical and metabolic blood and urine tests, two CT scans, an MRI and several EEG studies. Other symptoms reported included prolonged sleeping (up to 18–20 hours per day) and fever.

The diagnosis of MBP was considered and a referral was made to the hospital's Suspected Child Abuse and Neglect (SCAN) team. Investigation of the case revealed there had been 90 emergency department/office visits and 12 hospital admissions. Involvement of the Children's Aid Society was recommended.

Seizures

Seizures are seen as a presentation of MBP in 42% of cases.[8] In 1984, 32 children were reported[9] who had been extensively investigated and treated for factitious epilepsy. Many of these children had seizures as their sole false symptom. A small number also had genuine epilepsy diagnosed in the past. The "seizures" of MBP are characterized by the following features:

1. Report of occurrence commonly at night during sleep
2. Frequent attacks
3. History of episodes exclusively from parent
4. Allegedly witnessed by other observers, but not substantiated on careful questioning of the third party
5. Poor control with appropriate anti-convulsant drugs
6. Cessation when the child is placed in an alternate care setting and antiepileptic drugs are discontinued

A literature review failed to provide details of the seizure types seen in reported cases of MBP other than the description of generalized tonic/clonic (and rarely partial) seizures. Episodes may be febrile or, more commonly, afebrile. Parents frequently report episodes of status epilepticus resulting in emergency department visits. A case report of a child taught to feign seizures describes attacks of shaking or trembling with apparent unconsciousness and, on one occasion, a "postictal" arm paralysis that persisted for two days.[10] Associated symptoms of headache, cyanosis, vomiting, and lethargy are often provided by the parent.

The methods of production (or simulation) of seizures include falsification of history, poisoning, suffocation, and/or carotid sinus pressure. In younger children, partial suffocation can result in anoxic episodes giving the appearance of seizures.[11] There may also be substantial morbidity from investigations and prescription of combinations of anticonvulsant medication and diets to treat the presumed epilepsy often without satisfactory results.

The diagnosis of MBP is often retrospective based on the establishment of other MBP features.[12] When poisoning is suspected, analysis of blood, urine, and intravenous fluids must be requested. Pharmacokinetic evaluation using therapeutic drug monitoring techniques can assist in diagnosis.[13] Suffocation may be witnessed directly or through video surveillance.[14]

Disorders of Consciousness

An extensive literature review of MBP[15] found "central nervous system depression" as a clinical presentation in 19% of patients. Symptoms and signs included lethargy, prolonged sleep, and unconsciousness. The parent describes recurrent episodes of loss of consciousness requiring vigorous resuscitation or obscure spells[16] of altered consciousness, lethargy, and daytime sleepiness. These symptoms may result in a referral to a sleep disorders center. A case report of an infant with a history of episodes of alternating stupor and delirium was diagnosed as MBP after toxicology screening demonstrated aspirin, diphenhydramine, opiates, and barbiturates in the child's blood.[17] These neurological symptoms are usually produced by administration of sedatives, tranquilizers, and other medications[18] or by suffocation. Coma and/or seizures secondary to factitious hypoglycemia caused by the covert administration of insulin can be detected by the presence of low serum levels of C-peptide and hyperinsulinism.[19]

Apnea and Apparent Life-Threatening Events

Neurologists are frequently asked to consult on infants with apneic spells and apparent life-threatening events (ALTEs, formerly called "near miss sudden infant death syndrome"). The full extent of this problem and its management from a pulmonary perspective are treated in Chapter 6. In cases of MBP the child's neurological and clinical status is incongruently well when compared with the history. The apnea, if real, is usually produced by suffocation. The clinical signs of asphyxia may be minimal other than multiple petechiae on the face[20] or conjunctiva.[21] There is often an overlap with possible genuine secondary seizures. In addition to being assessed for apnea, children may have been subjected to neurological investigations and ineffective anticonvulsant treatment.[22] Evaluative techniques including EEG studies may be required for proper diagnosis and management.

Other Presentations

Other neurological presentations (see Table 19–1) have been reported including nystagmus,[23] hypotonia,[24] developmental delay[25-27] (cognitive and motor delay with hearing impairment), headaches and other migraine syndromes,[28,29] cyclic vomiting,[30] hyperactivity,[31,32] and weakness. Nonaccidental poisoning with medication and other toxic chemical compounds may produce acute or long term neurological signs and symptoms (see Table 19–1).

Of particular neurological interest is the production of myopathy by administration of Ipecac (emetine) causing a generalized reversible muscle weakness.[33,34] Electrodiagnostic studies are not specific in such instances.[35] Muscle histology in emetine myopathy among adult patients demonstrates myofibrillar degeneration and mitochondrial alterations.[36] Pediatric presentation is with mild motor delay.[37] In one reported case, severe hypotonia and inadequate sucking in a 6-week-old infant were found to be caused by Ipecac poisoning.[38] The mother had added syrup of ipecac to expressed breast milk. Analysis of blood, urine, breast milk, gastric contents, and intravenous or oral fluids administered to the child can lead to the diagnosis of MBP.

Table 19-1
Reported Nonaccidental Poisonings and Neurological MBP

Neurological Sign or Symptom	Drug or Chemical Compound Used*
Seizures	Salt, Tricyclic Antidepressants[†+] Phenothiazines[†@], Propranolol+ Insulin[†], Excess water, Hydrocarbons[†+] Metaldehyde
Altered levels of consciousness (lethargy, excessive sleepiness)	Anticonvulsants (barbiturates), Perphenazine, Aspirin, Acetaminophen, Hypnotics, Methadone, Cannabis, Diphenoxylate, Diphenhydramine, Chloral hydrate
Apnea/ALTE	Benzodiazepines
Ataxia	Sedative-hypnotics (barbiturates), Phentermine, Methaqualone
Syncope and dizziness	Chlorthalidone, Furosemide
Tremor	Salbutamol, Diphenylhydantoin
Movement Disorders	Phenothiazines, Metoclopramide, Antihistamines, Propranolol

*not listed in order of frequency
[†]also produce altered states of consciousness
+ also produce apnea
@ also produce ataxia

Conclusion

Of greatest concern to child neurologists are the long-term disabilities that may be seen in the child victims of MBP. Severe brain injury from asphyxia or poison administration may result in mental retardation,[39] motor handicap including severe spastic forms of cerebral palsy, and sensory disabilities such as cortical blindness. It is therefore incumbent upon neurologists to be familiar with MBP and to consider this possibility especially when confronted with a bizarre, seemingly inexplicable, pattern of chronic neurologic illness. Likewise, it is important a neurologist be included in the multidisciplinary diagnosis and management of MBP cases.

References

1. Meadow R. Fictitious epilepsy. *Lancet*. 1984; 2:25–28.
2. Rosenberg DA. Web of deceit: a literature review of Munchausen syndrome by proxy. *Child Abuse Negl*. 1987; 11:547–563.
3. Guandolo VL. Munchausen syndrome by proxy: an outpatient challenge. *Pediatrics*. 1985; 75:526–530.
4. Light MJ and Sheridan MS. Munchausen syndrome by proxy and apnea (MBPA). *Clin Pediatr*. 1990; 29:162–168.
5. Rosenberg, Web.
6. Croft RD and Jervis M. Munchausen's syndrome in a 4 year old. *Arch Dis Child*. 1989; 64:740–741.
7. McGuire TL and Feldman KW. Psychologic morbidity of children subjected to Munchausen syndrome by proxy. *Pediatrics*. 1988; 83:289–292.
8. Rosenberg, Web.
9. Meadow, Fictitious epilepsy.
10. Croft and Jervis, Munchausen's.
11. Meadow, Fictitious epilepsy.
12. Reece RM. Unusual manifestations of child abuse. *Pediatr Clin N Am*. 1990; 37:905–921.
13. Mahesh VK, Stern HP, Kearns GL, et al. Application of pharmacokinetics in the diagnosis of chemical abuse in Munchausen syndrome by proxy. *Clin Pediatr*. 1988; 27:243–246.
14. Southall DP, Stebbens VA, Rees SV, et al. Apnoeic episodes induced by smothering: two cases identified by covert video surveillance. *Br Med J*. 1987; 294:1637–1641.
15. Rosenberg, Web.
16. Griffith JL and Slovik LS. Munchausen syndrome by proxy and sleep disorders medicine. *Sleep*. 1989; 12:178–183.
17. Woody RC and Jones JG. Neurologic munchausen-by-proxy syndrome. *South Med J*. 1987; 80:247–248.
18. Meadow R. Munchausen syndrome by proxy. *Arch Dis Child*. 1982; 57:92–98.
19. Mayefsky JH, Samaik AP, and Postellon DC. Factitious hypoglycemia. *Pediatrics*. 1982; 69:804–805.
20. Meadow R. Poisoning. *Br Med J*. 1989; 298:1445–1446.
21. Levin A., personal communication.
22. Makar AF and Squier PJ. Munchausen syndrome by proxy: father as perpetrator. *Pediatrics*. 1990; 85:370–373.
23. Meadow R. Neurological and developmental variants of Munchausen syndrome by proxy. *Dev Med Child Neurol*. 1991; 33:267–272.
24. Berkner P, Kastner T, and Skolnick L. Chronic ipecac poisoning in infancy: a

case report. *Pediatrics.* 1988; 82:384–385.

25. Kravitz RM and Wilmott RW. Munchausen syndrome by proxy presenting as factitious apnea. *Clin Pediatr.* 1990; 29:587–592.

26. Alexander R, Smith W, and Stevenson R. Serial munchausen syndrome by proxy. *Pediatrics.* 1990; 86:581–585.

27. Stevenson RD and Alexander R. Munchausen syndrome by proxy presenting as a developmental disability. *J Dev Behav Pediatr.* 1990; 11:262–264.

28. Guandolo, MBP.

29. Mahesh et al., Applications.

30. Embry CK. Toxic cyclic vomiting in an 11-year-old girl. *J Am Acad Child Adol Psychiat.* 1987; 26:447–448.

31. Hvizdala EV and Gellady AM. Intentional poisoning of two siblings by prescription drugs. *Clin Pediatr.* 1978; 17:480–482.

32. Stevenson and Alexander. MBP.

33. Bennett HS, Spiro AJ, et al. Ipecac-induced myopathy simulating dermatomyositis. *Neurology.* 1982; 32:91–94.

34. Duane DD and Engel AG. Emetine myopathy. *Neurology.* 1970; 20:733–739.

35. Bennett, Spiro, et al. Ipecac-induced.

36. Duane and Engel, Emetine.

37. McClung HJ, Murray R, Braden NJ, et al. Intentional Ipecac poisoning in children. *Am J Dis Child.* 1988; 142:637–639.

38. Berkner P, Kastner T, and Skolnick L. Chronic Ipecac poisoning in infancy: a case report. *Pediatrics.* 1988; 82:384–385.

39. Samuels MP and Southall DP. Munchausen syndrome by proxy. *Br J Hosp Med.* 1992; 47:759–762.

20

Developmental Disorders and Failure to Thrive

Randell C. Alexander
Lori D. Frasier

Although death or significant physical handicap may result from any form of abuse, for most survivors it is the psychological/developmental state that is most severely affected. Thus when considering any form of child abuse, including Munchausen Syndrome by Proxy (MBP), the long-term impact on the individual must also be evaluated. Table 20–1 lists the possible ways in which MBP and types of developmental impairments may interrelate.

Developmental Disorders

Diagnosing developmental disorders requires that normal development be considered not only for its average sequence and temporal order, but also for normal ranges and variations. Motor milestones may not always fit the usual sequence, for example, when a child does not crawl but begins to walk first. Cognitive, emotional, moral, and other forms of development may also have a series of stops and starts.

Developmental delay is a term used when the developmental sequence lags significantly behind the normal range and variation. Children with mild delays may eventually catch up to their peers. The term is especially appropriate for children under 5 years of age for whom estimates of developmental competence are necessarily

Table 20–1
Spectrum of MBP and Developmental Impairments

MBP presenting as a developmental disability

MBP presenting with an impairment of an aspect of development

Association between developmental impairments and MBP

Development altered by MBP

Developmental disabilities resulting from MBP

---

more imprecise and for whom predictions of future performance cannot safely be made. Child abuse or the circumstances surrounding the abused child may induce developmental delays or disorders. Some delays may be transient, some amenable to treatment, and some permanent.

A *developmental disorder* usually implies a more significant dysfunction, one which is more obvious and may be more lasting than a delay. Learning disabilities, neuromotor dysfunctions, pervasive developmental disorder (a mental health diagnosis), and mental retardation are examples of more specific developmental disorders.

The most severe developmental impairments are referred to as developmental disabilities. Although this term may be used somewhat loosely by professionals to indicate significant impairment, attempts have been made to define it more strictly. The United States Congress enacted the Developmental Disabilities Assistance and Bill of Rights Act (DD Act)[1] in 1976. The DD Act defines developmental disability as a severe, chronic disability of a person 5 years of age or older that:

1. Is attributable to a mental or physical impairment or combination of mental and physical impairments
2. Is manifested before the person attains age 22
3. Is likely to continue indefinitely
4. Results in substantial functional limitations in three or more of the following areas of major life activity: (a) self-care, (b) receptive and expressive language, (c) learning, (d) mobility, (e) self-direction, (f) capacity for independent living, and (g) economic self-sufficiency
5. Reflects the person's need for a combination and sequence of

special, interdisciplinary, or generic care, treatment, or other services that are of lifelong or extended duration and are individually planned and coordinated.

When applied to children less than age 5, the terminology implies substantial developmental delay or specific congenital or acquired conditions with a high probability of resultant developmental disability if services are not provided. Although this definition is somewhat circular in that it defines disability as an impairment and it restricts developmental disabilities to the most severe end of the continuum, it has served as a useful basis for identifying children for needed services. More recently, the Americans with Disabilities Act (ADA)[2] was enacted, which defines disability to include: a physical or mental impairment that substantially limits one or more of the major life activities of the individual; a record of having such an impairment; or being regarded as having such an impairment. Major life activities include functions such as taking care of oneself, hearing, seeing, speaking, breathing, performing manual tasks, working, and learning. The passage of the ADA in 1990 is just beginning to be reflected in efforts to end discrimination against people with disabilities and to provide them equal opportunities. Similar legislative efforts are underway in other countries.

MBP Presenting as a Developmental Disability

Among its many varied presentations, MBP has been described in which the symptoms were alleged to consist of multiple developmental disabilities, even when the strict definition of the DD Act is used.[3,4]

An 11-month-old child was seen at a tertiary hospital developmental center with complex problems including cerebral palsy, gastrostomy dependence, feeding problems, vomiting, mental retardation, and hearing difficulties necessitating bilateral hearing aids. Episodic tachycardia, hypertonic posturing, and staring spells were also reported. The mother recounted a detailed history of perinatal asphyxia leading to hypoxic-ischemic encephalopathy. She also provided multiple sophisticated details such as Apgar scores of 3 and 6. Ultimately none of the symptoms could be verified. Once birth records were obtained, they revealed no evidence of fetal distress, Apgars of 6 and 9, and a normal physical examination at birth. During the admission when the diagnosis of MBP was made, multiple medical tests and procedures included normal EEG, esophagram, endoscopy with biopsies, behavioral audiometry, and brainstem evoked responses (ABR), and physical examinations. Cognitive, speech/language, fine, and gross motor testing were age appropriate. On admission no vomiting was witnessed by the staff, but on four occasions the mother reported emesis when she was alone with the child. Once when the nurse's aide briefly left the mother and child alone, the mother called saying the child had vomited. However, the "vomitus" looked like unaltered formula, was cold to touch, and had a discrete drop of blood floating on top, suggesting that the blood had been added afterwards. A child abuse report was made and emergency custody assumed by the court.

During this admission the hearing aids were discontinued, weight gain was excellent on oral foods (which the mother had previously largely withheld), and the gastrostomy tube was removed. The child thrived in all ways. Later the case was transferred to the family's home state where a normal psychiatric examination of the mother persuaded the court to return the child to her. She later unsuccessfully sued the physician and hospital.

The mother was a former dental technician and nursing student, previously married to a physician, with a significant psychiatric history including factitious illness of her own. Despite her statement that she was coming to the developmental center for the first time, she was remembered by several staff as having brought another daughter 2 years previously with a history of "near-miss SIDS," vomiting, gastroesophageal reflux, and "rule out cerebral palsy." This daughter had undergone a Nissen fundoplication. No abnormalities of this daughter were found at the developmental center.

Developmental Impairments Caused by MBP

In addition to the MBP perpetrator directly mimicking or alleging developmental disabilities, real developmental impairments may result from the attempt to produce illness. MBP can be accompanied by the production of signs, such as recurrent anoxia, that lead to significant morbidity,[5,6] including brain damage, which can leave a child with multiple developmental difficulties. The medical procedures inflicted upon the child in good faith also carry a risk of morbidity and death. For example, anesthesia is used in a number of medical procedures to investigate MBP allegations.[7] The risk of anesthesia death is relatively low for otherwise healthy children, but death can occur. Morbidity from anesthesia can manifest as persistent coma, brain infarcts, or damage to organ systems.

With a complex form of child abuse such as MBP, it is not surprising that effects include alteration of the normal processes of development. Physical impairments can result from central nervous system damage arising from suffocation, carotid artery pressure, or administration of drugs. The emotional/behavioral effects are more common and may be nearly as profound.[8,9] These include hyperactive and oppositional behaviors, withdrawal, passive tolerance of medical procedures (and possibly tolerance to production of signs/symptoms by the perpetrator), and with older children, school difficulties and cooperation with the perpetrator. Not only are the child victims exposed to the behaviors of the offenders and the consequences of any direct illness production, but they are repeatedly engaged with the medical environment. The negative effects of repeated or chronic hospitalization on development are well described in children with "legitimate" disease.[10,11] More hospitalizations may mean less schooling and estrangement from its socialization. The effect of keeping children on an apnea monitor for an abnormally prolonged period, restricting physical activity because of a presumed health condition, or maintaining the precautions necessary for children with seizure disorder is to decrease their stimulation and possibly harm their self-image. Perhaps the most basic impairment of development is the violation of trust between parents and children. As with other forms of child abuse, child victims may grow up to have dysfunctional relationships based upon a distorted concept of trust and what can be expected in interactions with others.

Even when no cause-effect relationship exists between developmental impairments and MBP, there is the possibility that naturally occurring disabilities place a child at risk of MBP. There is a known correlation between developmental disabilities and child abuse,[12,13] although no study to date has documented whether children with disabilities may have a higher rate of being MBP victims. Hypothetically, a parent who becomes involved in a medical environment, as with the birth of a premature baby, may learn the social milieu and the medical skills to successfully create a MBP scenario. Perhaps the idea of using the medical system for secondary gains evolves from familiarity with it, either because the perpetrator has a medical background or because the child has an impairment requiring greater medical attention.

Failure to Thrive (FTT)

In a pioneering textbook in the then new field of pediatrics, *Diseases of Infancy and Childhood*, children were described who "ceased to thrive."[14] In a later edition, the term "failure to thrive" was used.[15] Henry Dwight Chapin referred to "atrophic infants," wasting away in poor home environments.[16] Rene Spitz[17] popularized the notion that psychological factors were responsible for children's developmental deficits and malnutrition. His theory of "hospitalism" combined "anaclitic depression" with growth failure. "Maternal deprivation syndrome," the idea that children might waste away from a lack of love, arose from this viewpoint. However, careful studies of actual calorie consumption by institutionalized children demonstrated that whether or not they were in fact emotionally deprived, the basis of the FTT was that they consumed fewer calories than needed for normal growth.[18] The concept of organic and nonorganic failure to thrive arose from these concerns.

More recently the distinction between organic and nonorganic FTT has been questioned. Current models of FTT emphasize the characteristics of the parent, child, environment, and interactions among them.[19-22] Every child with FTT has both an organic (insufficient weight gain) and a nonorganic problem. By the time that FTT is diagnosed, organic and nonorganic factors are invariably intertwined. Thus most pediatricians in the United States simultaneously evaluate psychosocial and physiological factors to determine the etiology of the FTT and to help with its management.[23] FTT may be a life-threatening condition or have substantial developmental impact, even after the FTT itself is corrected. Estimates of the frequency of FTT range from 1 to 10% of all pediatric hospitalizations of children followed in rural outpatient clinics.[24]

DEFINING FTT

No definition of FTT is commonly accepted, despite its relative frequency in the population. The multiple causes and manifestations of FTT ensure that a single definition will not work. Most definitions of FTT actually refer to "failure to grow." FTT has been considered when a child is below the 3rd percentile of weight for height on a standard growth chart. Any child whose weight curve crosses two or more major "percentile lines" on the growth curve is sometimes thought to have FTT. Neither of these definitions works for all cases and there may be important exceptions. More generally, FTT is a relative growth pattern determined by a physician to be subnormal for a child, considering the underlying medical status. The developmental consequences of FTT may include impairments of brain growth, language development, and psychological function.

FTT AND MBP

A number of features of FTT caused by neglect mirror the situation encountered with MBP. Parents may lie about the dietary history of their child, overestimating the amount of calories actually consumed. This may occur before or during treatment efforts. The child may have a number of medical encounters with considerable testing. This may entail a great deal of unnecessary expense and trauma to the child. The child may improve when the parent is absent. In MBP cases when food is deliberately withheld, laxatives or enemas are given, or certain medical conditions such as vomiting or diarrhea are induced, the child may present with FTT.

FTT has been described as both a form and a component of MBP.[25] The similarities may include deception, presentation for medical care, and resolution of the situation in the care of others. However, many disagree with this characterization. Whereas MBP is rare, FTT is fairly common. The deception in FTT may not be particularly deliberate nor is it typically for the purposes of interacting with the medical system. Denial often is present, as in most forms of neglect, but in many cases the caretaker eventually can be taught to recognize the antecedents of the behavior. In contrast, MBP perpetrators almost never admit to their actions and are quite interested in obtaining medical attention. In instances of FTT, videotapes of parent-child interactions may show dysfunctional feeding patterns. One such pattern, seen by many clinicians, consists of the mother bringing a bottle near the child's mouth and pulling it away at the last minute. Sometimes the practice is so subtle that an observer in the room may be unaware that the child is not actually being fed. However, unlike the MBP perpetrator, the mother may not be aware of this pattern. Although the interaction is dysfunctional, not all dysfunctional interactions are MBP.

In her review of 117 MBP cases, Rosenberg[26] found that FTT was associated with 14%. Induced chronic disease was the most frequent cause, but the deliberate withholding of food also occurred. The dynamics of FTT and MBP must also be distinguished from parents who are overly rigorous about diet, perhaps concerned with the child's health or achieving an ideal of thinness.

Summary

As with any form of child abuse, MBP has much of its impact upon the child's development, interfering with emotional functioning, behavior, and trust. The alterations in normal development may range from transient delays to permanent developmental disabilities to death. MBP may also present as a developmental impairment. It is unknown whether children with developmental disabilities are at higher risk for MBP. Failure to thrive specifically has significant developmental consequences, and may be one of the ways in which MBP presents. FTT may be a consequence of the production of factitious disease, and although not usually considered to be a type of MBP, may share many of its dynamics.

References

1. Developmental Disabilities Assistance and Bill of Rights Act, 42 U.S.C.A. Section 6000 et seq. (West Supp. 1993).
2. Americans with Disabilities Act of 1990, 42 U.S.C.A. Section 12101 et seq. (West Supp. 1993) and implementing regulations.
3. Stevenson RD and Alexander RC. Munchausen syndrome by proxy presenting as a developmental disability. *Devel Behav Pediatr.* 1990; 11:262–264.
4. Kahn G and Goldman E. Munchausen syndrome by proxy: mother fabricates infant's hearing impairment. *Speech Hear Res.* 1991; 34:957–959.
5. Rosenberg DA. Web of deceit: a literature review of Munchausen syndrome by proxy. *Child Abuse Negl.* 1987; 11:547–563.

6. Alexander R, Smith W, and Stevenson R. Serial munchausen syndrome by proxy. *Pediatrics*. 1990; 86:581–585.
7. Kurlandsky L, Lukjoff JY, Zinkham WH, et al. Munchausen syndrome by proxy: definition of factitious bleeding in an infant by CR 51 labeling of erythrocytes. *Pediatrics*. 1979; 63:228–231.
8. McGuire TL and Feldman FW. Psychologic morbidity of children subjected to Munchausen syndrome by proxy. *Pediatrics*. 1989; 83:289–292.
9. Bools CN, Neale BA, and Meadow SR. Follow up of victims of fabricated illness (Munchausen syndrome by proxy). *Arch Dis Child*. 1993; 69:625–630.
10. Prugh DC, Staub EM, Kirschenbaum RM, et al. A study of the emotional reactions of children and families to hospitalization and illness. *Am J Orthopsych*. 1953; 23:70–106.
11. Robertson J. *Young Children in Hospitals*, 2nd ed. 1970; London, Tavistock.
12. Benedict MI, White RB, Wulff LM, et al. Reported maltreatment in children with multiple disabilities. *Child Abuse Negl*. 1990; 14:207–217.
13. Tharinger D, Burrows-Horton C, and Millea S. Sexual abuse and exploitation of children and adults with mental retardation and other handicaps. *Child Abuse Negl*. 1990; 14:301–312.
14. Holt LE. *Diseases of Infancy and Childhood*. 1899; New York; Appleton.
15. Holt LE, McIntosh R. *Holt's Diseases of Infancy and Childhood* 10th ed. 1933; New York: Appleton-Century.
16. Chapin HD. A plan of dealing with atrophic infants and children. *Arch Pediatr*. 1908; 25:491–496.
17. Spitz RA. Hospitalism: an inquiry into the genesis of psychiatric conditions in early childhood. *Psychoanalytic Study of the Child*. 1945; 1:53–74.
18. Whitten CF, Pettit MG, and Fischoff J. Evidence that growth failure from maternal deprivation is secondary to undereating. *JAMA*. 1969; 209:1675–1682.
19. Goldson E. Child abuse: a social-psychological-medical disorder. In: Gellert E (ed.). *Psychosocial Aspects of Pediatric Care*. 1978; New York: Grune and Stratton: pp. 229–243.
20. Engel GL. The need for a new medical model: a challenge for biomedicine. *Science*. 1977; 196:129–136.
21. Casey PH. Failure to thrive: a reconceptualization. *Devel Behav Pediatr*. 1983; 4:63–66.
22. Goldson E, Milla PJ, and Bentovim A. Failure to thrive: a transactional issue. *Fam Syst Med*. 1985; 3:205–213.
23. Alexander RC. Failure to thrive. *Advisor*. 1992; 5:1–13.
24. Mitchell WG, Gorrel RW, and Greenbert RA. Failure to thrive: a study in a primary care setting. Epidemiology and follow-up. *Pediatrics*. 1980; 65:971–977.
25. Bools CN, Neale BA, and Meadow R: Co-morbidity associated with fabricated illness (Munchausen syndrome by proxy). *Arch Dis Child*. 1992; 67:77–79.
26. Rosenberg DA. Web of deceit: a literature review of Munchausen syndrome by proxy. *Child Abuse Negl*. 1987; 11:547–563.

21

Adult Victims
Mircea Sigal and David Altmark

The label of Munchausen Syndrome by Proxy (MBP), or Factitious Disorder by Proxy with Physical Symptoms, as we believe it should be correctly named, may be applied to anyone whose planned, repetitive, compulsive behavior is directed to inflicting damage, and/or fabricating symptoms with the intent of causing the victim to be regarded as ill.

MBP is a disorder in which one individual produces symptoms in another for the purpose of indirectly assuming a sick role. Although typically this pattern of interaction occurs between mother and child, it can develop in other kinds of human interaction models in which both the victim and the perpetrator are adults. The diagnosis of MBP is given to the individual inducing the symptoms ("the perpetrator"). If there is no evidence that the person with the symptoms colluded in the intentional production of the symptoms, then the perpetrator is given the diagnosis of MBP and the individual with symptoms is diagnosed as Induced MBP or Induced Factitious Disorders. If collusion exists, then the perpetrator is given the diagnosis of MBP, and the victim should be diagnosed as suffering from Munchausen Syndrome or Factitious Disorders.[1]

This definition, which we see as too rigid, glosses over a whole range of bizarre human interactions. Until now, only a few cases of Munchausen Syndrome by Proxy with Adult Victims (MBP-Adult) have been reported. The first, described by the authors in 1986[2] and supplemented in 1991[3], is extensively described below. The second, described by Smith and Ardern in 1989,[4] refers to the factitious pathological interaction between two adults in which the victim was an elderly man. In 1984, Meadow[5] mentioned four adults with false epileptic seizures invented or induced by a relative.

We believe that these cases represent only the tip of the iceberg of a phenomenologically identifiable diagnostic entity, and that other cases were not described because the lack of an accepted diagnostic framework caused them to be understood as simply bizarre or criminal interactions between adults.

The adult variant of the syndrome could account for those gray areas of human interaction, not necessarily in the field of criminology, where for unconscious and sometimes conscious reasons, with or without some measure of collusion, one adult fabricates mental or physical symptoms in a significant partner. In our opinion, MBP-Adult could be reclassified into two variants:

1. MBP-Adult with physical signs and symptoms. Cases: "The Gasoline Man," "The Old Man with his Companion Lady and her Pet Dog"
2. MBP-Adult with psychological signs and symptoms ("Gaslight Phenomenon"). Case: "The Cuckold Man."

Illustrative Case Histories:

The Gasoline Man (Mr. L.)[6,7]

Mr. L. was first examined by us in 1986, while serving an exceptionally heavy sentence of 46 years in prison, having been accused and convicted of the murder of his wife in 1980 and of causing severe invalidity to his girlfriend in 1983. He had a history of difficulties in interpersonal relationships and disruptive behavior, beginning in early childhood. He married and had two children. His wife became ill in 1979, when atypical abscesses appeared all over her body. She lost weight and had to be hospitalized. The etiology of the abscesses remained unknown to the doctors, who were baffled by a clinical picture which did not resemble any known disease. With the decline of his wife's condition, Mr. L.'s behavior became more and more devoted. He gained the respect and admiration of both the medical and nursing staff. In fact, Mr. L. later confessed to the police that he had put sleeping pills in his wife's coffee and then injected her with gasoline in different parts of her body, thus accounting for the atypical abscesses. Mr. L. explained that he was afraid of his wife leaving him, and by injecting her with poisonous substances and making her ill, he created an opportunity for nursing her, thus forcing her to stay with him and at the same time gaining respect and admiration for his "exemplary behavior."

Three years after his wife's painful death, Mr. L. employed a 21-year-old girl to take care of his daughters. When she threatened to leave, he again put sleeping pills in the girl's coffee, and when she lost consciousness, he injected her with gasoline in the neck, breasts and buttocks. As the girl eventually became ill and paraplegic, Mr. L. again played the role of a caring and extremely cooperative boyfriend, asking the doctors for more laboratory tests and inviting specialists for consultation for her. Even after conviction, he nonetheless regarded his behavior as an expression of "love and caring" and not as criminal.

While in prison, Mr. L. was a model prisoner and was rewarded with numerous responsibilities inside the compound, including access to the medical clinic, where he enjoyed a certain popularity among the medical staff. He developed a possessive relationship with his cellmate, to whom he wrote letters, impersonating family members in order to gain access to and control of the cellmate's inner emotional life. Learning of the man's plan to escape prison, and threatened again with abandonment, Mr. L. returned to his previous behavioral pattern by putting his partner to sleep using sleeping pills mixed with alcohol which he had obtained in the medical clinic. He then injected turpentine into various parts of Mr. D.'s body and abused him sexually.

Psychiatric examination was performed in the psychiatric ward of the prison. Mr. L. was cooperative and did not express any signs of anxiety. His affect was not remarkable, was even shallow, considering the consequences of his acts. No cognitive defects or any signs of formal thought disorder were found. His thought content was dominated by a feeling of injustice inflicted upon him.

Psychodiagnostic examination that included Wechsler Adult Intelligence Test, Rorschach, Bender, Draw A Person, and Thematic Apperception Test was administered. The results indicated that Mr. L.'s I.Q. was 117. No distortion of reality testing was found. The tests suggested a narcissistic personality organization with a need for symbiotic relations with significant others. His emotional and sexual relationships with women evoked panic with latent homosexual characteristics. The Rorschach Test suggested that he tried to resolve the conflict by turning the female object into a patient, dependent on him, thus trying the object to him while avoiding any sexual threats.

The Old Man with his Companion Lady and her Pet Dog

This case, reported in 1989 by Smith and Ardern,[8] describes a 65-year-old patient with a very long history of medical, surgical, psychiatric, and dental referrals. As the authors point out, one of the most striking features noted was that no positive findings were elicited, despite thorough medical and lab checkups. Most of the symptoms were reported by the patient's girlfriend, with no confirmatory evidence. This companion, a lady 55 years old, had previously worked as a nurse. Before meeting the old man, she had a history of psychiatric admissions and was diagnosed as suffering from "reactive depression secondary to a hysterical personality."

For several years she had a history of mental and medical referrals to health care professionals, including what was described as a manipulative pattern of relationships. This included problems with her pet dog, with whom she went from professional to professional for advice. She spent large amounts of money on veterinary bills because her male dog "kept mounting legs, both animate and inanimate." After meeting her companion, her doctor-seeking behavior changed abruptly, and instead of presenting herself or the dog with physical symptoms or signs of mental distress, she became actively busy promoting her friend's referral for medical examinations and treatments.

The lady was finally diagnosed as suffering from MBP when it became evident that her companion's symptoms were factitious and that she had fabricated them. The shifting from a previous pattern of behavior that may warrant the label of Munchausen's Syndrome to MBP-Adult occurred when she began to receive more benefits from his illness behavior than from her own.

The Gaslight Phenomenon

The term *Gaslight phenomenon*, coined by Barton and Whitehead in 1969,[9] is based on a classic play, *The Gaslight*, by P. Hamilton published in 1939, in which a husband plots to get rid of his wife by driving her into a psychiatric institution. In the play, the husband manipulated the gas light in a way that made his wife's complaints about it seem as if she were psychotic.

Barton and Whitehead described three cases, one of which is discussed below. Additional cases were described by Smith and Sinanan,[10] Tyndal,[11] Lund and Gardiner,[12] and Cawthra and co-workers.[13] In those cases the presentation of mental illness was found to have been induced or imposed on the patient by some other person for that other person's gain. The gain may be the removal of the patient to hospital for financial reasons or as a solution for family disputes. Boulette and co-workers[14] describe a "mind control" variant of the wife battering phenomenon. The abusive male uses strategies of coercion and deception similar to those used in political or religious cults. A typical instance of the Gaslight Phenomenon is presented in the following case.

The Cuckold Man

Mr. A, a 48-year-old mechanic, was admitted to a psychiatric hospital because of an alleged history of violence against his wife. She said that he had changed during the last 6 months, becoming irritable and prone to unprovoked violent outbursts. She also claimed that his memory had deteriorated and he lost his way in familiar places.

The patient denied any violent behavior, but admitted that he felt tense and depressed because he felt that his wife had changed her attitude toward him and he thought that she might be seeing another man. He remained in the hospital for 12 days without specific treatment, and no psychopathological signs were observed.

Two weeks after his discharge, his wife reported that his mental condition had worsened and that he had physically attacked her. She asked for his readmission, and when the patient refused to be hospitalized, compulsory admission was considered. At that point, however, the patient's employer asked for an urgent appointment. He reported having overheard a conversation between two men who were discussing Mr. A. It was apparent from their conversation that one of them was Mrs. A's lover, and that the story of Mr. A's violent behavior had been concocted in an attempt to gain his admission to a mental hospital and to facilitate divorce, so that the lover could marry Mrs. A. When Mrs. A was seen and confronted with the employer's report, she agreed that she had plotted with her boyfriend to get rid of her husband, but she claimed that the boyfriend had led her on and she regretted her behavior.

Phenomenology

MBP-Adult as a discrete diagnostic entity encompasses a wide range of phenomena between two adults in which the victim is, consciously or unconsciously, abused by the significant and, most probably, dominant perpetrator. Thus, the active partner of this dyad usually uses the body, as well as sometimes the mind of his victim, to create factitious illness and thus control the passive partner.

The Gaslight Phenomenon as exemplified by "the Cuckold Man," presents an interesting classification problem because of the obvious gain on the part of the perpetrator. It is doubtful that it should be classified as a factitious disorder. However, the fabrication of psychological symptoms by a perpetrator on an unknowing victim may warrant this diagnosis, and could open new ways of understanding bizarre cases of marital abuse, sometimes described in legal terms as mental cruelty.

Both the Gasoline Man and the Old Man with his Companion Lady show a compulsive pattern of inducing or inventing physical symptoms in a significant other with the intention of fabricating factitious illness in the victim so that the perpetrator can be regarded as a solicitous and caring partner. They differ, however, in the fact that in the case of the Gasoline Man, no measure of collusion was present, while in the case of the Old Man a certain measure of cooperation on the part of the victim can be assumed. The Old Man, who had no evident cognitive impairment, may have acted partly as a passive victim and partly as an accomplice in the deception. Thus, the Companion Lady is to be diagnosed as MBP-Adult while the Old Man could warrant a diagnosis of Munchausen Syndrome.

The level of cooperation on the part of the victim is an interesting point which differentiates the adult variant from the classic mother and child syndrome. Why should an adult agree to be abused? The answer to this question opens several possibilities.

1. Victims may be unaware (unconscious, as in case of the Gasoline Man).
2. Victims may be incompetent because of cognitive defects such as dementia.
3. Victims may be involved in such dependent relationships with the perpetrators that they forfeit their will or self-defense to the dominant partner.
4. Victims may be frightened of the dominant partner.
5. Victims may be participating in a sadomasochistic relationship.

Another interesting aspect of this bizarre entity is the frequent shifting of the perpetrator's attention from one object to another. It has been pointed out[15] that some mothers who create factitious illness in their children suffered from Munchausen Syndrome before turning against their offspring. In the case of the Gasoline Man attention shifts from one woman to another and then to a homosexual partner. In the case of the Old Man with his Companion Lady, this shifting is from the perpetrator herself to her pet and then to her companion. This indicates that the object in itself is important only when it becomes the container of the perpetrator's aggressive, dependent, and narcissistic needs.

It can be assumed that this syndrome can be expressed as a part of paraphilic relationships. Paraphilias, formerly known as sexual perversions, are defined by the existence of a specialized pathological sexual fantasy and its behavioral expression that is repetitive in nature. Sexual arousal is pathognomonically linked to the particular fantasy. In the psychoanalytic model, paraphilias are understood as a failure to complete the normal developmental process toward heterosexual adjustment, and are triggered by the unconscious threat of castration by, or separation from, the object. The common ground between MBP-Adult and the paraphilias can be seen in the perpetrator's irresistible impulses, which may include sadistic features that are ego-syntonic. The sexual component includes sexual abuse and sadomasochistic interactions. The repetitive, compulsive behavior involving a relationship between a perpetrator with a significant sexual object in the context of threatened abandonment emphasizes the similarities between this behavior and the irresistible deviant sexual behavior seen in common paraphilias.[16]

The role of an unaware and trusting doctor playing into the hands of the perpetrator may not always be as innocent as it seems. The practitioner plays an important role in the deception process as an unsuspicious accomplice of the perpetrator. The physician's usually unconditional acceptance of the perpetrator as a caring and loving partner may be the result of unconscious projective counter-identification. Eventually, a three-way relationship between the medical staff, the perpetrator, and the victim may develop, which could be termed "deception a trois." Then, when the truth comes out and the real level of deception is discovered, the doctor realizes that (s)he was unconsciously an accomplice and becomes frustrated and angry.

Psychodynamic Considerations

The cases described in the literature of the adult variant of MBP offer scarce information about the dynamics underlying the perpetrator-victim dyad. However, it can be assumed that MBP-Adult can develop only in specific personality interactions in which there is a symbiotic relationship between a narcissistic active partner and a dependent victim. The existence of overt sadistic trends in the narcissistic perpetrator and the potential threat of abandonment (real or imagined) is a malignant mixture that may trigger the emergence of this potentially catastrophic syndrome.

MBP-Adult with psychological symptoms is a complex and multimotivated phenomenon that can be understood on several levels. According to Sears,[17] "the initiating of any kind of interpersonal interaction which tends to foster emotional conflict in another person, tends to drive him crazy." The motives underlying this behavior can be seen as the psychological equivalent of murder.

When the effort to drive the other person crazy is predominantly unconscious, it may represent the desire to expel, and thus get rid of, madness in oneself that may be seen in Induced Delusional Disorders (follie a deux). This rare disorder includes a dominant individual and one or more submissive and dependent partners in a closely knit and often isolated relationship. In this relationship, the dominant individual has an already established delusional disorder and the recipient individual passively adopts his or her partner's bizarre beliefs. The main difference between follie a deux and MBP-Adult is that in the former there exists a clear delusional dimension which is usually absent in the latter. However, the coexistence of a mixed disorder can be theoretically assumed.

In MBP-Adult the patient-doctor role can be seen as a reenactment of the early parent-child relationship where the physician is the authoritative, caring, and admired parent (who takes care of the patient), as well as the rejecting and punishing parent (who hurts the patient by administrating painful treatments).

Following Sears, who sees the child's cooperation with the mother in her effort to drive him crazy as based on genuine love for the mother, we can understand similar cooperation on the part of dependent adults in the context of a symbiotic relationship with a narcissistic and sadistic partner.

Management

Management of MBP with competent adult victims differs from the classic MBP with child victims. The helpless child can be legally protected by the authorities. Elderly people, incompetent because of cognitive defects, can also be legally protected. It is much more complex to manage a situation in which the victim is cooperating with the perpetrator. We believe that early identification, although difficult, is vital, and adequate awareness of the wide range of clinical and subclinical presentations of this syndrome is essential.

Meadow[18] described several markers of MBP that are discussed elsewhere in this book. In addition to unexplained illnesses in the victim that are temporally related to the presence of the perpetrator, it is important to understand the dynamics of the relationship between the victim and the care-giver/perpetrator. The following may be noted:

1. The perpetrator is usually of a higher social and educational standing than the victim.
2. Unexplained symptoms may have occurred in more than one person significantly related to the perpetrator.
3. Staff may feel that the care-giver is in fact more interested in impressing them than worried by the partner's illness.

Once MBP-Adult has been identified, management must focus on alerting victims and fostering their efforts toward independence. That may be, in fact, a matter of survival. Management of victims will depend on their level of dependence and on their compliance toward the perpetrator. Psychotherapy should be directed to reinforcing their ego-strength and reaching a higher level of understanding of the role imposed on them and of the reasons, conscious and unconscious, that led them to comply with the perpetrators. If no collusion is present, direct confrontation between the victim and the perpetrator is warranted and separation may be a lifesaving measure. When victims are unable to take care of themselves, court intervention and guardianship are indicated.

Psychotherapeutic intervention with perpetrators themselves is difficult because of their ego-syntonic narcissistic and sadistic trends, and will require long-term insight therapy. We must take into account that the perpetrators' personality organization is primitive and alloplastic, with a tendency to act out their impulses. They usually have very little motivation for intrapsychic change.

We believe that informing general practitioners and mental health professionals about the possibility of MBP-Adult is crucial for early detection and prevention of tragic events similar to those described in the cases presented here. Although MBP has been presented in the pediatric literature, we believe that the adult variant is heavily underreported.

Is the Perpetrator Among Us?

We have presented three extreme examples of symptom fabrication by proxy in adults. However, between these clinically evident psychopathological models and normal human interaction there exists a wide, gray area, in which the "proxy mechanism" and factitious symptom creation are present. We see this gray area as a continuum, where subclinical, unidentified factitious disorders by proxy may exist. Thus we can understand cases of sexual abuse in which, for instance, a psychotherapist might deliberately cultivate his female patient's dependence needs to satisfy a narcissistic craving for love and admiration. (In such cases sexual abuse may not be the goal in itself, but the means.) A classic example from literature may be seen in Shakespeare's *Othello*, where Iago slowly distills poison in Othello's mind, fabricating a delusional disorder, jealous type, in his victim. Although his conscious motives are envy and hatred, on a deeper level, more complex motivations can be inferred.

Perpetrators, victims, and unaware doctors in the classic triad of deception can be a more common phenomenon than presumed, and we hope that this book will serve to promote the knowledge that will allow for prevention, early identification, and treatment of this syndrome.

References

1. American Psychiatric Association. *Diagnostic and Statistical Manual of Mental Disorders*, Fourth Edition. Washington, D.C.:APA; 1994:725.
2. Sigal M, Altmark D, and Carmel I. Munchausen syndrome by adult proxy; a perpetrator abusing two adults. *J Nervous and Mental Dis.* 1986; 174:696–698.

3. Sigal M, Altmark D, and Gelkopf M. Munchausen syndrome by adult proxy revisited. *Isr J Psychiatry Related Sci.* 1991; 28:33–37.

4. Smith NJ, Ardern MH. More in sickness than in health—a case study of Munchausen by proxy in the elderly. *J Family Therapy.* 1989; 11:321–334.

5. Meadow R. Fictitious epilepsy. *Lancet.* 1984; 2:25–29.

6. Sigal, et al., Adult proxy and Sigal, et al., Revisited.

7. Sigal M, Carmel I, Altmark D, and Silfen P. Munchausen syndrome by adult proxy; a psycho-dynamic analysis. *J Medicine Law* 1988; 17:49–56.

8. Smith and Arden, More in sickness.

9. Barton R, Whitehead JA. The Gaslight Phenomenon. *Lancet.* 1969; I:1258–1260.

10. Smith CG, Sinanan K. The "gaslight" phenomenon reappears. A modification of the Ganser Syndrome. *Br J Psychiatry.* 1972; 120:685–686.

11. Tyndal M. The "gaslight phenomenon." *Br J Psychiatry.* 1973; 122:367–371.

11. Lund CA and Gardiner AQ. The gaslight phenomenon—an institutional variant, Br J Psychiatry. 1977; 131:533–534.

12. Cawthra R, Hassanyeh F. Imposed psychosis. *Br J Psychiatry.* 1987; 150:553–556, 1987.

14. Boulette TR and Andersen SM. "Mind control" and the battering of women. *Cultic Studies J.* 1986; 3:25–35.

15. Sigal M, Gelkopf M, and Meadow R. Munchausen by proxy syndrome: the triad of abuse, self-abuse, and deception. *Comprehensive Psychiatry.* 1989; 6:527–533.

16. Blackwell B. The Munchausen syndrome. *Br J Hosp Med.* 1968; 1:98.

17. Sears HF. The effort to drive the other person crazy—an element in the etiology and psychotherapy of schizophrenia. *Br J Med Psychology.* 1959; 32:1–18.

18. Meadow R. Munchausen syndrome by proxy. *Arch Dis Child.* 1982; 57:92–98.

II

The Role of the Professional

22

A Multidisciplinary Approach

Marcellina Mian

Maltreatment of a child by Munchausen Syndrome by Proxy (MBP) requires the participation of several people. The extended family, medical caretakers, legal system, child protection services, and other professionals can all be unwitting participants in this complicated problem. By the same token, some of these participants are potentially key in the identification and protection of the child who is the victim of MBP.

Need for a Multidisciplinary Team

In general, the problem of child abuse is most effectively addressed using a multidisciplinary model. This approach is particularly recommended in MBP because of the many factors that render this entity very complex and difficult.[1] Several factors make multidisciplinary management difficult but essential.

Professionals' Lack of Knowledge and Denial. As documented by Kaufman and co-workers,[2] many physicians do not have a working knowledge of MBP. Child protection agencies and the legal system have to deal with such cases in small but increasing numbers while suffering from continued lack of knowledge.[3,4] For some professionals, the barrier is an inability to accept that parents can act in this way toward their children. For others, a diagnostic entity which is factitious cannot be serious. Professionals are often shocked when they learn the full range and malevolence of abuse inflicted by the offending parent. The omission of factitious illness

271

from the differential diagnosis of a child is the largest impediment to early discovery of MBP.[5] In our experience, health care givers are more willing to entertain hitherto unfamiliar and unreported disease entities or variations than to believe a parent could be fabricating or causing symptoms. Only after exhaustive medical evaluations have ruled out the possibility of true organic disease are physicians ready to consider factitious illness.[6] For the health care givers to entertain the possibility of MBP may also require an admission and recognition that they have unwittingly caused some or all of the morbidity in a child.[7] Further, it involves admitting to having been duped. It is difficult to face the possibility of having been a harmful fool.

A study found that, prior to the suggestion of MBP as a diagnosis, nurses had very positive feelings about families.[8] When the suspicion of MBP was raised, they experienced intense feelings of shock, disbelief, and denial, at times to the point of nausea and repulsion. The authors postulated that the nurses felt caught between their own perceptions and the physician's diagnosis. To discount either one went against the nurses' basic motivation. Physicians and social workers are also conflicted over their own perceptions of a family once the deception is discovered.[9,10]

Failure of Communication. Failure of communication among caregivers allows the offending parent the opportunity to assume control of the situation. In one of our cases at The Hospital for Sick Children (Toronto), a mother would alternately call first the pediatrician or the neurologist and then the other, misinforming each of the other's opinion until she had obtained the hospitalization or medication change that she desired. Each of the physicians believed that he was acceding to a colleague's request. Because the two busy physicians seldom communicated directly, the child's medical management was almost entirely of the mother's design.

Tertiary care centers, with their technological advances, multiple consultants and time-pressured environments add to the possible confusion in these cases. Diagnostic tests may be contradictory, conflicting opinions common, communication fragmented, information retrieval difficult, and relationships stereotyped or strained. The shallowness of contact fails to correct and even enhances these distortions.[11,12] In addition, the review of the child's course once the diagnosis of MBP is considered becomes confounded. The sequence of events is not traceable. It is unclear at whose instigation the medical interventions were conducted. The mother can legitimately claim to have been following the doctor's orders, while in fact she was the one orchestrating the entire process.

Symbiotic Relationship Between the Perpetrator Parent and Victim Child. In MBP a combination of the mother's overprotectiveness and the child's separation anxiety leads to an abnormal symbiotic relationship between the two.[13–17] The mother is usually described as dedicated and doting, dutifully ministering to her child's needs, and presenting herself as her child's champion and protector. The child appears to need to be with the mother, to crave her care and attention. This combination of dutiful mother and overattached child are often taken at face value and, being unexpected in situations involving child abuse, makes it difficult for onlookers to believe that the parent could actually be harming the child.[18,19]

Parental Denial of Wrongdoing. The ability of parents in MBP to convince lay persons and professionals alike of their innocence cannot be overemphasized. The denial of parents confronted with the suspicion that they induced factitious illness is so convincing that physicians may begin to doubt the accuracy of their own diagnosis. The parent's hostile reaction toward medical professionals often includes counter-accusations of victimization, leading some legal professionals to develop distrust of those making the allegations.[20] Physicians may fear that parents may initiate legal action—which in today's litigious environment, may successfully result in a failure of the physician to pursue the diagnosis of MBP strongly. It is important to remember, however, that MBP has been successfully prosecuted. The problem is that the factors listed here may deter professionals from pursuing the matter to a definitive conclusion.

The Need for Confrontation of Parents and Child Protection. Most health professionals find the possibility of having to deal with anger, making a mistake, saying the wrong thing, or having to defend their position in a one-on-one confrontation or in a court of law very frightening. The accusation is so horrible that they are reluctant to intervene early for fear of being wrong.[21] The potential for parental decompensation on confrontation cannot be dismissed.[22,23] It can seem far easier to do more tests than to confront the very real possibility of MBP and its perpetrator. Yet the management of MBP requires confrontation of the parent and separation (often as a diagnostic maneuver) of parent and child.

The Need for a Long-term Plan. Children who are or are suspected of being MBP victims may have legitimate illnesses and accidents as well as their factitious ones. They also manifest symptoms and signs as a result of their abuse and the associated investigations, medications, and operations. Their psychological morbidity, including personal adoption of Munchausen Syndrome behavior, must be recognized and treated.[24,25] A comprehensive plan must be developed and implemented to meet all of these needs. Long-term planning must also address the need for long-term protection by provision of a caretaker, either a nonfamily custodian or a family member who believes the diagnosis and understands the risks of contact with the perpetrator. In cases where perpetrators have admitted their involvement and are allowed to continue contact with the children, ongoing supervision is mandatory. Without a well-developed and articulated long-term plan, the reasoning behind the need for supervision is lost and interest in continuing it wanes in the face of limited resources.

For all of these reasons, individual clinicians may find it difficult, if not impossible, to deal effectively with MBP families. A multidisciplinary team multiplies the chances for effective intervention by providing a broader knowledge base with varied perspectives and obligations while giving each individual on the team the support needed to address his or her concerns.

Composition of the Multidisciplinary Team

Many children's hospitals and tertiary care centers have multidisciplinary child abuse teams already in place. These teams are ideally suited to respond to cases of suspected MBP, with some additional specialized input as may be required in specific cases. If there is no team already constituted, it is advisable to form one when a case of MBP is suspected. All members of the team must recognize the validity of a diagnosis of MBP. Note that it is just as incumbent upon the team to prove the diagnosis of MBP as it is to prove that the child indeed does not have a true medical illness. It is preferable that team members have some experience either in child abuse in general or, ideally, in MBP itself. A team that harbors members who deny the existence of MBP as a real form of child abuse may be ineffective. Good team leadership is required to ensure that the team is formed, meetings are called, tasks are assigned, and decisions are made about a management plan and its implementation. The team leader must have the respect of all involved professionals in order to be effective both in keeping discussions on an objective and productive level and in implementing management plans which may be controversial. The following team composition is recommended.

Physician. This should preferably be a pediatrician because of pediatricians' special knowledge of children and their diseases as well as normal parent-child interactions. As someone who is seen as a helper, to whom the child's interests are paramount, the pediatrician starts off with the confidence of the family.[26] Family physicians may also be able to offer a holistic approach to the child's care, particularly when children make up a large part of their clinical practice and experience. When available, a pediatrician specializing and consulting in the field of child abuse medicine is most desirable.

Social Worker. Social work skills are important in the identification and management of MBP.[27] Social workers are skilled in interviewing and, if trained as mental health professionals, can assist with both the psychological issues of the parent-child dyad and the feeling issues among the health care professionals. Many social workers have specialized training or experience in health care issues or child abuse that will be useful for this function. They are also generally knowledgeable about resources in the community and about the practical workings of child abuse law. (Note that in some settings [see, for example, Chapter 24], the nurse takes the role here described for the social worker.)

These are the core members of the team. One of them should act as team leader. It is desirable that the following professionals also be members of the team.

Attending Physician. If possible a child abuse consultant should act as the core member described above, while the child's attending physician becomes an additional team member. The time requirements of the team leader may be unmanageable for the attending physician and the role of team leader might compromise the attending physician's direct relationship with the family. In cases where the attending physician is a true skeptic regarding the possibility of MBP, it will be the team's task to work with this individual to provide the best patient care possible without breaching codes of professional courtesy or violating the child's right to protection.

Nurse. This is the professional who is on the front line in contact with the child-parent unit. The nurse has the greatest opportunity to observe and perhaps intervene in MBP cases.[28] Nurses often have particular skills in communicating with parents and children, skills that can be invaluable in assessing the risk factors for MBP.

Hospital Administrator. Since some of the investigative steps to be considered for inpatients (e.g., videotaping) will potentially have repercussions for the hospital, it is wise to include a hospital administrative representative in the discussions as they proceed.[29-31] (See also Chapter 28.)

Legal Consultant. As some of the investigative steps may have legal implications, expert guidance is essential.[32] Protection of the hospital from liability and lawsuit, questions about mandated reporting of suspected child abuse, and access to documents when the family denies permission are just three areas in which counsel can assist.

Hospital Security Officer. At many steps the security of the child, the parent, or hospital staff may be in jeopardy. Having hospital security services participating in planning means that the best approach to intervention can be devised.[33] This often means that problems will be prevented through an appropriate use of authority. In contrast to other members of the team, whose approach is primarily that of helping professionals, security officers are accustomed to considering and confronting deception. Institutional security officers also generally have an understanding of police procedure and linkages to police departments. They can often provide advice on investigative techniques prior to the time when it is appropriate to involve police.

The following are desirable members of the working team but may not be immediately available, particularly in smaller health care settings. They can be consulted as needed. In tertiary hospitals these individuals may be called upon to join the team at relevant points in the progress of the case.

Medical Subspecialist(s). MBP cases often present with complex symptoms which do not make sense, have not been seen before, or appear bizarre even to experienced clinicians.[34–37] New and sophisticated diagnostic and treatment techniques are introduced at a rapid rate. Appropriate subspecialists can provide expert guidance in areas specific to particular cases and unfamiliar to other team members. For example, medical toxicologists have particular expertise in recognizing symptoms brought on by drugs or other poisons and carrying out the appropriate investigations.[38]

Psychiatrist. Given the potential for psychiatric diagnoses in parents suspected of MBP, psychiatric input can be very helpful. A psychiatrist is most effective when closely linked to a pediatrician and the medical care team in these cases.[39,40]

Other Mental Health Professionals. Some multidisciplinary teams have included psychologists, psychiatric nurses, and child care workers.[41,42] We have also found an art therapist very advantageous in helping children to express facts and feelings through nonverbal means.

Bioethicist. Many issues arising in MBP cases have ethical implications. There may be competition among patient rights, parental rights, child protection concerns, and staff obligations (which may be perceived differently by different people).[43–45]

The following people are not usually members of a hospital-based health care team but are needed in cases involving reporting of child abuse and alleged criminal activity. Direct involvement with the hospital team is helpful in educating these nonmedical personnel and in discharge planning.

Child Protection Worker. All cases of suspected MBP fall into the legal definitions of reportable child abuse in locations with mandatory reporting laws. After reporting has occurred, a child protection worker will be assigned to the case. This worker needs to become part of the investigative and intervention team.

Police. Their interest will be predominantly in matters pertaining to criminal prosecution. Their assistance in gathering evidence and providing protection can be very helpful.

Statistician. Sometimes the individual elements of a particular case are possible, but the whole is improbable. For example, a family may claim to have experienced multiple Sudden Infant Death Syndrome deaths or a child might supposedly have rare variants of several diseases and unusual side effects to many medicines. Symptoms might cluster around the presence of a single person, whether parent or hospital staff member. A statistician may be useful in demonstrating that the reported chain of events is so improbable as to make another hypothesis—MBP—more likely.

Tasks of the Multidisciplinary Team

Education and Support. If the team is a standing one, then it should take every opportunity to provide rounds, conferences, and other forms of inservice training on MBP to professionals with which it regularly comes in contact. If the team is formed in response to a specific case, then education must be focused toward the group of professionals who are likely to be involved with that case. This may require the distribution of relevant literature and special inservice sessions.[46,47] The team can also be available for informal consultation in the differential diagnosis of difficult cases, if only to raise the possibility of factitious illness when appropriate. Involvement of the team may actually be helpful in ruling *out* MBP in certain cases, thus obviating the need for reporting, confrontation, or child protection.

The team members also provide support to each other as well as support to those involved with the child's care by allowing hospital staff or other caretakers to share conflicted feelings. This facilitates the reframing process that must take place when a potential case is identified.[48] Because of the very nature of MBP and the response of many of the participants described above, the team will find much of its strength in open discussions within itself. In team discussions, for example, potentially hostile reactions of others may be seen for what they are, without deflecting the team members from their goal.

Immediate Protection of the Child. Given the 9% mortality rate cited in this disorder,[49] it is imperative that steps be taken to protect the child immediately, even before proceeding with further evaluation. Rosenberg's data also emphasize the need to protect other children in the family from serial involvement as MBP victims.[50] If a delay in accumulating more evidence may place the child at undue risk, then that delay needs to be reconsidered in terms of the child's safety.[51,52] If the team does not elect complete separation of child and parent, then constant vigilance must ensure that the potential perpetrator is not left alone with the child unobserved for even a moment. Supervision of parental contact with the child should be conducted by medically experienced individuals who understand the need for constant vigilance.[53,54] If events are being recorded in order to document or refute parental commission, it is essential that personnel be available to monitor the child while the recording is in progress to identify and intervene if and when an abusive act occurs.[55,56]

Gathering Information. This includes review of past medical records for the child in question, siblings, and the suspected parent. Original records must be sought and reviewed. The actual records must be obtained and read rather than relying on someone else's interpretation or report. The medical record review must be meticulous. We have found it useful to categorize retrieved information as follows: objective content including findings that were definitely proven; subjective reports; information open to interpretation (e.g., the diagnosis of otitis media without a description of the tympanic membrane); and unknown, contradictory, or questionable data. Classification should be as stringent as possible without using standards beyond reasonable medical practice. A review of the personal, social, and family history commonly reveals fabrication and often uncovers a possible motive for the mother's behavior.[57,58]

The team must also review data concerning the present illness. This includes medical information as well as data recorded by medical caretakers other than physicians, psychosocial observations, and circumstantial information.[59] For example, it was the careful review of the nursing bedside record in one case that revealed an unusual stooling pattern and alerted the physicians to possible factitious illness.[60] The team should review ongoing recordings of the child's recurring symptoms or response to treatment, coupled with recordings of parental presence or activity, to see if these events are linked temporally to each other.[61] Data must be detailed and objective. The source of information should always be recorded.[62] Alleged eyewitnesses should be interviewed to determine if events described by the suspected perpetrator did indeed occur, and to elucidate the facts of the event, from the vantage point of another observer. In cases of MBP, the perpetrator may give historical information that cannot be corroborated by other observers. Interviewing of the child victim, if old enough, regarding the possible cause of the illness may also be useful.[63] In a case reported by Waller, the answer to unexplained hematuria was provided by the patient, though never volunteered by him.[64] We have found art therapy very helpful in this regard. In a case involving suspicious recurrent burns, a 2-year-old girl drew a bathtub and was able to indicate that it was where she was burned, that her mother was involved, and that it had happened previously.

Ensuring Full Communication. Clear communication is essential to minimize confusion and maximize meaningful information gathering and good working relations with all concerned. All professionals must be aware of what is taking place so that expectations for each member of the health care team are clear. A clear chain of command must be established and, whenever possible, only one person put in charge of authorizing changes in the care plan. Parents and children should also be kept informed of diagnostic and therapeutic possibilities and procedures in such a way as to provide necessary reassurance without sabotaging the investigative process or provoking premature confrontation. Communication of substantive information with the parents should be carried out either by only one person (this is preferable) or as a team so as to minimize the chance of distortion and confusion.[65] Parents should be provided with psychosocial and practical support as needed.

Exploring All Diagnostic Possibilities. This requires careful and logical thinking on the part of the various clinicians involved. Each symptom, cluster of symptoms, or diagnostic category must be explored with a specialist in the field to determine the classical boundaries of the disorder under investigation as well as the common and atypical variants. Similarly, explanations of inconsistencies in historical data and parental behavior must be carefully analyzed. The team must be very vigilant during this exercise to maintain an openness to all reasonable diagnostic alternatives without stretching the bounds of credibility beyond reason. Although some atypical features, coincidences, mistakes, and other quirks may occur in some cases, the repeated need to invoke these in order to make a medical diagnosis other than MBP should be pointed out by the team leader as the team progresses in its discussions. Missing data needed to establish or refute a diagnosis should be identified. Clinicians, particularly subspecialists and skeptics, need to be asked, "What scientific information would you need to rule in or out the diagnosis in question, so that you would be satisfied that the patient does or does not have the disease as opposed to MBP?" (The team must be careful that the diagnostic evaluation requested is within reason so as to protect the child from further iatrogenic harm.) Striking this delicate balance can be one of the most difficult aspects of the team's work.

Formulation and Implementation of a Management Plan. Based on these initial five steps, the team will now be in a position to develop a unified course of action that addresses the child's immediate need for protection, assessment, and treatment of the medical concerns. This can be done while the child is already in the hospital, or an inpatient evaluation may be planned with this in mind.[66] As mentioned above, judicious decisions need to be made to allow for definitive diagnosis without subjecting the child to unnecessary or unnecessarily invasive procedures.[67] Rigorous technique needs to be applied to the collection of diagnostic specimens to avoid parental contamination.[68] Exclusion of the parent from contact with the child may be used as a diagnostic stratagem.[69] Finally, if surveillance or intrusive methods for the collection of definitive evidence are being considered, this requires very careful exploration with bioethicists, hospital administration, and legal authorities to ensure that such methods are not used prematurely or unnecessarily and that the family's right to confidentiality is preserved. The team must monitor the child's progress and the results of diagnostic procedures while revising the management plan as necessary, based on this information.

Reporting in Accordance with Local Child Protection Laws. The point at which child protection authorities are notified will depend on many factors, including those authorities' previous involvement.[70] When a critical mass of information has been collected that meets the statutory criteria for the reporting of suspected child abuse, a report must be made. From that point onward child welfare authorities and the police may be considered part of the working team. Different jurisdictions may have different laws and policies governing the type and degree of intervention possible. The hospital social worker and legal consultant are resources in understanding and working with the local situation.

Confrontation of the Parent Regarding Suspicions of MBP. This step above all others requires careful planning and orchestration. The point at which the parent needs to be confronted is that point at which the child's safety is in jeopardy *and* contingency plans are in place. The management plan cannot proceed without careful attention to this critical threshold. Confrontation may be necessary if further diagnostic intervention is not possible without parental permission or if referral to child protective services is planned. When confrontation is to occur, the team must be prepared with all the available facts. However, the child's safety from ongoing abuse must always take precedence over a perceived need for "just a bit more data," the collection or preparation of which might allow an MBP event to occur that could result in serious morbidity or mortality.

Confrontation has taken place in different ways. The strength and self-evident quality of the available evidence will determine the strategy to some extent. Meadow argues for first confronting the mother alone.[71] We have found it best to meet with both parents, even when one parent has not been actively involved in the child's hospitalization, as is often the case in MBP. The nonoffending parent has a right to know the evidence and implications regarding

MBP and, in some cases, may prove to be an ally for the child. The "confrontation team" should include the fewest number of people who can provide definitive information to the parents both regarding the medical facts and child protection, as well as an individual (perhaps of their own choosing) who they may see as an advocate. If there is the possibility of a criminal charge, the police may have some restrictions they wish to place on who attends the meeting and what is said, so prior consultation with law enforcement is vital.

The physician who has uncovered the deception should provide the relevant information to the parents in a clear and logical manner, as simply as possible. Parental questions should be answered but diversion into irrelevant detail should be avoided. The meeting must be controlled by the team leader. Otherwise, the perpetrator may attempt to diffuse and confuse the issue with diversion. By the end of the meeting it should be clear to the parents that it is the *team's* opinion that this is a case of MBP, that the child is being harmed by the parent's actions and that the child is in need of protection. A clear statement must follow regarding the legal implications and proposed plan of action.[72,73] The psychiatrist should be standing by in case the parents show signs of acute decompensation or suicidal ideation. Similarly, hospital security may be needed to provide for the safety of the child and others.[74,75] Child protection may also need to act promptly and should, therefore, have a protection plan ready to implement, if necessary.

Formulation of a Discharge Plan. Whether or not the diagnosis of MBP is validated and confrontation accomplished at the time of discharge, the team will need to formulate a plan that will allow for the child's ongoing medical assessment. Preferably the child will be followed by only one physician who is familiar with MBP. Mental health assessment and treatment of the child, if not already begun prior to discharge, should be arranged. Psychiatric assessment of the offending parent should be arranged.[76,77] Plans must be made to provide for the child's ongoing protection. The family must be assessed carefully and their dynamics understood before a plan involving protection by family members can be accepted. The family member chosen to provide protection for the child must clearly understand and believe the diagnosis of MBP as well as the risks of continued unsupervised contact between the child and perpetrator. Otherwise, family loyalties may result in a coalition of family members against the authorities rendering protective measures ineffective.[78] Out-of-home placement of the child outside the family circle may be necessary to protect the child adequately.[79,80]

If legal proceedings are planned, meetings should be held with the authorities concerned to prepare an effective child protection case. All facts should be presented clearly and in written form.[81]

Conclusions

Multidisciplinary teamwork is essential in the management of MBP. The perpetrators are exceptionally skilled at subterfuge, manipulation, and concealment. Only by drawing on the strengths of professionals from all disciplines involved with child health care can the cycle of MBP abuse be effectively broken.

References

1. Zitelli BJ, Seltman MF, and Shannon RM. Munchausen's syndrome by proxy and its professional participants. *Am J Dis Child*. 1987; 141:1099–1102.
2. Kaufman KL, Coury D, Pickrel E, and McCleery J. Munchausen syndrome by proxy: a survey of professionals' knowledge. *Child Abuse Negl*. 1989; 13:141–147.
3. Yorker BC and Kahan BB. The Munchausen syndrome by proxy variand of child abuse in the family courts. *Juv Fam Coutr J*. 1991; 42: 51–58.
4. Zitelli, Professional participants.
5. Rosenberg DA. Web of deceit: a literature review of Munchausen syndrome by proxy. *Child Abuse Negl*. 1987; 11:547–563.
6. Zitelli, Professional participants.
7. Rosenberg, Web.
8. Blix S and Brack G. The effects of a suspected case of Munchausen's syndrome by proxy on a pediatric nursing staff. *Gen Hosp Psychiatr*. 1988; 10:402–409.
9. Rosenberg, Web.
10. Zitelli, Professional participants.
11. Krener R and Adelman R. Parent salvage and parent sabotage in the care of chronically ill children. *Am J Dis Child*. 1988; 945–951.
12. Sapira JD. Munchausen's syndrome and the technological imperative. *South Med J*. 1981; 74:93–97.
13. Epstein MA, Markowitz RL, Gallo DM et al. Munchausen syndrome by proxy: considerations in diagnosis and confirmation by video surveillance. *Pediatrics* 1987; 80:220–224.

14. Guandolo VL. Munchausen syndrome by proxy: an outpatient challenge. *Pediatrics*. 1985; 75:526–530.
15. Meadow R. Munchausen syndrome by proxy. *Arch Dis Child*. 1982; 57:92–98.
16. Waller DA. Obstacles to the treatment of munchausen by proxy syndrome. *J Am Acad Child Psych*. 1983; 22:80–85.
17. Zitelli, Professional participants.
18. Waller, Obstacles.
19. Zitelli, Professional participants.
20. Waller, Obstacles.
21. Meadow R. Management of Munchausen syndrome by proxy. *Arch Dis Child*. 1985; 60:385–393.
22. Epstein et al., MBP.
23. Meadow, Management.
24. McGuire TL and Feldman KW. Psychologic morbidity of children subjected to Munchausen syndrome by proxy. *Pediatrics*. 1988; 83:289–292.
25. Bools CN, Neale BA, and Meadow SR. Follow up of victims of fabricated illness (Munchausen syndrome by proxy). *Arch Dis Child*. 1993; 69:625–630.
26. Meadow, Management.
27. Masterson J and Wilson J. Factitious illness in children: the social worker's role in identification and management. *Social Work Health Care*. 1987; 12:21–30.
28. Turk LJ, Hanrahan KM, and Weber ER. Munchausen syndrome by proxy: a nursing overview. *Issues Comp Pediatr Nursing*. 1990; 13:279–288.
29. Epstein et al., Considerations.
30. Meadow, Management.
31. Williams C and Bevan VT. The secret observation of children in hospital. *Lancet*. 1988; 2:780–781.
32. Epstein et al., Considerations.
33. Epstein, et al., Considerations.
34. Meadow, MBP.
35. Rosen et al., Two siblings.
36. Rosen CL, Frost JD, Bricker T, et al. Two siblings with recurrent infant apnea. *J Pediatr*. 1986; 109:1065–1067.
37. Zitelli, Professional participants.
38. Mahesh VK, Stern HP, Kearns GL, et al. Application of pharmacokinetics in the diagnosis of chemical abuse in Munchausen syndrome by proxy. *Clin Pediatr*. 1988: 27:243–246.
39. Bentovim A. Munchausen's syndrome and child psychiatrists. *Arch Dis Child*. 1985; 60:688.
40. Krener, Parent salvage.
41. Fialkov MJ: Peregrination in the problem pediatric patient. *Clin Pediatr*. 1984; 23:571–575.
42. Masterson, Factitious.
43. Meadow, Management.
44. Yorker and Kahan, Variant. 1991

45. Sadler JZ. Ethical and management considerations in factitious illness: one and the same. *Gen Hosp Psychiatry.* 1987; 9:31–36.
46. Blix and Brack, Effects.
47. Turk et al., Nursing overview.
48. Blix and Brack, Effects.
49. Rosenberg, Web.
50. Rosenberg, Web.
51. Meadow, Management.
52. Rosenberg, Web.
53. Meadow, Management.
54. Rosenberg, Web.
55. Epstein et al., Considerations.
56. Southall DP, Stebbens VA, Rees SV, et al. Apnoeic episodes induced by smothering: two cases identified by covert video surveillance. *Br Med J.* 1987; 294:1637–1641.
57. Griffith JL. The family systems of munchausen syndrome by proxy. *Fam Proc.* 1988; 27:423–437.
58. Meadow, Management.
59. Meadow, Management.
60. Epstein et al., Considerations.
61. Rosenberg, Web.
62. Meadow, Management.
63. Rosenberg, Web.
64. Waller, Obstacles.
65. Masterson, Factitious.
66. Fialkov, Perigrination.
67. Zitelli, Professional participants.
68. Rosenberg, Web.
69. Meadow, Management.
70. Meadow, Management.
71. Meadow, Management.
72. Meadow, Management.
73. Rosenberg, Web.
74. Epstein et al., Considerations.
75. Rosenberg, Web.
76. Rosenberg, Web.
77. Zitelli, Professional participants.
78. Griffith, Family systems.
79. Meadow, Management.
80. Rosenberg, Web.
81. Rosenberg, Web.

23

The Role of the Physician

Stephen Ludwig

The physician has many important roles in the care of the patient and family when there is suspected Munchausen Syndrome by Proxy (MBP). These roles range from modification of parental attitudes that may lead to patient overdependency, to the diagnosis and treatment of full-blown cases of MBP. In all of these roles, the physician is aided by working in a multidisciplinary context, whether it be a fully organized child abuse team or the collaboration of an office nurse and another physician colleague.

Prevention

MBP is a spectrum of disorders that range from parents simply overdramatizing their children's illnesses to flagrant injury. There are many steps in between: parents who keep their children home from school beyond what is needed for recovery; parents who take their children from doctor to doctor looking for a medical answer that may not exist; parents who encourage children to think of themselves as ill rather than healthy; and other examples of socially "acceptable" (or at least nonreportable) parental behaviors that may have a negative impact on the child's functional state and which may be mild or precursor forms of MBP. There are many everyday opportunities for the physician to practice prevention.

Prevention may be viewed in the traditional public health model as primary, secondary, or tertiary. In primary prevention, the physician attempts to stop a process before it begins. This requires the physician to be alert to the attitudes that patients hold about illness and wellness. The physician must be mindful of any child or parent who sees advantage or gain in being ill, as this is the root dynamic in MBP. In their seminal paper, Carey and Sibinga state: "the pediatrician should support the parents by helping them to deal with the specific illness and by promoting the capacity to cope with illness in general. If instead, the pediatrician is overly dominant or submissive, neglectful or punitive in handling the parents' needs they may become frightened, dependent, demanding, confused, or angry."[1] In MBP we must be concerned that we do not make parents feel too comfortable and overdependent, thereby encouraging prolonged or recurrent illness in the child. Collaborative, empowering relationships in which there is honest exchange of information and appropriate setting of limits would appear more appropriate than those which encourage parents to think of physicians as "gods" and the fulfillment of their fantasies.[2] Theory on "vulnerable children" also suggests that parents should receive clear information when a child's health problem has resolved, to prevent their feeling that "coddling" or precautions are still required long after the necessity for them has passed.[3] Although the literature on MBP has not progressed to the point that we know definitely what actions are facilitative and what are preventive, the giving of such information to all parents seems warranted. As pediatricians interacting with young children, we also do not want to plant these same unhealthy seeds in our young patients lest they become ailing, needy adults.

Secondary prevention occurs when a prompt and accurate diagnosis is made, thereby lessening morbidity and mortality. The key issue is to be alert to the diagnosis and to believe that the diagnosis exists and can be made on a regular basis. Those in primary care practice must be prepared to make the diagnosis and should not feel that MBP is an extremely rare or exotic possibility. Physicians working in secondary and tertiary care referral centers must not fall victim to the "only we can solve the problem" syndrome. Institutional egos may be primed for the possible overevaluation and overdiagnosis of a medical complaint in order to outdo a perceived rival or rival institution and make the diagnosis that "they" could not.

Prevention at the tertiary level pertains to the rehabilitation techniques that are used once the syndrome has injured the child, and the speed with which the family may be returned to healthy functioning. As yet, there have been no proven therapies for MBP. It seems clear that many families will need a variety of services and monitoring techniques before their problems are solved. To provide adequate services, the family should be assessed for strengths and weaknesses. The physician must take a major role in this activity.

Diagnosis

Diagnosis is a central right and role of the physician. What factors prompt the physician to make the diagnosis of MBP? First, the physician must be open to the possibility. As leader of the health care team, the physician plays a central gatekeeping role. A physician who does not believe in MBP or is not willing to listen to observations from other team members effectively stops an inquiry before it begins. Table 23–1 lists some of the high risk findings that have been noted in MBP cases. Familiarity with these findings along with the types of MBP presentations discussed in this book gives

Table 23–1
Diagnostic Characteristics of MBP

Illness in a child factitiously reported, simulated or produced by parent/primary caretaker

There may be history of unusual illness in other siblings or parent

Medical complaints may be common or bizarre in nature

Child's illness defies diagnosis or control of symptoms (e.g., the worst case of its kind, or failure to establish diagnosis at multiple health care sites or providers)

Acute symptoms or signs abate when child is separated from the parent

Characteristics of parent perpetrator
  most often mother
  father distant, uninvolved, marriage may be troubled
  mother friendly, calm, cooperative and well liked:
    a "model parent"
  may have medical background
  may have frequent symptoms, possibly Munchausen Syndrome
  spends long hours at bedside or in the hospital

---

the physician a starting point for diagnosis. That starting point, however, requires the same index of suspicion that physicians have had to learn for all child abuse. If patients are hospitalized, as often they are both because of the nature of the symptoms and the wish of the parent, there is a series of steps to be followed in confirming the suspected diagnosis. These are listed in Table 23–2. In these

Table 23–2
Process Guidelines for Confirming MBP[4]

---

1. Problem identification by physician or staff

2. Team meeting
   confront possible polarization by staff
   discussion of feelings and facts

3. Concerns validated or dismissed

4. Interim plan/data collection (more depth and objective medical data)
   specific nursing care plan
   daily communication with parents
   daily sharing of information by bedside team, with revision of plan as indicated
   physical adjustments to environment for safety's sake

5. Establishment of firm boundaries between staff and family, clarification of roles

6. Documentation of
   plan/goals
   interaction
     parent/child
     parent/staff
     staff/child
   interventions (medical and psychosocial)
   child's progress

7. Follow up team meeting
   compare and contrast parent data/staff data and data gleaned from evaluations
   decision to dismiss or pursue hypothesis of MBP
   explore feelings
   sharing of concern/decision with parents

permission obtained for voluntary collateral contacts if not
    already done
all group meetings should be recorded in medical record,
    note should include those present, content and plan

8. Collateral contacts
    status of other children
    parents' health status
    other agencies involved

9. Next team meeting
    attempt to establish consensus of team
    plan made re: how to approach parents
    if diagnosis of MBP is made, local child protective services
        agency contacted

10. Share diagnosis and plan with family

11. Encourage and broaden family's support system

12. Action requested from outside agencies as appropriate
    child protection services
    mental health
    visiting nurse/public health nurse

13. Team meeting (to include outside agents)
    establish intervention/follow-up needs

14. Safe setting for child established, continued support of family

15. Follow-up
    medical
    psychosocial
    legal

16. Staff debriefing.

---

days of managed care and strict utilization review, the physician must also be ready to justify such hospitalization, or its prolongation, as necessary to the proper diagnosis and welfare of the child when MBP is suspected.

For some conditions there may be medical procedures to unmask the diagnosis. The physician's prescription of equipment such as a "smart" infant apnea monitor (i.e., one with recording capability) will be helpful in telling the difference between true apnea, false alarms due to artifact, and times when the monitor was disconnected or unplugged. Measuring urine temperature may tell true fever from factitious fever—but only if the physician thinks to order it. Ordering certain laboratory tests—for example, levels of endogenous insulin versus levels of injected insulin—may be useful. Videotaping systems (with proper legal and administrative safeguards) have also proven helpful in unmasking MBP by filming parents in the act of harming their children. By the same token, physicians must also resist pressure from parents or colleagues for "just one more" unnecessary procedure, admission, or diagnostic test.

Treatment

Identifying and exposing the parental behavior is the first step in controlling such behaviors and treating the syndrome. If the diagnosis is confirmed, the next steps are reporting the findings to the parents and to the child protective service agency. Depending on the nature of the injury, a report may also be made to the police department. Although other members of the treatment team may substitute or assist, it is generally the attending physician's role to speak with parents about diagnosis and to make official reports. Next, there must be an assessment of how persistent the pattern of behavior has been and how likely it is to occur in the future. The physician is in the best position to resolve medical controversies and questions as this assessment proceeds, and may be able to facilitate information exchange with physician colleagues. The issue of continued placement of the child with the family during a period of therapy versus removal of the child from the family is discussed elsewhere. However, the physician's input will be of assistance to legal authorities and child protective workers in understanding the medical consequences of the abuse and the child's future medical needs. If the physician who has cared for the child prior to or through hospitalization is able to continue seeing the child on an outpatient basis, this continuity is extremely helpful both for the child's ongoing care and for legal case-building (e.g., the physician is able to testify that the child's symptoms have resolved during a period of foster care.)

Education and Research

The traditional physician roles of public education and research are always important: education to allow not only professional colleagues but the public to know about this syndrome and about how and why it occurs. In American society, physicians speak with particular authority and thus may be more effectively heard by other physicians and by the general public. Although some media reports are sensationalistic in their approach, others have a more responsible and educational tone. Like many other forms of child abuse, MBP is difficult for the average citizen to understand and accept. Knowing that it does occur with some frequency, it is the physician's job to break down these barriers of disbelief.

In the area of research there is much to be studied and learned. Until now, most physicians have dealt with one, two, or a small cluster of cases. Broader experience is a first step in further study. When numbers of cases are great enough, perhaps through multicenter collaboration, then there can be the kinds of investigations that reveal the best treatments, methods of prevention, and other associated information. Collaborating in such trials will require both commitment and generosity on the part of physicians.

Ethical Considerations

Physicians play an important role in the ethical decision making that entangles many MBP cases. Is it ethically proper to set up video surveillance around a patient's bed? Is it acceptable to limit a parent's visitation rights? Is it permissible for a physician to continue to order more and more laboratory tests and procedures while ignoring the possibility of MBP? Cases of MBP throw havoc into our notions of the rights of parents, children, families, health care practitioners, and hospitals. Indeed, all of these sets of civil and human rights are in a state of constant dynamic tension. MBP breaks all the rules and challenges the ethical underpinnings of our work as helping professionals. The use of the multidisciplinary approach will often be of help in resolving ethical issues or areas of controversy. Bringing together people of diverse backgrounds and experiences helps to ensure that a sense of honesty and fairness prevails.

References

1. Carey WB and Sibinga MS. Avoiding pediatric pathogenesis in the management of acute minor illness. *Pediatrics.* 1972; 49:553–562.
2. This is based on theorizing that women who are prone to MBP find in the pediatrician an idealized figure who meets their needs and gives them attention *when their child is sick.* See: Schreier HA and Libow JA. *Hurting for Love: Munchausen Syndrome by Proxy.* 1933; New York: Guilford Press.
3. Green M and Solnit AJ. Reactions to the threatened loss of a child: a vulnerable child syndrome. *Pediatrics.* 1964; 34:58–66.
4. Personal communication, Toni Seidl, ACSW, Children's Hospital of Philadelphia.

24

Nursing Care and Responsibilities

Pamela J. Stading and

Stephen J. Boros

Munchausen Syndrome by Proxy (MBP) has been widely described in the medical literature. Unfortunately, it is relatively new to the nursing literature. At the time this chapter was written, there were only 13 MBP publications in the nursing literature, with the first appearing in 1987.[1] A 1988 survey noted that only 10% of the nurses polled had any knowledge of or experience with MBP.[2] Fifty-five percent said they had never heard of the condition. Most stated they were professionally and personally unprepared to deal with such problems. This lack of awareness is a serious matter. It can lead to delayed identification, continued abuse and, in the extreme, child murder.[3] Pediatric nurses must become more familiar with this form of life-threatening child abuse. It is our job. It is our responsibility.

Like other forms of child abuse and neglect, MBP is best handled by a multidisciplinary team whose primary purpose is child protection.[4] It is imperative that all members of the team recognize not only their own roles and responsibilities, but the roles and responsibilities of other team members as well. Managing MBP does not allow the luxury of individual moralizing or outrage, but calls for intensely focused teamwork.[5] Nurses have unique positions on child protection teams. Typically nurses have the first and most constant contact with victims and their families. Outside the hospital, public health nurses may be the child's most available and consistent medical contacts. It is often the child victim's nurse who first suspects that all may not be as it seems. By simply following standard nursing documentation procedures, nurses can be in the best position to establish the chronology of suspicious events.[6]

Identification

Nurses, like other health care professionals, are trained to rely on parents' recollections of their children's medical problems. These medical histories are the diagnostic cornerstones for all subsequent investigations and therapies.[7] The fact that histories may be false and illness fabricated or induced is totally contrary to most medical and nursing training. Involved nursing and medical staffs may not be able, or want, to accept the possibility of child abuse.[8] Such ethical conflicts and ambivalence are extremely common. Unfortunately, they lead to delays in identification of MBP and implementation of appropriate child protection. Health care professionals need to recognize their own denials. This is often the first step in the successful identification of MBP.[9]

In almost all serious cases of MBP, the victims are eventually hospitalized. In the hospital, astute nurses can make major contributions toward successful identification and intervention.[10] Nurses are in the best position to monitor daily parent-child interaction and, while doing so, to evaluate the details of and inconsistencies in the patient's medical history.[11] When we suspect MBP at Children's Hospital of St. Paul, Minnesota, we immediately deploy a two-nurse evaluation team. A clinical nurse specialist coordinates the evaluation, verification and organization of all pertinent clinical information. A core group of primary nurses provides daily patient care and family monitoring. These roles are detailed in Table 24–1. Other members of the multidisciplinary team are capable of performing and supplementing some of these activities. This model reflects what has worked well for us. We try to play to the various strengths of all our team members, each focusing on the area relevant to his/her chosen field. We discuss our impressions, then collectively compile our evaluations in a "psychosocial journal."

Table 24–1
Staff Roles in MBP

The Clinical Nurse Specialist's Role

1. Develop a trusting relationship with the family.
   a. Provide the family with rationale for continued hospitalization. Prolonged hospitalizations are more often than not necessary in order to complete all necessary investigations. Nurses should never mention suspicions of MBP independently nor plans for covert surveillance.
   b. Update family on test results and diagnostic plans.
   c. Be available to discuss family concerns.

2. Identify a core group of nurses who will be responsible for primary care of the suspected victim while hospitalized.

3. Educate a core group of primary nurses regarding care plans, MBP warning signs, and classic perpetrator profiles.

4. Assist physicians in planning and coordinating diagnostic evaluations.

5. Coordinate multidisciplinary team meetings.

6. Assist in obtaining, reviewing, documenting, and verifying all discrepancies in the patient's and family's medical records.[12]

7. Coordinate conferences with extended family, school officials, social service agencies, and day-care providers regarding psychosocial issues.[13]

8. Review current medical and psychosocial records.

9. Update the multidisciplinary team on the progress of the investigation.

The Primary Nurse's Role

1. Provide an atmosphere of safety, security, and trust.

2. Provide for the patient's physical, developmental, and emotional needs.

3. Participate in diagnostic evaluations, making sure that laboratory specimens are protected.[14]

4. Assess and document child's eating toileting, and other behavioral status

5. Assess and document child's physical, emotional and developmental status.

6. Assess and document associations between the parent's presence and the child's signs and symptoms[15].

7. Assess and document the child's physical environment.

8. Assess and document interaction between parents and the patient, the health care team, and other family members.

The most important nursing activities during MBP investigations are assessment, documentation, verification, and collaboration. In carrying out these activities the clinical nurse specialist and primary nurse must function as a team.

Assessment

MEDICAL HISTORY

When obtaining medical histories, nurses should be mindful of the classic MBP warning signals. One or two episodes of naturally occurring disease do not exclude MBP.[16] Inconsistencies in stories are critical. All dates and locations of previous hospitalizations should be thoroughly documented. Comparing the history obtained by the nurse to the histories obtained by various physicians and social workers often highlights inconsistencies and suspicious events.

PHYSICAL EXAMINATION

Admission physical examinations are usually normal, although some victims of apnea induced by suffocation may show petechiae or bruises around their mouths, noses, or necks.[17] Overt signs of physical trauma are rare. Physical signs, when present, are often subtle. Bools and co-workers.[18] noted that approximately one-third of MBP victims show poor growth patterns and/or failure to thrive. Because they often have little control over anything in their lives except what they ingest, victims may choose not to eat in the perpetrator's presence, or not to eat at all.

The most important nursing activities during MBP investigations are assessment, documentation, verification, and collaboration. One hospital's patient care plan is shown in Table 24–2. In carrying out these activities the clinical nurse specialist and primary nurse must function as a team.

ENVIRONMENTAL ASSESSMENT

Nurses should consciously assess and reassess their patient's physical environment at the beginning of each shift and each time they enter or leave patients' rooms. Cardiorespiratory monitor alarm settings and IV fluid infusion rates must be regularly checked and rechecked. Items from outside the hospital such as food or beverages should be noted. Waste containers should be regularly examined for unusual items or items that may relate to patients' symptoms (e.g., mother's menstrual pads when a patient has hematuria). In one case, an MBP perpetrator was reading a popular

Table 24–2

The Children's Hospital of Philadelphia Department of Nursing Patient Care Plan for Munchausen Syndrome by Proxy

Date Initiated	Nursing Diagnosis	Planned Patient Outcome, Including Time Frame	Nursing Actions	Date Outcome Achieved
	Altered growth and development	Child will demonstrate developmental advancement pertinent to age in cognitive, psychomotor, and psychosocial areas.	–Make necessary psychiatric referrals –Determine baseline via Denver or other screening tool –Provide child and family with daily schedule and encourage structure. (Attach schedule to care plan.) –Maximize resources as appropriate (child life, PT, speech, etc.)	

	Potential for injury	Child will be protected from injury during hospitalization.	–Close observation of child when parents present.
			–Clearly outline physician, nurse, and parents' responsibilities (attach to care plan)
			–Maintain consistency in care and consistency with caregivers' assignments
			–Maintain boundaries with parents:
			  call by surname
			  nurses perform all care including feedings, temp. taking, etc.)	

	Ineffective family coping/ Altered parenting	Parents and family will demonstrate improved coping mechanisms and broaden support system	–Document parent-child interaction –Have staff role model for parents –Provide education as needed –Maximize interdisciplinary team (social work, child life, speech, feeding team, etc.)	

RN Signature_____

Reprinted with permisssion.

novel about a mother who murders her children.[19] All such observations should be recorded in the psychosocial record.

PERPETRATOR-VICTIM INTERACTION

Most MBP perpetrators seem to be caring, helping, loving parents. They often spend inordinate amounts of time at their victims' bedsides. They may become overtly anxious if prevented access to their victims.[20] Manifestations of unusual attentiveness (i.e., refusing to take breaks, skipping meals, volunteering to take over nursing duties, etc.) should be documented. Perpetrators seem extremely attached to their young victims. The relationship appears almost too good.[21] In fact, it is. Overt displays of parental affection and concern are part of the perpetrator's overall deception. When unaware they are being observed, perpetrators rarely handle, play with, or demonstrate any meaningful interaction with their children.[22] Whenever possible, nurses should observe, assess, and document such parent-child interactions. Infant feeding disorders are common. Perpetrators tend to treat older children as if they were younger, often attempting to orchestrate or control all their children's personal interactions. Older victims are often emotionally immature and demanding.[23] Toddlers and preschoolers can become withdrawn, hyperactive and, at times, aggressive. Interestingly, these "high strung" children, more often then not, respond passively or indifferently to painful medical procedures.[24] Nurses should assess and record children's responses to diagnostic procedures, especially those associated with discomfort or pain. Differences in responses when suspected perpetrators are present and when they are not can be important, even key, observations. Perpetrator-victim relationships can develop into two-way dependencies in which the perpetrator initiates the deception or assault and the victim helps it persist.[25] Child victims quickly learn that parental love is contingent on their being ill.

Constant parent-child surveillance is one of the most important aspects of any MBP investigation. This is difficult in today's hospitals. Most pediatric services encourage parental involvement in all facets of hospital child care and allow unlimited parental visitation.[26] To ensure constant and consistent surveillance, we assign one primary nurse each shift to each suspected child-victim. Depending on the type of abuse suspected, we also employ covert video surveillance. At Children's Hospital of St. Paul, covert video surveillance is instituted without parental knowledge after consusltation with our child abuse team and legal counsel. We do not believe either privacy rights or possible entrapment, though worthy of discussion, should contravene this potentially life-saving diagnostic procedure. We believe video monitors are medical diagnostic tools, not legal or law enforcement tools. They do not entice, they simply record. During video surveillance, we encourage parents to spend as much time with their children as possible. We also request they report any signs and symptoms they think are relevant to their child's alleged illness. Nurses record all child and parent behavior temporally related to these reports. Whenever a parent and child leave a video monitored room, a nurse accompanies them. Our goal is to keep suspected perpetrators and victims in sight for as long as possible.

PERPETRATOR–STAFF INTERACTION

MBP perpetrators seem to thrive in hospital environments and hospital personnel initially respond very positively to them.[27] Perpetrators tend to reinforce these positive feelings by praise and flattery.[28] It is not unusual for perpetrators to cultivate personal friendships among staff members. These "friends" can later become vigorous perpetrator-advocates and very vocal disbelievers in even the possibility of MBP. We believe these cultivated friendships are part of the perpetrator's plan. The game is to manipulate the medical system and especially to outwit the child's physicians.[29] It is essential that staff members remain as objective as possible and vigilant regarding their professional boundaries. To prevent primary nurses from being enmeshed in these deceptions, we inform them of our suspicions of MBP. We then formally review the clinical aspects of the condition and classic perpetrator profiles. Nurses then decide whether or not to continue their involvement. Some choose to withdraw from the case. Others, attracted by the drama of the situation, impulsively volunteer without fully understanding what they are getting into. All primary nurses must be fully aware of psychological and potential physical risks attendant to their involvement.

FAMILY DYNAMICS

Many MBP family relationships at first glance seem ideal. Eventually they prove dysfunctional in the extreme. The child victim and parent perpetrator are typically isolated from the rest of the family.[30] More often than not domestic partner relationships are volatile and/or disturbed. Perpetrators' spouses or partners are usually peripherally involved in the family, either geographically or emotionally distant.[31]

Verification

MEDICAL RECORD REVIEW

It is essential to review thoroughly all available medical records of the suspected victim and relevant family members[32]—generally a long and tedious job. When done properly, however, such a review can produce useful information regarding families' medical care usage patterns.[33] In our experience, perpetrators are surprisingly willing to allow the release of all medical records even when these records contain past suspicions of fabrication or foul play. Reviewers should be wary of such statements as, "those records were lost" or, "I'm not sure where he was hospitalized that time." Such statements cannot be accepted on faith. They require follow up. Phone calls to and/or visits with previous care providers can be extremely productive.

All suspected victims capable of speech should be interviewed, alone if possible. The interviews should gentle and pleasant but focused and probing. Questions regarding family secrets or special foods or medicines can produce surprising answers.[34] During any interview, the nurse should remember that child victims can be active or passive participants in the deceptions, or they may not be able to differentiate real symptoms from fabricated symptoms.

THE VICTIM'S SOCIAL MILIEU

During any MBP evaluation nurses must remember that fabrication and disinformation are integral parts of the entity they are investigating. All relevant information obtained from the suspected perpetrator, especially that related to family interactions, needs to be verified. Telephone interviews with extended family members, social workers, school officials, public health officials, day-care providers and neighbors supply useful outside perspectives regarding families' social environments.

All MBP investigations should include queries about the health, previous hospitalization(s) and/or unexpected deaths of siblings.

MBP is not necessarily limited to one child. Histories of Sudden Infant Death Syndrome (SIDS) in other siblings are particularly suspect.

Documentation

Complete, legible documentation is essential. If suspicions of MBP are correct, all patient records will go to court. We routinely keep two patient charts, the standard medical record and a separate psychosocial journal. The standard medical record contains all physician orders and progress notes, test results, and the usual nursing care notes. As always, this chart is kept on the ward at the nursing station. The term MBP is never mentioned in this record. (We believe that at one time or another, all parents read their children's medical records.) Perpetrators have been known to flee at the mere mention of MBP. The term is no longer arcane. Nurses must also be alert to guard all medical records and bedside flow sheets closely to ensure that perpetrators do not alter them.[35] Most perpetrators are well versed in hospital policies and procedures. Their notations in the medical record can be indistinguishable from those of physicians and nurses. If parents ask to review their child's medical records, a nurse or physician should always "assist" them to prevent factitious entries.

The psychosocial journal is a clandestine record available only to relevant nursing and medical personnel. It records personal interactions, conversations, potential inconsistencies, and staff members' impressions. This duplicate record keeping is tedious and time consuming. However, it can quickly point up inconsistencies and important observations. This journal becomes part of the child's regular medical record either at the time of discharge or whenever MBP is officially confirmed.

Teamwork

In today's acute care hospitals there are legions of health professionals, trainees, consultants, and other ancillary personnel. Communication is always a problem.[36] In any MBP investigation, clear, direct communication is essential. Without it the investigation will flounder and likely fail. There should be regular team meetings to discuss suspected victims' alleged medical problems and social circumstances, as well as to update medical and nursing care plans.[37] It is often in these meetings that nebulous feelings materialize into frank suspicions of fabricated or induced illness, or where incongruities between stories and objective findings become evident.[38] At Children's Hospital of St Paul, team meetings are organized by the clinical nurse specialist. Other team members include attending and consulting physicians, primary nurses, and social workers. We hold an initial meeting at the time of the suspected victim's admission, then at least weekly throughout the course of the investigation. We inform local police and child protection officials of our suspicions and our investigation plans. Most police and child protection personnel do not attend these regular meetings. However, they are always present whenever the diagnosis of MBP is confirmed and whenever suspected perpetrators are confronted.

Confrontation and Aftercare

Confrontations with suspected MBP perpetrators are emotionally charged, volatile, and potentially dangerous. They should never be carried out alone. In our experience, perpetrators' reactions have ranged from passive remorse to manic flight, and catatonic withdrawal to violent rage. One male perpetrator had to be physically restrained and removed from the hospital in handcuffs.[39] Anything can happen, and staff must be ready. Our confrontation team consists of the victim's attending physician, the nurse specialist, a social worker or child protection worker, and a police officer. Depending on the situation, the police officer is either present in the room where the confrontation is occurring or in a room adjacent. The demeanor of all health care personnel should be professional, firm, and focused on the welfare of the child victim.[40,41] Only law enforcement officials should address the issues of a perpetrator's responsibilities and/or rights. After the victim's family is informed of the medical staff's suspicions, child protection workers rapidly move to temporarily terminate the suspected perpetrator's parental rights. The victim is then placed in the custody of the court until the issues of the child's welfare are legally resolved. Following confrontations, children are removed from video surveillance and placed in safe areas where they are always in constant direct view of their primary nurse. The same group of primary nurses provides patient care before and after confrontation. Nursing roles during and after confrontation are shown in Table 24–3.

Table 24–3
Roles During and After Confrontation

The Clinical Nurse Specialist's Role

1. Cooperate fully with law enforcement and legal authorities.

2. Provide and clarify, if necessary, information requested by law enforcement and legal authorities.

3. Educate health care team, child protection workers, and law enforcement personnel regarding MBP, especially its risks and prognosis.[43]

4. Inform primary nurses regarding law enforcement and legal processes, and steps being taken to institute appropriate aftercare.

5. Provide emotional support for families by regularly updating them regarding the victim's medical status.[44]

6. Allow family members to express their emotions.[45]

7. Strictly supervise all visitors:
   A. The child victim must be in direct view of staff at all times.
   B. Nurses must directly supervise all visitations. They should never, for any reason, leave the victim alone with either the alleged perpetrator or family members.
   C. Strictly supervise any family member providing patient care.
   D. All food and drink for the victim should be provided by the hospital, and should never be left unattended during visitations.

8. Coordinate multidisciplinary aftercare/discharge meetings.

The Primary Nurse's Role

1. Provide the victim with consistent care and support during the remainder of the hospitalization.[46]

2. Assist in the supervision of visitation.

3. Address the child victim's physical, developmental and emotional needs.

4. Provide emotional support for the family by regularly updating them regarding the victim's medical status.[47]

5. Assess and document all interaction between parent and child, health care team, and other family members.

6. Assist in the provision and interpretation of information requested by law enforcement officials and/or courts.

7. Reinforce positive parenting behavior.[48]

8. Allow family members to express their emotions.[49]

Families of MBP victims are families in crisis. Once the diagnosis is made and the suspected perpetrator confronted, whatever tenuous mechanisms held the family together may begin to break down. Families need assurance that child victims will be well cared for until the legal issues are resolved and the families are able to regroup or, if need be, reconfigure. Positive parenting behavior needs to be reinforced to help families develop both the sense and reality of adequacy.[42]

OUTPATIENT ISSUES

Most cases of MBP are identified in hospitals. However, this form of child abuse usually first appears in outpatient settings. In large managed or military health care systems, MBP becomes extremely difficult to identify. Victims move back and forth between primary and tertiary care physicians, between one clinic and another, or from one base to another.[50] In such complex outpatient settings, it may be the public health or school nurse who initially raises concerns regarding a child's bizarre or suspicious health problems.

Guandolo[51] observed that in outpatient settings, MBP perpetrators behaved in ways similar to those described in acute care. They tend to be medically sophisticated. They are very friendly to office personnel and frequently discuss their children's medical problems with other parents or clinic staff. When referred to specialty physicians, they often fabricate bits and pieces of their children's medical histories, confusing both the specialists and the children's primary physicians.

Primary care physicians and their nurse associates or nurse practitioners are in the best position to coordinate most outpatient MBP evaluations. They may have the best perspective on their patients' general health.[52] However, they are also usually the first medical personnel deceived by MBP perpetrators. In addition to being physicians and nurses, primary care providers are often their patients' friends and neighbors. Given such relationships, the possibility of induced or fabricated illness may seem preposterous to the professionals. Even more than hospital-based personnel, primary care physicians and nurses must try to remain clinically objective and cognizant of their professional boundaries. As with hospital evaluations, a multidisciplinary team (i.e., physicians, clinic nurses, social workers, school and or public health nurses) should review the case to determine if child protection measures are warranted. However, such teams may be less available to community-based practitioners.

School nurses should document the number of and reasons for school absences. They should also note inconsistencies between children's and parents' descriptions of illnesses and symptoms, symptoms that are frequently reported to occur at home but never happen at school, and excessive parental requests for special services (e.g., nursing services, psychological testing, special education) especially when these services are not requested or supported by the children's health care providers.[53]

Public health nurses bring unique perspectives to MBP investigations. Their assessments come not from the hospital, but from the victims' homes. Perpetrator-victim interactions in the home are often quite different from those in the hospital. If a public health nurse has been involved with a suspected child victim, information about interactions such as feeding behavior, eye contact, touching, smiling, and conversing can be compared to that observed in the hospital. Scheduled and unscheduled public health nursing visits also provide information about families' compliance with medical recommendations. As part of their normal care, public health nurses regularly assess children's physical status. They note both physical growth and developmental milestones. Any physical abnormalities, developmental delays, or signs of trauma should be referred to a child's primary physician. Information on the status of siblings may also cause suspicion of MBP or contribute to ongoing investigations.

Public health nursing assessment of parental behavior in the home is always useful. Preoccupation with medical issues and terminology may be more obvious in the home than in the hospital. Public health nurses often observe medical textbooks and/or journals in the homes of those suspected of MBP. Individually such bits of information may seem irrelevant. However, they often become important pieces of the larger diagnostic puzzle. Since MBP perpetrators frequently change physicians and hospitals, public health nurses are often the victims' only consistent medical contacts and thus their only life-lines. Nursing suspicions of MBP that appear to fall upon deaf ears within the medical establishment can and should be referred directly to social service agencies and/or child protection services.

Staff Effects

The diagnosis of MBP can produce significant professional and personal conflicts within the health care team.[54] These conflicts stem from a clash of perceptions: the perpetrator as a loving and caring parent versus the perception of the same individual as a pathologic liar and child abuser.[55] When perpetrators have cultivated friendships, it is only natural that these new friends initially rally around the perpetrator when he/she is threatened. Friends help one another. Friends do not wish to think ill of one another. The perpetrator's advocates usually direct their anger toward the first person who mentions the possibility of foul play.[56] More than any other form of child abuse, MBP stirs up strong emotions among medical professionals. Staff members, particularly those closest to the perpetrator, are extremely vulnerable to feelings of complicity, guilt, and inadequacy.[57] Such nebulous feelings of guilt and inadequacy are not easy to deal with and may become problems when team members have to testify in court.[58]

Blix and Brack noted that most nurses were initially unable to accept the diagnosis of MBP. Following this disbelief, most became sickened and angry about being used as a vehicle for the abuse. Not only did the perpetrator abuse their patient during their watch, but time and again, he/she outwitted them. Some nurses, still disbelieving, may object to child protective referrals or measures. Once agencies outside medicine become involved, it is difficult, often impossible, for nurses involved in the initial MBP investigation to maintain contact with the victims.[59] Light and Sheridan[60] surveyed infant apnea monitoring programs that had experienced probable cases of MBP. The respondents, predominantly nurses, reported feelings of frustration in case management or with unrecognized MBP, "pain" or difficulty, team conflict, and fear. They recognized their own attempts to deny what they were seeing, and were thwarted when others around denied the possibility of MBP and blocked their efforts to intervene with patients. Caring for a victim of MBP is a significant professional and emotional event. Sixty-five percent of the nurses surveyed by Blix and Brack stated that their experience with MBP significantly altered their views of patients and families. They were more observant, more cautious, and less trusting.

Summary

We were all taught that caring for pediatric patients requires trust and cooperation between families and caregivers. When that trust is betrayed, it is difficult for anyone, nurse or other professional, not to be affected. However, life is not always pretty or as we would wish it to be. Knowledge of and experience with MBP places pediatric nurses in a better position to recognize and deal with the hard realities of all forms of child abuse.

References

1. Weber S. Munchausen syndrome by proxy. *J Pediatr Nurs.* 1987; 2:50–54.
2. Blix S and Brack G. The effects of a suspected case of Munchausen's syndrome by proxy on a pediatric nursing staff. *Gen Hosp Psychiatr.* 1988; 10:402–409.
3. Senner A and Ott MJ. Munchausen syndrome by proxy. *Issues Comp Ped Nurs.* 1989; 12:345–357.
4. Rosenberg DA. Web of deceit: a literature review of Munchausen syndrome by proxy. *Child Abuse Negl.* 1987; 11:547–563.
5. Manthei DJ, Pierce RL, Rothbaum RJ, et al. Munchausen syndrome by proxy: covert child abuse. *J Fam Violence.* 1988; 3:131–140.
6. Weber, MBP.
7. Meadow R. Munchausen syndrome by proxy: the hinterland of child abuse. *Lancet.* 1977; 2:343–345.
8. Samuels MP, McClaughlin W, Jacobsen RR, et al. Fourteen cases of imposed upper airway obstruction. *Arch Dis Child.* 1992; 67:162–170.
9. Rosenberg, Web.
10. Kaufman KL, Coury D, Pickrel E, et al. Munchausen syndrome by proxy: a survey of professionals' knowledge. *Child Abuse Negl.* 1989; 13:141–147.
11. Weber, MBP.
12. Meadow, Management.
13. Meadow, Management.
14. Meadow, Management and Plum HJ. Munchausen syndrome by proxy. In: *Proceedings of the 1992 Summer Meeting.* Waianae, Hawaii: National Association of Apnea Professionals. 1992; 33–48.
15. Meadow, Management.
16. Meadow R. Management of Munchausen syndrome by proxy. *Arch Dis Child.* 1985; 60:385–393.
17. Southall DP, Stebbens VA, Rees SV, et al. Apnoeic episodes induced by smothering: two cases identified by covert video surveillance. *Br Med J.* 1987; 294:1637–1641.
18. Bools CN, Neale BA, and Meadow SR. Co-morbidity associated with fabricated illness (Munchausen syndrome by proxy). *Arch Dis Child.* 1991; 67:77–79.

19. Levin A. Personal communication.
20. Sigal M, Gelkopf M, and Meadow SR. Munchausen by proxy syndrome: the triad of abuse, self-abuse and deception. *Comp Psych.* 1989; 30:527–533.
21. Meadow, Hinterland.
22. Samuels, Fourteen cases.
23. Chan DA, Salcedo JR, Atkins DM, et al. Munchausen syndrome by proxy: a review and case study. *J Pediatr Psychol.* 1986; 11:71–80.
24. McGuire TL and Feldman KW. Psychologic morbidity of children subjected to Munchausen syndrome by proxy. *Pediatrics.* 1988; 83:289–292.
25. Sigal, Triad.
26. Meadow, Management.
27. Rosenberg, Web.
28. Sigal, Triad.
29. Manthei, Covert child abuse.
30. Chan, Review and case study.
31. Guandolo VL. Munchausen syndrome by proxy: an outpatient challenge. *Pediatrics.* 1987; 75:526–530.
32. Mehl AL, Coble L, and Johnson S. Munchausen syndrome by proxy: a family affair. *Child Abuse Negl.* 1990; 14:577–585.
33. Eminson DM and Postlethwaite RJ. Factitious illness: recognition and management. *Arch Dis Child.* 1992; 67:1510–1516.
34. Meadow, Management.
35. Meadow, Management.
36. Krener R and Adelman R. Parent salvage and parent sabotage in the care of chronically ill children. *Am J Dis Child.* 1988; 142:945–951.
37. Manthei, Covert child abuse.
38. Stephenson RD and Alexander R. Munchausen syndrome by proxy presenting as developmental disability. *J Dev Beh Pediatr.* 1990; 11:262–264.
39. Boros SJ and Brubaker LC. Munchausen syndrome by proxy. *FBI Law Enforcement Bulletin.* 1992; 61:16–20.
40. Weber, MBP.
41. Sheridan MS. Munchausen syndrome by proxy. *Health Soc Work.* 1989; 14:53–58.
42. Weber, MBP.
43. Turk LJ, Hanrahan KM, and Weber ER. Munchausen syndrome by proxy: a nursing overview. *Issues Comp Pediatr Nursing.* 1990; 13:279–288.
44. Turk, Overview.
45. Turk, Overview.
46. Turk, Overview.
47. Turk, Overview.
48. Turk, Overview.
49. Turk, Overview.
50. Sullivan CA, Francis GL, Bain MW, et al. Munchausen syndrome by proxy: 1990: a portent for problems? *Clin Pediatr.* 1991; 30:112–116.
51. Guandolo, Outpatient challenge.

52. Sullivan, Portent.
53. Kahan BB and Yorker BC. Munchausen syndrome by proxy. *J School Health.* 1990; 60:108–110.
54. Sullivan, Portent.
55. Blix and Brack, Effects.
56. Jones JG, Butler HL, Hamilton B, et al. Munchausen syndrome by proxy. *Child Abuse Negl.* 1986; 10:33–40.
57. Chan, Review and case study.
58. Sigal et al., Triad.
59. Zitelli BJ, Seltman MF, and Shannon RM. Munchausen syndrome by proxy and its professional participants. *AJDC.* 1987; 141:1099–1102.
60. Light MJ and Sheridan MS. Unpublished data presented at The First North American Conference on Child Abuse and Neglect/Fourth National Child Abuse Conference. Toronto, Ont., June 8, 1991.

25

Social Work Intervention
Judith A. Henslee

Social workers are in a unique position to assist in the identification of, and treatment planning for, victims of Munchausen Syndrome by Proxy (MBP). Because of the high morbidity and mortality rates attributed to this syndrome, rapid, accurate identification of affected children is critical to their physical and emotional well-being. Social work professionals, whether in schools, community social service agencies, or hospitals, may find themselves in the uncomfortable position of being the first to recognize MBP.

Since MBP does, by definition, present with ongoing physical problems, the medical social worker is often included in treatment planning for the chronically ill child and family. As a member of the treatment team, this hospital-based social worker has ready access to medical records and physician and nursing input. Because social work involvement is viewed as an everyday component of the hospital experience, the caretaker is usually willing, if not eager, to share the social and medical histories of the child.

The school- or community-based social worker who first suspects MBP may meet with resistance from the family and even from medical professionals. Handling inquiries in a sensitive, tactful manner should facilitate the development of relationships with those involved in the care of the infant or child. Expressions of concern for the identified patient and family and an offer to extend social services as deemed appropriate, may serve to break down barriers to communication. The community-based social worker should be acutely aware of the serious potential consequences of a real or perceived threat to the perpetrator. Confrontation should not be considered until the identified patient is known to be in a safe setting and professional assistance is available to the perpetrator and family.

Intervention principles are similar in suspected MBP for both community- and hospital-based social workers. Social work intervention is multiphasic, beginning before or immediately after suspicions are raised and ending when resources for the victim, perpetrator, and family have been mobilized and follow up indicates that satisfactory resolution of the crisis has occurred. The social worker, functioning as case manager, is often responsible for reporting the case to child protective services (CPS), identifying and mobilizing community resources, and facilitating communication among multidisciplinary team members. Support must be readily available to the perpetrator when confronted, and a safe environment provided for the child.

The Social Work Assessment

MBP should be considered as part of the differential diagnosis whenever an infant or child presents with symptoms that are refractory to conventional therapy and for which no definitive explanation can be found. Once the syndrome is suspected, the social worker, acting as a member of a multidisciplinary team, often serves as primary investigator, comprehensively evaluating the child's and family's present and historical somatic, social, environmental, and intrapsychic systems.

Since medical social workers assume a supportive role when working with families of acutely and chronically ill children, their involvement with the parents is likely to be accepted without question. It may be a continuation of an already established role. The psychosocial dynamics involved in MBP remain obscure. However, perpetrators' needs for support, comfort, and escape from unrewarding interpersonal relationships appear to override their need to provide a safe, nourishing environment for the child.

HEALTH

The social work assessment should include evaluation, if possible, of the health histories of the index patient, all siblings, parents or caretakers, and grandparents.[1] Since historical reports and clinical observations often conflict in MBP, it is important to record details of all significant events. Frequently, the mother will report that life-threatening episodes have been observed by other individuals (e.g., other family members, day care workers). These events should be validated with those reportedly involved. Failure of the witnesses to confirm episodes may point to a perpetrator who is a help seeker,[2] fabricating symptoms in the child in an effort to gain admission to the medical system. Confirmation of the symptoms by the witnesses does not rule out MBP, and may point to the more malignant active inducer. In fact, a literature review found that as many as 75% of published cases involved actual production of illness by the mother.[3] Rosen identified an increased incidence of MBP in a subset of patients diagnosed as having two or more apparent life-threatening events (ALTEs) during infancy.[4] These MBP babies had multiple episodes requiring cardiopulmonary resuscitation beginning solely in the presence of one caretaker, but later witnessed by those called to provide emergency medical care. The ease of induction of cardiopulmonary arrest during infancy highlights the need to document temporal relationships between the onset of symptoms and the presence of witnesses.

Parents should be asked to sign medical record release forms so that accurate information can be exchanged with all facilities and physicians involved with the child's treatment and evaluation. Similar records should be obtained for siblings, and these should be reviewed for repeated doctor and hospital visits, obscure symptoms or illnesses, and unexplained death. The alleged perpetrator's medical history may also provide valuable information in the differential diagnosis of MBP. Meadow suggests that more than half of the mothers have features of Munchausen's Syndrome themselves, with some exhibiting signs and symptoms similar to those of their child.[5]

SOCIAL/ENVIRONMENTAL ASSESSMENT

The social work assessment should include evaluation of interpersonal relationships and the environment of the child and his family. Who is the primary caretaker? Does he or she appear mentally and physically capable of providing adequate care? With whom does the patient live? Are the parents together at this time? What are their occupations? Are marital conflicts apparent? Does the victim have siblings? Do they attend school? What is the attendance record? What is the family's socioeconomic status? Is housing adequate? Are funds available to meet the child's basic needs? Is substance abuse suspected or acknowledged? Dysfunctional family dynamics have been reported in association with MBP.[6] The father is often characterized as distant and uninvolved. The mother, although presenting as capable, may be insecure and unable to cope with life situations in a socially acceptable manner. Marital conflicts may be apparent. The perpetrator frequently has a medical background.

The need for food, shelter, or even drugs may lead to fabrication or induction of symptoms if financial gain is assured with hospital admission. Although this is considered to be a less frequent and probably secondary motivator, the possibility should be explored when direct financial aid is supplied to caretakers during hospitalization.[7] We recently encountered a patient who had been repeatedly admitted to a hospital for diarrhea and vomiting. The parents were provided a daily financial subsidy to cover the cost of room and board during their infant's illness. A staff gastroenterologist, suspicious of the baby's refractory symptoms, discovered formula in the baby's diaper bag to which the infant was severely allergic. Following confrontation, the gastrointestinal symptoms stopped, only to be followed by reported episodes of apnea. Admissions for apnea stopped after a documenting monitor was prescribed and episodes could no longer be fabricated.[8] The parents, who had a history of drug abuse, were using the financial subsidy to support their addictions during the infant's hospitalizations. This family fled to another state following referral to child protective services (CPS).

PSYCHOLOGICAL ASSESSMENT

Information should be obtained about caretakers' mental health status, including their own childhood experiences with illness. A history of emotional or psychiatric problems is common among perpetrators of MBP.[9] Although most are described as socially adept, histories of factitious illness, depression, and personality disorders have been reported.[10] The caretakers' ability to separate psychologically from their child should be examined.

No large-scale study of the psychological impact of MBP on the child victim has been reported. However, it has been noted that children who have been forced to assume the patient role over an extended period of time may begin to integrate the perpetrator's behavior.[11] This collusion may predispose the victim to development of Munchausen Syndrome, or lead to overconcern about health and physical well-being. Mercer and Perdue aptly state, "parental fabrication or induction of an illness in a child violates a basic trust that is necessary for the child's emotional maturation."[12]

Case Management

The social worker, acting as facilitator during case conferences, should share findings with other members of the multi-disciplinary team. If data from all participants is consistent with MBP, steps should be taken to ensure the immediate safety of the child. Although local child protection laws may vary, CPS should be notified whenever MBP is suspected. Since documentation of active induction of symptoms by the caretaker is the most certain method of obtaining alternative placement for the child and treatment for the perpetrator, use of video surveillance equipment might be considered. Issues of confidentiality and privacy should be dealt with by the facility's legal counsel. Alternatively, parental separation from the child, coupled with resolution of symptoms, provides indirect evidence for the diagnosis. If this approach is taken, the emotional impact of separation on the child should be considered, and extra support provided.

Once the diagnosis of MBP has been made by the team, CPS should be informed as required by law and plans formalized to provide a safe environment for the child. Following implementation of these plans at least two members of the treatment team, including the physician and social worker, should discuss the patient's history and findings with the perpetrator. Confrontation may create a crisis for the caretaker, and backup psychiatric support should be available.

The caretaker's partner, if any, should be informed of the child's situation, agencies involved, and recommendations for the perpetrator. The partner may deny that the perpetrator is capable of such wrongdoing and resist intervention until presented with irrefutable evidence. Placement and treatment plans should be clearly outlined, in writing, to prevent any future misunderstanding.

Liaison/Follow-Up

The social worker serves as a liaison between hospital team members, CPS workers, community agencies, and the infant and his/her family. An excellent example of effective coordination of services is found at Texas Children's Hospital, located in the Texas Medical

Center at Houston. Their Child Protection Committee, functioning continuously since 1976, is headed by a pediatrician and coordinated by the Director of Social Services. The team is responsible for the development of a case management plan including medical, legal, and psychosocial aspects, and follows the child as long as needed. Social workers assigned to the Child Protection Team have responsibility for the following:

1. Assessment of the family situation
2. Reporting that assessment to Child Protective Services
3. Advising the family that a report to CPS is being made
4. Charting custody orders or decisions
5. Working in conjunction with CPS to determine risk to the child during parental visits
6. Working in conjunction with the physician to assure the safety of the child during hospitalization
7. Advising key personnel of the child's high-risk status and steps to be taken should the parents attempt to visit or remove the child from the facility
8. Monitoring the child/family to provide psychosocial intervention as needed
9. Presenting the case during weekly Child Protection Team meetings for review and recommendations
10. Coordination of the Team's ongoing involvement with the case from the time of discharge until services are no longer deemed necessary.[13]

Because MBP is a potentially lethal form of child abuse, CPS should be actively involved in investigation of risk and in treatment planning. The aggressiveness with which they may act is largely dependent upon the strength of evidence supporting a diagnosis of MBP. If evidence is insufficient and foster care cannot be justified, the child may have to remain in a life-threatening situation. The social worker reporting a case of suspected MBP is therefore challenged to provide a comprehensive history detailing reasons for the diagnosis, including documentation of active induction if possible. Once confrontation has occurred, the referring social worker may be viewed as an antagonist by the perpetrator and family, making further intervention by this individual difficult, if not impossible. Referral to another caseworker may become necessary.

In cases where CPS intervenes with court support, treatment recommendations for the child and perpetrator are typically shared with the family. If these recommendations are carried out, placement of the victim with a capable family member may be considered. If the parents refuse assistance or fail to follow through with recommendations, foster placement is often the most viable alternative. Follow-up social work intervention, including periodic assessment of the child's health and emotional status, is an essential component of the successful treatment process.

A Case Study

The critical need for social work intervention, rapid recognition of MBP, protection of the child during and following interactions viewed as threatening to the mother, and coordination of efforts, is illustrated by the following history. This infant was treated at several different facilities. The pattern, so characteristic of MBP, was not recognized by staff of any of the treating institutions until after the infant's death, when comprehensive medical and social histories were reviewed.

PATIENT HISTORY

W.D., a 2-month-old, full-term Caucasian male, was referred to the Southwest SIDS (Sudden Infant Death Syndrome) Research Institute (SSRI) from a tertiary care facility for polygraphic evaluation of recurrent apparent life-threatening events (ALTE) of unknown etiology. The infant had been seen by multiple physicians since 3 weeks of age when his mother first reported an apneic episode. All evaluations, including 48-hour esophageal pH monitoring and esophageal biopsies, were normal. Twenty-four-hour Holter monitoring was negative for any dysrhythmia. Despite repeated, prolonged hospitalizations, no prolonged apnea or cyanosis was observed by hospital staff prior to the episode which led to W.D.'s death. The infant was placed on a nondocumenting home cardiorespiratory monitor and discharged on May 10 following parental instruction in cardiopulmonary resuscitation and monitor use. The mother learned procedures rapidly and seemed very concerned about her infant's condition.

On May 12, the mother called to report that W.D. had been admitted to a local hospital the previous day following respiratory arrest. Her flat affect when discussing this event was noted in the chart. On May 15, the mother advised the SSRI sleep study technician that she was in a "custody battle" over the infant and was divorcing an abusive husband. (The mother later repeated that the husband was abusive, but denied that he wanted custody of her children.) The infant remained hospitalized at the local facility until transfer to a tertiary care center for reevaluation on May 22. He remained there until May 26 at which time he was discharged home. All studies were considered to be within normal limits, all medication had been discontinued, and no further apneic episodes were observed. Normal findings were shared with the mother, who was encouraged to view her infant as "healthy." For the first time, her contention that the infant was critically ill was verbally challenged.

On May 30, emergency personnel were dispatched to the D. home in response to a call that W.D. was not breathing. Neither the paramedics nor physicians at the local hospital could find anything wrong with him, and, this time, instead of admitting him to the hospital as had been done in the past, they sent him home.

On the following day emergency personnel were again called to the infant's residence and found him not breathing. The baby was transported to the hospital and placed on life support. He died on June 1. The attending physician, believing the cause of death to be "(SIDS) secondary to apnea," failed to notify the county's Justice of the Peace. Consequently, neither an autopsy nor inquest, as required by law, were performed. Ms. D. was alone with the infant at the onset of all events.

On June 14, the first day that Ms. D. and W.D.'s 2-year-old sister, A.D., returned to their home following W.D.'s death, emergency personnel were called to the residence for A.D., who was reportedly not breathing. A.D. was found to be apneic and cyanotic and was transferred to a medical facility where a heartbeat was reestablished. She was placed on life support and was flown to a tertiary care center in a nearby city. Physicians again observed flat affect in the mother. Despite intensive care, A.D. died on June 16. Physicians at the hospital, suspicious of the death, contacted SSRI and reviewed W.D.'s medical records. Autopsy on A.D. determined the cause of death to be homicide. The drug screen was positive for diazepam. A review of records showed repeated doctors visits at multiple facilities.

A multidisciplinary meeting was held concerning W.D.'s death. The infant's history was strongly suggestive of MBP. Based upon these findings, an inquest was held, the body was exhumed and an autopsy was performed. Homicide (suffocation) was determined to be the probable cause of death. In a telephone interview, the pathologist stated that, "there is no disease entity known to man that presents this way."

At the time the children died, Ms. D. was a 19-year-old white female with a history of childhood instability and a chaotic, abusive marriage. She dropped out of school in the 11th grade, although she was described as bright and learned easily. She was taking care of young children in her home on June 23 when investigators came to her house and criminal charges were discussed. Despite the fact that within a 16-day period two children suffered fatal respiratory and cardiac arrest when in her sole care, the listing of homicide as the cause of death for both children, polygraphic indications that she was deceptive, and children's medical histories strongly suggestive of MBP, the mother was not indicted because of "insufficient evidence." She was presented by her attorney as a bereaved, grieving mother, the victim of professionals on a "witch hunt."

In retrospect, it appears that Ms. D. was initially a help seeker, falsely reporting life-threatening symptoms in her infant to obtain the support and concern lacking in her home. This support stopped abruptly after 6 weeks, when the mother was told by staff of two different facilities that her baby was fine and no longer needed any medication or hospitalization. These unexpected responses, with the implication that reported events were not significant, may have served to catalyze the transition of the mother from a help seeker to an active inducer. In an effort to prove that her infant continued to need hospitalization and medical care, it became necessary to produce documentable symptoms. Family, friends, and hospital personnel provided support to the mother, validating her need to obtain care for the infant, during the infant's final hospitalization. Tragically, the presumed suffocation resulted in the infant's death.

If the mother's continued need for support from the medical community caused the suffocation and ultimate death of the 2-year-old sibling only 16 days later, this case may represent the lethal extreme of MBP. The sibling was also found to have a life-long history of multiple medical contacts for fever, eye problems, ear problems, foot problems, accidents, and emotional problems. Certainly, this child's admission to pediatric intensive care reinstituted the fragile family support system that had rallied around the mother just days before, and returned her to a familiar environment free from the stresses of an abusive husband.

What could have been done differently to alter the tragic outcome for both children? In retrospect, signs of MBP were apparent in A.D.'s history long before W.D.'s birth. Although the mother doctor shopped with her daughter and no primary care physician was responsible for coordinating the baby's care, Mrs. D. was receiving public assistance that required periodic recertification for continuation of financial and medical benefits. If the social worker assigned to the family had suspected MBP, mobilized community support, and encouraged a designated clinic physician to oversee A.D.'s care, aggressive intervention might have averted further problems with A.D. and prevented a continuation of the help-seeking pattern with W.D.[14]

Failing intervention with the first child, suspicions should have been raised during W.D.'s second hospitalization, when two events had apparently occurred in the presence of only one caretaker, no event was documented in the hospital, and all test results were negative. Certainly, following referral to the tertiary care center, the infant's physical and social history, coupled with continued negative findings, should have resulted in a referral to hospital social services. The medical social worker should then have been in a position to complete social and historical assessments and communicate concerns to hospital physicians and staff. Through the use of a multidisciplinary team and case conference protocol, the diagnosis of MBP should have been considered and CPS informed. With proper management, provision of a safe, secure environment for both children, and controlled confrontation with support for the mother, it is possible that the deaths of both A.D. and W.D. could have been prevented. Unfortunately, with the exception of the social worker involved in Medicaid recertification, there is no documentation of any social work intervention prior to their death.

Failure of a single source to serve as treatment coordinator and the use of multiple facilities and multiple specialists within those facilities made detection of MBP difficult. The speed with which the symptoms evolved from fabricated to documentable serves to reinforce the need for provision of a safe environment for the child prior to any level of confrontation. As demonstrated by this case history, coordination of care, social work intervention, and rapid diagnosis are critically important to a successful outcome for victims of MBP.

Discussion

While it is important for social workers to be aware of MBP, it is equally important not to confuse this disorder with overanxious parenting. Parents who have previously lost a child to SIDS, for example, may feel particularly vulnerable and inadequate. This may predispose them to excessive reliance upon medical professionals when they have subsequent children. It has been our experience, however, that unlike the perpetrators of factitious illness, anxious SIDS parents want to be reassured that their infant is normal. They generally also resist painful or invasive procedures, and apologize for their frequent telephone calls. Their infants generally present only expected symptoms. Since their anxiety tends to lessen when the infant exceeds the age at which the sibling died, medical utilization trends may be of value.

Suspicion of MBP is often met with marked resistance from hospital staff, family members, legal professionals, and others. These responses underscore the critical need for multidisciplinary child protection teams and ongoing education of all professionals involved in the treatment and placement planning of children at risk for abuse. Social workers, functioning as group facilitators, may help staff members verbalize frustrations and deal with their feelings about specific MBP cases. Certainly social workers themselves may also feel betrayed by the perpetrator and benefit from an opportunity to share their anger and hurt with other professionals involved. Since those who enter the field of social work are well-versed in dealing with interpersonal relationships, they are in a unique position to offer insight into the dynamics of MBP, allaying feelings of guilt in professionals who unwittingly participate in the deception. The heightened awareness that follows an encounter with MBP serves as a safeguard against prolonged misdiagnosis of the syndrome in the future.

MBP presents a diagnostic and treatment challenge to the social worker involved. With early recognition and appropriate social work intervention, the chance for a positive outcome for the child and family is greatly enhanced.

References

1. Sheridan MS. Munchausen syndrome by proxy. *Health Social Work.* 1989; 14:53–58.
2. Libow JA and Schreier HA. Three forms of factitious illness: when is it Munchausen syndrome by proxy? *Am J Orthopsychiatr.* 1986; 56:602–611.
3. Rosenberg DA. Web of deceit: a literature review of Munchausen syndrome by proxy. *Child Abuse Negl.* 1987; 11:547–563.
4. Rosen CL, Frost JD, and Glaze DG. Child abuse and recurrent infant apnea. *J Pediatr.* 1986; 109:1065–1067.
5. Meadow R. Munchausen syndrome by proxy. *Arch Dis Child.* 1982; 57:92–98.
6. Mercer SO, and Perdue JD. Munchausen syndrome by proxy: social work's role. *Social Work.* 1993; 38:74–81.
7. Meadow R. Management of Munchausen syndrome by proxy. *Arch Dis Child.* 1985; 60:385–393.
8. See Chapter 7 for a discussion of this technology.
9. Mercer and Perdue, Social work's role.
10. Rosenberg, Web.
11. Fialkov MJ. Perigrination in the problem pediatric patient. *Clin Pediatr.* 1984; 23:571–575.
12. Mercer and Perdue, Social work's role, quote from p. 77.
13. Black DB. History, Texas Children's Hospital Child Protection Committee. (Unpublished text/correspondence, 1993).
14. This would, of course, have required that the public assistance caseworker be able to recognize and intervene into MBP. Education of community social workers about this entity and how it may present in their practice is an appropriate activity for hospital-based social workers.

26

A Police Perspective

Jack R. Shepherd

The complex myriad of factors that produce Munchausen Syndrome by Proxy (MBP) presents the ultimate challenge to any profession it touches. This is no less true for law enforcement than it is for health care. Although many of the objectives for health care professionals differ from those of law enforcement, when confronted with an issue such as MBP both professions find common ground in the goal of ensuring the safety of a child.

This chapter focuses on the law enforcement role in MBP. Law enforcement's responsibility requires that MBP be viewed as a form of criminal behavior. The investigator will endeavor to make a systematic inquiry to either prove or disprove an allegation, complaint, or incident report of a criminal nature. The characteristics of an effective investigation involving allegations of MBP are that it be professional, thorough, objective, timely, focused, and relevant to what is being alleged. Finally, for this type of an investigation to succeed it must be conducted in an orderly and structured manner that allows for the collection and preservation of direct (witnessed), circumstantial, or real (speaks for itself) evidence.

Barriers to Investigation

Whereas the amount of information concerning MBP has grown steadily, particularly over the last decade, only recently has law enforcement been utilized when this problem arises. Doctors are not police officers and they are frequently uncomfortable with the idea of a criminal investigation. Health care professionals are committed to helping sick people get better. It is foreign to their nature to assist in building evidence against individuals which in all likelihood will lead to their arrest and conviction. Medical professionals are more likely to view the victim from a patient perspective rather than a criminal justice perspective. The child is seen as sick or injured rather than as a victim of a criminal act, and the perpetrator is also seen as sick—the victim of a mental illness.

Compounding this issue are the attributes of the syndrome itself. Those reporting suspected MBP often meet resistance, skepticism, and ignorance. Authors such as Kaufman and Coury[1] have observed that in spite of more than 10 years of cases reported in professional journals, MBP is still hard to detect. The obstacles that interfere with intervention include the medical staff's perceptions of the parent as ideal, strong and convincing denial by the parent, professional skepticism concerning MBP, and the ease with which perpetrators move from one health care provider to another.

If the investigator on the receiving end of such allegations is not adequately educated about the syndrome, it may only delay the investigative process. Therefore, to avoid as much confusion as possible at the initial phases of a criminal investigation, any suspicions of MBP should be discussed with the prosecuting attorney's office. Given the overriding concerns medical institutions frequently have concerning the possibility of lawsuits and the confidentiality of patient records, it only seems logical to have the administration and legal staff of the hospital discussing this issue directly with the community's chief law enforcement official. The prosecutor's office can then select the most appropriate investigator to actually conduct the investigation.

Investigative Process

It will be the investigator's responsibility either alone or in concert with protective services to obtain the proper court orders for medical files, charts, and other records necessary to document the case. Depending on the nature of the alleged offense, the investigator is expected to satisfy what are known as the elements of the crime.[2] Any criminal activity has a set of legal definitions that must be met in order to both obtain an arrest warrant and satisfy the legal requirements for a successful prosecution. For example, should the

MBP result in the death of a child as it reportedly does between 9% and 22% of the time,[3-5] the investigator would have to satisfy the following elements, which are the legal standard for homicide in all states: (1) That there had been the killing of a human being with the absence of an excuse and (2) That the person suspected of the homicide committed the act willfully, deliberately, and with premeditation. Obviously, these important legal points can become extremely complex.

The initial stages of the investigation will proceed with the investigator collecting as much information as possible about the allegation, the suspect, and the victim(s). Interviews with health care professionals should be discreetly arranged. When interviewing medical staff, the investigator should look for the nature of the parent's conduct while the child is in the hospital. There should be a strong focus on any changes in the victim's status after visits or prolonged contact with the child by the parent. Although originally developed for physicians, Meadow's nine warning signals serve as an excellent investigative checklist:[6]

1. Inexplicably persistent or recurrent illnesses
2. Signs and symptoms that are inconsistent with the child's overall health or known patterns of disease
3. Atypical patterns of disease unknown even to experienced clinicians
4. Symptoms and signs that stop when the child is separated from the perpetrator
5. A parent who is particularly attentive and will not leave the bedside
6. The child cannot tolerate any treatment, particularly because of vomiting
7. A "very rare" disorder
8. "Belle indifference": the mother who does not seem as worried as the professional staff
9. Seizures that do not respond to proper levels of anticonvulsants.

The investigator should obtain the diagnostic impressions of others who treated the child and endeavor to compile a list of all hospital admissions, symptoms, and treatment provided. The health care professionals' impressions and clinical view of the situation should be carefully documented. Emphasis should be given to any pattern suggestive of a difficult diagnosis or the inability of staff to find anything conclusive. These findings should then be combined with any unusual or persistent problems the parent reports that do not respond to treatment.[7]

The investigation often takes place while the child is still under hospital care. All reasonable measures should be taken to avoid a confrontation with the suspected parent until the investigator is prepared. Only when the investigator is ready should the parent be advised that an investigation has occurred. Even when evidence is solid, strong denial can be expected, especially when dealing with mothers.[8] This denial has been known to be so convincing as to cause physicians to question the validity of their laboratory tests. The ability of the parent(s) to convince lay persons and professionals of their innocence cannot be overemphasized.[9] If the mother is confronted while the child is in the hospital, arrangements should be made with a psychiatric ward in anticipation that she might harm herself.[10]

When gathering data in MBP cases, investigators will seek out information thoroughly from a variety of sources. For example, a case involving a parent reporting seizures in a child may include the allegation of third-party verification. Investigators should aggressively pursue this, as they are likely to find the parent's assertions to be unfounded.[11] Investigators should look for a pattern of frequent geographic movement on the part of the family and attempt to interview former as well as present neighbors and immediate and extended family. The investigation will also require a check on the validity of the parent's stories about the child's past hospitalizations and treatments, as this information will be beneficial in demonstrating a pattern of factitious illnesses.[12] Since there is no single known precursor for this behavior there is a need to build a history based on the traits and actions of the parent.

It should not be expected that everyone associated with the case will embrace the notion of an investigation enthusiastically. Attending staff and nurses will frequently receive complimentary cards, letters, and gifts from the parent.[13,14] Anyone who makes an allegation against the parent may be met with strong criticism and hostility. It should be expected that the parent will attempt to form an unusually close relationship with the staff, which in turn will make for a more difficult investigation.

After basic interviewing and collection of supporting information, the investigator must turn full attention to forensic evidence. Specimens should be collected and guarded at the hospital. One of the functions that law enforcement should accomplish best is the collection and preservation of evidence. If laboratory specimens are still available, the investigator will obtain the proper court orders to secure, package, and bring about the examination of this form of evidence at a forensic laboratory. All existing reports relating to hospital laboratory work already conducted will also be obtained through proper channels.

Recording Evidence

The evidentiary phase of the investigation brings up the question of the use of recording equipment as a means of documenting the presence of MBP. This is not a new idea and can be controversial. A survey of apnea centers around the country revealed only six out of 51 programs had access to video equipment and even fewer programs ever used it.[15]

Any ethical questions regarding the use of video equipment should be resolved if its use literally focuses on the child whose life is potentially in jeopardy. The decision to use recording equipment should be made in conjunction with the law enforcement investigator, who will not only have access to the proper equipment but will additionally have the benefit of the prosecutor's guidance on legal issues including the need for a court order. This position should not imply that the cooperation and support of the hospital's physicians, nurses, security staff, administration, and attorneys will be ignored. Rather, the investigator has an expertise in criminal investigation that hospital personnel often lack, whereas they have medical expertise that the investigator lacks. The primary goal of everyone associated with the case must be the health and safety of the child. With this in mind, the investigation should be conducted with a true team approach.

Since the death of the child is a distinct possibility, the following approach to videotaping should be considered.[16]

1. Move the child to a multibed room.
2. Install a concealed pinhole camera lens in the child's original private room, with a closed circuit TV monitor in a separate room.
3. Attach a time-lapse video recorder to the TV.
4. Assign staff to watch the monitor.
5. Return child to private room.

Confidentiality must be maintained, therefore the closed circuit television should be positioned in a separate secured room accessible only to staff directly involved in the treatment of the child. The pinhole lens should be angled in such a way as to focus primarily on the child's bed area to avoid the issue of violating the parent's right to privacy.

Actual closed circuit monitoring is necessary so that staff can intervene immediately if the parent is observed doing something to harm the child. Videotape produces a permanent record for later use when confronting the parent and as evidence if the case goes to court.

It has been argued within the medical profession that a diagnosis of MBP supported by incontrovertible evidence is crucial to any subsequent court proceedings. The use of videotape is meant for the benefit and protection of the child. There should be no question of entrapment because the presence of video equipment does not mean a crime will be committed.[17]

Another important piece of medical equipment that should not be overlooked as a source of evidence is an infant apnea monitor. Apnea during infancy is relatively common. However, a number of authors have reported MBP presenting as apnea.[18-20] Many apnea monitors can be internally programmed to record valuable information that can later be down-loaded and evaluated. If the investigation begins within the hospital or the child has been admitted frequently for apneic episodes that cannot be explained, a documenting monitor should be considered. Suspicions should be heightened if there have been two or more episodes of apnea that result in mouth-to-mouth resuscitation. The investigator should also be alert for situations in which the episodes allegedly begin only in the presence of the parent, but are subsequently witnessed by others who have been summoned to help.[21]

The literature surrounding MBP frequently cites an absence of information regarding family characteristics. A complete social profile is often lacking because MBP was merely suspected or was only recognized after the family had sought medical advice elsewhere. The following case history represents an example of apnea-related MBP on the part of a mother. In this case three children died and the ensuing criminal investigation allowed for a detailed profile of the suspect. It also illustrates the value of an apnea monitor in documenting the suspect's criminal intent.

The social profile of the mother begins with allegations of sexual abuse involving her stepfather at age 14. She was an habitual runaway by age 15. Alcohol abuse was already a developing problem leading to her placement in a foster care facility after her involvement in an armed robbery. Shortly after placement she ran away and met a cross country truck driver with whom she eventually bore a female child while residing in another state.

The child had only lived for approximately 7 weeks when she allegedly succumbed to Sudden Infant Death Syndrome (SIDS) at a local hospital. Two years later the mother had another female baby with the same man which was adopted out at birth. Two years after this, she married another man and had her third child. This female child lived for 15 days before she also died as a result of breathing difficulties. The death certificate again officially listed the cause of death as SIDS. No autopsy was performed on either of the children who had died in her care. The mother has been routinely treated for alcohol and drug dependency at a local rehabilitation center. She also has a prison record for check forgery. When employed, she works as a waitress.

The 15-month-old male victim first came to the attention of local authorities as a result of several emergency calls alledging breathing difficulties placed by his mother, now age 22. His recent medical history included frequent visits and admissions to a pediatric clinic as well as referral to a neurologist. Hospital workups were extensive for infantile apnea and neurologic disorders. All findings were within normal limits. The child was ultimately admitted to a community hospital that maintained an apnea diagnostic service.

This child was born after the mother and father separated and was not fathered by the man to whom the mother was married. While he was under hospital care and during a series of tests over several days, his mother never left his side. She was highly inquisitive and well-versed concerning medical procedures. One of the attending physicians even remarked how supportive and compassionate she was over his frustration at attempting to find a solution to her child's breathing problems.

It was during this time that MBP was first suspected. The mother routinely reported a number of breathing crises which could not be confirmed by the hospital staff. More troubling was the discovery by a hospital technician of the mother deliberately removing a nasal thermistor connected to her child during a pneumogram. The mother was confronted, but continued to deny the accusations in spite of the eyewitness account. Due to her propensity for interfering with the hospital staff combined with the suspicions over MBP, the mother was threatened with a restraining order if she persisted in interfering with the child's care. Although counseling was offered, all attempts at intervention were rebuffed.

At the time the infant was scheduled to return home, his mother became more insistent about the need for an apnea monitor. She constantly brought up the subject and offered numerous reasons for its necessity to protect her child. (Investigators discovered much later that she had learned about apnea monitors while residing in another state. The equipment had been used on her other children.) An apnea monitor was prescribed when this child was discharged. The mother was given detailed instructions concerning its use and the device was under her sole control for a period of 4 days. Due to suspicions over MBP an internal recorder was placed in the monitor, allowing technicians to later review exactly what the monitor was sensing while attached to the child. The mother was deliberately not informed about this recorder.

For reasons unrelated to this case the original apnea monitor was removed from the house after the fourth day and was replaced with a more sophisticated model which also contained an internal recording module. A review of the mother's log entries over this initial period showed a total of six alarms including five for bradycardia and one for apnea. However, when the recorder was downloaded, the infant's heart and respiratory rates were all found to be normal. This overreporting resulted in a heightened concern over the possibilities of MBP and the second apnea monitor was closely inspected by technicians prior to releasing it to the mother on the fifth day.

At 6:41 the following morning, police were summoned to the victim's residence by the mother, who reported her baby not breathing. The responding officer and ambulance attendants attempted cardiopulmonary resuscitation, however, the infant was pronounced dead a short time later at a local hospital. The responding officer indicated that at the time of his arrival the baby was still warm, with a fixed stare and mottling of the skin. After arriving at the emergency room, the mother requested to hold her baby. She commented that if she could keep him warm, everything would be all right.

When the second apnea monitor was retrieved, the mother refused to provide her log or the electrical leads used to attach the baby to the monitor. A review of the monitor's recorder revealed some surprising information. It showed the victim was attached to the monitor at 8:36 P.M. At 4:49 A.M. the monitor was turned off. However, the following sequence of activities was then recorded: 5:25:21 A.M.—monitor turned on for 5 seconds, with no recorded pulmonary or respiratory activity; 5:26:50 A.M.—monitor turned on for 3 seconds, with no recorded pulmonary or respiratory activity; 5:29:04 A.M.—monitor turned on for 3 seconds, with no recorded pulmonary or respiratory activity.

The monitor would have signaled had there been any loose connections and additionally would have recorded on the internal memory a "loose lead" or electrode not attached properly to the infant. When the monitor was subsequently examined by technicians, it was discovered that several screws were missing from each of the side plates. While access to the internal components was not accomplished, it was obvious that someone had tampered with the device.

As the investigation unfolded, the mother agreed to be interviewed without the presence of legal counsel. Investigators did request the presence of the mother's counselor from the rehabilitation center where she had been treated for her addictions. When asked to provide an account of what had occurred during the early morning hours in question, she offered the following information.

She recalled that she breast fed her baby and put him in his crib at 10:30 P.M. He had the belt that holds the electrodes in place around his chest during the feeding. At 5:00 A.M., she stated, he awoke. She indicated he did not feed particularly well and seemed congested. She returned him to his crib until 6:00 A.M., when she said the monitor went off. She reset it but it alarmed again at 6:10 A.M. It was at this time she supposedly discovered he was not breathing at all and immediately began CPR. Shortly thereafter she called for assistance and within minutes an officer arrived followed by an ambulance crew.

During the entire interview with the suspect, she used medical terminology and referred to medical procedures frequently as she answered questions. When initially confronted with the discrepancies between her stories and the monitor's recording, she suggested that the apnea monitor unit probably malfunctioned. When queried about the missing screws from the side plates of the monitor, she blamed nephews who had been "playing" with the device. When asked why her babies repeatedly die, she responded: "God is mad at me for being a bad person." When asked if she was responsible for her baby's death, she replied, "I don't know, I black out sometimes." (She later recanted this statement claiming she did not understand the question.) When confronted with the issue of MBP, she angrily snapped at investigators, "Ask my family if I killed my children." Shortly after her second interview, she consented to taking a polygraph.

During the postinterview phase of the polygraphic examination, the suspect admitted to deliberately killing three of her four children. In a subsequent interview with investigators she demonstrated how she held her hand, a towel, pillow, or blanket over the mouth and nose of each victim. She said that she would hold her hand firmly in place until she could no longer detect movement or observe a rise or fall from the victim's chest. She related how she thought she had suffocated her first child, only to have the infant unexpectedly regain a heartbeat and die several days later at the hospital.

The first victim was described by her mother as sickly and listless from birth. She was also characterized as never smiling and frequently crying. However, prior to confessing the mother had this to say about her first born: "At 15 I got pregnant. . . . I quit using [drugs] and gave myself to my daughter. She was so sweet. Maybe I had her for the wrong reason but she gave me a purpose. She died on September 29th. They said she had spit up in her sleep and choked to death. Asphyxiation is what they called it. I felt I had nothing."

The suspect's second child was given up for adoption immediately after birth, which in all likelihood saved that child's life. The third child was considered to be a happier baby. However, mother described placing a blanket over her face 15 days after the birth, with no signs of remorse shown or explanation given. This baby was later described by the mother in the following manner: "She was a very good baby and once again I loved more than I thought possible. Found a purpose. I stayed clean and tried to be a good mother. On September sixth I got up and went to check her and she was dead. She had died about 5 A.M. of what is called SIDS. We never really had an answer because SIDS' cause is unknown. I started using IV drugs the day after her funeral."

The mother's idealized view of her last victim is revealing. "I was so happy and had so much love just for him. We had a real close relationship even though he was so little. He was just a special, special baby. . . . He was my entire world. Every hope and dream I had included him. He died September 25th of this year. I was standing right there but nothing we tried worked. I'm afraid I did CPR wrong or something. I gave him life and let him down the night he died." The final victim had no legitimate medical problems and followed the fate of his sisters.

During the course of the investigation a number of the mother's friends and acquaintances were interviewed. In every case, their accounts of her behavior corresponded to the MBP parent described in the literature. Investigators frequently were told about embellishments, lies, and deception on the part of the suspect. Even her mother refused to interact with her as the facts of the case became known.

The mother often lied convincingly to gain attention. A former roommate described how, on one occasion, the mother returned home on crutches after allegedly being struck by a car. She later changed her story to having been beaten by a drug dealer over an unpaid debt. It was ultimately discovered that she had deliberately injured herself to draw attention. She was repeatedly described as having a need for attention that was overwhelming.

During the investigation it had been argued by the mother that the apnea monitor had somehow malfunctioned. The Food and Drug Administration mandates the examination of apnea monitors after any death of an infant while on a monitor. In this case the monitor was examined at an independent federal laboratory and was found to be in perfect working condition. The mother was charged and convicted in the homicide of her last child and is currently incarcerated.

Victim and Suspect Profile

A beneficial perspective for the investigator is to view the child as a tool in the hands of the parent. The parent is attempting to gain something through the child. That something often appears to be attention.[22] The investigation may yield any number of false indicators of disease, including the parent altering urine, adding urine or menstrual discharge to specimens, adding salt to the blood, or altering thermometer readings. Other reported possibilities range from smearing blood on the victim's face or genital area to injecting drugs or producing rashes chemically or by sharp objects. The investigator should additionally be alert for the injection of oral or fecal excretions into the child. However, after reviewing 117 MBP cases one researcher concluded the two most common symptoms encountered are bleeding (44%) and seizures (42%).[23]

There is an equal possibility that the victim of MBP will be of either gender. In most instances the child will be young, if not preverbal. However, even if the child is old enough to communicate, it is not unusual to find the victim accepting the "illness" as real and assisting the parent in maintaining the charade. A symbiotic relationship develops between the parent and child. The child learns to play the role of "sick" in return for the parent's comfort and affection. From an investigative standpoint the parent-child relationship may be of such a complex nature as to defy an explanation. Patience and thorough documentation will assist in unraveling this "web of deceit."[24]

Attempting to describe why an adult, usually a mother, becomes involved in MBP is analogous to adequately explaining why an individual develops into a pedophile. There are some answers; however, there are far more questions. The investigator will find it useful to view the parent's thinking as quasidelusional. While there may not be discernible mental illness, the parent may be a pathological liar or experiencing dissociative behavior.[25] In many instances the MBP parent also suffers from Munchausen Syndrome.[26,27] This has most often been associated with mothers, although it might also be found with fathers. The parent with Munchausen Syndrome might additionally possess many of the following characteristics:[28]

1. Tendency toward self-dramatization
2. Incessant drawing of attention to self
3. Craving for excitement or activity
4. Overreaction to minor events

5. Irrational, angry outbursts or temper tantrums
6. Limited or strained interpersonal relationships
7. Self-centered and inconsiderate of others
8. History of manipulative suicidal threats or gestures
9. Marital difficulties, financial or other hardships
10. Factitious illnesses

The investigator must remain alert to the fact that the parent who is suspected of MBP is a cunning and highly motivated individual. Underestimating this adversary is a critical error. In one case, a mother was able to find no fewer than five different physicians who attested to her character. The life of a physician has been threatened in a MBP case.[29]

Even though there have been relatively few cases reported in the literature involving fathers as perpetrators, they should not be overlooked during the investigative process. Most MBP cases describe the mother's behavioral patterns in strikingly similar and repetitive fashion. Conversely, fathers in these cases are frequently referred to in such terms as passive and weak, uninvolved, emotionally or physically absent, distant and uncaring.[30] The nonintervention by one parent (father) in preventing the abuse committed by the other parent (mother) seems to encourage and perpetuate the abusing parent's dangerous actions.[31]

When fathers are suspects, the traditional profile of the perpetrator may be greatly altered. They may exhibit more dominant behaviors and are much less likely to bond with medical staff.[32] There is much we do not know about male suspects in MBP. It is still unclear whether MBP is primarily a female phenomenon or whether males have been underreported in the past. Some law enforcement investigators have begun to report fathers as suspects in MBP cases over the past several years. However, mothers presently continue to be the overwhelming perpetrators of this abuse.

Protection of Victims(s)

It is inadvisable to keep the MBP victim together with the family. The investigator should work closely with protective services to remove the child from the family as soon as possible. This strategy may even include full termination of parental rights. The investigator must also evaluate the possibility of multiple MBP victims within the same family. Estimates of this occurring range from 9% to 35%.[33] Hospital- and physician shopping is common with this syndrome, therefore no legal arrangements should be made without the approval of the medical team that originally diagnosed and reported the problem.[34]

Hospital staff should also recognize their own responsibility in the reporting process. MBP is a form of child abuse and as such must be reported to child protective services officials and/or law enforcement in all states. All health care providers and other mandated reporters should be versed in the reporting requirements of their state's child protection law. There is a high risk of significant injury if MBP is not discovered early. Determining who is going to report this form of suspected abuse and under what circumstances can avoid later repercussions.

Conclusion

The primary focus of any law enforcement involvement with MBP is on the health and safety of the child victim. However, the responsibility of law enforcement is to prove or disprove allegations of criminal activity. As a complex form of child maltreatment, MBP is best addressed through a team approach where many skills combine and evolve into a multidimensional safety net that surrounds and protects intended victim(s).

References

1. Kaufman KL and Coury D. Munchausen syndrome by proxy: a survey of professionals' knowledge. *Child Abuse Negl.* 1989; 13:141–147.
2. See the following chapter on legal issues.
3. Jones JG, Butler HL, Hamilton B, et al. Munchausen syndrome by proxy. *Child Abuse Negl.* 1986; 10:33–40.
4. Kaufman and Coury, MBP.
5. Rosenberg DA. Web of deceit: a literature review of Munchausen Syndrome by proxy. *Child Abuse Negl.* 1987; 11:547–563.
6. Meadow R. Munchausen syndrome by proxy. *Arch Dis Child.* 1982; 57:92–98.
7. Davis TA. Munchausen syndrome by proxy. *Forensic Sci Digest.* 1987; 13:41–50.
8. Light MJ and Sheridan MS. Munchausen syndrome and apnea (MBPA). *Clinical Pediatr.* 1989; 29:162–168.

9. Waller DA. Obstacles to the treatment of Munchausen by proxy syndrome. *J Amer Acad Child Psychiatr.* 1983; 22:80–85.
10. Epstein MA, Markowitz RL, Gallo DM, et al. Munchausen syndrome by proxy: considerations in diagnosis and confirmation by video surveillance. *Pediatrics.* 1987; 80:220–224.
11. Meadow R. Munchausen syndrome by proxy: the hinterland of child abuse. *Lancet.* 1977; 2:343–345.
12. Sigal M, Gelkopf M, and Levertov G. Medical and legal aspects of the Munchausen by proxy perpetrator. *Med and Law.* 1990; 9:739–749.
13. Waller, Obstacles.
14. Rosenberg, Web.
15. Light and Sheridan, MBPA.
16. Epstein et al., Considerations.
17. Frost JD, Glaze DG, and Rosen CL. Munchausen syndrome by proxy and video surveillance. *Am J Dis Child.* 1988; 142:917 [letter].
18. Light and Sheridan, MBPA.
19. Rosenberg, Web.
20. Alexander R, Smith W, and Stevenson R. Serial Munchausen syndrome by proxy. *Pediatrics.* 1990; 86:581–585.
21. Rosenberg, Web.
22. Sigal, Gelkopf, Levertov: Aspects.
23. Rosenberg, Web.
24. Rosenberg, Web.
25. Waller, Obstacles.
26. Alexander, Smith, and Stevenson, Serial MBP.
27. Meadow R. Management of Munchausen syndrome by proxy. *Arch Dis Child.* 1985; 60:385–393.
28. Davis, MBP.
29. Light and Sheridan, MBPA.
30. Orenstein DM and Wasserman AL. Munchausen syndrome by proxy simulating Cystic Fibrosis. *Pediatrics.* 1986; 78:621–624.
31. Guandolo VL. Munchausen syndrome by proxy: an outpatient challenge. *Pediatrics.* 1985:75:526–530.
32. Makar AF and Squier PJ. Munchausen syndrome by proxy: father as perpetrator. *Pediatrics.* 1990; 85:370–373.
33. Rosenberg, Web and Alexander, Smith, and Stevenson, Serial MBP.
34. Waller, Obstacles.

27

Legal Considerations

Henry J. Plum

"How often have I said to you Watson, that when you have eliminated the impossible, whatever remains, however improbable, must be the truth?"

—Sir Arthur Conan Doyle, The Sign of Four

Sherlock Holmes' statement to Watson characterizes the particular difficulty Munchausen Syndrome by Proxy (MBP) presents to the legal practitioner and investigator, because this particular diagnosis is often inconsistent with a cursory review of the presenting evidence. Therefore, the legal practitioner's approach requires a thorough analysis of the available evidence to ascertain what is disproved, as well as what is proved. Often what the data reveals will initially appear to be improbable. However, after further analysis, what appears improbable *may* eventually be proven to be the truth.

The diagnosis of MBP requires all practitioners, legal and medical, to reach a conclusion that is antithetical to their traditional view of caretakers and caretakers' relationships to children. A caretaker is one who protects, treats, and nourishes the child; the MBP perpetrator is one who endangers, exploits, and abuses the child. This realization is critical. Once it is made, case building, evidence gathering, and procedural steps taken to protect the child and hold the MBP perpetrator legally accountable are no different from those used in proving any other crime or intentional act of abuse.

This chapter addresses the issue of MBP from the perspective of the legal practitioner. This inquiry includes:

1. An examination of the various procedural alternatives that the legal practitioner may employ to successfully protect the victim of MBP from further exploitation, as well as to hold the MBP perpetrator legally accountable
2. A discussion of the strategies available for effective case building in both a criminal and civil context
3. Recommendations to assist in the gathering and presentation of evidence to the court in this type of case

Procedural Alternatives

The first critical step in developing an effective approach to MBP cases is understanding that these cases require the practitioner to effectively combine the protective intervention characteristics of the juvenile system with the accusatory, punitive, and deterrent qualities of the criminal system. Therefore, this step requires that the practitioner understand the different outcomes and procedures inherent in each system.

THE JUVENILE JUSTICE SYSTEM

The juvenile system,[1] through its focus on protection of the child, provides the vehicle through which the following may occur:

Detection and Diagnosis. Detection and diagnosis of intentional acts of child abuse and neglect are authorized under state child abuse reporting laws. These laws are part of the juvenile system. They provide the authority for the medical practitioner to examine physically a child suspected of being abused or neglected and utilize diagnostic procedures such as radiographic imaging techniques, photographs, laboratory tests, and other diagnostic steps to detect intentional injuries sustained by the child. These diagnostic procedures could also include surveillance techniques such as video cameras employed in a hospital setting for the purpose of determining whether intentional injuries were being inflicted on a child. Further, child abuse reporting laws provide an exemption from the normal expectations of confidentiality and privilege that apply to medical treatment and records, and waive liability for practitioners making reports in good faith.

Placing the Child into Protective Custody. This placement is another option available through the juvenile system. This authority is extended to law enforcement or frequently the local or state social services agency when there is a belief that a child is suffering from injury or illness or is in immediate danger from its surroundings, and some change in custody or location of the child is necessary in order to allow the child to be safe. The steps for a protective custody order usually require that the parent or guardian be notified and that judicial review of this protective order be provided in a very timely manner, often 24 to 72 hours depending upon the jurisdiction in which the alleged abuse or neglect occurs.

Removing Custody of the Child from a Primary Caretaker. The caretaker can be a parent or guardian who is also the MBP perpetrator. Removal is a procedural step available only in the juvenile system. This procedure requires the filing of a legal document called a petition that sets forth the factual and legal basis for accusing the MBP perpetrator of abusing the MBP victim. The criteria for such a transfer of custody will rest on a determination of status by either a judge or a jury that a child is dependent, neglected, abused, in need of protection or services (CHIPS), or a child in need of assistance (CHINA). The particular terminology will vary from state to state. However, the status of dependency, neglect, or CHIPS will rest on the specific determination that a child has sustained an intentionally induced injury or illness. Juvenile code statutes also generally allow the court to remove custody when a parent has failed or been unable to protect or prevent the child from sustaining intentional injuries. This concept is frequently included under neglect.

Alternative Dispositions on Behalf of the Child. These dispositions are available through court orders. Once the court has made a determination of dependency, neglect, CHIPS, or CHINA, these alternative dispositions will not only focus on the child's needs but will also address the needs of the MBP perpetrator in the context of a treatment plan for the purpose of reassuming the role of a primary caretaker. As part of this treatment plan, the court could require, for example, that the MBP perpetrator undergo treatment or counseling, or demonstrate rehabilitation as a precursor to regaining custody of the child. The court would have the option of transferring custody, as well as limiting the nature and frequency of contact between the MBP perpetrator and child while the treatment plan remains in effect.

Review of Court-Approved Treatment Plans on a Periodic Basis. This review is usually required by state statutes. If it is determined from the evidence that the MBP perpetrator has achieved the goals of the treatment plan, the juvenile court may authorize reunification with the child. However, if the treatment plan is not achieved in a timely fashion, the court then could consider other alternatives that might include permanent custody away from the perpetrator, severance of all parental rights to the child, or other less drastic alternatives.

Consideration of Other Procedural and Dispositional Options. Available through juvenile court proceedings, these include:

Court-ordered physical examination of the child.
Court-ordered treatment of the child.
Court-ordered psychological examination of the parent.
Court-ordered treatment of the parent as a condition of reunification with the child.
Court-appointed legal advocate (defense counsel or guardian ad litem) for the child.
Court-appointed legal counsel for the parent.
Court-ordered agency services for both the child and parent.
Court-ordered no-contact provisions for not only the parent but other individuals in relation to the child.
A lower burden of proof than that required in the criminal system (jurisdictions will vary). The amount of evidence required to establish the status of dependency, neglect, CHINA, or CHIPS is either a "preponderance of evidence" or "clear and convincing," depending on the jurisdiction. Either burden of proof is less than the criminal burden of proof, which is "beyond a reasonable doubt."
The civil rules of evidence prevail in most jurisdictions. Rights of confrontation and rights against self-incrimination are handled differently. In a criminal proceeding, the failure or refusal of the defendant (parent) to testify allows no negative inference to be drawn regarding the defendant's guilt. Such refusal or

failure to testify in a civil proceeding does allow the judge to draw a negative inference regarding the parent's guilt. In addition, the rules of discovering information through such vehicles as depositions or written interrogatories are available to the legal practitioner in juvenile proceedings.

It is important that legal counsel assisting health care and social service professionals not only understand but communicate clearly the current status, as well as the overall goals and end result of the juvenile proceedings to the other nonlegal professionals. Such communication at each step is important to achieve and maintain a unified interdisciplinary approach. Health care professionals need to understand why the juvenile court is not the vehicle through which parents can be punished, as well as how the differences between juvenile court and criminal courts affect case outcomes and evidence.

THE CRIMINAL JUSTICE SYSTEM

The procedural mechanisms and dispositional alternatives discussed above are unique to the juvenile system and may only be accessed through that system. They are not present in the criminal system. Yet the criminal system provides particular deterring qualities not available in the juvenile system. Therefore, the criminal system should not be ignored but rather be effectively employed when it is determined to be appropriate. The criminal system, through its emphasis on deterrence and accountability, provides the vehicle through which the following may occur:

Separation. The MBP perpetrator can be separated from the victim and community through the vehicle of bail and a no-contact order. In order to set bail, it will be necessary to formally charge the MBP perpetrator with a crime. If the evidence is insufficient and charges are not filed, the mechanism of bail is not available. Incarceration of the MBP perpetrator can be achieved through successful criminal prosecution. Depending on the particular criminal charge, the sentence levied could be extensive, which could effectively remove the MBP perpetrator from having access to the child, other children, and the community in general for a long period of time.

Court-Ordered Treatment. Treatment of the MBP perpetrator is available as a sentencing option. However, if the individual chooses not to participate in treatment, once the sentence is served, the perpetrator would not be legally prohibited under the criminal law from having further contact with the MBP victim, community, or other children.

COMBINING THE JUVENILE AND CRIMINAL SYSTEMS

As has been illustrated, the outcomes available through the criminal court are more restrictive than those within the juvenile system. Criminal proceedings are primarily focused on the accused rather than the victim. Therefore the options available to the juvenile court, such as transferring custody of the child or ordering treatment for the child and other family members, are not available in the criminal arena. Since the MBP case is one in which a child sustains an intentionally induced illness or injury at the hands of a primary caretaker, utilization of both the juvenile and criminal systems is not only recommended but advocated. It is axiomatic that the immediate and primary focus must be the safety and protection of the child victim, rather than the punishment of the perpetrator. The long-term focus might include criminal prosecution or rehabilitation of the perpetrator. Therefore, the decision to intervene should be driven by determinations within the following priority scheme:

1. Obtain sufficient evidence to justify obtaining a protective order from the juvenile court.
2. Gather sufficient evidence to justify filing a petition for dependency, abuse, CHINA, or CHIPS in juvenile court.
3. Evaluate the sufficiency of evidence to justify initiating proceedings in criminal court.

The protective order will not remain in effect if it is not supported by the filing of a dependency, CHIPS, CHINA, or other petition. Therefore, the practitioner must be gathering evidence and preparing for the initiation of such proceedings before the protective order is obtained. If the case is one in which the suspected perpetrator is inducing illness or injury, the protective order will serve both criminal and juvenile court purposes:

1. It will prevent reoccurrence of any future episodes through restricting the MBP perpetrator's access to the victim

2. It will establish that the presenting symptoms disappear once the perpetrator is denied the access or contact necessary to induce the illness, injury, or symptoms in the child. In effect, the axiom proposed by Holmes to Watson is proven. If you have eliminated the cause of the injuries or illnesses, their reoccurrence should be eliminated.

Frequently in MBP cases, evidence of direct exploitation or abuse is not available. The practitioner must then turn to the concept of circumstantial evidence, which is "the process of decision-making by which the judge or jury may reason from circumstances known or proved, to establish by inference the principal fact."[2] Circumstantial evidence is a legitimate method for establishing that a child was forced to sustain an induced illness or injury. Therefore, the use of the protective order and petition through the juvenile system not only achieves prevention of future injuries to the child but also supports the conclusion of the intentional infliction of injuries by preventing reccurrence in the future.

Strategies for Case Building

The legal practitioner must recognize that it is not necessary to prove the existence of MBP in order to acquire court jurisdiction or achieve a criminal conviction. Rather, it is critical for the practitioner to understand the phenomenon of MBP: The perpetrator is intentionally causing the symptoms of illness or injury in the victim. The burden of the legal practitioner in both the juvenile and the criminal court will be to establish that the injuries, illness, or symptoms of the victim were caused by the alleged perpetrator. Using the terminology "Munchausen Syndrome by Proxy" is not critical to the presentation of the case. What is critical is proving that the condition of the child was intentionally induced by another individual. In several cases, the courts have not allowed the introduction of the specific diagnosis of MBP.[3] However in some cases, the diagnosis has been permitted through the testimony of an expert witness.[4-6] Practitioners should consider introducing the MBP diagnosis in a manner similar to that for other underlying theories of intentional injury, such as the battered child syndrome.[7] When introducing MBP, however, it is recommended that it be used to explain the motive of the alleged perpetrator. I have found that because the particular syndrome captures the imagination of other professionals and investigators, one can be easily led astray in attempting to prove each element of the syndrome, rather than proving each element required by the particular statutory scheme of the criminal or juvenile law. Therefore, it is my recommendation that the theory be introduced toward the end of the case presentation.

When the direct evidence of abuse or exploitation is very strong, it certainly makes proving the case much easier. For example, if the evidence includes a videotaped image of a parent attempting to suffocate a child in the hospital, it does not require much legal acumen to issue criminal charges, obtain a no-contact order as a condition of bail, and obtain a corresponding protective order from the juvenile court.

Even with this type of overwhelming direct evidence, the legal practitioner must still be concerned with initiating juvenile proceedings along with criminal proceedings to ensure that the child will receive appropriate care and case planning while the MBP perpetrator is, in all likelihood, incarcerated. A review of alternative options may be very appropriate, ranging from the child's placement in foster care or with relatives, to permanent guardianship, or even termination of parental rights with subsequent adoption. As noted, these alternatives would not be available through a criminal prosecution, only through the juvenile court.

Unfortunately, in the vast majority of MBP cases, direct evidence such as a videotape of the parent causing the injury to the child is not available. Therefore, a slightly different approach is necessary. It is important to recognize that establishing intentional injury or illness induced by an individual over a period of time will require proof of three issues:

Evidence that the Condition of the Child Was not Caused by Other Means. This will require a fairly exhaustive analysis of each of the medical procedures the child has undergone and the elimination of other possible causes of the symptoms which the child presented. This is the reason why MBP is sometimes referred to as a diagnosis of exclusion. When all other reasons are excluded, what is left may be MBP.

Evidence that the Alleged Perpetrator had the Capacity and Opportunity to Cause the Injuries. Proving this element might begin with an analysis of symptoms to illustrate that they were intentionally induced. This would also include evidence that would establish that the MBP perpetrator had the capacity to induce the condition in the child, such as proof that the MBP perpetrator had prior medical training, knowledge, or experience; or received training in the hospital to cope with the child's condition. It would be necessary to show that the MBP perpetrator had access to the child. Often it is difficult to establish that the perpetrator had actual exclusive access to the child; however, it is important to establish that the perpetrator had the *opportunity* for exclusive access to the child.

Evidence of the Absence of Further Injuries, Illness, or Symptoms Once the Alleged MBP Perpetrator Has Had His or Her Access to the Victim Eliminated. The last element will be the linchpin in the presentation of the case to the court or jury. It demonstrates that the illnesses occurred only during the period when the alleged perpetrator had access to the MBP victim. This factor is critical because it forces the judge or jury to draw the improbable conclusion that the parent is an MBP perpetrator.

All three of these points are illustrated in one case this author prosecuted. The evidence established that a 4-month-old child had experienced nine separate episodes of cardiac arrest as well as approximately 40 episodes of cyanosis while a patient in a pediatric intensive care unit. A brain scan established the presence of air emboli shortly after an episode of cardiac arrest, whereas a subsequent brain scan revealed an absence of the emboli. The physician concluded that for this result to occur, someone would have had to intentionally induce air into the child's blood stream. A review of the medical chart revealed that each episode of cardiac arrest and cyanosis occurred within the same hours of the day, between 10:00 A.M. and 10:00 P.M. Evidence showed that the staff was on a rotation schedule throughout this period and no one staff member worked in the area during all of the episodes. The only individual who had access to the child at the time of each episode was the mother. In addition, the child never experienced any such episodes during the opposite 12-hour cycle, from 10:00 P.M. until 10:00 A.M., and the visitation log revealed that the mother was never present with the child during this noneventful cycle. After the mother was legally prohibited from having any access to the child, the child never experienced another episode of cardiac arrest or cyanosis. The jury drew the inference that the mother had intentionally induced the condition in the child despite the lack of direct evidence showing how she induced the air into the child's blood stream. In discussions after the conclusion of proceedings, the mother acknowledged that she used a syringe.

Gathering and Presenting Evidence

The presentation of any case involving circumstantial evidence presents additional challenges to attorneys. Since their function is to educate and persuade the judge or jury to accept their theory of the case, they must evaluate how this will be most effectively accomplished. Most cases depend on eyewitness testimony or other forms of direct evidence. In an MBP case, it is important for the practitioner to create the correct atmosphere for teaching the judge or jury. This will require reevaluation of the three critical elements discussed previously but examined here from the perspective of case presentation.

Presenting evidence that demonstrates that the child's condition was not caused by accidental or natural means will, by its very nature, require a detailed examination and explanation of medical diagnostic procedures used. This type of evidence can be very confusing and tedious to nonmedical people such as judges and juries. Therefore, use of demonstrative evidence, such as audiovisual aids, will be critical to the learning process of the jury or court. It is important that the primary witness or witnesses present this data in a clear and understandable manner. The witnesses should be prepared to present their testimony so that they educate the jury or judge in a positive fashion. The legal practitioner should consider the use of slides or transparencies containing summaries of critical procedures. If medical equipment was used extensively in treatment, it should be brought into the courtroom. Consider the possibility of using a doll with hook-ups to the various medical equipment and apparatus. The goal of this phase should be to allow the judge or jury to become familiar with the medical equipment, procedures, and methods of treatment. Where there is evidence of direct injuries, consider transferring photographs or X-rays to slides. This will allow the jury to see and understand the injuries.

The only limitation to the use of demonstrative evidence, beyond the boundaries of the imagination of the attorney and relevance, is whether it will assist the judge or jury in reaching a clearer understanding of the evidence and aid their judgment in that regard.

The second element of proof addresses the behavior of the alleged MBP perpetrator. An exhaustive review of the records will be required to locate the perpetrator's prior inconsistent or suspicious statements regarding the condition of the child. The investigators should interview parents of other children who were hospitalized at the same time. Often these lay witnesses will recall unusual coincidences and incriminating statements. This examination will also require a review of the nursing staff's notes to identify inconsistencies in the perpetrator's behavior and discussions. The prosecuting attorney needs to conduct a thorough analysis of the records and interview witnesses to ascertain inconsistent statements of the perpetrator. Often it is not one statement but rather the sheer volume of inconsistencies that is critical to the presentation of the case. Once this information is assembled, it is important to present it in a logical format. The use of charts or other methods by which the judge or jury can visualize the evidence, or the presentation of actual quotes of the parents can be effective. When presenting comparisons of times and particular events, the attorney should use a clear chart that can be easily explained and understood by the judge or jury.

The lack of symptoms once the child has been separated from the alleged perpetrator can be established very graphically with demonstrative evidence. Use of before and after photographs is effective. Demonstration of all of the presenting symptoms and then their absence following the date of the protective order is very persuasive.

In the event that a practitioner chooses to introduce the MBP theory, careful consideration should be given to how this will be presented. Certainly a qualified expert or experts will be necessary to present this information. In addition, the expert(s) selected will have to be familiar with all of the medical evidence. Finally, there are several characteristics of this syndrome that the expert will have to be able to draw together with the other evidence. The practitioner should review these thoroughly with the expert before this particular evidence is presented.

Because these cases often include substantial involvement of many professionals over a period of time, a strict chronological rendition of the facts becomes confusing and difficult to present. The practitioner might consider categorizing each of the witnesses by their profession. In this way, each group of professionals can then present their involvement in chronological order.

Conclusion

There is no hard and fast rule for presenting an MBP case. The general principles of logic, common sense, and clarity apply, coupled with the desire to teach the judge or jury. The MBP case poses a unique challenge for the legal practitioner because it requires an understanding of two systems, juvenile and criminal, and knowledge of how these systems can be used to protect an MBP victim. It also requires a multidisciplinary approach, bringing together professionals with disparate orientations such as law enforcement with a primary criminal/investigative focus, social services with a primary mental health/helping focus, and medicine with a primary scientific/technological focus. In addition, the legal practitioner must implement particular procedural alternatives to obtain the necessary medical diagnosis and evidence to present to the court. The legal practitioner must also become educated as to the various medical procedures employed to treat and diagnose the child. These cases require coordination, cooperation, and participation on an interdisciplinary level. Recognition of the interdependence between the legal and other disciplines, as well as working together as a team, is the critical ingredient to this interdisciplinary effort. If this occurs, the likelihood of protecting the MBP victim and holding the MBP perpetrator accountable is greatly improved.

References

1. In some jurisdictions, "family court" or other nomenclature is used rather than juvenile court. Since the courts that handle these cases are most commonly called juvenile courts, that term will be used throughout the paper.
2. *Black's Law Dictionary* (6th ed.) St. Paul, Minn.: West; 1990.
3. *Commonwealth v. Robinson*, 565 N.E.2d 1229 (Mass. App. Ct. 1991)
4. *People v. Phillips*, 175 Cal. Rptr. 703, 709, 122 Cal. App. 3d 69, 79 (Ct. App. 1981).

5. *In the Matter of Jessica Z.*, 135 Misc. 2d 520, 515 N.Y.S.2d 370 (Fam. Ct. 1987).
6. *State v. Lumbrera*, 845 P2d 609 (Kan. 1992)
7. *Estelle v. McGuire*, 502 U.S. [page not yet available], 116 L.Ed. 2d 385, 112 S. Ct. 475 (1991) on remand 956 F.2d 923 (1992).

28

The Role of the Hospital Administration[1]

Barbara M. Ostfeld

". . . the child is not free of risk merely by being in hospital."
—Rosenberg[2]

A mother who had been charged with poisoning her child during hospitalization denied responsibility and accused the hospital staff of administering the poison.[3] Although this parent's claim that her child was a victim of Munchausen Syndrome by *Professional* Proxy was not sustained, risk management consultants have begun advising hospital administrators of their potential liability for the morbidity and mortality caused by Munchausen Syndrome by Proxy (MBP)[4] both during and after hospitalization. Moreover, although the incidence of MBP is not known, the hospital's exposure in any given case is high. In a comprehensive review, Rosenberg[5] determined that in 95% of the cases studied involving illness production, the parent induced symptoms while the child was hospitalized. Thus, the hospital administration has joined the physician and the patient as a victim of MBP. This chapter explores the risks hospital administrations face from MBP and ways they can become proactive in addressing its challenge.

The Impact of MBP on Hospitals

ECONOMIC BURDEN

In the face of the MBP patient's pain and suffering, concerns about institutional costs, utilization burdens, and liability appear trivial.

However, the economic impact is by no means benign. In a health care climate that rewards cost containment, parents who fabricate or induce illness endanger the community by overloading children's services and threatening the economic viability of the institutions that provide them, as well as reducing the services potentially available to children with naturally occurring illness.

As the pressure to control legitimate health care costs increases, the economic burden of MBP is particularly distressing. These cases are notable for the involvement of pediatric subspecialties[6] and for costly invasive procedures.[7] Inpatient expenses for an infant whose foster mother was suspected of intentionally contaminating his central catheter[8] were comparable to the costs of a heart transplant plus one year of follow-up care.[9] Nicol and Eccles[10] presented a case of an infant whose symptoms were induced by salt poisoning lasting from 10 weeks to 1 year of age. By the time a diagnosis of MBP was made, the patient had been hospitalized for 29 weeks, received two CT scans, two blood transfusions, three radiographs, one electroencephalograph and 83 venipunctures. Fifty-one stool specimens had been submitted to the hospital laboratory. An audit of the medical records of another MBP victim[11] revealed that from birth to age seven the patient underwent 105 blood studies and 121 radiographs, among numerous other evaluations. She had been admitted to the hospital 27 times for 4.1 days of average duration, and was seen in the emergency room 11 times during the first year of her life. From birth to 20 months of age, a male infant with jejunal atresia was hospitalized 21 times for a variety of problems.[12] During this period he underwent procedures to place four Broviac catheters, four temporary catheters, and two subcutaneous ports. Following removal of the patient from a foster mother who was suspected of intentionally contaminating his catheter, the patient had no subsequent infections. The costs for his admissions were over $337,000.

Economists are prevented from assessing the full impact of MBP upon medical systems by the lack of accurate measures of incidence and prevalence. However, the examples cited above suggest that MBP patients could have an adverse effect on a hospital's utilization data. One effect of this could be to dissuade managed health care groups from selecting that hospital for their admissions. Another might be higher levels of review by managed care corporations. And, of course, the whole system of health care suffers when there is extensive and unnecessary delivery of services.

LIABILITY

Compounding the expenses accrued by hospitalization and care is the potential litigation associated with MBP. As more cases are adjudicated, hospital administrators may face more countersuits. In addition to charges that personnel were negligent or intentionally caused harm,[13] hospitals may find themselves liable for invasion of privacy stemming from emerging techniques for gathering incriminating evidence against parents. If unsuccessful in court, the hospital is vulnerable to countersuit and, more importantly, the child is at high risk for continued abuse.[14]

The use of a hidden video camera for covert surveillance of the hospitalized child and the parent has been reported for several years.[15-17] Although the technique has produced unequivocal evidence,[18] the decision to employ it involves ethical, legal, and clinical considerations that need to be carefully addressed by hospital administrators, attorneys, security officers, physicians, social workers, child protection service representatives, law enforcement agents and prosecutors.[19,20] Epstein and co-workers.[21] presented a case in which covert surveillance was used to determine that an 18-month-old's intractable diarrhea had been caused by his mother's surreptitious oral administration of substances including castor oil, milk of magnesia, and hypoglycemics. Following the diagnosis and separation from the mother, the child recovered and was successfully weaned from hyperalimentation. Despite the validation of the surveillance technique, the authors speculated that, ". . . at some future time the mother might bring suit against the hospital for such actions as invasion of privacy, worsening of her mental health, or the disruption of her family. Additionally, the father might sue on behalf of his child." Some authorities have also described searching of the suspected parent's belongings,[22] another method that potentially places hospitals at risk. Finally, a hospital that did not identify MBP or report it in timely fashion could also place itself at risk from action by public child protective services, parents, and from children themselves.

How Hospitals Can Protect Themselves

EDUCATION

MBP is difficult to diagnose. Increased awareness on the part of physicians, nurses, social workers, risk managers, and hospital administrators ultimately translates into a more accurate diagnosis and, thus, a better estimate of its true incidence and prevalence. Diagnostic rates that correctly reflect the problems and needs of a community enable service providers and systems to develop appropriate policies and programs. Hospital administrations can facilitate all of this through continuing education programs.

Education programs are needed to improve awareness[23] and to counter the resistance of professionals faced with addressing such aberrant behavior.[24] Unless these goals are pursued, there is a continuing risk that diagnoses will be overlooked or delayed. Rosenberg[25] noted that even in cases in which MBP was included in a differential diagnosis, an average of 1 year elapsed from the presentation of symptoms to its diagnosis. During that time the victim, the medical and nursing staff, and the hospital administration remained vulnerable. An important consequence to underdiagnosis is a reduction in vigilance and diagnostic confidence even among health care providers who are familiar with MBP.

Several studies have demonstrated that MBP is not yet well known, even among clinicians who work with high-risk pediatric populations. Participants in a regional child abuse conference were surveyed regarding their awareness of MBP. Despite their experience, only 50% had heard of MBP.[26] Preliminary data from an ongoing survey of physicians and mental health care professionals[27] further reinforces the need for more education. Among mental health clinicians who worked with a pediatric population, child psychiatrists were twice as likely as social workers to have knowledge of MBP, yet the latter discipline is more typically involved in the initial referral and diagnosis. Among primary care physicians, pediatricians were twice as likely as family practitioners to be aware of MBP. This limitation in knowledge comes in part from the variability in the availability of references in the academic literature of each discipline. For example, a recent survey of social work journals identified only two references to this topic.[28]

Reporting child abuse has been described as one of the most difficult tasks required of a health professional, particularly when there has been an ongoing relationship with the family.[29] In the case of MBP, the stress intensifies. Here, the evidence is not a bruise in the shape of a belt buckle, but seemingly legitimate symptoms of disease. What if the physician is incorrect in his or her assumptions and has simply failed to diagnose an unusual medical illness? Wouldn't the diagnosis of MBP be seen as self-serving and insensitive to those parents coping with legitimate illness? In a recent newspaper account reflecting a defense attorney's perspective, such an argument was indeed put forward.[30] Charges against a mother accused of causing her son's apnea were attributed to "overconfident doctors, in search of exotic and fashionable diagnoses, and courts, poorly equipped to handle complex cases of medical ambiguity, that unduly favored the hospital's expert witnesses."[31] The article went on to note that there was community resistance to the charge by parents of medically fragile children. They characterized themselves as feeling vulnerable to similar charges and described the lawsuit as "a witch hunt in which doctors, armed with circumstantial evidence, blame mothers for the unusual medical problems of their child."[32] Clearly, the consequences of misdiagnosing MBP are high and public, increasing the physician's need for clear markers, strong evidence, and the support of a knowledgeable multidisciplinary team.

Resistance to diagnosis is also fostered by the positive impression the parents make upon health care workers. Dedication to the child is, in fact, a hallmark of the MBP perpetrator. The initial reaction among physicians and nurses to a suggestion of MBP has been characterized by pain, disbelief, anger, and a sense of betrayal.[33,34] This reaction is experienced by members of other professions that interface with the medical team. Samuels and Southall noted that judges continue to have great difficulty believing that the syndrome exists even when provided with incontrovertible evidence obtained through covert video surveillance.[35] Unless professionals are part of specialized programs for the assessment of child abuse, it is highly unlikely at this time that they have participated in the workup of more than a few cases. Without much clinical experience to reinforce academic knowledge, they are apt to be conservative about including this syndrome in a differential diagnosis. Finally, they may seek reassurance in discounting MBP based on its assumed low frequency rates.

Reviews of indicators and techniques of differential diagnosis serve as an important educational tool to inform clinicians and counter resistance among those already knowledgeable. However, clinicians derive even more benefit from exposure to cases and experienced health care providers. Hospital administrations can assume a proactive stance by encouraging department heads in pediatrics, family medicine, nursing, and social services to identify experts in their fields and schedule grand rounds and special lectures on MBP. It is also important for administrators to address the benefits of continuing education for risk managers, hospital attorneys, and others within the health care delivery system who may be called upon to facilitate a diagnosis or defend against counter charges. It has been the experience of this author that these individuals are least likely to be knowledgeable about the disorder, a circumstance that may slow a hospital's progress in recognizing its vulnerability and formulating an appropriate policy. Hospitals should also extend education to community systems with which they are likely to interface on MBP cases, including representatives from child protective service agencies, law enforcement, and the prosecutor's office.[36,37] The legal community is even less likely than the medical community to be familiar with MBP. This limitation increases judicial resistance[38] and may interfere with legal support and protection for victims.[39] Once aware of the existence of the syndrome in its many forms, all parties are better able to judge the case on its merits.

DOCUMENTATION (INCLUDING VIDEO SURVEILLANCE)

MBP must be supported by unequivocal evidence, which is extremely difficult to obtain. If the evidence consists only of such traditional markers of concern as synchrony between the presence of mother and the onset of symptoms, it may be considered circumstantial. For the court to agree to set in motion the steps required for the child's protection, a strong case must be made.[40]

The elaborate medical records of MBP victims are a potential clue for raising suspicions. However, MBP parents typically respond to inquiries by changing healthcare providers and claiming that previous records were lost. Confidentiality laws preclude physicians and hospitals from pursuing these records without a release form. Efforts to obtain records through a court order cannot be made without showing cause, a process that requires disclosure of what may only be vague suspicions. The parent may temporarily terminate illness induction and seek care elsewhere. If the patient's family is insured by a managed health care program, all referrals and treatments must be reviewed by the primary care physician assigned to the patient. This physician serves as a gatekeeper and is in a position to obtain an overview that is unavailable to hospitals and physicians dealing with traditional health care systems. He or she can then red flag atypical utilization patterns. However, even managed health care programs are vulnerable; Sullivan describes an 8-year-old patient treated in such a system.[41] Although suspicions were raised by multiple rare diagnoses and "lost" medical records, the treating physicians were unable to document how the parent caused the symptoms. The child was weaned from a parentally induced program of apnea monitoring, bladder catheterization, hyperalimentation, and medications, and development normalized. Unfortunately, the parents had her readmitted to another medical center, where hyperalimentation and catherization were resumed.

Covert video surveillance has been successfully implemented in pediatric centers in the United States and England. A hidden camera enables a clinician, such as a nurse or a trained security guard, to monitor the interactions between parent and child. Endangering events (criteria defined in advance) are interrupted by the clinician with appropriate support personnel. Although it is not yet the standard of care, surveillance is moving into more regular use, particularly as it proves to be an intervention with high yield and short duration. Samuels[42] reported video confirmation of intentional suffocation in 18 of 19 cases in which circumstantial evidence was consistent with MBP. The average time required for documentation was 24 hours. Program and hospital administrators who have incorporated covert surveillance into their diagnosis have begun to communicate with colleagues about protocols that address the ethical and legal concerns.[43-45] Their recommendations follow closely the insights expressed in earlier articles.[46,47] These authors emphasized the need for collaboration among the medical, administrative, legal, social service, protective service, and law enforcement systems that serve children and protect individual liberties. Protocols for the use of covert video surveillance are just being established by hospitals. The reader is advised to follow the literature for the emergence of more refined standards and test cases.

There are several compelling concerns about covert surveillance: (1) it puts the child at risk for additional abuse; (2) if conducted by a hospital as part of the diagnostic process, it postpones the intervention of the state child protective service agency; and (3) it invades the privacy of the parent and child.[48] Any one of these concerns exposes the hospital to liability.

The first concern contrasts the risk that would result from failure to substantiate charges with the risk that results from failure to protect the child from exposure to one witnessed episode of induction. The physicians on the team must determine the vulnerability of the child. If a patient is medically fragile, any additional exposure to the suspected induction technique might prove lethal, particularly if the induction is accomplished too quickly to be interrupted. Some clinicians have attempted to use surveillance in instances when they believed that they could intervene before the induction resulted in morbidity. Samuels and co-workers.[49] elected to use video surveillance to document imposed upper airway obstruction. In their experience, this form of induction had been difficult to confirm through other means. They reasoned that if the charges were unsubstantiated, the perpetrator would continue to expose the child to episodes of suffocation. During the surveillance, the physicians minimized risk to the patient by interrupting the suffocation before there was any risk of cerebral hypoxia. To date, the author knows of no case in which surveillance has resulted in a fatality. However, the risk remains and must be addressed. If alternative methods of documentation are possible, they should be considered first.

The second concern focuses upon the physician's mandate to notify the child protective service system of suspected abuse and the system's legal responsibility to the child and the parent. Surveillance is undertaken to develop unequivocal evidence when suspicions are already considered to be well founded. Even without video confirmation, there is usually a sufficient level of suspicion to require that the case be reported to protective services. In turn, child protection workers must respond to their mandates to apprise the family of charges and protect the child from the parent, pending an investigation. If they act within the time frame mandated by most state laws, video documentation might not be accomplished. One program[50] has resolved this potential conflict through education. Children's protective services workers and members of the state's investigative units were apprised of the problems associated with documentation and the continued vulnerability of children when evidence against their parents is inconclusive. They participated in the multidisciplinary team that developed a protocol for covert video monitoring. This protocol allowed the protective services system to remain informed, but was also sensitive to the special requirements for surveillance in MBP.

The third concern addresses the family's loss of privacy. Although patient management in a hospital involves free entry of staff into patients' rooms and use of video cameras in selected areas such as intensive care, these systems are not covert. Hospitals that employ covert surveillance are sensitive to the ethical and legal ramifications. In one hospital,[51] the possibility of room surveillance has been incorporated into the general release form signed by all patients or their guardians upon admission. In another facility,[52] the hospital administration does not act until it is obliged to do so by a court order obtained by the law enforcement representatives on the multidisciplinary team.

UTILIZATION REVIEW AND RISK MANAGEMENT

Utilization review and risk management departments respond to reports of incidents that impinge on health care, and often monitor length of stay as well. However, as long as the treatment is consistent with the diagnosis, hospital utilization review committees may not be able to identify suspicious cases without the use of more sophisticated methods than length of stay. Moreover, not all cases of MBP involve prolonged hospitalizations. For example, Hosch[53] described a patient with multiple hospitalization whose average length of stay, 4 days, was identical to the national pediatric average.[54] Repeated presentations to emergency providers and repeated hospitalizations may be more appropriate than simple length of stay. Knowledge of such patterns and alertness to the possibility of MBP on the part of utilization reviewers potentially may be one method of early detection.

Utilization review and risk management departments also play a vital role in responding to potential countersuits by parents who claim that a patient's illness was induced by a staff member's negligence or intent. Intentional illness induction by a staff member has been referred to as Munchausen Syndrome by Professional Proxy (MBPP see Chapter 6). It can result in secondary gain for an employee who appears heroic by rescuing patients from acute distress. Its incidence is unknown and research into its etiology is lacking. In a case mentioned earlier,[55] the risk management department investigated a parent's charge that a staff member had been injecting her child with ammonia. The department successfully defended the hospital by examining discarded containers of ammonia found in the trash and demonstrating that the brand was not one the hospital stocked.

Utilization Review and other departments need to know about MBP and the possibility of such countercharges. They can then anticipate data needs and track patterns of incidents and staffing, for example, or participate in a differential diagnosis by gathering evidence to determine whether staff negligence or participation is possible. Routine review of which staff members report and respond to cardiopulmonary arrests ("codes") is one means of spotting emerging problems. It is conceivable, though still theoretical, that if such record-keeping is known throughout the hospital, it might serve as a deterrent to the occasional employee who is tempted to engage in MBPP. However, as with drug testing, the risk of false positives might also alarm employees and place the hospital at risk of allegations of unfair labor practices. Routinizing meaningful code critiques or adopting models from police departments who investigate all shootings by officers as a matter of policy might be helpful in this area. At the very least, risk managers ought to take seriously the labeling or self-designation of any staff member as "an angel of death" or equivalent.

Even if staff involvement is excluded, the hospital may still be open to liability for parental acts committed on its premises.[56] To obtain conclusive evidence, new systems such as covert surveillance and multidisciplinary team management are needed along with appropriate administrative policies.

MULTIDISCIPLINARY TEAMS

The multidisciplinary team is an important resource throughout the management of suspected MBP. A hospital administration's support of the extended process of team building and its expectation that such teams will be both meaningful and egalitarian are important precursors to effective team functioning and thus to the effective diagnosis and treatment of MBP. Involvement by representatives of all systems that serve an advocacy role for children is both instructive and supportive. As an increasing number of facilities establish such teams and as community agencies increasingly participate in them, sharing among such teams will become a logical next step. Regionalization of the protocols they develop will contribute to the development of a uniform and credible system of child protection.

Conclusion

Hospitalization does not protect a victim of MBP. Abusing parents continue to fabricate or induce illness, exposing the hospital to liability and economic repercussions. A timely diagnosis benefits the victim, the physician, and the hospital. Hospitals need to determine how their programs and policies impinge on diagnosis and what they can do to support the diagnostic process. Awareness of MBP by medical and administrative staff is often limited. Existing hospital databases and management systems do not always provide adequate support for the diagnostic team. As administrators and health care providers become aware of MBP, diagnostic rates will more accurately reflect true incidence and prevalence. By reviewing systems and policies, hospitals can develop effective programs for tracking suspicious events and gathering evidence. Finally, hospital administrators can develop a multidisciplinary forum in collaboration with their community's law enforcement and children's protective service systems. The members of such a team can guide each other in the development of policies that serve all parties affected by MBP in accordance with the hospital's interests and the community's laws.

References

1. Portions of this chapter were presented at the American Psychiatric Association meeting, Philadelphia, May 24, 1994.
2. Rosenberg DA. Web of deceit: a literature review of Munchausen syndrome by proxy. *Child Abuse Negl.* 1987; 11:547–563.
3. American Health Consultants. Munchausen syndrome by proxy. *Hospital Risk Management.* 1993; 15:39–46.
4. Melfi MH. Munchausen Syndrome by Proxy: "Please protect me from my parents." Presented at the 14th annual conference of the American Society for Healthcare Risk Management, 1992.
5. Rosenberg, Web.
6. Rosenberg, Web.

7. Leonard KF and Farrell PA. Munchausen's syndrome by proxy: A little-known type of abuse. *Postgraduate Med.* 1992; 91:197–204.

8. Frederick V, Leudtke GS, Barrett FF, et al. Munchausen syndrome by proxy: recurrent central catheter sepsis. *Pediatr Inf Dis J.* 1990; 9:440–442.

9. Smith L. The right cure for health care. *Fortune.* 1992; 126(8):88–89.

10. Nicol AR and Eccles M. Psychotherapy for Munchausen syndrome by proxy. *Arch Dis Child.* 1985; 60:344–348.

11. Hosch I. Munchausen syndrome by proxy. *Am J Mat Child Nurs.* 1987; 12:48–52.

12. Frederick et al., MBP.

13. American Health Consultants, MBP.

14. Sullivan CA, Francis GL, Bain MW, et al. Munchausen syndrome by proxy: 1990. *Clin Pediatr.* 1991; 30:112–116.

15. Rosen CL, Frost JD, and Bricker T. Two siblings with recurrent cardiorespiratory arrest: MBP or child abuse? *Pediatrics.* 1983; 71:715–720.

16. Epstein MA, Markowitz RL, Gallo DM, et al. Munchausen syndrome by proxy: considerations in diagnosis and confirmation by video surveillance. *Pediatrics.* 1987; 80:220–224.

17. Southall DP, Stebbens VA, Rees SV, et al. Apnoeic episodes induced by smothering: two cases identified by covert video surveillance. *Br Med J.* 1987; 294:1637–1641.

18. Samuels MP, McClaughlin W, Jacobson RR, et al. Fourteen cases of imposed upper airway obstruction. *Arch Dis Child.* 1992; 67:162–170.

19. Epstein et al., MBP.

20. Williams C and Bevan VT. The secret observation of children in hospital. *Lancet.* 1988; I:780–781.

21. Epstein et al. Considerations. Quote p. 223.

22. Personal communication, Roy Meadow to Mary Sheridan.

23. Kaufman KL, Coury D, Pickrel, et al. Munchausen syndrome by proxy: a survey of professionals' knowledge. *Child Abuse Negl.* 1989; 13:141–147.

24. Blix S and Brack G. The effects of a suspected case of Munchausen's syndrome by proxy on a pediatric nursing staff. *General Hosp Psychiatr.* 1988; 10:402–409.

25. Rosenberg, Web.

26. Kaufman, et al., Survey.

27. Ostfeld B, Feldman M, Hiatt M, et al. Physician awareness of Munchausen syndrome by proxy. *Pediatr Res.* 1993; 30:120A.

28. Mercer SO and Perdue JD. Munchausen syndrome by proxy: social work's role. *Social Work.* 1993; 38:74–81.

29. Kornberg AE. Recognizing and reporting child abuse. In: Ludwig S, Kornberg AE, eds. *Child Abuse: A Medical Reference.* (2nd ed). 1992; New York: Churchill Livingstone: 13–24.

30. Barbanel J. When a mother is blamed for her child's unusual illness. *NY Times.* Oct. 11, 1992: Metro 41 ff.

31. Barbanel, When, p. 45.

32. Barbanel, When, p. 41.

33. Blix and Brack, Effects.
34. Light MJ and Sheridan MS. Munchausen syndrome by proxy and apnea (MBPA). *Clin Pediatr.* 1990; 29:162–168.
35. Samuels MP and Southall DP. Munchausen syndrome by proxy. *Br J Hosp Med.* 1992; 47:759–762.
36. Epstein MA, et al. Considerations.
37. American Health Consultants, MBP.
38. American Health Consultants, MBP.
39. Samuels MP, Southall DP, MBP.
40. Samuels MP, Southall DP. MBP.
41. Sullivan CA, Francis GL, Bain MW, et al. Munchausen syndrome by proxy: 1990. *Clin Pediatr.* 1991; 30:112–116.
42. Samuels, M. ALTEs and Munchausen syndrome by proxy. Paper presented at the Eleventh Annual Conference on Apnea in Infancy. Annenberg Center at Eisenhower Medical Center, Rancho Mirage, CA; 1993.
43. American Health Consultants, MBP.
44. Sherman A, Cochran S. MBP: the silent killer. Paper presented at Georgia Council on Child Abuse Seminar, Atlanta, 1993.
45. Siebel M, Whelan-Williams S, Baker, T. Munchausen syndrome by proxy: a hospital's challenge. Paper presented at Fourth European Conference on Child Abuse & Neglect, Padua, Italy, 1993.
46. Epstein MA, et al. Considerations.
47. Williams C and Beven VT. Secret.
48. Williams C and Beven VT. Secret.
49. Samuels et al. Fourteen.
50. Seibel et al,Challenge.
51. Sherman A and Cochran S. Silent.
52. Seibel et al., Challenge.
53. Hosch. MBP.
54. Commission on Professional and Hospital Activities. *Pediatric Length of Stay by Diagnosis and Operation.* 1991; Ann Arbor, MI: Healthcare Knowledge Resources.
55. American Health Consultants, MBP.
56. Melfi M. Please.

29

The Role of Psychiatry

Geoffrey C. Fisher

In 1982 Meadow wrote that enlisting psychiatric help with cases of Munchausen Syndrome by Proxy (MBP) was, in his experience, of limited value.[1] Later in the same paper he comments that those perpetrators who were seen by psychiatry emerged without clear diagnostic labels. In 1985 he noted that many perpetrators were assessed as normal by psychiatrists and in some instances the assessing psychiatrist found it hard to believe the suspicions about the mother.[2]

These critiques of psychiatrists are valid, however there is a paucity of information on how psychiatrists should behave. Some cases appear to have been handled well[3-5] with psychiatric input benefiting the pediatric team, while in other circumstances psychiatric involvement may be less helpful or frankly inappropriate. In my experience, even with ample pediatric evidence of deception, there has been doubt and disbelief by other psychiatrists. By far the greatest barrier to diagnosis and effective management is the attitude and knowledge of physicians, especially psychiatrists.

The available literature does not give clear guidelines for psychiatrists as it does for pediatricians. Most reports and papers are written for pediatric journals or those dedicated to specialized practice (e.g., child abuse), journals psychiatrists do not routinely read. In addition, these reports tend to "highlight the most serious cases and those with the worst outcome,"[6] that is, "classical" or "prototypical" presentations of the active induction of illness. There are fewer reviews of less spectacular, but probably more common, presentations. Hence there is a risk of acquiring prejudiced information.

Surprisingly few psychiatrists have a sound understanding of what MBP is and what it is not. Some psychiatrists believe the perpetrator's behavior is unconscious or that the perpetrator must have Munchausen Syndrome and project personal psychopathology, by proxy, onto the child. Others have formed opinions (including those for legal proceedings) on the presence (or usually the absence) of the syndrome based only on individual psychiatric assessment of the alleged perpetrator, without consultation with the pediatric team or review of the child's medical records. In a syndrome that has exaggeration and deception as its basis there is a danger of clinical error or medico-legal problems without very careful gathering and thorough review of information.

A further difficulty identified by Meadow[7] is a belief that psychiatrists only manage willing and motivated patients. Victims of MBP do not generally ask for assistance, nor do most of the perpetrators. Yet serious psychological, psychiatric, and social situations are usually present. In a syndrome with extensive and varied victim morbidity, including a significant mortality, the luxury of refusing to see unwilling patients has to be resisted. Developing skills and techniques of rapport building and engagement are essential for the efficient management of this population. Even if the patient remains resistant to direct psychiatric involvement, useful consultation and support can be given to staff attempting to manage the child and family.

As virtually nothing has been written defining a role for the psychiatrist, this chapter briefly discusses some theoretical issues about the concept of MBP that have direct psychiatric implications, and then outlines some practical guidelines for management.

Theoretical Aspects

Efficient psychiatric assessment and management of cases of MBP must rest firmly on a sound understanding of what MBP is and is *not*. Before one can devise a reliable, coherent, and competent approach to the psychiatric assessment and treatment of victims and perpetrators, a detailed discussion of some of the conceptual pitfalls is required.

A suitable place to begin this discussion is with the obvious point of who usually raises the suspicion of an illness fabricated in a child. In most cases it is a pediatrician or other professional with medical knowledge who astutely notices discrepancies between the patient's history of illness, physical examination, and investigation findings, or an unusual course to a child's illness. When such suspicions are raised, a provisional diagnosis of MBP will be considered. However this diagnosis of MBP only describes *observed* irregularities and incongruities. Hence it is only an observational description with connotations regarding cause. In other words, it is no more than a description of a clinical situation. Only at this point in the process of diagnosis do speculation and conjecture occur regarding possible causes of the situation, one of these being suggestions about an alleged perpetrator's mental status.

This simple consideration of who raises the suspicion has far-reaching consequences. The most important is that the diagnosis is a medical one and *not* a psychiatric one. It is surprising to me how frequently this obvious point is missed or misunderstood by a wide variety of professionals—especially, it appears, by child protection and legal professionals. The ramifications of this are equally wide ranging. It means that there are *two stages* of investigation. The first is the careful consideration of medical evidence. If the suspicions remain valid, the second issue is the assessment of victim impact, both medical and psychological, and perpetrator behaviors leading to the fabrication. In some respects the psychologist or psychiatrist becomes a secondary professional in the process of understanding the encountered situation. It also means that when a psychiatrist is asked to assess an alleged victim or perpetrator, he or she needs to rely heavily on the medical opinion of the pediatrician advancing the suspicions. These ramifications also extend to the psychiatrist giving expert testimony in a court of law in a case of suspected MBP. The psychiatrist cannot, in expert opinion evidence, pass judgment on the medical evidence for and against a particular illness being "false." I have personally noticed a defense counsel startegy of asking an outside psychiatrist to assess an alleged perpetrator in order to answer the question of whether MBP is present or not. Clearly this cannot be done unless the psychiatrist is also a recognized expert and practicing clinician in the physical manifestations of the medical disorder in question. Not only does this indicate a lack of knowledge by attorneys, but even more so, if a psychiatrist does pass an opinion on such issues, this is a serious breach of professional competence.

Part of the problem inherent in understanding MBP is the use of terminology and what this suggests to psychiatrists. The term MBP derives from Asher's description of Munchausen syndrome.[8] Although useful, the name can be misleading. It implies that there is an "illness," called MBP, that perpetrators "have." More important, it may suggest that perpetrators have Munchausen Syndrome themselves and manifest their psychopathology via their child. This is mistaken, as few perpetrators appear to have Munchausen Syndrome.

Given the trend against the use of eponyms, Morris[9] suggested using the term Factitious Illness by Proxy (FIP) instead of MBP. The term Factitious Illness (FI) is included in the *Diagnostic and Statistical Manual of Mental Disorders*, Fourth Edition (DSM-IV),[10] where it replaces the term Munchausen Syndrome and is a purely descriptive term assuming no etiological basis. The DSM system of diagnosis attempts to define various mental disorders by means of the history of the symptoms and observable mental status features, without assuming knowledge of etiological factors. Thus a diagnosis of FI is made when certain criteria are met. FIP is derived from FI. Although discarding the eponym may appear to be progress, implied Munchausen Syndrome is only replaced by implied FI in a perpetrator. In our paper, "Is Munchausen Syndrome by Proxy really a syndrome?"[11] we strongly argue that the terms MBP and FIP be severely restricted to those cases in which a perpetrator clearly has Munchausen Syndrome or FI *and* because of unique, individual psychodynamic reasons, manifests psychopathology via a child. Support for this position is implicit in the work of Eminson and Postlewaithe.[12] These authors describe a two-dimensional model to explain MBP (see Fig. 29–1). The first dimension describes the appropriateness of parents' desires to consult sources of medical care. At the midpoint of this dimension is the "normal range," where there is general agreement between parent and clinician about the need for medical intervention. Well outside the normal range are situations in which the parents' desires are markedly different from the clinicians' opinions. At one pole there is neglect of children's needs, and at the opposite pole classical MBP.

When assessing and treating cases of child neglect, the clinician does not diagnose an illness known as child neglect in the perpetra-

FIGURE 29–1

Parent's desire to consult for their child's symptoms.

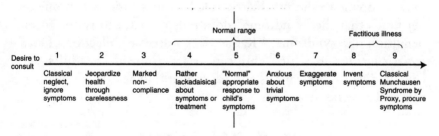

Reprinted by permission of BMJ Publishing Group.

tor. Rather, there are combinations of parental social, psychological, and psychiatric pathology that lead to a child's welfare being neglected. The circumstances encountered when a fabricated illness has been discovered in a child are exactly the same. That is, there are various social, psychological, and psychiatric pathways leading to the behavior of a parent exaggerating or fabricating an illness in a child. *Only one* of these pathways is the presence of Munchausen Syndrome in a parent.

This conceptualization has many advantages for all professionals involved in assessing and treating cases of MBP, not least for psychiatrists. As already discussed, implicit assumptions about possible perpetrator illness are avoided. In addition, professional roles are clarified. The pediatrician's medical duty to assess the clinical evidence is obvious, and the psychiatrist becomes free to investigate and speculate on the numerous psychosocial and psychopathological pathways leading to the perpetrator's behavior and the situation of fabrication. Some of these pathways are more amenable to assessment and treatment than others. For example, major depressive disorder responds better to intervention than serious personality disorder. Both of these can, theoretically, be part of the etiological pathway towards the behavior of "telling lies," the reasons for which are legion.

Not every case of suspected MBP can be proven, and Meadow describes a category known as "not quite MBP."[13,14] Eminson and Postlewaite have a portion of their first dimension that includes exaggeration without induction. Similar social and psychological pathways operate with the exaggeration of symptoms in children by parents.

Developing a valid psychiatric role becomes easier when one understands that the "syndrome" does not, in fact, satisfy the formal definition of a syndrome.[15] Rather, it is a diverse collection of *medical situations* in which children are victimized by adults with equally diverse motivations and psychopathologies. This psychiatric role will now be described.

The Psychiatrist's Role

GENERAL CONSIDERATIONS

Assessment and management of MBP is a joint pediatric/psychiatric venture. Early on, the diagnosis is ventured by a pediatrician whose duty is to complete necessary medical investigations and confirm or refute the suspicions. During this stage speculations about what may lie behind the alleged fabrications and perpetrator behavior will occur. At this point consultation with psychiatry should be considered. In larger centers this may be easily accomplished. However in smaller centers, and particularly in rural areas, intermittent visiting consultation by an overworked general psychiatrist may be all that is available. When a psychiatrist is unavailable, the initial consultation may be with a psychologist, social worker, or other mental health professional who may or may not have a thorough understanding of MBP, and whose ability to help may be limited by the lack of medical training. If a psychiatrist is available but uninformed about MBP, he or she must be prepared to be educated.

The pediatrician must also have an understanding about what psychiatry can and cannot do, and needs to be clear about the purpose of the consultation. A common reason for failure at all levels in psychiatric consultation is lack of clarity on the part of the person making the request. Common reasons for psychiatric consultation include support in a difficult situation; assistance with diagnosis; help in acquiring information, maintaining rapport with a difficult parent, or relating to other professionals; or a need for assessment of the child and/or parent.

Sometimes a nonphysician or a psychiatrist may initially raise the suspicion of MBP. We have recently reported a possible case of the fabrication of psychiatric illness in a child.[16] Occasionally there may be resistance or even opposition to this suggestion from the pediatric staff. This situation may arise when a professional becomes concerned about abnormal illness behavior in a parent or a parent seems overly concerned about illnesses in the child, or because of excessive criticisms of physicians "not doing their jobs" or not taking the parent seriously. When this situation arises, a competent pediatrician should always be consulted to provide an opinion on the child's illness. Unfortunately, issues of who is qualified to make such a judgment, or differential power or status dynamics may become significant. These situations must be handled carefully and sensitively.

In a well-functioning, cohesive treatment team all members should feel sufficiently comfortable to raise and discuss various opinions. However, some multidisciplinary teams may not function well; members may be under stress for other reasons, or there may be personality differences or status and power issues that interfere with communication. Whatever the reason, the venturing of a suspicion of MBP, particularly if this comes from a nonmedical member, can drastically influence team functioning. If a team already has difficulties, such a suggestion may not only worsen team functioning but ultimately impact the management and safety of the child. Clearly the consulting psychiatrist, social worker, or psychologist has a role in assisting the team to navigate these hazards.

THE INITIAL CONSULTATION

It is suggested that the initial consultation with the psychiatrist should occur in confidence both from the family and other members of the pediatric team. It is not uncommon for alleged perpetrators to overstep boundaries with health professionals, who are sometimes incorporated into the family system. If a family becomes aware of the suspicions at an early stage the case may be lost. Also, other physicians may not take kindly to questioning of their diagnostic acumen. Occasionally conflictual relationships may have developed among physicians or team members. Psychiatric advice on how these may be handled can be valuable. Professionals seeking consultation may doubt their suspicions and the psychiatrist must allow for frank discussion of these uncertainties as well as the relevant medical issues. Psychiatrists must always remember that they are dealing with colleagues and a medical condition, and respect the expertise of those considering the diagnosis.

In all instances, psychiatrists must review the complete medical record. Careful reading of the family medical and social history is essential. Particular attention should be given to past abuse histories, child protection suspicions, individual and family psychiatric histories, and the number of professionals involved. Social and family histories are often inadequately completed by general physicians but are essential in MBP, particularly the timing of any significant psychological, social or family stressors that may correlate with presentations of illness. If good histories are lacking, the psychiatrist should advise on the information to be obtained. Nursing notes are particularly valuable as they often contain sound observations of child and parental behaviors and interactions. Thus a function of the initial consultation is to plan strategies of amassing and organizing clinical information. It also serves to plan coordinated pediatric/psychiatric management. For instance, a medical social worker may already be involved; if not, one should be carefully selected. Social workers can assist in collecting missing data and history, and as they are usually already part of the pediatric team less suspicion may be aroused. Early contact between the alleged perpetrator and/or child and the psychiatrist may be not be helpful except in unusual circumstances such as obviously abnormal parent or child behaviors.

SUBSEQUENT CONSULTATIONS

New information should be meticulously reviewed and decisions made about additional, carefully selected, clinicians joining to form a core investigation and management team. Once again confidentiality is essential, as is regular contact among team members. Sufficient information may be available for the psychiatrist to speculate on perpetrator motivation (for example, illness or psychodynamic factors) and whether direct evaluation of either the child or perpetrator is necessary.

If direct assessment is requested the psychiatrist may be placed in a potentially difficult situation. Careful consideration of how a psychiatric assessment may be presented to a family is required. The family may already be suspicious, and it is common for many patients to assume that if psychiatric appraisal is needed then someone suspects the child victim's condition is not real or that they are mentally unstable. The psychiatrist may be introduced as part of the team, or the focus may be on the stress, for the child and parent, of a complex illness. Most families will accept these approaches, but some will refuse. When the family refuses, the pediatrician should remain in contact with the family and consult frequently with the psychiatrist around issues of communication and case management.

PSYCHIATRIC ASSESSMENT OF THE ALLEGED PERPETRATOR

The psychiatrist's first priority is engagement and rapport building. Interrogation must be avoided. Behind the successful social facade so often described in the literature, alleged perpetrators (usually mothers) are defensive and sensitive to criticism. To maximize rapport it may be necessary to delay formal history taking and detailed evaluation of mental status, especially if the parent is questioning or suspicious. Clearly, however, if major psychopathology is suspected (either based on previously gathered history or the subject's presentation at the interview), early assessment of mental status is obligatory.

The primary focus of the evaluation is to assess and describe the alleged perpetrator's mental status in terms of risk for the child. This can be a difficult situation for a psychiatrist who may identify factors indicating acute or serious risk for the child but also acute treatment needs for a parent. Unpalatable and fraught with ethical dilemmas though the decision may be, the child's safety must always take priority. The worst scenario is serious child risk combined with serious perpetrator psychopathology; for example, major depressive illness with suicidal ideation. Complicating the situation is often symbiosis, or an enmeshed relationship between the child and mother. Frequently mothers will say that their child "is everything to them" or that they "live for their child." If the presentation of a child as sick is a method for a mother to obtain nurturance or satisfy her own internal needs, then a recommendation for action on child safety may precipitate acute and dramatic psychological distress or crisis in a parent, even self harm. Fortunately these scenarios appear to be rare.

The caregiver must be suffering at some level to perpetrate the abuse. Engaging the alleged perpetrator in conversation about stress will often reveal a lifestyle revolving around the child and illness. Questions such as "how do you cope?" or "what is it like for you?" can be helpful and presented to the patient as the psychiatrist needing to understand strengths and weaknesses. This line of questioning can lead into discussions of relationships and supports. Care is needed in questioning like this as there is a fine line between rapport and collusion. The aim is for the person to feel listened to and understood. Initially any stress may be denied and a picture of an efficient, capable person heroically managing a very sick child may be presented. However, behind this facade the suffering can be intense and many interviews may be needed before a parent will feel comfortable enough to talk about stresses or any feeling of inadequacy. On the other hand some subjects persist in presenting a coping facade, and little more can be done.

Obtaining medical, psychiatric, and social history is essential. Extensive past medical histories, frequently of rare conditions, are common and often similar to the child's current illness.[17-21] Fabrications may extend into other areas one ends up not knowing where truth ends and lies begin.[22-24] Hence assessment can be time-consuming and uncertain. Past histories of mental disorders are common. There is an association with adult factitious illness in some cases,[25-34] though in other cases this association is less clear.[35-42] Possibly some 10–30% of perpetrators may have factitious symptoms that may amount to Munchausen Syndrome. It is noteworthy that there are few descriptions of dissociative disorders, which could explain some features of a perpetrator's behavior, though cases reported by Geelhoed and Pemberton[43] and Rosen[44] may suggest dissociation. Occasionally a curious mixture of fabricated and functional illness is encountered.[45] Depression, suicidal gestures, personality disorders, anxiety attacks, and functional illnesses have been reported.[46-58] Maternal somatization disorder has been described.[59,60] In cases of child poisoning there may be a higher incidence of maternal "mental disturbance."[61] Interestingly, frank psychotic illnesses have not been reported in association with MBP, though some reports suggest them.[62-66]

It is important also to assess the perpetrator's social situation thoroughly, as this may relate clearly to the presentation of the child. Loss of employment, recent family stressors (for example, the

death of a close relative), poverty, and marital breakup may all precipitate health-care-seeking behaviors in vulnerable persons in the
absence of obvious mental illness. Many of these people may be vulnerable by way of dependent personality traits, lack of self-confidence, poor self esteem and self worth, or because of constant
battles with poverty, unemployment, and poor housing. Approximately two-thirds of the alleged perpetrators I have dealt with are
single, struggling, isolated, unsupported, poor, depressed women,
separated from their families of origin, which in turn were equally
unsupportive and dysfunctional. About half of the perpetrators were
victims of abuse and in all cases they were exposed, in their formative years, to environments where emotional abuse and erosion of
self-esteem were daily occurrences. I do not know how common
this type of psychosocial deprivation is in cases of MBP, although
there are indications of it in the literature[67-71] and it may be a selec-
tion bias on my part because of my work in a government-funded
hospital child abuse program. Not only is this an area for sensitive,
socially informed psychiatric assessment, but also it is a fruitful area
for further research.

Early authors did not report institutional life or excesses of deprivation in the mothers' childhoods, but past histories of physical
and/or sexual abuse or emotional neglect appear common[72-83]. Detailed evaluation of abuse experiences is essential as these experiences may underlie perpetrator psychodynamic functioning and may
have later treatment implications. Questioning about current family
violence should be done, as abusive episodes may relate temporally
to the presentation of a child as ill. Exploration of the alleged perpetrator's perceptions of growing up and early experiences of personal
and family illness should be completed. Histories of any attention
seeking behaviors (overdoses, wrist slashing, behavioral problems,
lying, delinquency, and particularly factitious illness) during childhood and teenage years should also be obtained. Most common,
however, are mixed pictures of varied psychiatric illness, social
problems, and family dysfunction, past and present.

When sufficient rapport has developed, a thorough current mental status examination is mandatory. Particular diagnostic attention
should be given to affective disorders, dissociative states, psychotic
conditions, intellectual impairment, substance abuse, personality
disorder, and the adult sequelae of childhood abuse. Psychological

assessment can be valuable and may be acceptable to the alleged perpetrator. I have found it a useful strategy to tell parents that additional psychological assessment can help identify their strengths and weaknesses.

No psychiatric opinion of a parent in any case involving children can be considered complete without personal observation of parent-child interactions by the psychiatrist. This may be done in an interview setting or via a one-way screen depending upon the age of the child and the information required. (Since some authors describe marked changes in behavior when alleged perpetrators know they are being observed, varied settings and conditions may be desirable.) Assessment of parenting capacity is essential. An excellent review of the components to this can be found in Steinhauer's book *The Least Detrimental Alternative*.[84] All too often psychiatrists (particularly those external to the pediatric team, such as those retained by parents, attorneys, or child protection agencies) will formulate opinions on parenting capacity without any observation of the parent and child together, review of the pediatric medical record, or formal assessment of parenting skills. Unfortunately the average adult psychiatrist is relatively inexperienced or has not been trained in these methods. If opinions on the custody of a child are to be ventured, such assessments are essential.

Following the psychiatric assessment of the alleged perpetrator, a clear written and verbal report should be given to the pediatric team. Ideally this should outline diagnostic opinions, prognosis, treatment options, and a description of how these relate to the development of the parent's fabricating behavior. An opinion must also be given on any parental factors that have a direct impact on child safety.

The psychiatrist also has a role in the disclosure of medical suspicions to a parent. The process of disclosure should be carefully planned jointly by the psychiatrist and the team. If good rapport and engagement has been established, the psychiatrist may be in a unique position to offer assistance to the parent. In my experience, carefully managing engagement and disclosure has resulted in a number of perpetrators accepting psychiatric treatment.

If a degree of engagement has been adequately established, the offending parent will probably have disclosed meaningful personal information to the psychiatrist. (This is certainly my experience.) If the psychiatrist can acknowledge and accurately empathize with a parent's suffering, rapport and engagement will be strengthened. Even so, with proficient deceivers the risks of collusion and the presence of only illusory rapport and engagement must always be kept in mind. The psychiatrist should arrange to accompany the parent to the meeting with carefully selected team members when the medical suspicions are to be discussed. Prior to any meeting, members of the pediatric team should have a working knowledge of the perpetrator's social situation, psychiatric diagnosis, and the practical implications of that diagnosis (such as propensity for anger, aggression, or precipitation of suicidal ideation). Such information will assist the team in formulating how the information is to be presented and what, if any, backup may be required. Backup may mean anything from alerting an adult psychiatric inpatient unit about a possible problem to having hospital security personnel discretely at hand. Obviously, everything cannot be planned, but general precautions can be taken.

The pediatrician should present medical suspicions and evidence gently and clearly to the parent. Suggesting to the parent that various team members worry as much about the child *and parent's* welfare as the parent does may be a useful strategy, as embedded in statements like this are messages that the pediatric team acknowledges that the parent is suffering. The psychiatrist can reinforce the acknowledgement of parental suffering and offer support. Unfortunately very few of us appear to have any extensive experience with a process like this, and I am unsure how successful it will be in all cases. From general experience of managing severely personality disordered individuals (such as borderline personality disorder) or those suffering from depressive illness, strongly indicating that their distress has been heard is always a powerful strategy. There may, however, be potential problems with an approach like this. I believe that this strategy is most helpful with those perpetrators who correspond more closely with Libow and Schreier's category of help seekers.[85] I suspect that this group of perpetrators may have a higher incidence of psychosocial deprivation and/or conditions such as depressive illness, and may be more open to external acknowledgement of their distress.

A suspicious and anxious parent may suspect collaboration between the psychiatrist and pediatric team, or that the meeting is obviously stage managed. With those perpetrators who are severely personality disordered, or who strongly maintain their denial (rather like Libow and Schreier's active inducers) such an approach will be less successful. In any case, nothing will be lost by attempting such an approach as it is conceivable that some seed may be planted, even with the most severely denying and personality disordered person, that may come to fruition in the future.

Occasionally a psychiatrist may be asked to see alleged perpetrators for the first time after disclosure of suspicions to them and and their families. Generally there is little a psychiatrist can do in these situations. The accused are usually hostile, angry, denying, and suspicious of the psychiatrist's motives. Often they believe the psychiatrist only hopes to obtain further "evidence" to be used against them. Histories are minimized and efforts are made to present a normal mental state. This is particularly so in cases where an outside psychiatrist has been retained. The psychiatrist must remember that it takes skill to perpetrate complex fabrications or maintain them over long periods of time. Intelligent, possibly personality disordered, patients can easily mislead psychiatrists, particularly if the medical information and documentation have not been thoroughly reviewed.

Some parents are calm after disclosure,[86,87] while others attempt self-harm or become overtly depressed.[88-94] Inpatient or outpatient psychiatric treatment is accepted by a few, while others "run," with their families, only to seek medical involvement elsewhere. Attempted abduction of a child is a real risk.[95]

Descriptions of perpetrator treatment are scant.[96-100] Some readily accept treatment and are relieved.[101,102] There are unproven clinical suspicions that those who continue in denial and refusal may have a greater degree of personality disorder. Any psychiatric illness should be actively treated with medication, psychotherapy, or a combination of both, as indicated. Family management, including family therapy, may also be indicated. Other treatment modalities such as parent skills education and training, anger management techniques, assertiveness training, and social skills work are valuable. Cognitive behavioral therapy may be an option, as many perpetrators operate with a multitude of self-defeating thoughts and statements. Providing assistance to the parent or family in the home, if possible, should be considered, as home aides can assist the mother in developing a healthy social network away from medical contacts.

Rarely, successful treatment of the perpetrator may be achieved without actual reference to the discovered fabrications. A common dynamic our research group has identified is that many perpetrators were objectified or had numerous experiences of disconfirmation when they were children, often via their own abusive ordeals or from living in environments where sick role behavior was a vehicle for obtaining nurturance. As adults they objectify their own children, and cannot view them as independent beings (symbiosis). Some perpetrators readily engage in conversation about these childhood experiences; if they can be dealt with in psychotherapy then reduction of help-seeking behaviors and subsequent risk to the children is possible without overtly addressing any fabrications. Clearly, however, careful analysis of the degree of risk to the child is needed before any decision is taken to manage a case in this fashion.

PSYCHIATRIC ASSESSMENT OF THE CHILD

The psychiatrist may be asked to evaluate the child. Once again, clear questions are needed from the pediatric team. The setting and age of the child determine how the assesement should proceed. Sometimes access to and engagement of parents may be best achieved via assessment of the child. For those children in hospital and still in the care of their parents, consent is required for psychiatric assessment. Once again various pretexts may be needed and the pediatrician should carefully explain to the parent(s) why the psychiatric evaluation is indicated. Older children should be told about the evaluation and their consent sought. A suitable approach for older children is to explain that the attending doctor would like to know how they feel about their "being ill" with so many problems. By sharing this the children can help the doctors work out the best treatment plan. The name of the psychiatrist should be given and the children should be told that the meeting will take place shortly. Children may be nervous and, as they are victims, the initial approach should be as supportive as possible.

In some circumstances children may have already been removed from the care of their parents by a child protection agency and may either be in hospital or in a foster family. In these cases the risks to the children will probably have been serious and acute. Not only will there be significant victimization issues, even life-threatening episodes, but also the stresses of removal from the family. As symbiosis is a two-way phenomenon, some of these children will be fearful and apprehensive. In other older children there may have been conscious or unconscious collusion between the children and perpetrators, and the children may fear disaster or harm befalling their parents because of their absence from the home. Other children are relieved to be out of the home. Whatever the circumstances, careful preparation of children for psychiatric assessment is essential.

With infant victims, psychiatric assessments require the full and active involvement of the parents. Observational data from nursing staff is of the utmost value as this may reveal enmeshment, symbiosis, poor parenting techniques, overindulgence, or unusual and bizarre parenting beliefs and practices; however, it does not replace the psychiatrist's own observations. Psychiatric appraisal should involve a developmental assessment and observation of parent-child interactions, not only on the unit or in the office but in a suitable child-orientated playroom. The use of a one-way mirror is recommended. With consent, the session may be videotaped, and rating instruments are available for assessing the quality of infant-parent relationships. The psychiatrist must have a thorough knowledge of attachment theory and behaviors to accomplish these observational studies. Observations of feeding routines are particularly revealing in studying parent-infant interactions. Again various pretexts may be needed to accomplish these observational interviews.

Children from about age 2 years can be interviewed individually, preferably in a quiet private room with age-appropriate activities, not on the open ward. Techniques of engagement and rapport-building vary with age and these are comprehensively reviewed by Philip J. Barker in *Clinical Interviews with Children and Adolescents*.[103] Often the entire first session may be concerned with settling and engaging the child, but this is time well spent. The children may be fearful for many reasons. Some have little self-confidence or self-esteem because of their family environments or other abuse. Some may have been threatened not to tell. The rule with all of these victims is to be slow and gentle. Engaging the child in drawing, building blocks, or play in a sand tray are useful introductions to the interviews. Once rapport has been established, an age-appropriate standard childhood mental status examination should be completed. Enquiry into day care/school, family constellation and activities, friendships, likes and dislikes, fears, phobias, and wishes should be done. Encouraging the children to draw pictures of themselves and their families provides opportunities for examining their perceptions. Important information on intellectual and academic abilities, family style, and stresses may also be gleaned.

These measures should be routine for all childhood assessments. However, in cases of suspected MBP more specific information is needed. How this is acquired will depend on the age of the children involved. Older children may be able to verbalize their experiences of illness and direct questioning may be used. With younger children, observation of themes to play may be all the psychiatrist has to go on. Play themes may reveal fears, phobias, preoccupations with illness (such as treating "sick dolls" and the like) or death, fears of abandonment and loss, or depictions of sickness within the family. If these are not spontaneously divulged in play, gentle encouragement by providing toy doctor kits and bandages can be helpful, but care must be taken not to lead the interview too directly. If children are in hospital, talking about their experiences is very useful. It is also important—but difficult—to elicit children's perceptions of their parents' behaviors around illness. Play in a doll house with figures representing family members can be used to obtain information on family functioning. "Lets pretend" games in which it is suggested that one of the play figures is ill are also useful. Through such games, children may provide very clear depictions of what may have occurred. Sometimes inferences may be made about how children perceive the emotional availability of one or both parents.

Also obligatory with all age groups is an exploration of any other forms of abuse (physical and/or sexual) the children may have been subjected to. This can be done either via direct questioning, observation of play themes, or indirect projective evaluation.

It is important to encourage any children who may have been abused, either directly or more subtly, and make frequent positive comments about how well they are doing. The use of a technique known as "the one down" can be very helpful with these children. The use of carefully chosen phrases such as "I'm having difficulty here, and you're so good at talking about this, can you help me understand . . .?" empowers children by placing them in the position of assisting the examiner. They can also be told, "you're a great help to me, and when you help me, I can help you."

Even with the most gentle interview by a skilled psychiatrist, some children will remain so inhibited that only uncertain inferences can be made. At these times consultation with a psychologist about the use of indirect assessment techniques may be indicated. Projective assessments of the children's perceptions of self, the family, illness, fears, and relationships may be completed. When there is developmental delay, either independent of the fabrications (for example as a result of prematurity or a developmental syndrome such as pervasive developmental disorder), or directly associated with induced illness (for example the sequelae of repeated anoxic episodes, poisonings, or medical procedures[104]), a developmental and intellectual psychological appraisal is mandatory. Sometimes the psychiatrist may recommend neuropsychological evaluation. Investigations should be chosen on the basis of sound clinical judgement to refute or confirm a clinical concern, not to appease a parent. Fortunately psychiatric and psychological investigations are noninvasive and do not cause significant iatrogenic pathology, though at times they can be distressing or stressful to children.

In addition to psychiatric symptomatology and developmental delay, many of these children are socially handicapped, especially those with long histories of "illness."[105] Social delay is well known with many cases of childhood chronic illness and seems especially prevalent in children with epilepsy. Often the social delay is secondary to parental overprotection. The psychiatric appraisal should thus assess the child's social and interpersonal skills. For older children, secondary handicaps such as academic failure, the stigma of illness, and limitations of play and social life may be significant.[106,107] The individual assessment may suggest difficulties in these areas, but a clearer understanding can usually be obtained from day care, school, or nursing staff. With the appropriate consents the psychiatrist should consult with these individuals.

There are few reported evaluations of victims. McGuire and Feldman[108] report developmentally appropriate reactions such as feeding disorders in infants, and withdrawal and hyperactivity in preschoolers. Adolescents may present with "hysterical" (functional) disorders and Munchausen-like behaviors themselves. Rosenberg[109] reported an overly compliant child with poor self-concept who felt little connection with family members and denied important relationships. Maternal figures were perceived as punitive and insensitive to his experiences of pain. Also, fears of poisoning and death have been recorded.[110,111] In a recently reported case we noted the child had fears of victimization, rejection, and abandonment, and a poor self-image.[112] Bools, Neale, and Meadow[113] studied 54 children who had been subjected to fabricated illnesses. Just over one half of them were living with their biological mothers. The authors note, "It is worrying that a substantial number of children continued to be the subjects of their mothers' fabrications, in some cases for a number of years after the initial discovery of the index fabrications and after interventions by professionals." Additional problems were also noted with many of these children, including relationship difficulties between the mothers and children, conduct disorders, and school difficulties. Twenty-four of the children had been placed out of the home with other families. Significant psychological difficulties were common, either related to preexisting disorders or as a reaction to the change in the family. The authors particularly point out five children who had been smothered and whose psychological disturbance clearly was related to their experiences. These children had fears and avoidance of specific places or situations, sleep problems (including nightmares), and features of Post Traumatic Stress Disorder. Although the study was methodologically difficult to complete, the conclusion that "the presence of such extreme disturbance in so many of the children several years after the abuse is of great concern" is salutary. These authors comment on the similarity of MBP victims to victims of physical abuse. The essential message of this study is that the outcome for victims is not optimistic, though better outcomes may be associated with the presence of an active, involved father (or other relative), therapeutic relationships for the perpetrators, or the perpetrators meeting their own needs in other ways, for example, through remarriage.

Depressive reactions or even illness may be theoretically precipitated in the victim, but there is a lack of reported data. Little is known about the long-term effects of being subjected to multiple fabrications or induction of illness. McGuire and Feldman note that these children have "had their psychological development thwarted at the most basic level—basic parental trust."[114] Evidence from attachment theory would suggest later possible emergence of personality disorders resulting from such early psychological trauma or inappropriate attachments. Insufficient evidence is currently available; however, some children as they grow older come to believe they are really ill and collude with the parent who wants them to be ill.[115] This suggests that some distortion of personality development may occur. Other children may lose their ability to identify whether genuine illness is present or not.[116] Meadow[117] notes a number of cases in adults and older children that may indicate the presence of such long-term personality deviations. All of these realms must be explored in diagnostic interviews, particularly with older children, and usually a number of interviews are necessary to gain an accurate understanding of the child's lifestyle.

Following the individual appraisal of the child, a clear and concise summary and formulation must be presented to the pediatric team. Excessive use of psychiatric and psychological jargon should be avoided. The pediatrician and child protection agency usually require information on the presence of major psychiatric pathology, an opinion on risk, additional evidence that fabrication is or is not occurring, and suggestions for management and treatment. Usually some feedback will need to be given to the parents. Each member of the core team must be clear on what will be told to the parents, in case of misinformation or manipulation of information. Early or careless disclosure of findings that may alert parental suspicions must be avoided. Close communication among the selected team members is essential at this time. If the psychiatrist identifies significant psychopathology in the child and believes that this is a direct result of parental behaviors, this constitutes child abuse under most state and provincial child protection legislation. Reporting of the opinion to child protection services is mandatory in these circumstances. In cases where there may be a risk of abduction or early discharge from hospital against medical advice, the local child protective agency may need to be informed and full discussions should occur with them before any feedback to the parents. Although often unpalatable and uncomfortable, this psychiatric duty cannot be evaded.

Even less is known about treating these youngsters. Infants at high risk or in life-threatening situations, particularly when the parent is deemed a poor treatment candidate, should be placed in foster homes. A long-term, secure, consistent, nurturing, and warm environment is treatment in itself for infants and very young children.

Distortions of attachment may be overcome in time, and a secure base for healthy personality development established. Unfortunately, many foster care agencies are unable to provide long-term placement with a single family, although all efforts must be made to achieve this. For older children who are unable to live with their own families, similar requirements for security are essential. However, many of these children suffer grief and loss when they are removed from their own families. In these cases individual psychotherapy may be added to the treatment plan. Sometimes specific treatment strategies are needed to deal with fears, phobias, depression, and behavioral disturbances. All treatment modalities should be considered, including psychopharmacology, relaxation therapy, desensitization procedures, hypnosis in special circumstances (for example hospital or doctor phobias), social skills training, and specialized academic assistance. Work with foster parents is essential to assist them in providing a stable home environment, understanding what has happened to the children in their care, and for instituting treatment programs within the home.

Foster care may be temporary or permanent, perhaps with later adoption. In temporary care, when the child will be returned to the parent(s), a satisfactory treatment outcome will depend on the parent(s)' capacity to create a secure environment without presenting the child for unnecessary medical care. The same applies when the child either remains with the parent or is returned following a hospital admission. In other words, treatment of the child depends a great deal on successful parent management. Combinations of treatment may be envisaged, such as intensive perpetrator management, parent skills training, family management and therapy, and individual child therapy. The psychiatrist is in a unique position to coordinate such multimodal treatment strategies.

FAMILY ASSESSMENT AND TREATMENT

The literature of MBP is replete with examples of dysfunctional families and disturbed marital relationship.[118-125] Following the individual assessment of the alleged perpetrator and/or child, discussion with the pediatric team should occur about psychiatric diagnostic impressions and whether the motivations driving the fabrications lie mainly within the realm of individual psychopathology or as an emergent property of a dysfunctional family system.

When there is serious individual perpetrator psychopathology, family systems assessment may assist in describing the process or culture within which the fabrications arose, but family therapy may be relatively contraindicated until the perpetrator has been adequately treated. For example, serious major depressive illness or psychosis must be dealt with primarily on an individual basis. Severely personality disordered individuals, especially sociopathic individuals, can be so manipulative and destructive to family therapy treatment attempts that the modality is contraindicated.

When the fabrications appear to have arisen from the functioning of the family system itself, early family assessment is indicated. Such an assessment may be conducted by the psychiatrist or by a skilled family therapist (familiar with MBP and knowledgable about individual psychodynamics and illnesses) selected and appointed by the core management team. In some cases the presentation of the child may correlate with episodes of family stress or crisis (e.g., family violence or the father's absence). Illness may serve a special role in the family as a means of connecting members or as a way of regulating intimacy between the marital couple, either by bringing them closer or by maintaining distance. If it is clear that such issues are the primary driving pathway behind the fabrications, then family or marital therapy should be attempted. However, once again, this should be done only when the situation is deemed safe from pediatric and child protection perspectives.

Administrative, Ethical, Legal and Medico-Legal Issues

The psychiatrist's work with MBP is fraught with administrative, ethical, and potential legal and medico-legal problems. Careful and diligent reading of all available medical, pediatric, and other reports is essential. Setting aside enough time amid a busy practice to do this, as well as discussing the case with team members, can be problematic. Whether one likes it or not, these cases are time-consuming and complex. In countries where payment for psychiatrists is based on fees for direct patient contact and procedures, and does not include compensation for reviewing extensive documentation or lengthy phone discussions with the many health care professionals usually involved, an individual practitioner may be discouraged at the prospect of an MBP case. Cursory and possibly negligent background information gathering may be a very real risk.

Clear documentation is essential for the pediatric team and child protection agencies, and is of paramount importance if there are later legal procedings. Reports should record what is actually observed and end with clear opinions written in plain language, avoiding as much as possible the use of jargon (sometimes, accurately, known as psychobabble!) Often there is a delay of many months between expressing an opinion and discussing it in court. Thorough documentation and clear notes are the best preparation for later testimony.

When a case of MBP goes to court, generally the psychiatrist is called upon to give expert testimony. This means that, unlike witnesses after the fact, who speak only to observable matters, the psychiatrist is qualified to pass an opinion on the case and to make recommendations for management. A divergence of legal and medical practices may become evident at this juncture. Attorneys tend to focus on the presenting facts. In MBP this usually means being limited to the actual event that precipitated the child protection procedings. Unfortunately in MBP this "final event," as it were, is almost always only a small part of a long-standing pattern of perpetrator behavior. It is essential that any written psychiatric report or oral evidence that may support a diagnosis of MBP contain as complete a history as possible, documenting as many previous episodes of suspected and confirmed fabrication as can be presented. The psychiatrist should also diligently describe any other significant perpetrator behaviors, past history, and family dynamics that convey to the court the *development* of the fabrications. Essentially the aim is to paint a picture of how the fabrication that led to the procedings developed, in a way that is understandable to nonmedical professionals.

Complicating matters further is the fact that many physicians have fears of court-related work. Physicians are generally poor in training junior colleagues to work with the legal and child protection professions. If psychiatrists have such apprehensions, they should always seek consultation from experienced colleagues and attorneys.

Psychiatrists may find themselves conflicted between confidentiality and duty. This is particularly so when rapport has been well established with an alleged perpetrator and much highly personal information has been entrusted to the psychiatrist. This same information may also have significant implications for child safety and future prognosis, including whether a child remains with a family. For child protection reasons the information may need to be disclosed, yet it has been given in confidence. Revealing this information to others can easily be construed by the perpetrator as a betrayal, and many have been emotionally betrayed many times throughout their lives. But such disclosure may be necessary for the safety of the child. At other times psychiatric assessment may reveal significant perpetrator psychopathology and need for treatment along with a recommendation for the removal of the child from the family. Such recommendations could precipitate the perpetrator into acute and possibly life-threatening crisis. There are no hard and fast rules that can be applied. Discussion should continue, relying on personal experience and the concept of medical practice "in good faith."

The ethical question in these circumstances is whether the psychiatrist's primary duty lies with the perpetrator or the child at risk. Obviously the psychiatrist has a duty toward both persons, and if possible the situation must be managed in a way that allows for this. In all cases it should be clarified with alleged perpetrators that the results of the assessment will be of value to their child's doctor as well as themselves. They should be told that the psychiatric assessment was a referral from the child's doctor and the findings will be discussed with that doctor. Most alleged perpetrators agree and their consent should be documented. It may be decided that, based on the psychiatrist's opinion, reporting to child protection is required. Another member of the pediatric team may assume responsibility for reporting, thus freeing the psychiatrist to work with the alleged perpetrator. The drawback to this approach is that later, for instance during legal procedings, it may come to the perpetrator's attention that the removal of the child was based upon the psychiatric findings. This betrayal, and its sequelae, may pose a significant risk to the relationship between the psychiatrist and the alleged perpetrator. Another option is for the assessing psychiatrist to have a colleague to whom the parent may be referred for ongoing treatment. However, if the referring psychiatrist comes to be seen as a betrayer, the new therapeutic relationship may be contaminated.

Other problems include lack of knowledge of MBP by psychiatric colleagues, and problems with coordinating management when several therapists are involved. In my experience, if there is reasonable rapport and engagement with the alleged perpetrator I have found it a reasonable approach to tell the parent that I have discussed the case with their child's doctor and that there do appear to be concerns about the child's welfare that I share. If this is done in a supportive manner, the weathering of and dealing with the issues of betrayal has been possible (so far!).

Summary

Little has been written in the literature to assist the psychiatrist in management of these complex cases. Unfortunately much if not most of this chapter is based not upon empirically derived research but on hard earned, and at times stressful clinical experience. In his critiques of psychiatric involvement, Meadow challenges psychiatry to create methods and approaches to assessment and treatment that may not be part of traditional psychiatric training and practice. Psychiatrists must accept this challenge.

References

1. Meadow R. Munchausen syndrome by proxy. *Arch Dis Child.* 1982; 57:92–98.
2. Meadow R. Management of Munchausen syndrome by proxy. *Arch Dis Child.* 1985; 60:385–393.
3. Nicol AR and Eccles M. Psychotherapy for Munchausen syndrome by proxy. *Arch Dis Child.* 1985; 60:345–348.
4. Mitchell I, Brummitt J, DeForest J, and Fisher GC. Apnea and factitious illness (Munchausen syndrome) by proxy. *Pediatrics.* 1993; 92:810–814.
5. Fisher GC, Mitchell I, and Murdoch DM. Munchausen syndrome by proxy: the question of psychiatric illness in a child. *Br J Psychiatry.* 1993; 162:701–703.
6. Meadow, R. Letter. *Child Abuse Negl.* 1990; 14:289.
7. Meadow R. Fictitious epilepsy. *Lancet.* 1984; 2:25–28.
8. Asher R. Munchausen's syndrome. *Lancet.* 1951: 1:339–341.
9. Morris, M. Munchausen's syndrome and factitious illness. *Curr Opinion Psychiatr.* 1991; 4:225–230.
10. Washington, D.C.: American Psychiatric Assn., 1994.
11. Fisher GC and Mitchell I. *Arch Dis Child.* In press.

12. Eminson DM and Postlethwaite RJ. Factitious illness: recognition and management. *Arch Dis Child.* 1992; 67:1510–1516.
13. Meadow, Management.
14. Meadow, R. Factitious illness: the hinterland of child abuse. *Recent Advances in Pediatrics*, No. 7. 1984; Edinburgh: Churchill Livingston: 217–232.
15. Fisher and Mitchell, Really a syndrome?
16. Fisher, et al., Question.
17. Meadow, Munchausen syndrome by proxy.
18. Meadow, Factitious.
19. Hodge D, Schwartz W, Sargent J, et al. The bacteriologically battered baby: another case of Munchausen syndrome by proxy. Ann Emerg Med. 1982; 11:205–207.
20. Ackerman NB and Strobel CT. Polle syndrome: chronic diarrhea in a Munchausen child. *Gastroenterology.* 1981; 81:1140–1142.
21. Goebel J, Gremse DA, and Artman M. Cardiomyopathy from ipecac administration in Munchausen syndrome by proxy. *Pediatrics.* 1993; 92:601–603.
22. Fisher, et al., Question.
23. Guandolo VL. Munchausen syndrome by proxy: an outpatient challenge. *Pediatrics.* 1985; 75:526–530.
24. Jones JG, Butler HL, Hamilton B, et al. Munchausen syndrome by proxy. *Child Abuse Negl.* 1986; 10:33–40.
25. Hodge, et al., Bacteriologically.
26. Goebel, et al., Cardiomyopathy.
27. Jones, et al., et al., MBP.
28. Alexander R, Smith W, and Stevenson R. Serial Munchausen syndrome by proxy. *Pediatrics.* 1990; 86: 581–585.
29. McKinlay I. Munchausen syndrome by proxy. *Br Med J.* 1986; 293:1308 (letter).
30. Mehl AL, Coble L, and Johnsons. Munchausen syndrome by proxy: a family affair. *Child Abuse Negl.* 1990; 14:577–585.
31. Palmer AJ and Yoshimura GJ. Munchausen syndrome by proxy. *J Amer Acad Child Psychiatry.* 1984; 23:503–508.
32. Richardson G. Munchausen syndrome by proxy. *Am Fam Physician.* 1987; 36:119–123.
33. Rosenberg DA. Web of deceit: A literature review of Munchausen syndrome by proxy. *Child Abuse Negl.* 1987; 11:457–563.
34. Verity CM, Winckworth C, and Burman D. Polle syndrome: children of Munchausen. *Br Med J.* 1979; 2:422–423.
35. Meadow, Factitious.
36. Ackerman and Strobel, Polle syndrome.
37. Jones, et al., MBP.
38. Kahan BB and Yorker BC. Munchausen syndrome by proxy. *J Sch Health.* 1990; 60:108–110.
39. Lee D. Munchausen syndrome by proxy in twins. *Arch Dis Child.* 1979; 54:646–647.

40. Pickering L. Munchausen syndrome by proxy. *Am J Dis Child*. 1981; 135:288 (letter).
41. Sullivan CA, Francis GL, Bain MW, et al. Munchausen syndrome by proxy 1990: a portent for problems. *Clin Pediatr*. 1991; 30: 112–116.
42. White ST, Voter K, and Perry J. Surreptitious warferin ingestion. *Child Abuse Negl*. 1985; 9:349–352.
43. Geelhoed GC and Pemberton PJ. SIDS, seizures, or 'sophogeal reflux? *Med J Aust*. 1985; 143:357–358.
44. Rosen CL, Frost JD, Bricker T, et al. Two siblings with recurrent cardiorespiratory arrest: Munchausen syndrome by proxy or child abuse? *Pediatrics*. 1983; 71:715–720.
45. Palmer and Yoshimura, MBP.
46. Fisher, et al., Question.
47. Hodge, et al., Bacteriologically.
48. Ackerman and Strobel, Polle.
49. Alexander, et al., Serial.
50. Geelhood and Pemberton, SIDS.
51. Rosen, et al., Two siblings.
52. Atoynatan TH, O'Reilly E, and Loin L. Munchausen syndrome by proxy. Child Psychiatr Hum Dev. 1988; 19:3–13.
53. Chan DA, Salcedo JR, Atkins M., et al. Munchausen syndrome by proxy: a review and case study. *J Pediatr Psychol*. 1986; 11:71–80.
54. Fleisher D and Ament ME. Diarrhea, red diapers, and child abuse. *Clin Pediatr*. 1977; 17:820–824.
55. Griffith JL and Slovick LS. Munchausen syndrome by proxy and sleep disorders medicine. *Sleep*. 1989; 12:178–183.
56. Hosch IA. Munchausen syndrome by proxy. MCN. 1987; 12:48–52.
57. Shnaps Y, Frand M, Rotem Y, et al. The chemically abused child. *Pediatrics*. 1981; 68:119–121.
58. Stevenson RD, Alexander R. Munchausen syndrome by proxy presenting as a developmental disability. *J Dev Beh Pediatr*. 1990; 11:262–264.
59. Griffith and Slovick, Sleep Disorders.
60. Wood PR, Fowlkes J, Holden P, et al. Fever of unknown origin for six years: Munchausen syndrome by proxy. *J Fam Prac*. 1989; 28:391–395.
61. Shnaps, et al., Chemically abused.
62. Chan, et al., Review.
63. Fleisher and Ament, Diarrhea.
64. Holborrow PL. A variant of Munchausen's syndrome by proxy. *J Am Acad Child Psychiatr*. 1984; 24:238 (letter).
65. Kravitz RM and Wilmott R. Munchausen syndrome by proxy presenting as factitious apnea. *Clin Pediatr*. 1990; 29:587–592.
66. Ravenscroft K and Hochkeiser J, cited in Atoynatan, O'Reilly, and Loin, MBP.
67. Lee, Twins.
68. Griffith and Slovick, Sleep.
69. Hosch, MBP.

70. Bourchier D. Bleeding ears: case report of Munchausen syndrome by proxy. *Aust Pediatr J.* 1983; 19:256–257.

71. Manning SC, Casselbrant M, and Lammers D. Otolaryngologic manifestations of child abuse. *Int J Pediatr Otorhinolaryngol.* 1990; 20:7–16.

72. Mitchell, et al., Apnea.

73. Ackerman and Strobel, Polle.

74. Geeohoed and Pemberton, SIDS.

75. Atoynatank et al., MBP.

76. Griffith and Slovik, Sleep.

77. Hosch, MBP.

78. Shnaps, et al., Chemically.

79. Wood, et al., Fever.

80. Black D. The extended munchausen syndrome: a family case. *Br J Psychiatr.* 1986; 145:300–301 (letter).

81. Main DJ, Douglas JE, and Tamanika HM. Munchausen's syndrome by proxy. *Med J Aust.* 1986; 145:300–301 (letter).

82. Woody RC and Jones JG. Neurologic Munchausen-by-proxy. *South Med J.* 1987; 80:247–248.

83. Zitelli BJ, Seltman MF, and Shannon RM. Munchausen syndrome by proxy and its professional participants. *Am J Dis Child.* 1987; 141:1099–1102.

84. Steinhauer PD. 1991; Toronto: University of Toronto Press.

85. Libow JA and Schreier HA. Three forms of factitious illness in children: when is it Munchausen syndrome by proxy? *Am J Orthopsychiat.* 1986; 56:602–611.

86. Chan, et al., Review.

87. Clayton PT, Counahan R, and Chantler C. Munchausen syndrome by proxy. *Lancet.* 1978; 1:102–103 (letter).

88. Meadow, Factitious.

89. Ackerman and Strobel, Polle.

90. Rosenberg, Web.

91. Verity, et al., Polle.

92. Rosen, et al., Two siblings.

93. Chan, et al., Review.

94. Fleisher and Ament, Diarrhea.

95. (personal case).

96. Nicol and Eccles, Psychotherapy.

97. Ackerman and Strobel, Polle.

98. Jones, et al., MBP.

99. Black, Extended.

100. Zitelli, et al., Professional participants.

101. Libow and Schreier, Three forms.

102. Clayton, et al., MBP.

103. 1990; New York: Norton.

104. Meadow R. Munchausen syndrome by proxy and brain damage. *Dev Med Child Neurol.* 1984; 26:669–676.

105. Guandolo, Outpatient.

106. Meadow, Fictitious.
107. Sigal M, Gelkopf M, and Levertov G. Munchausen by proxy syndrome: the triad of abuse, self abuse and deception. *Comp Psychiatr*. 1989; 30:527–533.
108. McGuire TL and Feldman KW. Psychologic morbidity of children subjected to Munchausen syndrome by proxy. *Pediatrics*. 1988; 83:289–292.
109. Rosenberg, Web.
110. Hvizdala EV and Gellady AM. Intentional poisoning of two siblings by prescription drugs. *Clin Pediatr*. 1978; 17:480–483.
111. Rogers D, Tripp J, Bentovim A, et al. Non-accidental poisoning: An extended syndrome of child abuse. *Br Med J*. 1976; (April 3): 793–796.
112. Fisher, et al., Question.
113. Bools CN, Neale BA, and Meadow SR. Follow up of victims of fabricated illness (Munchausen syndrome by proxy). *Arch Dis Child*. 1993; 69:625–630.
114. McGuire and Feldman, morbidity, quote p. 291.
115. Meadow, Fictitious.
116. Sigal, et al., Triad.
117. Fictitious.
118. Jones, et al., MBP.
119. Atoynatan, et al., MBP.
120. Kravitz and Wilmott, Factitious apnea.
121. Black, Extended.
122. Woody and Jones, Neurologic.
123. Lansky LL. An unusual case of childhood chloral hydrate poisoning. *Am J Dis Child*. 1974; 127:275–276.
124. Griffith JL. The family systems of Munchausen syndrome by proxy. *Fam Proc*. 1988; 29:423–437.
125. Yorker BC and Kahan BB. Munchausen syndrome by proxy as a form of child abuse. *Arch Psychiatr Nurs*. 1990; 4:313–318.

30

The Role of Child Abuse Agencies and Foster Care

Joseph M. Pape

Public child protective services agencies are charged by law with receiving and investigating reports of suspected child abuse or neglect, and with implementing plans to ensure children's ongoing safety. Once a referral of Munchausen Syndrome by Proxy (MBP) or a referral containing information that implies warning signals for MBP has been received by the child protection agency, specific protocol should be followed to ensure the safety and well-being of the alleged child victim. The referral source should be identified and if a medical professional is making the referral, explicit documentation should be gathered.

This chapter provides guidelines to the child welfare professional, beginning with the intake department receiving the initial referral and progressing to the ongoing placement department that serves the child and family while the child is in foster care. In addition, transfer proceedings from one department to the next are addressed, as well as the responsibilities of all child welfare employees throughout this process. The chapter presumes that the child welfare professional already understands the concept and dynamics of MBP. Child welfare agencies have a responsibility to include such information in the basic training that their employees receive, and to ensure that those employees who receive referrals from hospitals or follow up such referrals are adequately prepared. Child protective workers should also be aware that situations analogous to MBP have occurred nonmedical contexts, including persistent factitious allegations of physical and sexual abuse.[1]

Phase I: The Intake Department

Workers who receive and investigate reports of suspected child abuse and neglect should be alert for signs of MBP. All cases with elements of MBP should be rated "Priority I" with immediate response in an organized fashion preferred. A Priority I rating indicates imminent risk to a child's life, mental or physical health, or safety, and requires a one-hour response time with a face-to-face contact with the alleged victim.[2] This response time is critical given the grave consequences possible with MBP.

It is imperative to remember that the child welfare professional's role is not necessarily to prove a specific diagnosis of MBP, but rather (if it is true) to demonstrate the increased number of illnesses and medical emergencies that exist when the child is in the presence of the suspected perpetrator. A careful history must be taken from the person making the referral, and the intake worker must make certain that he or she understands what is being alleged. Some consultation with the referring or another health professional may be required for the intake worker to understand the medical condition which is alleged and why the suspected perpetrator's behavior is potentially harmful.

In making the investigation, the intake worker should approach the family in a supportive and caring fashion. The parents should know from the beginning that the agency's role is to ensure the safety of the child. The perpetrator should be aware that the medical and social work professionals are concerned for the child's increased health risks when in his/her presence. A detailed medical history of all family members must be gathered, not only for documentation purposes and understanding of possibly etiology, but also because often more than one child in a family is or has been the victim of MBP. Histories of other children who have died are particularly significant. The intake worker should focus on gathering the names of all health care professionals who have been involved in the care of the family. Appropriate releases of information should be signed for each professional, and records requested.

The intake worker should interview each family member thoroughly. The mother (who is most likely to be the perpetrator) should be made aware that there are concerns for the child due to the severe medical problems and/or long history of hospitalizations. She will probably react defensively. The literature suggests that the mother will generally deny any part in the child's presenting medical difficulties. The available data also suggests that the mother may remain calm despite the seriousness of the child's illness. Often an emotional reaction can only be invoked by an implication that she may play some part in the child's illness. The mother may be very convincing in her statements and behaviors, but these cannot be taken at face value if important facts contradict them. As Zitelli states "the seeming friendliness, cooperation, and closeness of the mother and child encompass desirable social qualities and are taken at face value, hence the social worker may be caught in the web of complicity."[3] The child welfare worker must be very careful not to doubt a well-formulated medical diagnosis. I was involved in the case of a 5-month-old infant in which the nurses' notes indicated many questions and concerns about the high number of documented cyanotic episodes when the child was with the mother. The nurses were very suspicious that the mother was playing a role in these episodes. However, the medical social worker saw the mother as a caring, affectionate, and concerned parent. The social worker interpreted as signs of caring and concern that the mother spent all of her time with the child and that the child would eat and rest for no one but the mother. The child was released from the hospital in the mother's care, and 3 days later he was pronounced dead.

At the same time, child welfare professionals must be careful to make their own differential diagnosis and not jump too quickly to the conclusion that a given situation represents MBP. For example, frequent emergency room visits may result from all the factors that lead to medical neglect. Occasionally, too, health care professionals might not pursue diagnosis sufficiently, and might unfairly blame a parent. Some cases might require intervention, yet fall in the "hinterland" of MBP.[4]

It is imperative that all professionals communicate openly and share feelings and intuitions. It is also imperative that child welfare professionals gather information in an objective and professional manner. They may not be able to take everything from their social work colleagues at face value, but should evaluate it just as they do information from other professionals. Once concerns from the medical professionals are expressed, it will be the child welfare worker's responsibility to gather factual evidence to support or refute these claims. All concerns should be recorded in a clear and reader-sensitive fashion. Reports fraught with jargon—social work or medical—will only confuse and frustrate legal participants at a future date.

If the factual evidence supports the concerns, it will be necessary to approach the court to request that temporary custody of the alleged child victim be placed with the appropriate child welfare agency. The options of placing the victim with relatives or allowing the child to remain in the home should be thoroughly scrutinized. When a written diagnosis of MBP is made by a medical professional, it is my opinion that placement in a licensed foster home is the only way of ensuring the safety and well-being of the alleged child victim. This may seem to contradict the basic philosophy of child welfare practice that makes its first priority the maintenance of intact families. In MBP cases, however, the exceptional high morbidity and mortality rates must be weighed against maintaining the child in a home where parental access or influence is easy.

Once the initial assessment has been completed, all releases of information have been sent to the appropriate professionals, and the child is secured in a foster home, the case should be transferred from the intake department to the ongoing placement unit for further servicing.

Phase II: The Placement Caseworker

The placement worker's role is a continuation of the intake worker's. There are important differences, however. The intake worker's main role was to gather all pertinent information and ensure that the agency, and subsequently the court, had access to this information. The placement worker needs to gather further information for long-term planning as well as to supervise the child in temporary placement. The placement worker will have additional contact with the child, the mother, and other significant family members. This worker should use the process recording method of documentation, which involves writing verbatim the entire interview with the mother, father, witnesses (if any) to the child's medical symptoms, and any other significant parties.

All visits between the suspected perpetrator and the alleged child victim must be strictly supervised. The child should never be left unattended, even for very brief periods of time. The child was removed from the parent to ensure safety, and that safety is the highest priority. It is recommended that food, drink, or medicines not be allowed into the visits. This ensures that no one can contaminate or manipulate the child into presenting factitious medical problems.

The worker should strive to appear professional at all times. A nonjudgmental approach is vital, with the worker displaying empathy for the family's present situation. It is important to remember that the removal of a child is a genuine crisis to all family members. The placement worker may have to be confrontive yet supportive of the parents.

Once the necessary documentation has been gathered, the sequence of events resulting in the child's hospitalization, the trips to the family physician, and consultation with experts should be laid out in chronological fashion. Each situation should be reviewed carefully with the possible perpetrator. That person's explanation of the child's illness and each presentation to a medical facility should be documented specifically. These explanations can then be compared to the medical conclusions of the involved physicians and other medical staff.

If the child welfare agency is fortunate enough to have an epidemiologist or biostatistician as consultant, all medical reports should be shared. The information could then be reviewed and the likelihood of the events evaluated. For example, the epidemiologist may be able to state in a given case that the association of medical problems and the presence of the suspected inducer is far beyond chance. Utilizing an epidemiologist allows the agency to submit a scientific report based entirely on medical facts and independent of any conjecture or opinion on the part of the agency or any other involved party.

When the suspected perpetrator is confronted, the likely outcome will be denial. This is often associated with hostility toward medical and social work professionals. The denial of suspected perpetrators is such that they will hope to gain support for their position by turning to others who know them well, including other medical professionals. This denial will not only present an obstacle to subsequent management of the child and family but, if it persists, may also be accompanied by a continuation of the abuse. This should be a signal for the agency to continue court-ordered separation, or at least supervision if the court is unwilling to extend the separation period.

A long-term plan should be developed. The parents should be given specific goals that must be achieved prior to the return of the child. For example, a structured visitation schedule must be adhered to. The mother and other family members must seek psychological evaluations and treatment, if recommended, which may require long-term intervention to ensure that all identified areas of pathology are addressed.

If the case plan objectives are met, the child will eventually return home. Unfortunately, experience indicates that case plan goal attainment is the exception rather than the rule in cases of MBP. In the event that the perpetrator is unable to accept or admit a role in the illness or injury to the child, the agency should begin permanency planning for the child. That is, the agency must make plans for the child's permanent placement with another family.

A placement with relatives could be very dangerous in a case of MBP. The relative would have to be a very strong individual to be capable of preventing unsupervised interaction between the child and perpetrator. Maintaining such a placement would be difficult, as the perpetrator would continually attempt to discredit the new caretaker and disrupt the placement. A relative placement would be viewed as least restrictive but it would take a very determined and courageous individual to keep the child victim free from harm.

If no such relative exists and a determination is made by the agency to secure permanent custody of the child victim, a case must be prepared for court presentation. Again, it is imperative for the worker to remember the goal: not necessarily to prove a case of MBP, but rather to show that the child is at risk when in the presence of a particular person.

The material for court presentation is best presented in pictorial fashion so that the court understands exactly the degree of risk the child experiences when in the presence of the mother. The report from the epidemiologist is generally viewed as specific, unbiased, and easily understood. Physicians should be asked to write their reports concisely and in lay terminology. The goal is not to impress the court with knowledge of medical terms but rather to prove that the child is at risk if allowed to return to the home. The use of graphs or charts in court presentation helps to depict vividly the facts of the case and the danger to the child.

Figure 30–1 is an example of a simple pie graph showing the total months of life for a particular child and the small percentage of time the child lived with the mother. In this illustration, the child was with the mother 12.5% of her life. Charts like this one can be presented to the court with hospital reports depicting the number of hospitalizations while the child was in the mother's care. In this case, 87.5 of the child's life was free of hospital visits. However, in the short time that the child was with her mother, she was hospitalized seven times.

Figure 30–2 is a graph presented in conjunction with Figure 30–1. It depicts the same life span as Figure 30–1. Note the accelerated number of hospitalizations in a 2-month period when the child was with the mother. When the child was placed in foster care for eight months, however, not one hospitalization or apnea episode occurred.

Figure 30–3 shows a sibling of the child depicted in Figures 30–1 and 30–2. This child was hospitalized 17 times in little more than 5 months. One hospitalization lasted 28 days. The child was returned home on January 30th and rehospitalized on February 1st. The child remained in the hospital from February 1st to February 5th. The

FIGURE 30–1
Pie graph showing infant's time with and away from mother.

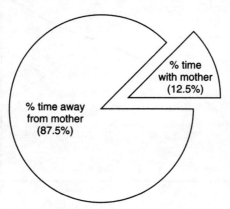

FIGURE 30–2
Number of incidents per month for infant represented in Figure 30–1.

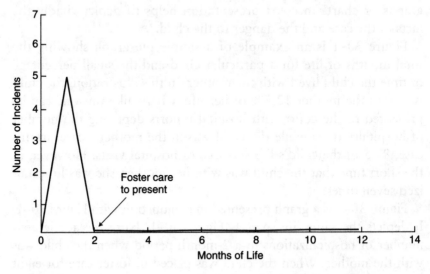

FIGURE 30–3
Number of incidents per month for a sibling of the infant in Figures 30–1 and 30–2.

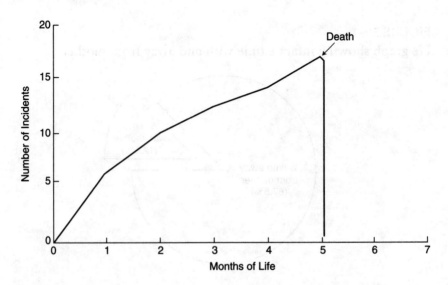

child was then returned home and was pronounced dead on February 8th. Again, this graph shows dramatically the degree of danger to the child and siblings when in the presence of the mother.

Figure 30–4 shows a child who had six hospitalizations in a 4-month period. The child was subsequently removed from the mother and remained in foster care for 30 months. During that time there were no hospitalizations. When the child was returned to the mother for a 2-month period, eight hospitalizations occurred. The child was then returned to foster care and to date no further hospitalizations have occurred.

In each of the previous chapters, various professionals have outlined their roles and responsibilities. It is my belief that the child protective placement worker and the presentations to the court act as a thread to weave all of the professional responsibilities together. Often extensive investigation, coordination, explanation of legal processes, and encouragement is required for the successful accomplishment of this task.

Phase III: Foster Parents

The foster parents in an MBP case need to be more actively involved than average foster parents. It is essential that the physician

FIGURE 30–4
Number of incidents for a third infant.

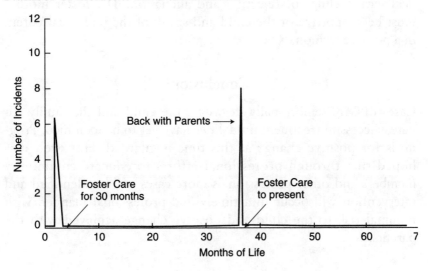

diagnosing MBP remain involved with the child. No matter which pediatrician the foster parents are accustomed to using, they should continue with the child's own pediatrician to ensure continuity.

The usual child welfare practice is to encourage a relationship between the natural mother and the foster parent. However, this may not be a good idea in cases of MBP. An MBP mother's narcissistic attitudes and vehement denial are counterproductive in any type of true relationship formulation.

The foster mother should be encouraged to keep a daily log of the child's activities and development. A "life book" should be maintained, as in all placement cases. In the MBP victim's life book, specific developmental milestones should be documented. There should be a notation each day that the child did or did not have any type of medical symptom. The absence of medical symptoms, particularly those that the perpetrator reported, while the child is not in the presence of the perpetrator will strengthen the agency's position if the matter must go to court. The foster parents should review the log with their caseworker on a weekly basis. The caseworker should summarize the log and secure the documentation within the case file. Throughout the case, the foster parents must work very closely with the placement caseworker. Information must be shared freely and documentation must be concise and complete.

It is important for a child victim of MBP to receive therapy to deal with feelings of rejection and alienation. The foster mother must be supportive of the child and speak of the biological parent in a positive fashion.

Conclusion

Cases of MBP emotionally devastate the child and the family. To date, successful treatment modalities have yet to be identified. Prognosis for positive change at this time is guarded. However, it is hoped that through professional efforts to educate community members and other professionals more cases will be identified and intervention will occur in a timely and professional manner, with minimal risk to the child and positive change achieved with the parents.

Dr. Meadow writes: ". . . These cases are a reminder that at times doctors must accept the parents' history . . . with more than usual skepticism. We may teach, and I believe should teach, that mothers are always right; but at the same time we must recognize that when mothers are wrong they can be terribly wrong."[5] We must believe in the sanctity of the relationship between mothers and their children, yet accept the fact that not all relationships between mothers and their children are positive and healthy. As this single fact is contrary to the average caseworker's belief system, it may be the single greatest hurdle to overcome in preventing the loss of children to MBP.

References

1. Meadow R. False allegations of abuse and Munchausen syndrome by proxy. *Arch Dis Child*. 1993; 68:444–447.
2. The details of some policies discussed in this chapter are specific to various regional agencies.
3. Zitelli BJ, Seltman MF, and Shannon RM. Munchausen's syndrome by proxy and its professional participants. *Am J Dis Child*. 1987; 141:1099–1102. Quote p. 1101.
4. Cantwell, HB. Child protective services in parental mismanagement of diabetes. *Diabetes Educator* 1984; 9(4):41–43.
5. Meadow R. Munchausen syndrome by proxy: The hinterland of child abuse. *Lancet* 1977; 2:343–345, quote p. 345.

31

Is Family Preservation, Reunification, and Successful Treatment a Possibility?

A Round Table Chaired by Toni Seidl

Toni Seidl

The cornerstone of child protection has been planning for the child's best interests. The justification for the intrusion into family life is based on the often contradictory missions of child protection and family preservation. Defining best interests, however, may be exceedingly difficult, especially with the frequently elusive, occasionally controversial, and often not legally provable diagnosis of Munchausen Syndrome by Proxy (MBP).

Removing a child from any family system and then later reunifying the family is complex. Extraordinary obstacles and dilemmas are encountered when the family in question appears intact and normative by the usual evaluative standards, or when professionals are unfamiliar with the diagnosis of MBP. Returning the child who has been removed from her family creates many anxieties and dilemmas for health care practitioners. This is an unwieldy issue precisely because we have few, if any, proven parameters of successful intervention available when working with the dynamic of MBP. Minimal collaborative research has been done on intervention with MBP. What data we do have is, at best, impressionistic and often purely anecdotal. Most intervention models created to address

411

MBP dynamics are not specific to the disorder, and therefore address hypothesized stressors and presumptive psychopathology.

What, then, are the components of decision-making as they pertain to the reunification of children removed from their parents' care, custody, and supervision as a result of MBP? How do we best manage parents who place their own needs above the needs of their children to the point where those children have to be removed for safety's sake? In other words, what would be the standard for child protection for families diagnosed with MBP? Reunification is best attained when conceptualized as a thoughtful and progressive process, rather than a single act or event.

What should the process of reunification look like in cases of MBP? I believe that the standard and the process should comport with those generally established for child abuse and neglect. Risk to the index child should be minimized. To accomplish this with MBP families, the alleged perpetrator's complex needs and the family's implicit collusion have to be: (1) precisely identified, (2) psychologically and socially assessed, (3) owned by the perpetrator, and (4) extinguished. This sequence should have been articulated and planned during the assessment phase of the case and again at adjudication. Subsequently the process should be formalized as a template for change in the Family Service Plan (FSD), with delineation of specific tasks to be accomplished by all parties involved during the victim's placement.

Reunification should be attempted only if it is considered to be a viable option for the child, not because it is "time for it" or because the parents and their attorneys are demanding it. It should only be considered following successful and well-monitored parental visitation. "Child advocacy"[1] is the guiding principle when considering the potential for reunification of children and their families. All children affected by MBP are entitled to—and should have—a guardian ad litem[2] thoroughly involved. Only through active and uncompromised legal advocacy can the child's needs be kept as the focal point in an adult-oriented and adversarial court system.

Reentry of a child into a family previously considered to be unhealthy and having a negative impact on the child's growth and development has historically been a much struggled-with and loosely evaluated concept and process. Little research has been available in planning for reunification, which has caused the experience frequently to be idiosyncratic, inconsistent and unsuccessful. Fortunately, three researchers[3] evaluated the effectiveness of family reunification services in cases where children were at risk significant enough for them to be returned to foster care. The model used was a case study–based Professional Review Action Group (PRAG). The interventions of the social agency, policies, and professional training efforts were examined. Especially relevant for this discussion was their focus on parental behaviors, interactions, and expectations. Practice standards based on this work were subsequently formalized by the Marion County, Indiana, Public Welfare Department. The benchmarks delineated therein have particular applicability to MBP victims and their families.[4]

One would want to confirm that the perpetrator has acknowledged the abuse. Of prime importance is the perpetrator's self-awareness, particularly as it relates to MBP and acknowledgment of her destructive behaviors. The perpetrator must be honest with all of the therapeutic providers and actively commit to problem-solving. Just expressing affection and commitment to the child while continuing to deny the dangerous activity is not acceptable. Such denial is always a contraindication to the return of a child, no matter how functional the family appears on the surface.

Of equal importance is the noninvolved parent's acknowledgement that the MBP activity and threat are real and potentially lethal. It is imperative that the perpetrator's partner feels able, empowered, and obligated to intervene on the child victim's behalf. In short, this person must be willing and able to risk jeopardizing his or her relationship with the perpetrator on behalf of the child. If the victim is old enough, both of the parents should make that commitment in the child's presence with professionals witnessing. The mutually established safety plan should be shared with the child. If it is developmentally appropriate, the child should have his or her own safety strategy, which should include an understanding of MBP risk behaviors and a list of helpful friends, neighbors, and professional advocates to call upon for immediate support, direction, and assistance. Again, permission for this should be articulated directly by the parents to the child in the presence of the professional team.

Of additional importance is the creation of a viable support system for the perpetrator and the perpetrator's partner. Roles and responsibilities of the professionals providing services need to be included in planning for the sake of parity and accountability.

This type of protection agreement serves the victim and the family best when it is crafted during one or more family meetings, with all of these participants present and actively involved. This protection plan should be considered to be a living document, to be reviewed and revised at regular intervals and whenever clinically indicated during the life of the case. Sanctions for noncompliance with the established contract also need to be agreed upon and included in the plan.

Unquestionably, an imperative for those professionals involved in child abuse work—and particularly in MBP—is the establishment of collaborative research efforts. Such efforts will serve to protect children more adequately, lessen our sense of impotence, and move toward the creation of a "gold standard" for the correct identification and treatment of the MBP family system. What follows is the beginning of a dialogue among experienced providers of care and theoreticians that will, we hope, stimulate thought and research on this confounding disease.

MARY S. SHERIDAN, PH.D., ACSW: CONSIDER THE "INFRASTRUCTURE"

Considerations such as those suggested by Ms. Seidl are basic. But another sort of resource must also be considered, which might be called infrastructural. Along with asking about family resources, and what a family needs for us to feel comfortable with reunification, it is equally important to ask about community resources and what we would want before we would feel safe in returning an MBP victim to the home. Child protective agencies vary from region to region, but they are characteristically crisis-responsive, overworked, and often staffed by relatively inexperienced and transient workers. For safe reunification, some agency should be able to make an honest commitment to long-term supervision and intervention that the family may not refuse. Court systems and judges differ in their sophistication and willingness to impose oversight or enforce compliance. The ability of a clinician to trust the court system would be an important determinant of what could be done with a family. Some regions are rich in psychiatric resources, homemaker services, or specialized health care. In other areas these are not available, or are available only to those who can pay.

Too often, I believe, we assess only the family to decide what is possible. The community also has a part in determining what can be done with families. Given ideal resources—which means long-term social support for the family as a whole, therapy (at a minimum) for the perpetrating parent, and consistent, vigilant health care—family preservation should be possible in at least some situations of MBP. Whether it is desirable, particularly when we do not have adequate treatment and supervisory services, is a social policy question that raises issues of competing interests and perceptions on the part of victim and others of who is at fault.

ALEX V. LEVIN, M.D., FRCSC: CONSIDER THE SIBLINGS AND THE EFFECT OF SEPARATION

The primary concern when considering family preservation—allowing the child victim to remain in the care of the perpetrator—in a case of MBP must always be the child's safety. Will the perpetrator, given access to the child victim, injure the child or continue the MBP scenario? To achieve any measure of satisfaction regarding the child's safety, the child care team must receive at the very minimum a "confession" from the perpetrating parent. In fact, this disclosure alone has in some cases resulted in an abrupt halt of the MBP behavior. Yet, confession alone may be insufficient. By admitting to their abusive acts, perpetrators may be hopeful that "the system" will indeed offer them more access to the child, by which their continuing perpetration may occur.

Thus it becomes important that the perpetrator's admission is supported by the recognition of MBP and the perpetrator's role in its propagation by other adults involved with the child victim's care, in particular the perpetrator's spouse/partner. These individuals must demonstrate a clear understanding of the risk to the child. Diligent assessment of the home situation is critical to obtain some level of security in understanding the familial relationships that may allow unwanted or unsupervised contact between the parent and child. One must also consider carefully the risk to other, previously unaffected siblings in the home. The removal of one child victim does not guarantee protection of others left in the care of the perpetrator. Written statements documenting the protective responsibility of the family members in addition to their acknowledgment of the diagnosis and its implication may be quite helpful should further problems occur after placement has been made.

We must guard against further traumatization of the child caused by separation from his family unit. Family preservation/reunification may be possible in MBP if the above criteria are met and a solid vigilant professional support system is in place. Too often, lack of education and failure to believe in the diagnosis may lead law enforcement, legal, or child protection systems to err on the side of leniency in the protection of the MBP child victim. Professionals well versed in this field must honor their commitment to continued advocacy for the child through ongoing involvement, education, and research.

CHARLES F. JOHNSON, M.D.: FAMILY PRESERVATION AS A FEDERAL PRIORITY

A major goal of family preservation is to avoid placement of abused children. Proponents of preservation recognize that the structure and values of families vary but that the welfare of children is best served, whenever possible, when children remain in the their families. Success requires that (1) families have the potential and desire to change, (2) the safety of the child is assured, (3) all recommended services are available, and (4) the plan is supported by professionals. Professionals who mistrust home interventions and wish to guarantee that a child not be reabused by a specific perpetrator will favor separation.

Skepticism about the efficacy of family preservation is based on the results of controlled studies which to date have not indicated uniform effectiveness. Cost saving over immediate separation and placement of abused children has been demonstrated by family preservation. The federal government committed itself to family preservation with the passage of the Family Preservation Act (P.L. 103-66) in August 1993 to provide states with 1 billion dollars over a 5-year period. Depending on the cost of services and numbers of families to be served this amount may prove to be inadequate.

Professionals dealing with the complex issue of MBP can expect to be challenged if they recommend separation of a child victim from the offending parent. Support for this recommendation will require indication of possible jeopardy to the child that could result from family preservation as well as the advantages to accrue from separation. A physician who has established the diagnosis of MBP and confronted a deceptive parent who has placed a child's life in danger may have lost perspective and credibility when making placement recommendations. Placement recommendations supported by a multidisciplinary staff that has carefully assessed all risk factors may be more compelling.

Preservation of families and cost effectiveness are laudable, but the primary goal of all professionals is to serve the best interest of children. Factors that would increase the possibility for continued abuse, the desires of the family, and the level of medical and psychological care for the child should be determined carefully. Management of a child damaged by MBP may increase existing family stressors. Ultimately placement decisions must be based on the psychological state and cooperation of the parents, chronicity and severity of abuse, and availability of a realistic case plan that mandates regular follow-up guided by one knowledgeable and available physician.

To determine with more certainty which, if any, cases of MBP would benefit from family preservation will require information from controlled studies. The variability of the manifestations of MBP and family dynamics may hinder the performance of adequately controlled research.

MARCELLINA MIAN, M.D.: FAMILY PRESERVATION IS NOT POSSIBLE

There are no data to indicate that treatment of MBP offenders is effective and a great deal of data to indicate that MBP is dangerous to the child victim's life and physical and emotional well-being. In my experience, offending parents choose to oppose the diagnosis rather than seek treatment. Their energies are directed toward continued thwarting or deception of child protection strategies. The specifics of the situation may change: New symptoms may be introduced, the offending parent may form a relationship with a new mate, or health care or child protection personnel may change. All of these factors lead to a whole new cycle of diagnostic and child protection dilemmas. Therefore, in my opinion, family preservation is not possible in MBP.

Close supervision in the home is a very tempting option. In our jurisdiction, courts have ordered "24-hour supervision" when a finding is made that a child is in need of protection, but circumstances lead the judge to believe that complete removal of the child from the home is too drastic a step. MBP and its diagnostic conundrum presents just such a set of circumstances. This supervision has been ordered to be provided by the nonoffending parent, a relative, a friend, or a nurse employed by the family. In one case, a rotating schedule was set up to involve the entire community of the same ethnic origin as the family.

In our experience, this form of supervision does not work. Allegiances through family ties, employment obligations, or cultural loyalties mitigate against child advocacy and vigilance. In these circumstances we have documented reabuse, disappearance of the family, and the maintenance of a barely tolerable situation because no single infraction or worrisome instance was sufficient to escalate child protective action. In fact, over time, the courts view the appearance of "no new abuse" to constitute a safe environment for the child. The onus of proof for child advocates then reaches unattainable levels.

STEPHEN LUDWIG, M.D.: THE IMPORTANCE OF ASSESSMENT

When considering MBP, a range of distributed behaviors, I must first ask question: "Where is the family located along the Munchausen continuum?" Is this a family that functions adequately in many different dimensions, yet has a specific problem in their reaction to stress and their dependency needs? Or, at the other end of the continuum, is this a family totally unable to function except around the issues of their child's illness? Would this family unit fall apart if their child were well?

These questions raise issues of *pervasiveness* of the disorder and judgments about how much of the family function is wellness-based versus how much is illness-based. Making such assessments is difficult particularly when assessing at only one point in time. It takes a long-term knowledge of a family to see how they are capable of functioning. Every family unit has its ups and downs and cycles of "normal" life events. How does the family in question move in response to these changes of family stretch and strain? This can only be judged over time.

The issue of *admission of responsibilities* is also an important assessment factor, in my judgment. MBP is so clandestine that there must be some admission of guilt and acceptance of parental responsibility for successful therapeutic intervention to occur. If "how the child became ill" remains a secret, then it always remains a point of contention in the therapeutic relationship. If it becomes a "yes you did"/"no I didn't" contest, no effective change can ever take place. Parents must be willing to take responsibility for their own actions in order for the actions not to occur again.

I would also assess the family on issues of *lethality* and *intent*. These, too, are difficult measures to make. They are similar to the issues one assesses in cases of suicide. Lethality is the potential of the form of MBP to do harm. Some forms of MBP, such as suffocation, have the potential to result in more harm (lethality) than others such as MBP pseudohematuria.

Finally, *intent* refers to the expected result the parent seeks. If a parent states that (s)he inflicted harm to the child with the intent that something untoward might really happen to the child, the situation is a high-risk one.

By using these four factors—pervasiveness, admission of responsibility, lethality, and intent—one can begin to make a determination about placing a child with the family. The final element in the formula is the community's ability to provide services.

If there is any significant risk, the child should be kept away from the family. Reunification should be undertaken when the family is deemed safe and the community can provide a high level of surveillance on the situation. Even under the best circumstances, MBP is difficult to treat as the problem is very basic or primitive. This makes family reunification a desirable but often unachievable goal in the minds of most child advocates.

JUDITH A. HENSLEE, LMSW: DIFFERENTIAL DIAGNOSIS AND POSSIBLE SECONDARY GAINS

If the behavior of the perpetrator has been limited to fabrication of symptoms (i.e., no evidence exists that symptoms of any kind have been induced), *and* the perpetrator responds to confrontation appropriately, return of the victim to the home might be considered. This decision should be made on the basis of the perpetrator and family's willingness to obtain counseling, an assessment of the perpetrator's emotional status that strongly suggests that active induction of symptoms is not a likely outcome, and the availability of close, ongoing community support. Continuation of medical care is a critical component of this support system.

In cases in which the perpetrator is believed to be actively inducing symptoms, separation would seem prudent. In the absence of the perpetrator, return to the immediate or extended family might be considered. However, the potential for the perpetrator to return to the home should always be considered, and any visitation by this individual should be closely supervised by appropriate personnel. After a period of separation, reunification with the perpetrator might be cautiously considered if psychiatric evaluation demonstrates that the risk for active induction of symptoms has become very low, a strong community support system is in place, and all medical care of the victim is centrally coordinated.

Occasionally, the perpetrator in MBP is motivated by secondary financial gain. In certain hospitals in Texas, for example, parents of hospitalized children are provided with daily food and housing allowances. The parent of one of our patients repeatedly induced severe gastrointestinal symptoms and fabricated apnea in her infant, for which the baby was admitted to a tertiary care center on multiple occasions. The infant was returned to the home following each admission. It was later discovered that both parents were drug addicted, and the food and housing subsidies, available only when the infant was hospitalized, were being used to support their addictions. Although this case is very different from the "typical" MBP, it clearly demonstrates the need for careful assessment of the child's psychosocial environment prior to discharge to the family whenever MBP is suspected. In this example, as long as the potential for financial gain remained, the home was not a safe environment for the infant. Indeed, these parents would have benefited from drug rehabilitation services before reunification of the family was considered under any circumstances.

Despite the perceived benefits of family reunification, the child's safety is of critical importance when making short- and long-term plans for the victim of MBP. Because of the potential for serious injury or even death, great care must be taken when contemplating the return of this child to his family. Each case should be assessed individually, and the potential for reunification evaluated periodically. Through long-term intervention and family counseling, successful reunification seems an achievable goal in selected cases.

References

1. Gelles R. Abandon re-unification goal for abusive families and replace with child protection. *Brown Univ Child Adolescent Behavior Letter.* 1992; 8:5.
2. An attorney or other advocate, generally a neutral party, who represents the child's interests, particularly in court.
3. Hess P, Folarson G, and Jefferson A. Effectiveness of family re-unification services: an innovative evaluative model. *Social Work.* 1992; 37:4.
4. Hess P, Folarson G, and Jefferson A. *Family Protection Plan: Outline for Discussion with Family.* From materials developed for use in the Marion County Department of Public Welfare (Indianapolis In.) 1990, through a collaborative project between Indiana State Department of Public Welfare, District VII and Indiana University School of Social Work, funded in part by the U.S. Department of Health and Human Services, Administration for Children Youth and Families.

32

Research in Munchausen Syndrome by Proxy

Ian Mitchell

Research, to some degree, is the duty of all health care professionals. Factual information is needed to identify and provide
optimal treatment for any disease entity, including Munchausen
Syndrome by Proxy (MBP). Hypotheses regarding the causes of the
disease can be developed, then followed by tests or experiments to
verify or refute initial ideas. Many of the facts about MBP are in
this book. However, the case reports and small series cited raise
more questions than answers. These questions, evidence of continuing puzzles in a condition that has such a major impact on the children and families involved, mandates further research.

Little detailed research has been done on MBP. The techniques
of research for it have not been well developed. Legally acceptable
and ethically appropriate techniques for identification of cases,
standardized examination of family members, and initiation of
long-term follow-up are essential. A registry, despite legal and ethical difficulties, might well be important for long-term follow-up.
Research should also focus on professionals involved, in addition to
families.

Experimental investigations of MBP have been rare. The discrepancy between extensive description—mainly by case report, occasionally by small series—and description of underlying principles is
perhaps intrinsic to a relatively new disorder. It is certainly intrinsic
to a disorder with a spectrum of manifestations, in which definition
and diagnostic criteria are not universally accepted. The variety of

its presentations increases the difficulty in initiating prospective investigations.

The name used for this "disorder" may serve as a barrier to some studies, particularly those related to incidence. The use of "Munchausen" and "Munchausen by Proxy" as titles serves wonderfully to dramatize and draw attention to patterns of individual and parental behavior. Recently there has been a trend in medicine away from historical eponyms and toward factual descriptors. Certainly separating variants of factitious illness[1,2] and extreme illness exaggeration[3] as separate disorders will not help. All of these are part of the same spectrum.

What are the questions we need to answer?

1. An understanding of the incidence of MBP in medical and allied health practice, especially family medicine and pediatrics, social work, child welfare law, and other subspecialties.

Determining the incidence of MBP has been surprisingly difficult. Attempts have been made for particular diagnostic groups, such as apnea and asthma.[4,5,6] In most studies there is no denominator, and thus incidence cannot be accurately identified. Other medical, psychological, and social presentations need to be examined in the same way, but the incidence of MBP overall may be impossible to determine, even with such detailed research.

The frequency of MBP outlined in apnea and asthma was estimated because specific historical data was collected. There may be need for similar data to be sought in all parent/physician interactions. For example, family histories may need more detailed descriptors of the interaction between the child's illness and concurrent life events in the family. MBP is a reminder to inquire into the real reason for the child's being presented to a physician at a particular time.[7] Studies might examine whether this information about MBP, which is already in the pediatric literature, has changed physician behavior.

2. A listing of etiological factors in parents or families that lead to this unusual pattern of behavior.

Some families and parents have been assessed because of MBP, but no overall concepts of etiology have developed. Psychiatric/psychological abnormalities and illness-related behaviors in the parents, or in the family as a whole (including multiple generations) would seem to be important, and could be a very fruitful area of research. Yet there are difficulties in this area because of the nature of the syndrome. Families often fail to cooperate, and examinations done by court order are often less than satisfactory. Psychosocial research in other directions, such as long-term follow-up of victims and perpetrators, may give us more clues to etiology than detailed psychiatric examination at the time of discharge. The results of such research, however, will not come quickly.

3. Information on management, which will first be a description of strategies that have been found to be successful. As some strategies have been reported to be both successful and unsuccessful, identification of factors that lead to success and failure is needed.

Management strategies reported in the literature vary widely. They include confrontation, support, prosecution, and out-of-home placement. The circumstances in which one mode of management might work and others might not work are unclear and require detailed study. Such studies must be collaborative and interdisciplinary. Predictive tools need to be developed to evaluate management strategies. Virtually nothing has been investigated in the line of prevention.

In many case reports, management has been limited to removal of the child from the family, often permanently, with or without criminal prosecution of the parents. It is not clear that this will either address the needs of the parents or the needs for protection of existing or subsequent siblings. (This may, however, be the correct management strategy in the specific cases reported, which tend to be the most extreme examples of MBP.) Research may help us find situations in which treatment of the family may be successful without permanently separating the child from the family.

The response of the legal system to MBP has been reported but not well studied. Problems are indicated in many of the case reports, such as a lack of understanding of the syndrome, refusing to order victims to be removed from the home, returning them to the home on the basis of symptom resolution, or placing them with unsuitable guardians. For example, legal authorities have discharged children to the care of grandparents, not recognizing that their abuse of the perpetrator as a child may be part of the genesis of the MBP. Psychiatric and medical consultation to the courts may be inadequate or incomplete, and specific legal techniques or precedents may need to be developed to deal with MBP, as when video surveillance is requested. Legal authorities may also see MBP as an issue of prosecution rather than looking at the long-term needs of the child.[8] At present we do not know whether a civil or criminal approach is more effective in generating insight, changing behavior, and reducing feelings of victimization.

Physician behavior has been commented upon but not researched in detail.[9] Much of the morbidity of MBP is caused by unnecessary investigation or treatment. The reasons for these investigations and invasive treatments are still not clear, but one factor may be that physicians are taught from medical school to elicit and believe the history of the parents, and thus trust the information received. This advice is passed to all pediatric trainees. While this trust may be misplaced, there is little information available to help the pediatrician, whether trainee or practicing, to know when skepticism is appropriate.

Diagnosis is reached by many different methods and the varying processes are poorly understood. It does not always follow a logical pattern! Some physicians need diagnostic certainty, but as in other branches of medicine,[10] this is rarely available in pediatrics. Despite this lack of certainty, evaluation may continue. If MBP is a possibility and is not recognized, or the diagnosis is not believed, not only may the evaluation continue, but potentially dangerous tests may be used. If MBP is raised as a diagnosis, many physicians would see it as a diagnosis of exclusion and thus justify further exhaustive investigations.

These explanations for the unnecessary investigation and treatment relating to the diagnostic process are undoubtedly true in some cases. However, the underlying relationship between pediatricians and parents is also poorly understood, and there is a complex relationship between giving help and needing help. Some of the dynamic of this relationship may lead to delay in the diagnosis of MBP, and the overall relationship is itself worthy of study.

4. The outcomes of children involved in MBP and their siblings, in survival and health, is not known in detail. Likewise, the inci-

dence and nature of adverse emotional/psychological effects on children and families is unknown, but these must be great. Research should also be directed to family function before and after diagnosis.

There is a mortality rate in MBP for both index cases and their siblings, but its extent is unclear. A better knowledge of the mortality rate will help us decide on treatment strategies and how frequently we should resort to permanent removal of the child from the parents. Detailed study of mortality in MBP might also indicate the situations in which children are at most risk. Mortality may vary by medical presentation; without more comprehensive statistics, mortality rates for specific disorders may be applied to MBP as a whole. Unfortunately the most severe cases tend to be reported, so overall mortality may be exaggerated. This, in turn, distorts our concepts of prevention and treatment.

One report of 27 MBP cases presenting with suffocation and apnea found that 18 of the cases had elder siblings who had died.[11] Many of these deaths had been classified as Sudden Infant Death Syndrome (SIDS). This information again confirms that there is a mortality with MBP, but tells us nothing about the likelihood of SIDS being a result of MBP except indirectly, Differences in epidemiology of the death in those children are contrasted with death in SIDS. Another author has suggested that 10% of deaths classified as due to SIDS may be infanticide, an unknown portion of which is related to MBP.[12] It is difficult to know how accurate such figures will prove to be. Reliable information to identify children who are at high risk is not available.

Formal follow-up studies giving information on outcome apart from mortality are rare. Some information on long term results comes from studies completed by Meadow and colleagues.[13,14] This group presents data on 54 child victims of MBP. Of those successfully followed up, 49% had outcomes that were unacceptable.[15] In the parallel study there was significant morbidity in siblings of the index cases.[16]

Although these studies of long-term follow up are outstanding, it is also instructive to examine problems faced by this research group. They had knowledge of 100 families in which a child had suffered from the effects of fabricated illness. The families had been identified from varying sources, and of the 100 it was initially thought there would be enough information to study 62. In fact, there was insufficient information on six, and two of the children had subsequently died. Thus only 54 were available of the original 100. In addition to the problem of ascertainment, an additional problem was the wide range of severity, duration, and variety of fabrications used. Multiple sources of information were used to improve the objectivity of the data. There were common social services throughout the United Kingdom that facilitated the study. Such a study would be very difficult when children move from one legal jurisdiction to another and when there are no shared procedures among the jurisdictions. Improved knowledge of long term outcome can only occur if we have long term information on *all* the patients.

A registry of MBP cases would seem to be essential to achieve consistent information on long-term outcome. Long-term follow-up of families is needed. Such comprehensive research can only be done by full cooperation among medical, legal, and social agencies. The inadequacy of present follow-up arrangements and the need for a registry is illustrated by two of the many published reports. In the first, factitious bleeding was reported with survival of the child.[17] In another report published later, that same child was reported to have been found dead, with the cause of death given as "sudden infant death" in a child beyond infancy.[18] This sort of misinformation cannot be unique.

There are major difficulties to be overcome before a registry can be established. The ethical and legal issues of a registry need to be examined in detail, and appropriate safeguards developed. There will be concerns about confidentiality of the information, about who can add names, and about who has access to information. These objections, and those of cost, might be fatal to such a project. Parents who are subject to MBP allegations often change physicians. They also change their residence and such a move might be to another legal jurisdiction. Thus registries need to be linked to be fully effective, and this is another reason they may be deemed unacceptable. In the short term, institutions such as pediatric centers should identify cases and follow them closely to examine the feasibility of a registry, and to allow discovery of other issues. Areas in which national or managed care systems already exist can also serve as proving grounds for registries and other research endeavors, particularly because of their focus on identifying and diminishing overutilization of services. In such situations, however, care must be exercised that the focus remains therapeutic rather than punitive.

The suggestion of a registry exposes flaws in our present identification of cases—which cannot be registered until they are recognized. There is a lack of precision in diagnosis and a lack of agreement on what constitutes a full assessment. The former can be formalized, and the latter should include full psychological and social assessment, with evaluation of the family by skilled professionals using standardized techniques (which need to be developed).

Ethical Issues

The ethical issues of research in MBP itself are important. From one standpoint, given the morbidity and mortality of the syndrome, it would be unethical *not* to pursue the research. Yet some published studies raise further issues, as with covert video surveillance or the searching of belongings. These issues of secrecy and concealment also need further ethical discussion. In the early stages of management of MBP there is some concealment of the diagnosis from the family (and sometimes concealment of suspicions from child protective authorities) until the issue is secure and arrangements have been made for further investigation or the protection of the child. Particularly if research is involved, parental consent will have to be sought and the process carefully reviewed by institutional research boards (IRBs). Whether parents are likely to consent for research at a time when they are being accused of deception and investigated for abuse, and how such research will co-exist with clinical care are issues that still must be worked out.

The management of MBP is troublesome, time-consuming, and often not financially rewarding for the health care and other practitioners involved. There may be adverse publicity and even legal or personal risk directed against individuals and institutions. Thus there are many reasons it may be advantageous to avoid identifying cases and thus avoid the long process of management. This concern, that there may be vested interests against the identification of cases, raises a further ethical issue for researchers. Should they report cases, identified in their research, to child protection agencies?

What if they are given access to records or other materials only on condition that they will *not* make such reports?[19] Should institutions permit and encourage studies that may benefit children and families, but that also run the risk of adverse publicity and certainly will require funding for staff time? There will be a variety of answers to these questions, but they need to be addressed by individual researchers and IRBs. The issue of MBP is too important not to be subject to detailed study.

Summary

Research techniques needed to answer these questions will vary. Detailed analyses of cases will reveal some information, but this will differ from larger cross-sectional studies. Large series of cases of MBP are uncommon. The history and spectrum, and the medical manifestations by bodily function have been well documented in this book, but few publications address underlying principles. Although there are recent attempts to construct a framework[20,21] these have not yet been validated by other authors.

References

1. Libow JA and Schreier HA. Three forms of factitious illness in children: when is it Munchausen syndrome by proxy? *Am J Orthopsychiat.* 1986; 56:602–611.
2. Woodcott P. Aeto T, Rutt R, et al. Doctor shopping with the child as proxy patient: a variant of child abuse. *J Pediatr.* 1982; 101:297–301.
3. Masterson J, Dunworth R, and Williams N. Extreme illness exaggeration in pediatric patients: a variant of Munchausen's by proxy? *Am J Orthopsychiat.* 1988; 58:188–195.
4. Rosen CL, Frost JD, and Glaze DG. Child abuse and recurrent infant apnea. *J Pediatr.* 1986; 109:1065–1067.
5. Light MJ and Sheridan MS. Munchausen syndrome by proxy and apnea. *Clin Pediatr.* 1990; 29:162–168.
6. Godding V and Kruth M. Compliance with treatment of asthma and Munchausen syndrome by proxy. *Arch Dis Child.* 1991; 66:956–960.
7. Bass LW and Cohen RL. Ostensible vs. actual reasons for seeking pediatric attention: another look at the parental ticket of admission. *Pediatrics.* 1982; 70:870–874.
8. Peters JM. Criminal prosecution of child abuse: recent trends. *Pediatric Annals.* 1989; 18:505–509.
9. Zitelli BJ, Seltman MF, and Shanon RM. Munchausen's syndrome by proxy and its professional participants. *Am J Dis Child.* 1987; 141:1099–1102.

10. Kassirer JP. Our stubborn quest for diagnostic uncertainty: a cause of excessive testing. *N Engl J Med.* 1989; 1320:1489–1491.
11. Meadow R. Suffocation, recurrent apnea, and sudden infant death. *J Pediatr.* 1990; 117:351–357.
12. Emery JL. Infanticide, filicide, and cot death. *Arch Dis Child.* 1985; 60:505–507.
13. Bools CN, Neale BA, and Meadow SR. Follow up of victims of fabricated illness (Munchausen syndrome by proxy). *Arch Dis Child.* 1993; 69:625–630.
14. Bools CN, Neale BA, and Meadow SR. Co-morbidity associated with fabricated illness (Munchausen syndrome by proxy). *Arch Dis Child.* 1992; 67:77–79.
15. Bools, et al., Follow up.
16. Bools, et al., Co-morbidity.
17. Kurlandsky L, Lukoff JY, Zinkham WH, et al. Munchausen syndrome by proxy: definition of factitious bleeding in an infant by [51]CR labeling of erythrocytes. *Pediatrics.* 1979; 63:228–231.
18. Kessler RW quoted in Waller DA. Obstacles to the treatment of Munchausen by proxy syndrome. *J Am Acad Child Psychiatr.* 1983; 22:80–85. Quotation from p. 81.
19. Personal communication, Mary Sheridan.
20. Eminson DM and Postlewaite RJ. Factitious illness: recognition and management. *Arch Dis Child.* 1992; 67:1510–1516.
21. Robins PM and Sesan R. Munchausen syndrome by proxy: another women's disorder. *Professional Psychology: Research and Practice.* 1991; 22:285–290.

33

Summary

Mary S. Sheridan and Alex V. Levin

This chapter is intended to be a brief summary of the major points made by all of the authors in this book. In order to keep the material useful and manageable, there are no citations from the literature. However, it should be understood that material is derived from each of the preceding authors, and that their work, in turn, is indebted to the various sources they have cited. The reader is referred to each chapter and its supporting literature for a fuller description of the observations noted here. The reader is also cautioned that this material reflects understandings that were accurate at the time of writing (1995), but which may become inaccurate as new knowledge is generated.

Munchausen Syndrome by Proxy (MBP), which some have called Factitious Disorder by Proxy, is the deliberate creation of illness or its appearance in a child or other dependent, done primarily because of the secondary gains the caretaker derives from attention associated with that illness. It was first identified by Professor S. Roy Meadow in 1977. The caretaker may be, or may appear to be, obsessed with the idea that the victim is genuinely ill. Illness creation may include *actions* such as poisoning, smothering, or manipulation of laboratory or other data; *withholding of care* such as not giving medications that would prevent illness; and *false reporting* of symptoms or events. It is a form of abuse occurring most often with mothers as perpetrators and young children as victims, although other perpetrators (fathers, caretakers) and other victims (spouses, companions, animals) have been reported. It is differentiated from other forms of abuse and neglect primarily by its intent and calculated chronicity. Its incidence is unknown. There have, however, been a large number of cases reported by health care professionals throughout the world.

Frequent characteristics of MBP include:

1. Repetitive presentation of the victim for diagnosis and treatment.
2. Symptoms that are improbable, defy conventional explanations, or form rare syndromes. Alternatively, a series of events, each possible in itself, but unlikely when taken as a whole.
3. Symptoms fail to respond to treatments that "should" work, or treatments that are repeatedly not tolerated.
4. On close inquiry, the invariable association of the perpetrator with the occurrence of symptoms.
5. If "witnesses" other than the perpetrator are questioned closely, they are not able to conclusively support the picture presented by the perpetrator.
6. Cessation of symptoms when perpetrator and victim are separated.
7. A perpetrator who often appears devoted to the victim (if not overenmeshed) and exemplary in caretaking.
8. Significant morbidity and mortality, sometimes through the well-intentioned evaluations of a health care provider seeking to obtain a diagnosis or treat fabricated signs and symptoms.
9. Histories of unusual or similar health problems and/or deaths among the victim's siblings.
10. An apparently normal psychiatric profile in the perpetrator, (with the exception of possible Munchausen Syndrome) but life experiences that have taught the perpetrator to confuse love and illness, or impaired the perpetrator's ability to see the victim as a separate individual with rights.
11. Frequent (not invariable) family constellation of a suspected perpetrator who is usually the mother, who has some training or interest in health care, combined with a passive, abusive, or absent partner. In some cases, illness episodes correlate with the absence of or abuse by the partner. In some cases, the suspected perpetrator appears to have a reason for anger at health care professionals.

Many students of the disorder caution against using the term MBP as a diagnosis (and particularly as a condition which the perpetrator or victim "has"). Rather, they suggest that it is a behavioral descriptor. It is often more important in practice to protect the victim from behaviors than to label the behaviors.

MBP must be understood within context. The most relevant contexts are psychosocial (it is a form of deception), legal (it is a form of abuse), and medical (the same diagnostic criteria apply to MBP as to any other entity that must be ruled in or ruled out). It must be differentiated carefully from other diagnoses, including other forms of abuse and neglect, true illness with appropriate parental persistence, Vulnerable Child Syndrome, and disorders caused by social problems. MBP must also be understood as a spectrum of disorders ranging from mild exaggeration to lethal induction. There is at present no consensus on how many incidences of fabrication are "required" for the diagnosis. Motivations of the perpetrator are probably not uniform, and may include components of help-seeking; a delusion that the illness is real; rage at the victim, health care provider(s), or significant others; and tangible secondary gain. The victim may come to believe that the dysfunction is genuine and participate in associated lifestyle restrictions or, passively or actively, in the deception itself. There are also analogs to MBP ("Munchausen's by Professional Proxy") in some of the helping professions, when individuals can "look good" by responding capably to the fires, "codes," and other situations they induce.

Presentations

MBP may present as virtually any medical condition. The most commonly recognized forms of MBP have been various physical illnesses. Multisystem complaints are common. The presence of genuine illness does not exclude the possibility of MBP. The following are common known presentations.

RESPIRATORY

1. Apnea may be feigned by false history or produced by nonaccidental suffocation. The report of multiple episodes of apnea requiring cardiopulmonary resuscitation, with no cause discovered, should raise suspicions of MBP particularly if the victim is be-

yond the usual age (<1 year) for Apparent Life Threatening
Events (ALTE) or Sudden Infant Death Syndrome (SIDS). The
use of recording monitors is suggested to help clarify whether
apnea is real, feigned, or induced. The report of more than one
sudden infant death in a family, particularly when those deaths do
not "fit" usual parameters for SIDS should raise suspicions of
MBP.

2. Other pulmonary conditions or symptoms, such as asthma,
bronchopulmonary dysplasia, chest pain, and cystic fibrosis,
have been fabricated.
3. The appearance of bleeding from the airway may be produced
through local trauma, poisoning with anticoagulants, or
through exogenous blood (often the perpetrator's).

GASTROINTESTINAL

1. Vomiting may be produced through poisoning or stimulation
of the posterior pharynx. If vomiting is not observed by health
care providers, the history may be fraudulent.
2. Gastrointestinal bleeding can be produced through trauma,
poisoning, or recurrent vomiting. Bleeding can be simulated
with exogenous blood, substances that have the appearance of
blood, or falsified history.
3. Chronic diarrhea with secondary failure to thrive or electrolyte
disturbance can be produced by laxatives.

HEMATOLOGICAL

1. Bleeding may be simulated through the use of exogenous
blood, substances that look like blood, or false history.
2. True bleeding can be produced through trauma, manipulation
of intravenous and other catheters, or administration of drugs
such as anticoagulants. The evaluation of possible MBP bleeding begins with a determination of whether the sample is truly
blood, and whether its source is the patient.
3. Anemia may develop because of blood loss, drug withholding
(e.g., iron), or iatrogenically from multiple blood tests to diagnose other disease features.
4. Abnormalities in blood laboratory values may occasionally be
seen as a side-effect of attempts to create, diagnose, or treat
factitious illness.

INFECTION AND FEVER

1. Infection can be induced through the administration of patho-
genic material, foreign proteins, or pyrogens. Patients with an
indwelling central line or other catheter have a ready route for
the creation of infection. The appearance of unusual or multiple organisms on culture may suggest that the infection is factitious. Infection can be simulated through manipulation of lab
specimens.
2. Fevers can be simulated through manipulating thermometers or
the site of the temperature reading, and altering fever charts.
When fever is the only symptom, follows an inappropriate pattern, or is so high as to be improbable, MBP should be considered.

DERMATOLOGIC

1. Rashes can be caused by irritating the skin through mechanical
trauma, applying caustics, or painting with dye.
2. Bruising may be caused by external trauma, (look for features
that may reveal the source), and by drugs that cause bleeding
or inhibit clotting.
3. Intentionally produced burns, as from caustics, may be confused with unusual skin conditions, infections, or allergies.
4. Skin infections can be caused by breaking the surface of the
skin with a contaminated instrument or by injecting contaminated material.

All of these dermalogic signs should be differentiated from folk
medicine practices that involve applications to the skin that sometimes burn or bruise.

ALLERGIC

Allergies are more often reported as an associated feature with
other factitious illness. Multiple allergies and unusual allergies are
particularly suspect. Fabrication often occurs at the level of history.
Food allergies, with food restrictions even to the point of failure to
thrive, may be reported among patients in whom MBP is suspected.

OCULAR

1. Noxious substances can be instilled into the eyes or around the

eyes causing skin abnormalities, conjunctivitis, pupil abnormalities, periocular infection and visual loss.

2. Strabismus, nystagmus, and pupil abnormalities may result
   from systemic poisoning.

RENAL

1. Hematuria can be simulated through the addition of exogenous
   blood or dye to urine samples. To prevent this, urine collection
   in suspected MBP should be closely supervised.
2. Proteinuria can be simulated by adding egg albumin to urine
   samples.
3. Bacteriuria can be simulated through contaminating urine samples. Infection or bleeding can result from instrumentation of
   the urethra, either as part of disease production or attempts at
   diagnosis.
4. Urinary calculi can be simulated through false history and the
   production of exogenous gravel or stones.
5. The appearance of other renal disorders may be induced
   through biochemical side-effects of poisoning (e.g., table salt)
   or urine sample contamination.
6. Genuine renal dysfunction and hypertension may result from
   poisoning.
7. Factitious hypertension is usually traceable to altered blood
   pressure records.

OTORHINOLARYNGOLOGIC

1. Trauma to the ears, nose, mouth, and throat can cause bleeding, ruptured ear drum, hearing loss, scarring, palatal injury,
   and retropharyngeal abscess. Oropharyngeal injury may be a
   marker for subsequent induced foreign body ingestion.
2. Poisoning may cause bleeding by disruption of coagulation, or
   burning/inflaming the oropharynx.

NEUROLOGICAL

1. Seizures occurring in MBP are of three types: false reports;
   acute, genuine seizures caused by poisoning, suffocation, or
   carotid sinus pressure; or chronic genuine seizures as a result of
   attempts to induce illness (e.g., through prolonged or repeated
   suffocation).

2. Disorders of consciousness may be the result of poisoning or suffocation.
3. Nystagmus, hypotonia, headaches, behavioral disorders or retardation, cyclic vomiting, and weakness may be the result of poisoning and anoxia. Myopathy may be induced by ipecac poisoning. Cerebral palsy, blindness, and other permanent handicaps may result from severe abuse.

DEVELOPMENTAL DELAY AND FAILURE TO THRIVE

1. These may be alleged, in which case objective markers such as testing and weight will be appropriate.
2. They may also be a side-effect of efforts to induce illness (e.g., frequent laxatives) or even to diagnose (e.g., prolonged hospitalization, surgery).
3. Failure to thrive may be the result of excessive restrictions imposed by the perpetrator (e.g., the victim supposedly has multiple allergies and is so restricted in food that weight cannot be maintained).
4. The disturbed relationship between perpetrator and victim may result in long-term failure of appropriate psychological growth or nonorganic failure to thrive.

PSYCHIATRIC ILLNESS

Little is known about this area. Because of the subjectivity of much mental health diagnosis, extreme care must be used in concluding that a particular situation reflects MBP. However, anecdotal and published reports do exist of situations in which a caretaker or dominant partner creates the appearance of psychiatric illness in a victim. Care must be taken to differentiate true MBP from other forms of abuse or exploitation in which a judgment of psychiatric illness is one means to tangible gain, and from situations in which a naive or trusting patient or caretaker is convinced by a practitioner that a certain illness exists. In addition, studies of MBP victims years after their abuse suggest a higher than normal incidence of behavioral, school, and psychiatric problems, including factitious illness.

FALSE CLAIMS OF ABUSE

Careful differentiation is necessary from situations in which there is an obvious secondary gain (e.g., custody disputes, stressed relationships in which trust has been lost) and those in which the person making the allegation may be obsessed with the possibility that abuse has occurred (closer to or indistinguishable from some forms of MBP).

Evaluation and Management

The first and most critical phase in the diagnosis of MBP is the generation of appropriate suspicion when confronted by a suggestive clinical scenario. Diagnosis is a dynamic process; MBP should not be ruled in or ruled out until sufficient evidence is available. One must carefully separate real, induced, and factitious disease. Many diagnostic modalities may be necessary both to rule out organic disease and to rule in the diagnosis of MBP. These may include the following.

Covert Videotaping. This method is well suited to hospital use, where it has been applied successfully. If undertaken, videotaping must always be done in a planned manner, with continuous observation by trained personnel who are in a position to intervene immediately if the perpetrator's behavior threatens to harm the victim. Covert videotaping has been criticized as intrusive into the trust relationship between parent and hospital, and as potentially placing the victim at risk of further physical harm or psychological trauma.

Supporters of videotaping counter that it is a fast and incontrovertible means of determining what is causing the symptoms in the victim, and that sufficient protection can be built in so that further injury will not occur. Some methods (two cameras, blanket release forms as part of admission consents) have been devised to answer the legal objections, but such methods have still been challenged as deceptive. As the law is changing rapidly in this area, and varies from region to region, the professionals are advised to consult the appropriate administrative and legal resources before undertaking covert surveillance.

Separation of Victim and Alleged Perpetrator. If symptoms abate in the absence of the perpetrator, particularly if no other changes are made, the hypothesis that the perpetrator was the cause of the symptoms is strengthened. Statistical analysis is sometimes used to show that alternative hypotheses are not likely. Separation protects the victim, but may cause significant psychological trauma. Brief separations can be enforced by hospitalizing the victim, although the ability of the perpetrator to cause symptoms within the hospital should not be underestimated. Longer separation as a form of diagnosis or treatment usually requires child protective and legal authorities.

THE MULTIDISCIPLINARY TEAM

After the diagnosis of MBP has been confirmed, one must take action to protect the child and potentially the child's siblings. MBP must be judged not only on the harm that has actually occurred, but also on the risk for injury that might occur if the perpetrator's behavior is allowed to continue. The process of confrontation, assessment of risk, protection, and (if possible) treatment requires utilizing or establishing a coordinated multidisciplinary approach.

MBP cases are difficult to manage because the disorder may be unfamiliar to the practitioner or staff, unpleasant to accept as a real entity, and threatening to the relationships that have often been formed between perpetrator and health care professionals. Parents may flatly and convincingly deny that they have had any part in illness fabrication. Effective management of the situation and protection of victim, perpetrator, and professionals depends on the willingness of all participants in the process to respect each other's viewpoints, communicate openly, and plan well. It may be necessary to form an ad hoc team to address the situation. Ideally, the person with suspicions should have recourse to a functioning child protection team with experience in MBP.

The following professionals are proposed for an effective team. In small facilities and rural areas, some of these members may be unavailable, or available only on a consultant basis. Core team members are indicated by an asterisk, and one of these will generally take the role of team leader. There is some overlapping of roles, and local conditions will determine appropriate division of labor. It is important that role issues be resolved in advance and to the reasonable satisfaction of all participants, as MBP cases provide fruitful ground for exploiting interpersonal differences.

1. *Attending physician of patient

2. *Child abuse physician
3. *Primary nurse(s) of patient
4. *Social worker
5. Nurse specialist
6. Hospital administrator
7. Hospital attorney/legal consultant
8. Hospital security and/or law enforcement
9. Appropriate consultant physician specialists
10. Psychiatrist/psychologist
11. Ethicist
12. Child protection agency worker

The multidisciplinary team has three general goals: protecting the suspected victim, assisting in the diagnosis and management of suspected MBP cases, and supporting those involved. Although the process must be individualized, it usually includes the following elements:

1. Suspicions are received and evaluated.
2. Information is gathered. As much as possible, all original records pertaining to the index patient's health history and that of pertinent family members (particularly siblings and alleged perpetrator) are obtained and reviewed. At the same time, careful recording of symptoms and the possible perpetrator's behavior is begun. Historical information provided by the possible perpetrator is verified to establish patterns of truth-telling or falsity.
3. All diagnostic possibilities are explored.
4. Lines of communication are opened to those who have a "need to know" while appropriately safeguarding confidentiality and preventing information release that could sabotage management plans.
5. If suspicions appear justified, a management plan will be implemented. This plan may include:
   a. Writing a unified patient care plan to be followed by all personnel.
   b. Clarifying roles and responsibilities.
   c. Assuring the safety of the victim through close observation and other methods.
   d. Carefully documenting observations.

e. Reporting to child protective authorities as required by law.

f. Planning for the protection of charts and laboratory specimens from alteration or contamination.

g. Instituting safe, ethical, and properly approved strategies (diagnostic separation, possibly videotaping, close observation) to catch the perpetrator "in the act."

h. Confronting the perpetrator. This must be done with adequate support available for the perpetrator, who may decompensate psychiatrically, and only when there is a plan in place for the immediate protection of the victim and staff as necessary

i. Formulating a discharge and after-care plan. This plan must take into account community conditions and resources. It should be communicated thoroughly in writing to all prospective participants. The establishment of a new care team, composed of those who will be involved after discharge, may be appropriate.

j. Staff debriefing. This addresses the emotional impact of the experience on participants.

k. Institutional follow-up. Management of a specific case may offer the opportunity for Grand Rounds presentations or other educational, preventive, or research activities.

Future Directions

Professionals knowledgeable about MBP have other roles and functions. These include educating health care providers about the existence of MBP; learning how to prevent its occurrence; diagnosing MBP sooner; and further research into areas such as frequency, antecedents, new forms, and methods of treatment.

Bibliography

Abram HS and Hollender MH. Factitious blood disease. *South Med J.* 1974; 67:691–696.

Abrol RP, Heck A, Gleckel L, et al. Self-induced hematuria. *J Natl Med Assoc.* 1990; 82:127–128.

Ackerman AB, Mosher DT, and Schwamm HA. Factitial Weber-Christian syndrome. *JAMA.* 1966; 198:731–736.

Ackerman NB, Jr., Strobel CT. Polle Syndrome: chronic diarrhea in Munchausen's child. *Gastroenterology.* 1981; 81:1140–1142.

Adler R and Touyz S. Ganser syndrome in a 10 year old boy—an 8 year followup. *Aust N Z J Psychiatry.* 1989; 23:124–126.

Adruaenssens P, Eggermont E. Het syndroom van Munchausen by proxy: De fatale driehoek moeder-arts-kind [Munchausen syndrome by proxy: The fatal triangle: Mother-doctor-child]. *Kind en Adolesc.* 1991; 12:185–188.

Aduan RP, Fauci AS, Dale DC, et al. Factitious fever and self-induced infection: A report of 32 cases and review of the literature. *Ann Intern Med.* 1979; 90:230–242.

Agle DP, Ratnoff OD, and Spring GK. The anticoagulant malingerer: Psychiatric studies of 3 patients. *Ann Int Med.* 1970; 73:67–72.

Alexander R, Smith W, and Stevenson R. Serial Munchausen syndrome by proxy. *Pediatrics.* 1990; 86:581–585.

Al-Mugeiren M and Ganelin RS. A suspected case of Munchausen's syndrome by proxy in a Saudi child. *Ann Saudi Med.* 1990; 662.

Amegavie L, Marzouk O, Mullen J, et al: Munchausen's syndrome by proxy: a warning for health professionals. *Br Med J.* 1986; 293:855–856.

American Health Consultants. Munchausen syndrome by proxy. *Hosp Risk Mangement.* 1993; 15:39–46.

American Psychiatric Assn. *Diagnostic and Statistical Manual of Mental Disorders* IV ed. 1994; Washington, DC: American Psychiatric Assn.

Amir J. Polymicrobial bacteremia and child abuse. *Am J Dis Child.* 1989; 143:444 [Letter].

Asher R. Munchausen's syndrome. *Lancet.* 1951; 1:339–341.

Atoynatan TH, O'Reilly E, and Loin L. Munchausen Syndrome by Proxy. *Child Psychiatry Human Dev.* 1988; 19:3–13.

Ayass M, Bussing R, and Mehta P. Munchausen syndrome presenting as hemophilia: a convenient and economical "steal" of disease and treatment. *Pediatr Hematol Oncol.* 1993; 10:241–244.

Babcock J, Hartman K, Pedersen A, et al. Rodenticide-induced coagulopathy in a young child. A case of Munchausen syndrome by proxy. *Am J Pediatr Hematol Oncol.* 1993; 15:126–30.

Baldwin MA. Munchausen syndrome by proxy: Neurological manifestations. *J Neurosci Nurs*. 1994; 26:18–23.

Barbanel J. When a mother is blamed for her child's unusual illness. *New York Times*. Oct 11, 1992; pg 41.

Barton R and Whitehead JA. The gaslight phenomenon. *Lancet*. 1969; 1:1258–1260.

Bauman WA and Yalow RS. Child abuse: Parenteral insulin administration. *J Pediatr*. 1981; 99:588–591.

Bass LW and Cohen RL. Ostensible versus actual reasons for seeking pediatric attention: another look at the parental ticket of admission. *Pediatrics*. 1982; 70:870–874.

Bass M, Kravath RE, and Glass L. Death-scene investigation in sudden infant death. *N Engl J Med*. 1986; 315:100–105.

Bath AP, Murty GE, and Gibbin KP. Munchausen syndrome by proxy: otolaryngologists beware! *J Laryngol Otol*. 1993; 107:151–2.

Beeber B and Cunningham N. Fatal child abuse and sudden infant death syndrome (SIDS): a critical diagnostic decision. *Pediatrics*. 1994; 93:539–540.

Bennett HS, Spiro AJ, Pollack MA, et al. Ipecac-induced myopathy simulating dermatomyositis. *Neurology*. 1982; 32:91–94.

Bentovim A. Munchausen's syndrome and child psychiatrists. *Arch Dis Child*. 1985; 60:688 [Letter].

Berger D. Child abuse simulating "near-miss" sudden infant death syndrome. *J Pediatr*. 1979; 95:554–556.

Berkner P, Kastner T, and Skolnick, L. Chronic ipecac poisoning in infancy: A case report. *Pediatrics*. 1988; 82:384–386.

Bhatia, RS. Pseudo sickness. *J Assoc Physicians India*. 1990; 38:514.

Black D. The extended Munchausen syndrome: a family case. *Brit J Psychiatry*. 1981; 138:466–469.

Blix S and Brack G. The effects of a suspected case of Munchausen's syndrome by proxy on a pediatric nursing staff. *Gen Hosp Psychiatry*. 1988; 10:402–409.

Bonadio WA. Polymicrobial bacteremia in children. *Am J Dis Child*. 1988; 142:1158–1160.

Bools CN, Neale BA, and Meadow, SR. Co-morbidity associated with fabricated illness (Munchausen syndrome by proxy). *Arch Dis Child*. 1992; 67:77–79.

———. Follow-up of victims of fabricated illness (Munchausen syndrome by proxy). *Arch Dis Child*. 1993; 69:625–630.

———. Munchausen syndrome by proxy: A study of psychopathology. *Child Abuse Negl*. 1994; 18:773–788.

Boros SJ and Brubaker LC. Munchausen syndrome by proxy. *FBI Law Enforcement Bull*. 1992; 61:16–20.

Bourchier D. Bleeding ears: case report of Munchausen syndrome by proxy. *Aust Paediatr J*. 1983; 19:256–257.

Boyce WT. The vulnerable child: new evidence, new approaches. *Adv Pediatr*. 1992; 39:1–33.

Brahams D. Video surveillance and child abuse. *Lancet*. 1993; 342:944.

Burman D, Stevens D. Munchausen family. *Lancet*. 1977; 2:456 [Letter].

Byard RW. Factitious patients with fictitious disorders: a note on Munchausen's syndrome. *Med J Aust.* 1992; 156:507–8 [Letter, comment].

Byard RW and Beal SM. Munchausen syndrome by proxy: repetitive infantile apnoea and homicide. *J Paediatr Child Health.* 1993; 29:77–9.

Byard RW and Burnell RH. Covert video surveillance in Munchausen syndrome by proxy. Ethical compromise or essential technique? *Med J Aust.* 1994; 160:352–356.

Cantwell HB. Child protective services in parental mismanagement of diabetes. *Diabetes Educator.* 1984; 10:41–43.

Carey WB and Sibinga MS. Avoiding pediatric pathogenesis in the management of acute minor illness. *Pediatrics.* 1972; 49:553–562.

Carlson J, Fernlund P, Ivarsson SA, et al. Munchausen syndrome by proxy: An unexpected cause of severe chronic diarrhoea in a child. *Acta Paediatr.* 1994; 83:119–121.

Caruso M, Bregani P, DiNatale B, et al. Ipoglicemia indotta. Un insolito caso di maltrattamento infantile. [Induced hypoglycemia. An unusual case of child abuse]. *Minerva Pediatr.* 1989; 41:525.

Ceronsky J. Articles on child abuse. *Clin Pediatr.* 1989; 28:33 [Letter with responses].

Chadwick DL. The diagnosis of inflicted injury in infants and young children. *Pediatr Ann.* 1992; 21:477–83.

Chan DA, Salcedo JR, Atkins DM, et al. Munchausen syndrome by proxy: A review and case study. *J Pediatr Psychol.* 1986; 11:71–80.

Clark GD, Key JD, Rutherford P, et al. Munchausen's syndrome by proxy (child abuse) presenting as apparent autoerythrocyte sensitization syndrome: an unusual presentation of Polle Syndrome. *Pediatrics.* 1984; 74:1100–1102.

Clarke E and Melnick SC. The Munchausen syndrome or the problem of hospital hoboes. *Am J Med.* 1958; 25:6–12.

Clayton PT, Counahan R, and Chantler C. Munchausen syndrome by proxy. *Lancet.* 1978; 1:102–103. [Letter].

Cohle SD, Trestrail JD 3rd, Graham MA, et al. Fatal pepper aspiration. *Am J Dis Child.* 1988; 142:633–636.

Cole A. Fatal attraction. *Nurs Times.* 1993; 89:20–1.

Colletti RB and Wasserman RC. Recurrent infantile vomiting due to intentional ipecac poisoning. *J Pediatr Gastro Nutr.* 1989; 8:394–396.

Cotterill JA. Self-stigmatization: Artefact dermatitis. *Br J Hosp Med.* 1992; 47:115–119.

Craig L and Biley F. Munchausen by proxy: Fact, not fiction. *Nursing.* (London) 1991; 4:11.

Cristobal MC, Aguilar A, Urbina F, et al. Self-inflicted tongue ulcer: An unusual form of factitious disorder. *J Am Acad Dermatol.* 1987; 17:339–341.

Croft RD and Jervis M. Munchausen's syndrome in a 4 year old. *Arch Dis Child.* 1989; 64:740.

Crouse KA. Munchausen syndrome by proxy: Recognizing the victim. *Pediatr Nurs.* 1992; 18:249–52.

David AS, Farrell M. Suffocation and videos. *Br Med J.* 1987; 295:116 [Letter].

David TJ. Spying on mothers. *Lancet.* 1994; 344:133 [Letter].

Davies N. *Murder on Ward Four.* 1993; London: Chatto and Windus.

Davis TA: Munchausen syndrome by proxy. *Forensic Sci.* 1987; 13:41–50.

Day L, Kelly C, Reed G, et al. Fatal cardiomyopathy: Suspected child abuse by chronic ipecac administration. *Vet Hum Toxicol.* 1989; 31:255–257.

Deonna T, Marcoz JP, Meyer HU, et al. Epilepsie factice: "Syndrome de Münchhausen par procuration." Une aytre facette de l'enfant maltraité: comas à répétition chez un enfant de 4 ans par intoxication non accidentelle [Factitious epilspsy. "Munchausen syndrome by proxy." Another aspect child abuse: repeated coma in a 4 year old caused by nonaccidental poisoning]. *Rev Méd Suisse Romande.* 1985; 105:995–1002.

Dershewitz R, Vestal B, Maclaren NK, et al. Transient hepatomegaly and hypoglycemia: A consequence of malicious insulin administration. *Am J Dis Child.* 1976; 130:998–999.

deToni T, Gastaldi R, Scarsi S, et al. La sindrome di Munchausen per procura. Descrizione di un Caso [Munchausen syndrome by proxy. Description of a case]. *Minerva Pediatr.* 1987; 39:33–36.

Diagnosing recurrent suffocation of children. *Lancet.* 1992; 340:87.

DiMaio VJ. SIDS or Murder? *Pediatrics.* 1988; 81:747–748 [Letter].

Dine MS. Tranquilizer poisoning: An example of child abuse. *Pediatrics.* 1965; 36:782–785.

Dine MS and McGovern ME. Intentional poisoning of children—an overlooked category of child abuse: report of seven cases and review of the literature. *Pediatrics.* 1982; 70:32–35.

The disorder no one suspects. *Sui Generis.* 1987; 9:3–9.

Dockery WK. Fatal intentional salt poisoning associated with a radiopaque mass. *Pediatrics.* 1991: 964–965.

Douchain F. Lithiase urinaire "factice": Syndrome de Munchausen par procuration? [Factitious urinary lithiasis: Munchausen syndrome by proxy?] *Presse Med.* 1987; 16:179.

Drell MJ. More on Munchausen syndrome by proxy. *J Am Acad Child Adolesc Psychiatry.* 1988; 27:140.

Duane DD and Engel AG. Emetine myopathy. *Neurology.* 1970; 20:733–739.

Duff A. Pyrexia of unusual origin. *Bri Med J.* 1951; 2:549 [Letter].

Eckhardt A. [Artifical diseases (self-induced diseases)-a review).] *Nervenarzt.* 1992; 63:409–15.

Eden OB and McNinch AW. Voodoo, videos and fits; another presentation of truancy. *Eur J Pediatr.* 1992; 151:918 [Letter].

Edwards MS and Butler KM. 'Hyperthermia of trickery' in an adolescent. *Pediatr Infect Dis J.* 1987; 6:411–414.

Egginton J. The bad mother. *Good Housekeeping.* 119:247–249, 253 (April 1989).

———. *From Cradle to Grave.* 1989; New York: William Morrowv & Company.

Elkind P. *The Death Shift: The True Story of Nurse Genene Jones and the Texas Baby Murders.* 1989; New York: Viking.

Embry CK. Toxic cyclic vomiting in an 11-year old girl. *J Am Acad Child Adol Psychiatry.* 1987; 26:447–448.

Emery JL. Child abuse and "near-miss cot death." *Br Med J.* 1981; 282:821 [Letter].

———. Infanticide, filicide, and cot death. *Arch Dis Child.* 1985; 60:505–507 [Letter].

———. Child abuse, sudden infant death syndrome, and unexpected infant death. *Am J Dis Child.* 1993; 147:1097–1100.

Eminson DM and Postlethwaite RJ. Factitious illness: Recognition and management. *Arch Dis Child.* 1992; 67:1510–1516.

Epstein MA, Markowitz RL, Gallo DM, et al. Munchausen syndrome by proxy: Considerations in diagnosis and confirmation by video surveillance. *Pediatrics.* 1987; 80:220–224.

Ernst TN and Philp M. Severe iron deficiency anemia. An example of covert child abuse (Munchausen syndrome by proxy). *West J Med.* 1986; 144:358–359.

Evans D. Covert video surveillance in Munchausen's syndrome by proxy. *Br Med J.* 308:341–342 [Letter].

Facey S. Munchausen syndrome by proxy. *Nurs Times.* 1993; 89:54–6.

Feenstra J, Merth IT, and Treffers PD. Een geval van het syndroom van Munchausen bij proxy [A case of Munchausen syndrome by proxy.] *Tijdschr Kindergeneeskunde.* 1988; 56:148–53.

Feldman K and Robertson WO. Salt poisoning: Presenting symptom of child abuse. *Vet Human Toxicol.* 1979; 21:341–343.

Feldman KW, Christopher DM, and Opheim KB. Munchausen syndrome/bulimia by proxy: ipecac as a toxin in child abuse. *Child Abuse Neg.* 1989; 13:257–261.

Feldman MD and Ford CV. *Patient or Pretender: Inside the Strange World of Factitious Disorders.* 1994; New York: Wiley.

Feldman MD. Spying on mothers. *Lancet.* 344:132 [Letter].

Fenton AC, Wailoo MP, and Tanner MS. Severe failure to thrive and diarrhoea caused by laxative abuse. *Arch Dis Child.* 1988; 63:978–979.

Fialkov MJ. Peregrination in the problem pediatric patient. The pediatric munchausen syndrome? *Clin Pediatr.* 1984; 23:571–575.

Fischler RS. Poisoning: a syndrome of child abuse. *Am Fam Physician.* 1983; 28:103–108.

Fisher G and Mitchell I. Munchausen's Syndrome by Proxy (Factitious Illness by Proxy). *Curr Opin Psychiatry.* 1992; 5:224–227.

Fisher G, Mitchell I, and Murdoch D. Munchausen's syndrome by proxy: the question of psychiatric illness in a child. *Br J Psychiatry.* 1993; 162:701–703.

Fleisher D and Ament ME. Diarrhea, red diapers, and child abuse. *Clin Pediatr.* 1977; 17:820–824.

Ford CV, Stein R, Kelly MP, et al. Factitial aplastic anemia. *J Nerv Ment Dis.* 1984; 172:369–372.

Ford CV and Zaner RM. Response to the article "Ethical and management considerations in factitious illness: one and the same." *Gen Hosp Psychiatry.* 1987; 9:37–39.

Foreman DM and Farsides C. Ethical use of covert videoing techniques in detecting Munchausen syndrome by proxy. *Br Med J.* 1993; 307:611–613.

Fowler BA and Weissberg JB. Arsine poisoning *N Engl J Med.* 1974; 291:1171–1174.

Frederick V, Luedtke GS, Barrett FF, et al. Munchausen syndrome by proxy: recurrent central catheter sepsis. *Pediatr Inf Dis J.* 1990; 9:440–442.

Friedman EM. Caustic ingestions and foreign body aspirations: An overlooked form of child abuse. *Ann Otol Rhinol Laryngol.* 1987; 96:709–712.

Frost JD Jr., Glaze, DG, and Rosen CL. Munchausen's syndrome by proxy and video surveillance. *Am J Dis Child.* 1988; 142:917 [Letter].

Fox J. Covert video surveillance of children. Role of police. *Br Med J.* 1993; 308:1145 [Letter].

Garty B. Garlic Burns. *Pediatrics.* 1993; 91:658–659.

Geelhoed GC and Pemberton PJ. SIDS, seizures or 'sophageal reflux? *Med J Aust.* 1985; 143:357–358.

Gellis S and Feingold M. Cao Gio: pseudobattering in Vietnamese children. *Am J Dis Child.* 1976; 130:857–858 ["Picture of the Month"].

Gilbert RW, Pierse PM, and Mitchell DP. Cryptic otalgia: A case of munchausen syndrome in a pediatric patient. *J Otolaryngol.* 1987; 16:231–233.

Gilbert-Barness E. Is sudden infant death syndrome a cause of death? *Am J Dis Child.* 1993; 147:25–26.

Ginies JL, Goulet O, Champion G, et al. Syndrome de Munchausen par procuration et pseudo-obstruction intestinale chronique [Munchausen syndrome by proxy and chronic intestinal pseudo-obstruction]. *Arch Fr Pediatr.* 1989; 46:267–269.

Godding V and Kruth M. Compliance with treatment of asthma and munchausen syndrome by proxy. *Arch Dis Child.* 1991; 66:956–60.

Goebel J, Gremse DA, and Artman M. Cardiomyopathy from ipecac administration in munchausen syndrome by proxy. *Pediatrics.* 1993; 92:601–603.

Goodwin J, Sahd D, and Rada RT. False allegations and false denials of incest; clinical myths and clinical realities. In: Goodwin J (ed). *Sexual Abuse: Incest Victims and Their Families.* 1989; Chicago: yearbook.

Goss PW and McDougall PN. Munchausen syndrome by proxy: a cause of preterm delivery. *Med J Aust.* 1992; 157:814–817.

Grace A, Kalinkiewicz M, and Drake-Lee AB. Covert manifestations of child abuse. *Br Med J.* 1984; 289:1041–1042.

Grace A and Grace S. Child abuse within the ear, nose and throat. *J Otolaryngol.* 1987; 16:108–111.

Greene JW, Craft L, and Ghishan F. Acetaminophen poisoning in infancy. *Am J Dis Child.* 1983; 137:386–387.

Greenfeld D. Feigned psychosis in a 14 year old girl. *Hosp Community Psychiatry.* 1987; 38:73–75.

Griffith JL. The family systems of Munchausen syndrome by proxy. *Fam Proc.* 1988; 27:423–437.

Griffith JL and Slovik LS. Munchausen syndrome by proxy and sleep disorders medicine. *Sleep.* 1989; 12:178–183.

Guandolo VL. Munchausen syndrome by proxy: An outpatient challenge. *Pediatrics*. 1985; 75:526–530.

Gunter M and Boos R. Significance of "abnormal reaction susceptibility of adolescents in Munchausen by proxy syndrome. Simulation, folie a deux, induced artefact diseasex or what else? *Nervenarzt*. 1994; 65:307–312.

Hale V and Evseichick O. Fraudulent fever. *Amer J Nurs*. 1943; 43:992–994.

Halsey NA, Frentz JM, Tucker TW, et al. Recurrent nosocomial polymicrobial sepsis secondary to child abuse. *Lancet*. 1983; 2:558–560.

Hawkings JR, Jones KS, Sim M, et al. Deliberate disability. *Br Med J*. 1956; 1:361–367.

Herzberg JH and Wolff SM. Chronic factitious fever in puberty and adolescence: A diagnostic challenge to the family physician. *Psychiatry Med*. 1972; 3:205–212.

Hickson GB, Greene JW, Ghishan FK, et al. Apparent intentional poisoning of an infant with acetaminophen. *Am J Dis Child*. 1983; 137:917.

Hill RM, Barer J, Hill LL, et al. An investigation of recurrent pine oil poisoning in an infant by the use of gas chromatographic-mass spectrometric methods. *J Pediatr*. 1975; 87:115–118.

Hodge D, Schwartz W, Sargent J, et al. The bacteriologically battered baby: Another case of Munchausen by Proxy. *Ann Emerg Med*. 1982; 11:205–207.

Holborow PL. A variant of Munchausen's syndrome by proxy. *J Am Acad Child Psychiatry*. 1985; 24:238.

Holmberg L. Munchausen's by proxy syndrome. *Pediatr Hematol Oncol*. 1993; 10:iii–iv [Editorial, comment].

Hood I, Mirchandani H, Monforte J, et al. Immunohistochemical demonstration of homicidal insulin injection site. *Arch Pathol Lab Med*. 1986; 110:973–974.

Hosch IA. Munchausen syndrome by proxy. *MCN*. 1987; 12:48–52.

Hulstijn-Dirkmaat GM, Raes BC, and Monnens LA. Het Beleid na het Stellen van de Diagnose 'MBP' [Management Following Diagnosis of Munchausen syndrome by proxy]. *Nederlands Tijdschr Geneeskunde*. 1987; 131:2372.

Hunt CE. Sudden infant death syndrome and subsequent siblings. *Pediatrics* 1995; 95:430–432.

Hvizdala EV and Gellady AM. Intentional poisoning of two siblings by prescription drugs: an unusual form of child abuse. *Clin Pediatr*. 1978; 17:480–482.

Iarsen F. [Munchausen syndrome. A rare condition requiring many resources]. *Nord Med*. 1991; 106:330–2.

Ifere OA, Yakubu AM, Aikhionbare HA, et al. Munchausen syndrome by proxy: an experience from Nigeria. *Ann Trop Paediatr*. 1993; 13:281–284.

Investigation of SIDS. *N Engl J Med*. 1986; 315:1675–1677 [Letter].

Jani S, White M, Rosenberg LA, et al. Munchausen syndrome by proxy. *Int J Psychiatry Med*. 1992; 22:343–9.

Jiminez-Hernandez JL, Lopez-Ibor-Alino JJ, Yturriaga-Matarranz RY, et al. El syndrome de Munchausen por poderes: Un tipo especial de ninos maltratados [Munchausen syndrome by proxy: A special type of child abuse]. *Actas Luso-Esp Neurol Psiquiatr*. 1987; 15:333–343.

Johnson CF. Constricting bands: manifestations of possible child abuse. *Clin Pediatr*. 1988; 27:439–444.

Johnson CF. Inflicted injury versus accidental injury. *Pediatr Clin N Am.* 1990; 37:791–814.

Johnson CF, Coury DL. Bruising and hemophilia: Accident or child abuse? *Child Abuse Negl.* 1988; 12:409–415.

Johnson CF, Kaufman KL, and Callendar C. The hand as a target organ in child abuse. *Clin Pediatr.* 1990; 29:66–72.

Johnson CF and Showers J. Injury variables in child abuse. *Child Abuse Negl.* 1985; 9:207–215.

Johnson G, Mullan B, and Rich G. A case of factitious disorder presenting as plumbism. *Med J Aust.* 1987; 146:264–266.

Johnson JE, Carpenter BL, Benton J, et al. Hemorrhagic colitis and pseudomelanosis coli in ipecac ingestion by proxy. *J Pediatr Gastro Nutr.* 1991; 12:501–506.

Johnson P. Diagnosis of recurrent suffocation of children. *Lancet.* 1992; 340:481 [Letter].

Johnson P and Morley C. Spying on mothers. *Lancet.* 1994; 344:132–133.

Jones D. Reliable and fictitious accounts of sexual abuse to children. *J Interpersonal Violence.* 1987; 2:27–45.

Jones DPH. Dermatitis artefacta in mother and baby as child abuse. *Br J Psychiatry.* 1983; 143:199–200.

Jones JG, Butler HL, Hamilton B, et al. Munchausen syndrome by proxy. *Child Abuse Negl.* 1986; 10:33–40.

Jones VF, Badgett JT, Minella JL, et al. The role of the male caretaker in Munchausen syndrome by proxy. *Clin Pediatr.* 1993; 32:245–7.

Juredini J. Obstetric factitious disorder and Munchausen syndrome by proxy. *J Nerv Mental Dis.* 1993; 181:135–137.

Justus PG, Kreutziger SS, and Kitchens CS. Probing the dynamics of munchausen's syndrome. *Ann Intern Med.* 1980; 93:120–127.

Kahan BB and Yorker BC. Munchausen syndrome by proxy. *J School Health.* 1990; 60:108–110.

———. Munchausen syndrome by proxy: Clinical review and legal issues. *Behav Sci Law.* 1991; 9:73–83.

Kahn G and Goldman E. Munchausen syndrome by proxy: Mother fabricates infant's hearing impairment. *J Speech Hear Res.* 1991; 34:957–959.

Kaissirer JP. Our stubborn quest for diagnostic uncertainty: a cause of excessive testing. *N Engl J Med.* 1989; 320:1489–1491.

Kaminer Y and Robbins DR. Insulin misuse: A review of an overlooked psychiatric problem. *Psychosomatics.* 1989; 30:19–24.

Kaufman KL, Coury D, Pickrel E, et al. Munchausen syndrome by proxy: a survey of professionals' knowledge. *Child Abuse Negl.* 1989; 13:141–147.

Kellerman J. *Devil's Walz.* 1992; New York: Little, Brown.

Kellner CH and Eth S: Code blue-factitious cyanosis. *J Nerv Mental Dis.* 1982; 170:371–372.

Kempe CH: Uncommon manifestations of the battered child syndrome. *Am J Dis Child.* 1975; 129:1265.

Kinscherff R, Famularo R. Extreme Munchausen syndrome by proxy: the case for termination of parental rights. *Juv Fam Court J*. 1991; 41–53.

Koch C and Hoiby N. Severe child abuse presenting as polymicrobial bacteremia. *Acta Pediatr Scand*. 1988; 77:940–943.

Kohl S, Pickering LK, and Dupree E. Child abuse presenting as immunodeficiency disease. *J Pediatr*. 1978; 93:466–468.

Koopman HM and Feenstra J. [Fraud in medicine with the child as victim: munchausen syndrome by proxy—a review of the literature]. *Tijdschr Kindergeneeskunde*. 1988; 56:141–148.

Kovac CS and Toth EL. Factitious diabetes mellitus and spontaneous hypoglycemia. *Diabetes Care*. 1993; 16:1294.

Kravitz RM and Wilmott RW. Munchausen syndrome by proxy presenting as factitious apnea. *Clin Pediatr*. 1990; 29:587–592.

Krener R and Adelman R. Parent salvage and parent sabotage in the care of chronically ill children. *Am J Dis Child*. 1988; 142:945–951.

Ksiazyk J, Socha J, Rujner J, et al. Zespol 'MBP' Jako Szczegolny Przklad Bledu Diagnostycznego [Munchausen syndrome by proxy as an example of diagnostic error]. *Polski Tygodnik Lekarski*. 1990; 45:255–256.

Kurlandsky L, Lukoff JY, Zinkham WH, et al. Munchausen syndrome by proxy: definition of factitious bleeding in an infant by ⁵¹CR labeling of erythrocytes. *Pediatrics*. 1979; 63:228–231.

Labbe J. Self-induced urinary tract infection in boys. *Pediatrics*. 1984; 74:1136 [Letter].

Lacey SR, Cooper C, Runyan DK, et al. Munchausen syndrome by proxy: Patterns of presentation to pediatric surgeons. *J Pediatr Surg*. 1993; 28:827–32.

Lansky LL. An unusual case of childhood chloral hydrate poisoning. *Am J Dis Child*. 1974; 127:275–276.

Lansky SB, Erickson HM. Prevention of child murder. *J Amer Acad Child Psychiatr*. 1974; 13:691–698.

Laws JW. Pyrexia of unusual origin. *Bri Med J*. 1951; 2:157–158.

Lazoritz S. Munchausen by proxy or Meadow's Syndrome? *Lancet*. 1987; 2:631 [Letter].

Lee DA. Munchausen syndrome by proxy in twins. *Arch Dis Child*. 1979; 54:646–647.

Leeder E. Supermom or child abuser? Treatment of the Munchausen mother. *Women and Ther*. 1990; 9:69–88.

Leonard KF and Farrell PA. Munchausen's syndrome by proxy: a little known type of abuse. *Postgrad Med*. 1992; 92:197–204.

Lerman P. [Munchausen syndrome by proxy or polle syndrome]. *Harefuah*. 1986; 110:248–250.

Lesnik-Oberstein M. 'MBP' in de Kindergeneeskunde [Munchausen syndrome by proxy in pediatrics]. *Nederlands Tijdschr Geneeskunde*. 1986; 130–221.

Lesnik-Oberstein M. Munchausen syndrome by proxy. *Child Abuse Negl*. 1986; 10:133 [Letter].

Lewis E. Secret observation of children in hospital. *Lancet*. 1988; 1:998.

Libow JA and Schreier HA. Three forms of factitious illness in children: When is it Munchausen syndrome by proxy? *Am J Orthopsychiat*. 1986; 56:602–611.

Light MJ and Sheridan MS. Munchausen syndrome by proxy and apnea (MBPA). *Clin Pediatr*. 1990; 29:162–168.

Lim LC, Yap HK, and Lim JW. Munchausen syndrome by proxy. *J Singapore Paediatr Soc*. 1991; 33:59–62.

Lipsitt DR. The factitious patient who sues. *Am J Psychiatry*. 1986; 143:1482 [Letter].

Liston TE, Levine PL, Anderson C. Polymicrobial bacteremia due to Polle Syndrome: The child abuse variant of Munchausen by proxy. *Pediatrics*. 1983; 72:211–213.

Livingston R. Maternal somatization disorder and Munchausen syndrome by proxy. *Psychosomatics*. 1987; 28:213–214, 217.

Lopez-Linares M: Sindrome de Munchausen Infantil [Childhood Munchausen syndrome]. *An Esp Pediatr*. 1986; 25:225–226.

Lorber J. Unexplained episodes of coma in a 2 year old. *Lancet*. 1978; 2:472–473.

Lorber J, Reckless JPD, and Watson JBG. Nonaccidental poisoning: the elusive diagnosis. *Arch Dis Child*. 1980; 55:643–647.

Loredo-Abdala A, Sierra-G de Quevado JJ, Oldak-Skvirsky D, et al. Sindrome de Munchausen en ninos: Informe de dos casos [Munchausen syndrome in children: Report of 2 cases]. *Bol Med Hosp Mexico*. 1991; 48:121–125.

Luce JM. The legacy of Baron Munchausen. *Pharos*. 1978; 41:19–23.

Ludwig J and Mann RJ. Münchhausen versus munchausen. *Mayo Clin Proc*. 1983; 58:767–769.

Lund CA and Gardiner AQ. The gaslight phenomenon—an institutional variant. *Br J Psychiatry*. 1977; 131:533–534.

Lunn J. Implications of the Allitt inquiry. *Br J Nurs*. 1994; 3:201–202 [Editorial].

Lyall EG, Stirling HF, Crofton PM, et al. Albuminuric growth failure. A case of Munchausen syndrome by proxy. *Acta Pediatr*. 1992; 81:373–376.

Lyons G. Munchausen syndrome by proxy. *New Law J*. July 9, 1993.

Macdonald HA. Munchausen syndrome by proxy. *N Z Med J*. 1993; Jul 14; 106:292 [Letter].

MacDonald TM. Myalgic encephalomyelitis by proxy. *Br Med J*. 1989; 299: 1030–1031.

MacNeal WJ. Hyperthermia, genuine and spurious. *Arch Int Med*. 1939; 64: 800–808.

Magnay AR, Debelle G, Proops DW, et al. Munchausen syndrome by proxy unmasked by nasal signs. *J Laryngol Otol*. 1994; 108:336–338.

Mahesh VK, Stern HP, Kearns GL, et al. Application of pharmacokinetics in the diagnosis of chemical abuse in Munchausen syndrome by proxy. Clin Pediatr 1988: 27:243–246.

Makar AF and Squier PJ. Munchausen syndrome by proxy: father as a perpetrator. *Pediatrics*. 1990; 85:370–373.

Malatack JJ, Wiener ES, Gartner JC Jr, et al. Munchausen syndrome by proxy: A new complication of central venous catherization. *Pediatrics*. 1985; 75:523–525.

Manning SC, Casselbrant M, and Lammers D. Otolaryngologic manifestations of child abuse. *Int J Pediatr Otorhinlaryngol.* 1990; 20:7–16.

Manthei DJ, Pierce RL, Rothbaum RJ, et al. Munchausen syndrome by proxy: Covert child abuse. *J Fam Viol.* 1988; 3:131–140.

Marcovitch H. Inexplicable pulmonary oedema. *Br Med J.* 1989; 298:1383 [Letter].

Markantonakis A. Munchausen's syndrome by proxy. *Br J Psychiatry.* 1989; 155:130–131.

Maslanka AM; Scott SK: LSD overdose in an eight-month-old-boy. *J Emerg Med.* 1992; 10:481–3.

Masterson J, Dunworth R, Williams N. Extreme illness exaggeration in pediatric patients: A variant of Munchausen's by proxy? *Am J Orthopsychiatr.* 1988; 58:188–195.

Masterson J and Wilson J. Factitious illness in children: The social worker's role in identifiaction and management. *Social Work Health Care.* 1987; 12:21–30.

Mayefsky JH, Sarnaik AP, and Postellon DC. Factitous hypoglycemia. *Pediatrics.* 1982; 69:804–805.

McClung HJ. Prolonged fever of unknown origin in children. *Amer J Dis Child.* 1972; 124:544–550.

McClung HJ, Murray R, Braden NJ, et al. Intentional ipecac poisoning in children. *Am J Dis Child.* 1988; 142:637–639.

McDowell HP and Fielding DW. Traumatic perforation of the hypopharynx—an unusual form of abuse. *Arch Dis Child.* 1984; 59:888–889.

McGuire TL and Feldman KW. Psychologic morbidity of children subjected to Munchausen syndrome by proxy. *Pediatrics.* 1989; 83:289–292.

McKinlay I. Munchausen's syndrome. *Br Med J.* 1986; 293:1308 [Letter].

McSweeney JJ and Hoffman RP. Munchausen's syndrome by proxy mistaken for IDDM. *Diabetes Care.* 1991; 14:928–929 [Letter].

Meadow R. Munchausen syndrome by proxy: the hinterland of child abuse. *Lancet.* 1977; 2:343–345.

———. Munchausen syndrome by proxy. *Arch Dis Child.* 1982; 57:92–98.

———. Munchausen syndrome by proxy and pseudo-epilepsy. *Arch Dis Child.* 1982; 57:811–812.

———. Factitious illness—the hinterland of child abuse. In: Meadow R (ed). *Recent Advances in Paediatrics.* No 7. 1984; Edinburgh: Churchill Livingstone.

———. Fictitious epilepsy. *Lancet.* 1984; 2:25–28.

———. Munchausen by proxy and brain damage. *Dev Med Child Neurol.* 1984; 26:669–676.

———. Management of Munchausen syndrome by proxy. *Arch Dis Child.* 1985; 60:385–393.

———. Video recording and child abuse. *Br Med J.* 1987; 294:1629–1630.

———. ABC of Child Abuse: Poisoning. *Br Med J.* 1989; 298:1445–1446.

———. ABC of Child Abuse: Suffocation. *Br Med J.* 1989; 298:1572–1573.

———. Suffocation, recurrent apnea, and sudden infant death. *J Pediatr.* 1990; 117:351–357.

———. Neurological and developmental variants of munchausen syndrome by proxy. *Dev Med Child Neurol.* 1991; 33:270–272.

————. False allegations of abuse and Munchausen syndrome by proxy. *Arch Dis Child.* 1993; 68:444–447.

————. Non-accidental salt poisoning. *Arch Dis Child.* 1993; 68:448–452.

————. (ed). *ABC of Child Abuse.* 1989; London?: British Medical Journal Press.

Meadow R and Lennert T. Munchausen by proxy or polle syndrome: which term is correct? *Pediatrics.* 1984; 74:554–556.

Mechanic D. The concept of illness behavior. *J Chron Dis.* 1961; 15:189–194.

Mehl AL, Coble L, and Johnson S. Munchausen syndrome by proxy: a family affair. *Child Abuse Negl.* 1990; 14:577–585.

Mehta P and Bussing R. Factitious coagulopathy due to munchausen syndrome by proxy. *Am J Pediatr Hematol Oncol.* 1993; 15:124–5 [Editorial].

Mercer SO and Perdue JD. Munchausen syndrome by proxy: Social work's role. *Social Work.* 1993; 38:74–81.

Metz ME. De munchhausen-moder. Het munchhausen-syndroom by proxy en de relatie met de nagebootste stoornissen [The munchausen mother: Munchausen syndrome by proxy]. *Tijdschr Psychiatrie.* 1989; 31:574–586.

Mills RW and Burke S. Gastrointestinal bleeding in a 15 month old male: A presentation of munchausen's syndrome by proxy. *Clin Pediatr.* 1990; 29:474–477.

Minford AMB: Child abuse presenting as apparent "near miss" sudden infant death syndrome. *Br Med J.* 1981; 282:521.

Mitchell I, Brummitt J, and DeForest J. Apnea and Munchausen's syndrome by proxy. *Pediatr Pulmonol.* 1987; 3:457 [Abstract].

Mitchell I, Brummitt J, DeForest J, et al. Apnea and factitious illness (Munchausen's syndrome) by proxy. *Pediatrics.* 1993; 92:810–814.

Money J: Munchausen's syndrome by proxy: Update. *J Pediatr Psychol.* 1986; 11:583–584.

————. Paleodigms and paleodigmatics: a new theoretical construct applicable to Munchausen's syndrome by proxy, child-abuse dwarfism, paraphilias, anorexia nervosa, and other syndromes. *Am J Psychother.* 1989; 43:15–24.

Money J, Annecillo C, and Hutchison JW. Forensic and family psychiatry in abuse dwarfism: Munchausen's syndrome by proxy, atonement, and addiction to abuse. *J Sex Marital Ther.* 1985; 11:30–40.

Money J and Werlwas J: Folie a deux in the parents of psychosocial dwarfs: two cases. *Bull Am Acad Psychiatr Law.* 1976; 4:351–361.

Moore K and Reed D. *Deadly Medicine.* 1988; New York: St. Martin's.

Morgan B. Covert surveillance in Munchausen's syndrome by proxy. *Br Med J.* 1994; 308:1715–1716 [Letter].

————. Spying on mothers. *Lancet.* 1994; 344:132 [Letter].

Morgan MEI, Manning DJ, Williams WJ, et al. Fictitious epilepsy. *Lancet.* 1984; 2:232–233.

Morley C. Diagnosis of recurrent suffocation of children. *Lancet.* 1992; 340:481 [Letter].

Morley CJ: Experts differ over diagnostic criteria for Munchausen syndrome by proxy. *Br J Hosp Med.* 1992; 48:197–8 [Letter].

Morris B. Child abuse manifested as factitious apnea. *South Med J.* 1985; 78:1013–1014.

Morris M. Munchausen's syndrome and factitious illness. *Current Opinion Psychiatry.* 1992; 4:225–230.

Morris TM and Reay HA. A battered baby with pharyngeal atresia. *J Laryngol Otol.* 1971; 85:729–731.

Morrow PL. Caffeine toxicity: A case of child abuse by drug ingestion. *J Forensic Sci.* 1987; 32:1801–1805.

My sister-in-law was starving her baby. *Good Housekeeping.* 1991; 213:26, 28–29 (October).

Nading JH and Duval-Arnould B. Factitious diabetes mellitus confirmed by ascorbic acid. *Arch Dis Child.* 1984; 59:166–7.

Neale B, Bools C, and Meadow R. Problems in the assessment and management of Munchausen syndrome by proxy abuse. *Child Society.* 1991; 5:324–333.

Ney PG, Moore C, McPhee J, et al. Child abuse: A study of the child's perspective. *Child Abuse Negl.* 1986; 10:511–518.

Nicol AR and Eccles M. Psychotherapy for Munchausen syndrome by proxy. *Arch Dis Child.* 1985; 60:344–348.

Obiako MN. Eardrum perforation as evidence of child abuse. *Child Abuse Negl.* 1987; 11:149–151.

Oppenoorth WH. Behandeling vn het Munchhausen syndroom "by proxy" met klinisch psychiatrische gezinsbehandeling en hypnotherapie: Een gevalsbeschrijving [Treatment of Munchausen syndrome by proxy with clinical psychiatric family therapy and hypnotherapy: a case description]. *Tijdschr Psychotherapie.* 1992; 18:12–21.

O'Reilly R and Aggeler PM. Overt anticoagulant ingestion: study of 25 patients and review of world literature. *Medicine.* 1976; 55:389–399.

Orenstein DM and Wasserman AL. Munchausen Syndrome by proxy simulating cystic fibrosis. *Pediatrics.* 1986; 78:621–624.

Orme R. Imposed upper airway obstruction in small children. *Arch Dis Child.* 1992; 67:663——(p 663 only—this is a letter).

Orr DP, Golden M. Surreptitious insulin administration: is it an iatrogenic syndrome? *Am J Dis Child.* 1987; 141:830–832 [Letter].

Orton CI. Loss of columella and septum from an unusual form of child abuse. *Plast Reconstr Surg.* 1975; 56:345–348.

Osborne JP. Non-accidental poisoning and child abuse. *Br Med J.* 1976; 1:1211. (Letter).

O'Shea B. Meadow's syndrome. *Irish J Psychother.* 1987; 4:6–8.

Outwater KM, Lipnick RN, Luban NL, et al. Factitious hematuria: diagnosis by minor blood group typing. *J Pediatr.* 1981; 98:95–97.

Overholser JC. Differential diagnosis of malingering and factitious disorder with physical symptoms. *Behavioral Sci Law.* 1990; 8:55–65.

Palmer AJ and Yoshimura GJ. Munchausen syndrome by proxy. *J Am Acad Child Psychiatry.* 1984; 23:503–508.

Pankrantz L. Historical note on pseudoseizures. *Neurology.* 1989; 39:750 [Letter].

Parker G and Barrett E. Factitious patients with factitious disorders: a note on munchausen's syndrome. *Med J Aust.* 1991; 16:155–772.

Pearson DJ. Pseudo food allergy. *Br Med J.* 1986; 292:221–222.

Pickel S, Anderson C, and Holliday MA. Thirsting and hypernatrimic dehydration—a form of child abuse. *Pediatrics*. 1970; 45:54–59.

Pickering D. Salicylate poisoning: the diagnosis when its possibility is denied by the parents. *Acta Paediatr Scand*. 1964; 53:501–504.

Pickering D, Mondrieff M, and Etches PC. Non-accidental poisoning and child abuse. *Br Med J*. 1976; 1:1210–1211.

Pickering LK, Kohl S. Munchausen syndrome by proxy. *Am J Dis Child*. 1981; 135:288–289.

Pickford E, Buchanan N, and McLaughlan S. Munchausen syndrome by proxy: a family anthology. *Med J Aust*. 1988; 148:646–650.

Plum HJ. Munchausen syndrome by proxy. In: Sheridan, MS (ed). *Proceedings of the 1992 Summer Meeting*. 1993; Waianae, Hawaii: National Association of Apnea Professionals.

Porter GE, Heitsch GM, and Miller MM. Munchausen syndrome by proxy. *Med J Aust*. 1993; 158:720 [letter].

Praakken A B, Den-Hartog L, and Weelkens JJ. [A new variant of munchausen's syndrome by proxy: the father in an active role.] *Tijdschr Kindergeneeskd*. 1991; 59:91–94.

Priestley BL, Harrison CJ, Gerrard MP, et al. Paediatrics—Part II. *Postgrad Med J*. 1993; 69:268–81.

Proesmans W, Sina J, Debucquoy P, et al. Recurrent acute renal failure due to non-accidental poisoning with glafenin in a child. *Clin Nephrol*. 1981; 16:207–210.

Raff MJ, Stodghill WB, and Roy TM. Fraudulent feculent fever in a female fabulist. *South Med J*. 1975; 68:360–362.

Rahilly PM. The pneumographic and medical investigation of infants suffering apparent life threatening episodes. *J Paediatr Child Health*. 1991; 27:349–353.

Rand DC. Munchausen syndrome by proxy: integration of classic and contempory types. *Issues Child Abuse Accusations*. 1990; 2:83–89.

Rappaport SR and Hochstadt NJ. Munchausen syndrome by proxy (MBSP): An intergenerational perspective. *J Mental Health Couns*. 1993; 15:278–289.

Raspe RE. *The Adventures of Baron Munchausen*. 1969; New York: Pantheon.

Raymond CA. Munchausen's may occur in younger persons. *JAMA*. 1987; 257:3332.

Read NW, Krejs GJ, Read MG, et al. Chronic diarrhea of unknown origin. *Gastroent*. 1980; 78:264–271.

Reece RM. Unusual manifestations of child abuse. *Pediatr Clin N Am*. 1990; 37:905–921.

———. Fatal child abuse and sudden infant death syndrome: A critical diagnostic decision. *Pediatrics*. 1993; 91:423–429.

Rendle-Short J. Non-accidental barbiturate poisoning of children. *Lancet*. 1978; 2:1212.

Richardson GF. Munchausen syndrome by proxy. *Am Fam Physician*. 1987; 36:119–123.

Robbins KB, and Sheridan MS. A case of Munchausen syndrome by proxy in a pediatric tourist. *Proc Straub Foundation.* 1994; 58:53–55.

Robins PM, Sesan R. Munchausen syndrome by proxy: Another women's disorder. *Prof Psychol Res Practice.* 1991; 22:285–290.

Rogers D, Tripp J, Bentovim A, et al. Non-accidental poisoning: An extended syndrome of child abuse. *Br Med J.* 1976; 1:793–796.

Rosen CL, Frost JD, Bricker T, et al. Two siblings with recurrent cardiorespiratory arrest: Munchausen syndrome by proxy or child abuse? *Pediatrics.* 1983; 71:715–720.

Rosen CL, Frost JD Jr, and Glaze DG: Child abuse and recurrent infant apnea. *J Pediatr.* 1986; 109:1065–1067.

Rosenberg DA. Web of deceit: a literature review of munchausen syndrome by proxy. *Child Abuse Negl.* 1987; 11:547–563.

———. Web of deceit. *Child Abuse Negl.* 1990; 14:290 [Letter].

———. Munchausen syndrome by proxy. in Reece R, ed. *Child Abuse: Medical Diagnosis and Management.* 1994; Philadelphia: Lea and Febiger.

Roth D. How "mild" is "mild" Munchausen syndrome by proxy? *Isr J Psychiatry Relat Sci.* 1990; 27:160–167.

Roueche B. Annals of medicine: the dinosaur collection. *New Yorker.* May 12, 1986; 102–111.

Rubin LG, Angelides A, Davidson M, et al. Recurrent sepsis and gastrointestinal ulceration due to child abuse. *Arch Dis Child.* 1986; 61:903–905.

Rumans LW and Vosti KL. Factitious and fraudulent fever. *Am J Med.* 1978; 65:745–755.

Sadler JZ. Ethical and management considerations in factitious illness: One and the same. *Gen Hosp Psychiatry.* 1987; 9:31–39.

Salinger S. A case of malignant recurring nasal hemorrhage of undetermined etiology. *Ann Oto Rhino Laryngol.* 1944; 53:583–588.

Salmon RF, Arant BS Jr, Baum MG, et al. Factitious hematuria with underlying renal abnormalities. *Pediatrics.* 1988; 82:377–379.

Samuels MP, McClaughlin W, Jacobson RR, et al. Fourteen cases of imposed upper airway obstruction. *Arch Dis Child.* 1992; 67:162–170.

Samuels MP, Poets CF, Noyes JP, et al. Diagnosis and management after life threatening events in infants and young children who received cardiopulmonary resuscitation. *Br Med J.* 1993; 306:489–92.

Samuels MP and Southall DP. Munchausen syndrome by proxy. *Br J Hosp Med.* 1992; 47:759–762.

———. Covert surveillance in Munchausen's syndrome by proxy. Welfare of the child must come first. *Br Med J.* 1994; 308:1101–1102 [Letter].

Sapira JD. Munchausen's syndrome and the technological imperative. *South Med J.* 1981; 74:193–196.

Saulsbury FT, Chobanian MC, and Wilson WG. Child abuse: Parenteral hydrocarbon administration. *Pediatrics.* 1984; 73:719–722.

Savard G, Andermann F, and Teitelbaum J. Epileptic Munchausen's syndrome: A form of pseudoseizures distinct from hysteria and malingering. *Neurology.* 1988; 38:1628–1629.

Schneider R, Klosinski G. Travellers in five worlds: adolescents with ganser's syndrome. *Acta Paedopsychiatr.* 1989; 52:150–155.

Schnur S. Malingering responsible for long-continued, unexplained fever. *South Med J.* 1940; 33:768–769.

Schreier HA: The perversion of mothering: Munchausen syndrome by proxy. *Bull Menninger Clin* 1992; 56:421–437.

Schreier HA and Libow JA. *Hurting for Love, Munchausen by Proxy Syndrome.* 1993; New York: Guilford Press.

———. Munchausen syndrome by proxy: diagnosis and prevalence. *Am J Orthopsychiatry.* 1993; 63:318–21.

Schreier HA and Libow JA. Munchausen by proxy syndrome: A clinical fable of our times. *J Am Acad Child Adolesc Psychiatry.* 1994;33:904–905.

Sears HF. The effort to drive the other person crazy—an element in the etiology and psychotheraphy of schizophrenia. *Br J Med Psychol* 1959; 32:1–18.

Senner A and Ott MJ. Munchausen syndrome by proxy. *Issues Compr Ped Nurs.* 1989; 12:345–357.

Shafer N and Shafer R. Factitious diseases including Munchausen's syndrome. *NY State J Med.* 1980; 80:594–604.

Shaner A and Eth S. Pseudoadolescent Munchausen syndrome. *Comp Psychiatry.* 1988; 29:561–565.

Shaywitz BA, Siegel NJ, and Pearson HA. Megavitamins for minimal brain dysfunction: a potentially dangerous therapy. *J Am Med Assn.* 1977; 238:1749–1750.

Shehadeh N, Benderly A, Erde P, et al. Factitious hyponatremia in a child. *Am J Dis Child.* 1984; 138:1085–only (Letter).

Sheldon SH. Munchausen syndrome by proxy. *Pediatrics.* 1985; 76:855–856.

Sheridan MS. Munchausen syndrome by proxy. *Health Soc Work.* 1989; 14:53–58.

———. Parents' reporting of symptoms in their children: Physicians' perceptions. *Hawaii Med J.* 1994; 53:216–217, 221–222.

———. Response to symptoms and use of medication: a survey. *Proc Straub Fdn.* 1994; 58:10–12.

Shnaps Y, Frand M, Rotem Y, et al. The chemically abused child. *Pediatrics.* 1981; 68:119–121.

Sigal MD, Altmark D, and Carmel I. Munchausen syndrome by adult proxy: A perpetrator abusing two adults. *J Nerv Ment Dis.* 1986; 174:696–698.

Sigal M, Altmark D, Gelkopf M. Munchausen syndrome by adult proxy revisited. *Isr J Psychiatry Relat Sci.* 1991; 28:33–36.

Sigal M, Carmel I, Altmark D, et al. Munchausen syndrome by proxy: A psychodynamic analysis. *Med Law.* 1988; 17:49–56.

Sigal M, Gelkopf M, and Levertov G. Medical and legal aspects of the munchausen by proxy perpetrator. *Med Law.* 1990; 9:739–749.

Sigal M, Gelkopf M, Meadow RS [sic]. Munchausen by proxy syndrome: The triad of abuse, self-abuse, and deception. *Compr Psychiatry*. 1989; 30:527–533.

Simon FA. Uncommon type of child abuse. *J Pediatr*. 1980; 96:785-only (Letter).

Single T and Henry LH. An unusual case of Munchausen syndrome by proxy. *Aust N Z J Psychiatr*. 1991; 25:422–425.

Smith CG and Sinanan K. The "gaslight" phenomenon reappears. A modification of the Ganser syndrome. *Br J Psychiatry*. 1972; 120:685–686.

Smith NJ and Ardern MH. More in sickness than in health: a case study of Munchausen by proxy in the elderly. *J Fam Therapy*. 1989; 11:321–334.

Smith K and Killam P. Munchausen syndrome by proxy. *MCN AM J Matern Child Nurs*. 1994; 19:214–221.

Sneed RC. Breed [Sneed] or Meadow?—Munchausen or Münchhausen? *Pediatrics*. 1989; 83:1078 [Letter, erratum appears in *Pediatrics* 84:582].

Sneed RC, Bell RF. The dauphin of Munchausen: Factitious passage of renal stones in a child. *Pediatrics*. 1976; 58:127–129.

Sofinowski RE and Butler PM. Munchausen syndrome by proxy: a review. *Texas Med*. 1991; 87:66–69.

Souid AK, Korins K. Keith D, et al. Unexplained menorrhagia and hematuria: a case report of Munchausen's syndrome by proxy. *Pediatr Hematol Oncol*. 1993; 10:245–248.

Southall DP, Samuels MP, and Stebbens VA. Suffocation and sudden infant death syndrome. *Br Med J*. 1989; 299:178.

Southall DP, Stebbens VA, Rees SV, et al: Apnoeic episodes induced by smothering: Two cases identified by covert video surveillance. *Br Med J*. 1987; 294:1637–1641.

Spiro HR. Chronic factitious illness: Munchausen's syndrome. *Arch Gen Psychiatry*. 1968; 18:569–579.

Spying on mothers. *Lancet*. 343:1373–1374 [Editorial].

Stankler L. Factitious skin lesions in a mother and two sons. *Br J Dermatol*. 1977; 97:217–219.

Stephenson T. Beyond belief. *Law Soc Gazette*. June 23, 1993:28–29.

Stevenson RD and Alexander R. Munchausen syndrome by proxy presenting as a developmental disability. *J Dev Behav Pediatr*. 1990; 11:262–264.

Stiehm ER. The psychologic fallout from Chernobyl. *Am J Dis Child*. 1992; 146:761-2.

Steinschneider A. Prolonged apnea and the sudden infant death syndrome: Clinical and laboratory observations. *Pediatrics*. 1972; 50:646–654. [Ed note: this article does not discuss MBP per se, but in 1994 a mother whose children are discussed in this article confessed, then recanted, to inducing apnea.]

Stone FB. Munchausen-by-proxy syndrome: an unusual form of child abuse. *J Contemp Social Work*. April 1989; 243–246.

Strassburg HM, Peuckert W. Not "Polle syndrome," please. *Lancet*. 1984; 1:166 [Letter].

Sugar JA, Belfer M, Israel E, et al. A 3-year-old boy's chronic diarrhea and unexplained death. *J Am Acad Child Adolesc Psychiatry*. 1991; 30:1015-21.

Sullivan CA, Francis GL, Bain MW, et al. Munchausen syndrome by proxy: 1990: a portent for problems? *Clin Pediatr.* 1991; 30:112–116.

Sutphen JL and Saulsbury FT. Intentional ipecac poisoning: Munchausen syndrome by proxy. *Pediatrics.* 1986; 82:453–456.

Taylor D and Bentovim A. Recurrent nonaccidentally inflicted chemical eye injuries to siblings. *J Pediatr Ophthalmol.* 1976; 13:238–242.

Taylor S and Hyler SE. Update on factitious disorders. *Int J Psychiatry Med.* 1993; 23:81–94.

Tenney G. Covert surveillance in Munchausen syndrome by proxy: an infringement of human rights. *Br Med J.* 1994; 308:1100–1101.

Thach BT. Sudden infant death syndrome: old causes rediscovered? *N Eng J Med.* 1986; 315:126–128 [Editorial].

Thoennes N and Tjaden P. The extent, nature and validity of sexual abuse allegations in custody/visitation disputes. *Child Abuse Neglect.* 1990; 14:151–163.

Tojo A, Nanba S, Kimura K, et al. Factitious proteinuria in a young girl. *Clinical Nephrology.* 1990; 33:299–302.

Toro J, Martinez A, Guimera ME, et al. Un case de "syndrome de polle" or "sindrome de Munchhausen porpoderes" [A case of polle syndrome or munchausen syndrome by proxy]. *Rev Depart Psiquiatr Facultad Med Barcelona.* 1986; 13:147–152.

Towbin A. Sudden infant death (cot death) related to spinal injury. *Lancet.* 1967; 1:940.

Tucker LE, Hayes JR, Viteri AL, et al. Factitial bleeding: Successful management with psychotherapy. *Dig Dis Sci.* 1979; 24:570–572.

Turk LJ, Hanrahan KM, and Weber ER. Munchausen syndrome by proxy: a nursing overview. *Issues Comp Pediatr Nurs.* 1990; 13:279–288.

Tyndal M. The "gaslight phenomenon." *Br J Psychiatry.* 1973; 122:367–338 [Letter].

Vaisrub S. Baron munchausen and the abused child. *JAMA.* 1977; 238:2265 [Editorial].

Verity CM, Winckworth C, Burman D, et al. Polle syndrome: children of Munchausen. *Br Med J.* 1979; 2:422–423.

Volk D. Factitious diarrhea in two children. *Am J Dis Child.* 1982; 136:1027 [Letter].

Waller DA. Obstacles to the treatment of Munchausen by proxy syndrome. *J Am Acad Child Psychiatry.* 1983; 22:80–85.

Waring WW. The persistent parent. *Am J Dis Child.* 1992; 146:753–756.

Warner JO and Hathaway MJ. Allergic form of Meadow's syndrome (Munchausen by proxy). *Arch Dis Child.* 1984; 59:151–156.

Watson JB, Davies JM, and Hunter JL. Nonaccidental poisoning in childhood. *Arch Dis Child.* 1979; 54:143–144.

Weber S. Munchausen syndrome by proxy. *J Pediatr Nurs.* 1987; 2:50–54.

Welliver JR. Unusual injuries. In: Ludwig S, Kornberg AE, eds. *Child Abuse: A Medical Reference,* 2nd ed. 1992; New York: Churchill Livingstone.

Wells LA. Varieties of imposture. *Perspectives Biol Med.* 1986; 29:588–610.

Wheatley R. Covert surveillance in Munchausen's syndrome by proxy. Clinical investigation, not research activity. *Br Med J.* 1994; 308:1101 [Letter].

Wheeler RA, Ade-Ajayi N, and Kiely EM. Covert surveillance in Munchausen's syndrome by proxy. At risk children may present to surgeons. *Br Med J.* 1994; 308:1101 [Letter].

White ST, Voter K, and Perry J. Sureptitious warfarin ingestion. *Child Abuse Negl.* 1985; 9:349–352.

Willging JP, Bower CM, and Cotton RT. Physical abuse of children. A retrospective review and an otolaryngology perspective. *Arch Otolaryngol Head Neck Surg.* 1992; 118:584–90.

Williams C. Munchausen syndrome by proxy: a bizarre form of child abuse. *Family Law.* 1986; 16:32–34.

Williams C and Bevan VT. The secret observation of children in hospital. *Lancet.* 1988; 2:780–781.

Wood PR, Fowlkes J, Holden P, et al. Fever of unknown origin for six years: Munchausen syndrome by proxy. *J Fam Pract.* 1989; 28:391–395.

Woody RC and Jones JG. Neurologic Munchausen-by-proxy syndrome. *South Med J.* 1987; 80:247–248.

Woollcott P Jr, Aceto T Jr, Rutt C, et al. Doctor shopping with the child as proxy patient: A variant of child abuse. *J Pediatr.* 1982; 101:297–301.

Wyllie E, Friedman D, Rothner AD, et al. Psychogenic seizures in children and adolescents: Outcome after diagnosis by ictal video and electroencephalographic recording. *Pediatrics.* 1990; 85:480–484.

Yeatman GW, Shaw C, Barlow MJ, et al. Pseudobattering in Vietnamese children. *Pediatrics.* 1976; 58:616–618.

Yomtovian R and Swanger R. Munchausen syndrome by proxy documented by discrepant blood typing. *Am J Clin Pathol.* 1991; 95:232–233.

Yorker BC and Kahan BB. Munchausen syndrome by proxy as a form of child abuse. *Arch Psychiatr Nurs.* 1990; 4:313–318.

———. The Munchausen syndrome by proxy variant of child abuse in the family courts. *Juv Family Court J.* 1991; 42:51–57.

Yudkin S: Six children with coughs: The second diagnosis. *Lancet.* 1961; 2:561–563.

Zitelli BJ, Seltman MF, and Shannon RM. Munchausen's syndrome by proxy and its professional participants. *Am J Dis Child.* 1987; 141:1099–1102.

Zohar Y, Avidan G, Shvili Y, et al. Otolaryngologic cases of Munchausen's syndrome. *Laryngoscope.* 1987; 97:201–203.

Index

About the Contributors

Randell Alexander, M.D., is Associate Professor of Pediatrics and on the staff of the Division of Disabilities at the University of Iowa. He is on the Boards of the American Professional Society on Abuse of Children (APSAC) and the National Committee to Prevent Child Abuse, and is a member of the U.S. Advisory Board on Child Abuse and Neglect. He co-chairs the child fatality review committee for the Iowa Department of Human Services, and chairs the Governor of Iowa's Advisory Board on Child Abuse and Neglect.

David Altmark, M.D., is Head, Psychiatric Emergency Unit, Lev Hasharon Mental Health Medical Center, Netania, Israel.

Stephen J. Boros, M.D., was Director of Neonatology and Medical Director of the Infant Apnea Program, Children's Hospital, St. Paul, Minnesota. He was the author of several articles about Munchausen Syndrome by Proxy, a cause to which he was devoted. His chapter for this book was his last completed manuscript prior to his death in 1994.

Joseph M. Campos, Ph.D., is Director, Microbiology Laboratory and Director, Laboratory Informatics, Children's National Medical Center, Washington, DC. and Professor of Pediatrics, Pathology, and Microbiology at George Washington University Medical Center.

Cindy Christian, M.D., is Assistant Professor, Department of Pediatrics, University of Pennsylvania School of Medicine; Medical Director, Child Abuse Services, Children's Hospital of Philadelphia; and Consulting Pediatrician, SCAN, Inc., Philadelphia.

Emil Chuang, M.D., was, when this chapter was written, Fellow in Pediatric Gastroenterology and Nutrition at Children's Hospital, Philadelphia.

Martin A. Finkel, DO, FACOP, is Medical Director and Founder of the Center for Children's Support, Stratford, NJ. He is Associate Clinical Professor of Pediatrics and Acting Chair, Department of Pediatrics, School of Osteopathic Medicine, University of Medicine and Dentistry of New Jersey. He co-chairs the Governor's Task Force on Child Abuse and Neglect in New Jersey.

Geoff C. Fisher, M.B., MRC Psych, FRCP(C), is a psychiatrist, Alberta Children's Hospital, Calgary, and author of articles about Munchausen Syndrome by Proxy and speculations on the role and nature of child psychiatry.

Lori D. Frasier, M.D., is an associate in the Department of Pediatrics, University of Iowa College of Medicine. She specializes in pediatrics and in the evaluation of abused and neglected children.

Judith A. Henslee, LMSW, is co-founder and Program Coordinator, Southwest SIDS Research Institute, Brazosport Memorial Hospital, Lake Jackson, Texas.

Fred Henretig, M.D., is Director of Clinical Toxicology, Children's Hospital of Philadelphia, and Medical Director of the Poison Control Center of Philadelphia. He is Associate Professor of Pediatrics at the University of Pennsylvania School of Medicine.

Dirk Huyer, M.D., is a physician with the Suspected Child Abuse and Neglect (SCAN) Program at the Hospital for Sick Children, Toronto, Ont. He has extensive experience in various aspects of child abuse including MBP.

Charles F. Johnson, M.D., is the director of the Child Abuse Program (a "Center of Excellence") at Children's Hospital, Columbus, OH. He is also a professor of Pediatrics at the Ohio State University College of Medicine. The author of multiple publications, he is editor of SCAN, the newsletter of the Section on Child Abuse, and a member of the Committee on Child Abuse of the American Academy of Pediatrics.

Michael J. Light, M.B., MRCP(UK), is Professor of Pediatrics and Chief of Pediatric Pulmonary, University of California at San Diego.

Stephen Ludwig, M.D., is Chief of the Division of General Pediatrics, Children's Hospital of Philadelphia, and Professor of Pediatrics at the University of Pennsylvania School of Medicine. He is Educational Consultant for SCAN, Inc., a long-term service delivery program in Philadelphia for abused and neglected children. He also edits *Child Abuse and Neglect: A Medical Reference.*

Daune L. MacGregor, M.D., FRCP, is Director of the Developmental Evaluation Unit and a staff neurologist at the Hospital for Sick Children, Toronto, and Associate Professor of pediatrics at the University of Toronto. She has studied neurodevelopmental assessment at the Hospital for Sick Children, London, and studied the multidisciplinary approach to children with special needs in Boston.

Marcellina Mian, M.D., is a pediatrician, and director of the Suspected Child Abuse and Neglect (SCAN) Program at the Hospital for Sick Children, Toronto, Ont. She is Associate Professor of Pediatrics at the University of Toronto, has been active in the field of child abuse for many years, and is a recognized expert in the identification and management of suspected victims and their families.

Roy Meadow, B.M., FRCP, is Professor and Head of the Department of Paediatrics and Child Health at St. James's University Hospital, Leeds. England. A pediatric nephrologist by training, he is the world's foremost authority on Munchausen Syndrome by Proxy. He is president of the British Paediatric Association.

Ian Mitchell, MBChB, FRCP(C), FCCP, is Professor of Pediatrics, The University of Calgary, and Vice President, Medical Services, Alberta Children's Hospital. He is a specialist in pediatric respiratory medicine with a special interest in apnea, Sudden Infant Death Syndrome, and MBP.

Barbara M. Ostfeld, Ph.D., is Director of Pediatric Psychology, St. Peter's Medical Center, and Associate Professor of Pediatrics and Psychiatry, University of Medicine and Dentistry of New Jersey, Robert Wood Johnson Medical School, New Brunswick, NJ.

Joseph M. Pape, Jr., MSSA, LSW, is Intake Caseworker IV, Trumbull County Children Services Board, Warren, OH.

David A. Piccoli, M.D., is Section Chief of Gastroenterology and Hepatology, Children's Hospital of Philadelphia, and Associate Professor of Pediatrics at the University of Pennsylvania School of Medicine. He has published extensively.

Henry J. Plum, J.D., is an attorney in private practice, Wauwatosa, Wisconsin, and a former prosecutor. He lectures and consults widely on Munchausen Syndrome by Proxy.

Donna Rosenberg, M.D., is Assistant Professor of Pediatrics, University of Colorado (Denver), and a forensic pediatrician with the Colorado Child Fatality Review Team.

Toni Seidl, R.N., ACSW, is Social Work Supervisor and Child Abuse/Sexual Abuse Coordinator at Children's Hospital of Philadelphia. She is Clinical Associate Professor at the University of Pennsylvania School of Medicine, and a member of the Field Cabinet of the University of Pennsylvania School of Social Work.

Jack R. Shepherd is Detective First Lieutenant with the Michigan Department of State Police.

Mircea Sigal, M.D., is Director, Lev Hasharon Mental Health Medical Center, Netania, Israel, and Professor, Newport University, California.

Pamela J. Stading, R.N., MPH, is Clinical Nurse Specialist, Infant Apnea Program, Children's Hospital of St. Paul, MN. She has been involved with the development of clinical pathways for inpatient management of apnea-related diagnoses and Munchausen Syndrome by Proxy.

About the Editors

ALEX V. LEVIN, M.D., FAAP, FAAO, FRCSC, is a pediatrician and pediatric ophthalmologist, having completed a residency in pediatrics at the Children's Hospital of Philadelphia, a residency in ophthalmology at Wills Eye Hospital in Philadelphia, and a Fellowship in pediatric ophthalmology at The Hospital for Sick Children in Toronto. He was a full-time geographic child abuse pediatrician at the Children's Hospital of Philadelphia and maintains an active interest in the ophthalmic manifestations of child abuse in his current practice as a pediatric ophthalmologist at the Hospital for Sick Children.

MARY S. SHERIDAN, Ph.D., ACSW, is a medical social worker who developed an interest in Munchausen Syndrome by Proxy while working in the field of infant apnea. Her career and personal research have focused on interactions between people and health care technology, as well as on the judgments that patients and professionals make about illness. She has published widely in the social work and health care literature. She was co-founder and first president of the National Association of Apnea Professionals, for which she chairs the Munchausen by Proxy Network. She is Research Manager, Straub Foundation, Honolulu, and on the faculty of Hawaii Pacific University.

DATE DUE